MARRIAGE, SCRIPTURE, AND THE CHURCH

THEOLOGICAL DISCERNMENT
ON THE QUESTION OF
SAME-SEX UNION

DARRIN W. SNYDER BELOUSEK

Baker Academic

a division of Baker Publishing Group
Grand Rapids, Michigan

© 2021 by Darrin W. Snyder Belousek

Published by Baker Academic
a division of Baker Publishing Group
PO Box 6287, Grand Rapids, MI 49516-6287
www.bakeracademic.com

Printed in the United States of America

Library of Congress Cataloging-in-Publication Data
Names: Snyder Belousek, Darrin W., 1969– author.
Title: Marriage, scripture, and the church : theological discernment on the question of same-sex union / Darrin W. Snyder Belousek.
Description: Grand Rapids, Michigan : Baker Academic, a division of Baker Publishing Group, 2021. | Includes bibliographical references and index.
Identifiers: LCCN 2020037108 | ISBN 9781540961839 (paperback) | ISBN 9781540964403 (casebound)
Subjects: LCSH: Same-sex marriage—Religious aspects—Christianity. | Marriage—Religious aspects—Christianity.
Classification: LCC BT707.6 .S69 2021 | DDC 241/.63—dc23
LC record available at https://lccn.loc.gov/2020037108

21 22 23 24 25 26 27   7 6 5 4 3 2 1

"This extraordinary book offers a comprehensive engagement with the current arguments favoring same-sex marriage from a Christian perspective. Snyder Belousek's tone is balanced and charitable, and his judgments are well reasoned and persuasive. Ultimately, its greatest contribution may consist in recentering the eschatological marriage of God and creation in Christian theology and pastoral practice, thereby teaching all of us, of whatever sexual orientation or state of life, to conceive our vocations in a fresh and striking light. This is the one book on this topic that everyone should read."

—**Matthew Levering**, Mundelein Seminary

"*Marriage, Scripture, and the Church* is a must-read book. Snyder Belousek presents an irenic, wholistic, and refreshing reminder of marriage's three facets—procreation, partnership, and prefiguring Christ and the church—and celibacy's prefiguring of the resurrection age, which are not present in same-sex unions."

—**Aída Besançon Spencer**, Gordon-Conwell Theological Seminary; coeditor of *Marriage at the Crossroads* and *Christian Egalitarian Leadership*

"Would you like a well-written, carefully researched study of marriage in the Christian tradition, intended as the basis for contemporary discussions about sexual practices and longings? Snyder Belousek's irenic study engages the reader from the start, without making heterosexual monogamy an idol and without denigrating those who struggle with the cogency of his presentation."

—**J. Andrew Dearman**, Fuller Theological Seminary

"The account of biblical marriage advanced in this volume is remarkable. Snyder Belousek maintains fidelity toward Scripture while highlighting the need to frame our doctrines in ways that address all manner of contemporary challenges. In particular, he is equally honest about challenges that exist within traditionalist faith communities as he is about the challenge of doctrinal innovations that do not remain faithful to Scripture. For example, Snyder Belousek is intentional about framing his account of biblical marriage in ways that are compelling to sexual minorities who adhere to a traditionalist perspective on marriage. For some of these individuals it is not always clear that the historic Christian account of marriage is truly good for all people. Snyder Belousek takes this challenge seriously, and with abundant care he outlines a theology of marriage that is both biblically faithful and pastorally sensitive for all believers, whether gay or straight. I look forward to adding this volume to my short list of recommended resources on the topic of biblical marriage."

—**Nate Collins**, president and founder of Revoice

"Those of us who write and teach about sexuality are well aware that there is a dearth of books offering a solid theological rationale for marriage. This is particularly true if what we are wanting is a current, well-written, thoroughly researched book, deeply rooted in scriptural teaching and the riches of the Christian tradition. And it is almost too much to hope for that this traditional view will be infused with the gospel, with the compassion, of Jesus Christ. Yet this is precisely what Snyder Belousek offers us in this wonderful book on marriage."

—**Mark Thiessen Nation**, Eastern Mennonite Seminary

"Like no other book, *Marriage, Scripture, and the Church* brilliantly frames our current disagreements on sexuality in terms of the doctrine of marriage. It carefully guides the reader through Scripture, church history, doctrine, and current arguments to highlight the different rationales for changing our doctrine and the consequences of doing so. It offers a positive vision and model of how the church might discern God's truth."

—**Andrew Goddard**, Ridley Hall, Cambridge,
and Westminster Theological Centre

"In the wide mix of books and articles on these interrelated topics, *Marriage, Scripture, and the Church* will make a much-needed contribution. Scholars from every position will need to take Darrin's work into consideration. I highly recommend it."

—**Willard Swartley†**, Anabaptist Mennonite Biblical Seminary

"Snyder Belousek deals with the question of same-sex union in a way that is not only judicious and fair but also generous and kind. His careful and thorough review of both Scripture and church tradition emphasizes the importance of understanding this issue within the context of a robust Christian theology of marriage."

—**Christina S. Hitchcock**, University of Sioux Falls;
author of *The Significance of Singleness*

"*Marriage, Scripture, and the Church* is a significant step away from lobbing Bible verses at the opposition like grenades, where, after the dust settles, all that seems left are damaged psyches and broken relationships. Snyder Belousek offers a rigorous treatment of Christian Scripture, theology, and history in an effort to discern, along with the larger church, what marriage can be and not just what type of sexual activity is allowed or forbidden."

—**Dennis R. Edwards**, North Park Theological Seminary

Dedicated to the memory of
Willard M. Swartley
beloved teacher, mentor, brother

Contents

Part 4 | Seeking a Direction: *Which Way to Walk*

Acknowledgments

At several stages during my study and writing, I have conversed or corresponded with, and sought counsel or received comments from, in personal meetings and by social media, various brothers and sisters. My thanks to Andrew Austin, Trevor Bechtel, Don Blosser, Neal Blough, Corben Boshart, David Cramer, Steve Dintaman, Alex Dye, Peter Erb, Berry Friesen, Ivan Friesen, Ted Grimsrud, Ryan Harker, Emily Hedrick, Randy Keeler, Gerald Mast, Harold Miller, Mark Thiessen Nation, Tim Otto, Ray Person, Gordon Preece, Christopher Roberts, John Roth, Mary Schertz, Gerald Schlabach, Rachel Stella, Isaac Villegas, and Phil Waite. Extra thanks to several persons who generously read and commented on the draft manuscript: Tim Erdel, Meghan Good, Wesley Hill, John Rempel, James Rissler, and Elmer Thiessen. Some of these sisters and brothers share my perspective in this matter; some do not. Nonetheless, by offering his or her conversation, comment, counsel, or correction, each one has participated in the mutual admonition that is essential to the integrity of the church as the body of Christ. Thanks to Robert Hosack at Baker Academic for seeing potential in my proposal and supporting publication of this book. Thanks to Wesley Hill, whose witness and writing have inspired many people and shaped my approach, for gracing this book with his afterword. Posthumous thanks to Willard Swartley, whose counsel and encouragement stimulated and sustained my writing of this book. Finally, special thanks to my wife, Paula, for her partnership in marriage, her pastoring of the church, and her patience with this book.

Some of the ideas in this book were first worked out in a short article published previously in two venues: "Marriage Practice, Biblical Interpretation, and Discernment," in *The Mennonite*, January 1, 2016, 44–47, and "What Is 'Good' and 'Acceptable'? Marriage Practice, Biblical Interpretation, and the Church's Discernment," in *Canadian Mennonite*, February 15, 2016, 4–6.

Living in the Midst

A PERSONAL INTRODUCTION

Search me, O God, and know my heart;
test me and know my thoughts.
Psalm 139:23

Before You Read This Book

Should Christians embrace gay people as brothers and sisters? Should the church bless same-sex couples in marriage? Each of us has some personal experience relating to these questions, whether we are aware of it, or reflect on it, or not. No one's history or identity grants a special privilege, an exemption from criticism or a presumption in favor of one's preferred view, on any question. Yet personal histories and identities do influence how we read Scripture, ask questions, and assess answers. It is thus important to recall and tell one's experience in the course of discerning with the church. I will relate briefly a formative experience in my life that has had continuing effect on my perspective.

Some thirty years ago, while a first-year philosophy graduate student, I found myself, for the first time, getting to know gay folks in a personal way. Erik, my campus roommate, introduced me to Andy, his friend and fellow music student, and through them I met Thomas, another philosophy student and church musician. Each was Christian—and gay. By knowing them, I saw how a Christian institution could be inhospitable to the gay sons and daughters of mother church, and how some Christians could show hostility toward their gay sisters and brothers. Despite this, they loved the church and desired to serve the church. Erik was music director and youth minister of a congregation (until his untimely death); Andy is a choir director at a Christian university; Thomas is an ordained priest and philosophy professor. During that time, they invited me to attend recitals and concerts, typically held in a church, and worship services at the campus church, in which they sometimes performed. Without realizing it, by welcoming me into their company they helped draw me back toward the church, from which I had wandered away during college. I am grateful for their hospitality and for the gifts with which God has blessed them and they have blessed the church. These brothers have remained in my heart along my journey of following Jesus and have been present to my mind as I have written this book.

Discernment by the church concerning these questions, whether at a personal or congregational or denominational level, must include testimonies of Christians that identify as gay, lesbian, bisexual, or asexual.[1] In addition to listening to family members, fellow congregants, and friends, I commend reading autobiographical accounts of Christians telling their journeys with faith and sexuality, Scripture and the church.[2] Discernment should take stock of how the church historically has perceived and responded to sexual minorities.[3] Discernment would benefit also from knowing the larger patterns of religious experience of sexual minorities in Western society, which could correct misperceptions of the faith lives of sexual minorities.[4] A discerning church must be aware that sexual minorities have suffered painful experiences, caused by society and the church, and acknowledge the need to lament maltreatment of sexual minorities, repent of abusive practices, and reconcile

---

1. Heated disputes have arisen among evangelical Christians over sexuality terminology. Some prefer "gay" and "lesbian" while others prefer "same-sex oriented" or "same-sex attracted." Some accept identifying as a "gay Christian" while others object to combining sexual identity with Christian identity. I use "sexual minorities" when referring generally to persons grouped under various acronyms (e.g., LGBTQIA). I also use "gay believer" when referring specifically to Christians that identify as gay or lesbian, or same-sex oriented or same-sex attracted. My intent is to accommodate varied ways individual Christians describe or identify themselves without overly complicating terminology or arbitrating terminological disputes. On sexuality terminology in the church's discernment, see appendix A in the online supplement.

2. Among various accounts I have read: Bennett, *War of Loves*; Butterfield, *Secret Thoughts of an Unlikely Convert*; Coles, *Single, Gay, Christian*; N. Collins, *All but Invisible*; Eileen, *8 Essential Thoughts*; Gilson, *Born Again This Way*; Hallett, *Still Learning to Love*; Hill, *Washed and Waiting*; Keen, *Scripture, Ethics, and the Possibility of Same-Sex Relationships*; Lee, *Torn*; Otto, *Oriented to Faith*; J. Perry, *Gay Girl, Good God*; Selmys, *Sexual Authenticity*; Shaw, *Same-Sex Attraction and the Church*; Tushnet, *Gay and Catholic*; Vasey, *Strangers and Friends*; Vines, *God and the Gay Christian*; White, *Stranger at the Gate*; Yuan and Yuan, *Out of a Far Country*.

3. See Keen, *Scripture, Ethics, and the Possibility of Same-Sex Relationships*, 1–15.

4. See Marin, *Us versus Us*.

with mistreated members.[5] Christians cannot discern faithfully as Christ's body apart from confessing where we fall short of God's glory and opening ourselves to renewal by the Holy Spirit.

Discernment also requires asking how and why these questions have become a debate of major proportion—disproportion, some would say—in the church today. This debate has acquired such importance in the church and become so disruptive of the church, in part at least, because it involves deeper theological issues and interacts with larger cultural dynamics. Theologically, this debate involves beliefs and values that each side sees as defining faithfulness: many traditionalists see this debate as testing allegiance to biblical authority or doctrinal orthodoxy or ethical purity; many innovationists see this debate as testing commitment to human dignity and human rights. Culturally, this debate interacts with differences of geography, identity, and class, a phenomenon I've observed in my denomination: (sub)urban white-majority, professional-class congregations tend toward an innovationist view; (sub)urban racial/ethnic-minority, and rural white-majority, working-class congregations tend toward a traditionalist view. Theologically and culturally, this debate has crystallized, and come to symbolize, fears and suspicions. Lamentably, sexual minorities have been made targets of these fears and suspicions—and so, understandably, have become fearful and suspicious of the church. Discerning honestly calls us to acknowledge our fears and suspicions, to recognize the hurts and hopes behind them—and to name these in the midst of the church.

The same-sex-union debate has generated many—sometimes fierce, even vitriolic—words from both sides. Taking due care with our words, especially concerning those with whom we disagree, is crucial to the church's integrity and witness. Christians cannot discern soundly or witness winsomely while on the rhetorical attack against one another. Whatever convictions we hold or passions we feel, we must remember that at the other end of our words stand sisters and brothers—and that our words are overheard by a listening world. To practice mutual charity and fidelity even as we disagree, let us agree that barbed words are unbecoming of the peaceable people we are called to be as followers of Jesus and members of his body. Above all, when speaking of persons who experience same-sex attraction, or who have same-sex orientation, or who identify as sexual minorities—whether sisters and brothers within the church, or neighbors and strangers within society—let us bear in heart and mind that we are speaking not of an "issue" to be discussed or ignored, nor of an "agenda" to be advanced or resisted, but of human beings made in God's image.[6]

5. See Cannon et al., *Forgive Us*, 135–52.
6. See Sprinkle, *People to Be Loved*, 177–86.

It has become too easy to make prejudicial presumptions about the motives of those with whom we disagree—and then to self-righteously impugn their person rather than consider their position. Traditionalists too easily accuse advocates of innovation of "abandoning the Bible" (as opposed to their own commitment to biblical authority). Innovationists too often disparage defenders of tradition as motivated simply by "bigotry" and "hate" (as opposed to their own attitudes of tolerance and love). Within the bonds of charity and fidelity, we may conscientiously critique each other's arguments and respectfully question each other's decisions. Yet instead of presuming to judge the hearts of others and declare my opponents to be God's enemies, I should petition God to "search me," "test me," "know my thoughts," "see if there is any wicked way in me, and lead me in the way everlasting" (Ps. 139:23–24).

Even when we do assess positions rather than assail persons, it has become typical to name one's own view in positive terms but name the other's view in negative terms, such as "inclusive vs. exclusive" or "biblical vs. liberal." Such rhetorical slanting is typical of our political milieu. To practice mutual charity and fidelity even as we disagree, we should avoid as far as possible using negative terms to name others' views. While no pair of terms may prove satisfactory to everyone, I will use "traditional/traditionalist" to identify the view that the church should maintain its doctrine of marriage as male-female union and "innovational/innovationist" to identify the view that the church should revise its doctrine of marriage to sanction same-sex union. Both terms bear positive connotation—"traditional/traditionalist" connotes holding fast to a valued heritage, "innovational/innovationist" connotes advocating change toward a desired goal—and each term fairly, albeit imperfectly, reflects how various proponents of each view have presented themselves.[7]

And when we consider views with which we disagree, it is tempting to portray another's view in ways that misrepresent it, making it mean otherwise than what was actually stated or likely intended or making it seem weaker—less biblical, less logical, less coherent, less compassionate—than it really is. Again, to practice mutual charity and fidelity even as we disagree, we should aim to represent a view with which we disagree in such a way that its author would recognize it and in a way that will assist others in understanding it.

7. Traditionalist and innovationist views are not monolithic. Each view exhibits variations in biblical interpretation, theological perspective, and pastoral approach. Holben, *What Christians Think about Homosexuality*, surveys six viewpoints, four traditionalist (condemnation, promise of healing, costly discipleship, and pastoral accommodation) and two innovationist (affirmation and liberation). Sprinkle, *Two Views on Homosexuality, the Bible, and the Church*, actually features four different perspectives, two traditionalist and two innovationist.

This does not require us to remain neutral between conflicting views or to refrain from critiquing opposing views, but it does call us to take due care in how we represent others' views. All parties to this debate, as members of Christ's body, have obligations of charity and fidelity toward other believers, while exercising perseverance in sound doctrine and patience under divine providence.[8]

The apostle Paul addressed an early church beset by disagreements and divisions. He counseled believers that, as those who had been reconciled in Christ to one another and to God, they ought to "lead a life worthy of the calling to which [they had] been called." This means "bearing with one another in love, making every effort to maintain the unity of the Spirit in the bond of peace," and "speaking the truth in love" (Eph. 4:1, 2–3, 15). I expect my readers to hold me to these standards.

Why I Wrote This Book

This book presents my path of thinking through the question of same-sex union. My intent at the start was not to write a book but to discern with the church. I was prompted by events within my denomination, Mennonite Church USA.

Over the years some pastors and congregations in my denomination have published statements or adopted policies to welcome same-sex couples as members and authorize pastors to bless same-sex couples—and some pastors have openly presided at such ceremonies. Some of these congregations and their pastors have been reproved, while others have been approved, by their overseeing conferences. Then two conferences of the denomination credentialed ministers living in same-sex partnerships. These actions, which contravened the denominational confession of faith and a denomination-wide agreement, galvanized debate and generated disruption. The denominational delegate assembly responded by adopting a resolution of "forbearance of differences" on sex and marriage. In the wake of all this, some conferences separated from the denomination and some congregations shifted conferences to align with like-minded congregations. And throughout all this, many sexual-minority members have felt excluded from and scapegoated by denominational processes and policies.

Intersecting with institutional actions and reactions are interpersonal relationships and situations. Having sojourned in both progressive urban congregations and conservative rural congregations of my denomination,

8. See Davis, *Forbearance*.

having studied and taught within denominational academic institutions, and having served with my denominational mission agency, I know Christians on all sides and in many situations. I know Christians who have entered same-sex partnerships, or have opened marriages to pursue same-sex relationships, or have left marriages to explore new sexual identities. I know pastors, teachers, and members who advocate for, or have presided at, blessings of same-sex couples. I also know pastors, teachers, and members who object to these institutional decisions and are troubled by our denominational direction. I know folks who have switched congregations or exited the denomination because of this and folks who have resolved to remain despite disagreeing with these decisions and the direction they portend. Living in the midst of the institutional and the interpersonal, I felt compelled to undertake a sustained study of this question.

While my motivation and this book's origin are personal and particular, I intend for this book to partake of the larger debate and contribute to ongoing discernment within the wider church. I have engaged throughout the book with writers and sources from across the ecclesial spectrum: Anglican, Baptist, Catholic, Episcopalian, Lutheran, Mennonite, Methodist, Orthodox, Presbyterian, and so on. While my confessional perspective and formational background are Anabaptist and evangelical, I have also been shaped significantly, theologically and spiritually, by Catholic and Orthodox traditions. I have mined the treasures of the church to help me in thinking theologically and discerning faithfully concerning sex and marriage. While this book is a scholarly work and interacts extensively with biblical, theological, and historical scholarship, I intend the book for the whole church, not only or primarily the academy. I have endeavored to present matters in a clear manner accessible to a church-wide audience and hope that this book will prove edifying for many: pastors, elders, and laity in the congregation or parish; scholars, teachers, and students in the college or seminary; and leaders serving in denominational positions or parachurch institutions.

I offer this book to the church cautiously, aware that what I write may elicit passionate reactions or touch pained places for some readers. I do so honestly, seeking to be fair with opposing viewpoints but not pretending to be neutral on the matter. I do so modestly, cognizant of assumptions and limitations in my approach and acknowledging that my arguments and assessments might fall short or miss the mark. I do so humbly, not presuming to perfectly understand the whole matter or ultimately settle every question. I do so fraternally, as a fellow laborer in the Lord's vineyard, inviting thoughtful consideration and, where I have erred, faithful correction.

Why the Church Needs This Book

The past several years have seen a flurry of books published from both sides of the debate. And here is another book! What is it about? How is it different? And why bother with it?

This book's central focus is the theology of marriage and interpretation of Scripture as these bear on whether the church should revise its doctrine of marriage in order to sanction same-sex union as true marriage and bless same-sex couples with its nuptial rite.[9] This book's aims are both constructive and critical: to elaborate a biblical-traditional theology of marriage and consider the innovation of same-sex union from that perspective; to analyze and assess Scripture-based arguments in favor of sanctioning same-sex union; and to do each of those with a view toward garnering wisdom that can guide the church in discernment and goad the church to reflection and action.

This book approaches the matter from a different angle than others. Whether written from an innovationist view or a traditionalist view, too many books and blogs in the debate have focused too narrowly on biblical texts that refer explicitly or pertain directly to same-sex intercourse. The debated question of this back-and-forth is whether Scripture strictly forbids same-sex intercourse, or not: Is same-sex intercourse always sin, or not? The debate then revolves around traditional versus revisionist readings of particular texts. Addressing that question and interpreting those texts is a necessary aspect of discerning this matter.[10] I offer my analysis of that question and interpretation of those texts in the online supplement to this book. That approach is inadequate, however, for several reasons.

First, whether approached from the innovationist side or the traditionalist side, this debate centers on a negative question of what Scripture forbids in sexual relations and then fixes on a particular set of texts. This approach can easily lose sight of marriage as the positive frame for the negative question and thus overlook Scripture's witness to marriage as the wider context for those texts on sexual relations. The church's teaching, based on Scripture's witness, has always maintained that sexual relations belong properly to the marriage covenant. From the perspective of Christian teaching, then, any question of sexual relations is properly a question of marriage. The typical approach to the same-sex-union question does not occasion biblical-theological consideration of what marriage is, why marriage matters, and how the church's doctrine of marriage bears upon the question of same-sex union.

---

9. Throughout the book, I use "sanction" with the positive sense of "to authorize" or "give official approval"—in the language of the church, "to declare holy."

10. See Gagnon, *Bible and Homosexual Practice*.

Shifting to a marriage frame for the same-sex-union question has the advantage of drawing the church's tradition into our discussion. While same-sex intercourse has been a subject of comment (and condemnation) within the church across centuries,[11] the church has sustained a tradition of reflecting theologically on marriage. Bishops and theologians of East and West (Tertullian, Clement, Methodius, Gregory, Chrysostom, Augustine, etc.) engaged in an extended debate during the second to the fourth centuries on the status of marriage in the age of Christ. Revisiting that marriage debate among early Christians will offer lessons to help guide discernment in the church today—and will pose questions that both traditionalists and innovationists must take seriously.

Framing the same-sex-union question as a marriage matter will generate questions, often neglected in the usual debate, that bear upon both traditionalist and innovationist views. A narrow focus on biblical texts concerning same-sex intercourse lets both parties to the debate avoid dealing with theological questions about marriage: it allows innovationists to avoid weighing how sanctioning same-sex union would alter the traditional doctrine of marriage; and it allows traditionalists to avoid wrestling with how accepting other practices (e.g., habitual contraception and divorce-remarriage) already implicates the traditional doctrine of marriage. Focusing specifically on same-sex intercourse also implicitly treats the same-sex-union question as a "special issue" divorced from other questions of sexual ethics. Debating same-sex union thus distracts us from obvious problems of sexual discipline (e.g., pornography use and premarital cohabitation) within our congregations. Framing the same-sex-union question as a marriage matter recalls the church to consistent scrutiny of sexual sin and consistent teaching of sexual chastity for all believers.

Framing the same-sex-union question as a marriage matter, hopefully, will benefit the church in another way. Christians in Western society, including evangelicals, are confused about marriage. On the one hand, some Christian subcultures have almost idolized marriage. Teens are exhorted to keep themselves "pure" by abstaining from sex while reserving themselves for a spouse; teens are taught that marital sex is the "ultimate" expression of love and "pinnacle" of intimacy. Enjoying sex in marriage is the promise for the faithful and "pure." At the same time, teens receive a mixed message—sex is dirty and defiling, so save it for your spouse!—that confuses and shames. In this vision of marriage, which weds a secular script about sex to the Christian doctrine of marriage, emphasis on sex between husband and wife almost

---

11. See Fortson and Grams, *Unchanging Witness.*

eclipses the vision of God's love in Christ for the church as the meaning of marriage and the goal of Christian life.[12]

On the other hand, Western Christians are at risk of forgetting how to say what marriage is and losing their reflex of seeing sex as belonging to marriage. Many Christian young adults, including from evangelical congregations, arrive at college already having absorbed a secular mindset on sex and marriage, covered with a veneer of Christian vocabulary.[13] Christian colleges and seminaries also can neglect the church's doctrine of sex and marriage. In a recent conversation with a young pastor fresh from seminary, I mentioned this book and my approach. The pastor responded, "I had never thought of this issue in relation to marriage." Even the scholarly guild of Christian ethics is in danger of forsaking marriage as the proper frame for Christian thinking about sexual relationships. At a recent conference of Christian ethicists, I attended a presentation that addressed the sexual culture of college campuses. The presenter, with audience approval, dismissed the Christian virtue of chastity, and the corresponding Christian standard that sex belongs only within marriage, as "passé" and impractical. The church needs to reclaim a distinctively Christian theology of sex and marriage—and a chastened vision of the purpose and place of sex and marriage in the divine plan and human vocation.

In part 2, accordingly, I frame the question of same-sex union as a matter of marriage, present a traditional interpretation of Scripture and theology of marriage, and then consider same-sex union with respect to traditional doctrine. Chapter 3 elaborates a traditional view of what marriage is, what marriage is for, and what marriage signifies, as presented in the biblical narrative and as represented by Christian tradition. Chapter 4 engages with Jesus's teaching on marriage and considers its implications for interpreting Genesis, discerning the same-sex-union question, and assessing the purpose and place of marriage in the church. Chapter 5 revisits marriage debates in the apostolic and patristic eras of the early church and draws lessons for discernment in the church today. Chapter 6 then considers same-sex union, along with other contemporary alterations to marriage (nonpermanent, nonmonogamous, and nonprocreative marriage), in relation to Scripture and tradition, and examines the theological implications of these alterations.

Second, the typical traditionalist approach to the debate, focused on ethics of sex and exegesis of texts, often overlooks the fact that innovationists have offered affirmative arguments, based on Scripture, in support of same-sex

12. See Callaway, *Breaking the Marriage Idol*.
13. See Rine, "What Is Marriage to Evangelical Millennials?"

union. Traditionalists have too often supposed that critiquing revisionist readings of biblical texts about same-sex intercourse is sufficient to carry the debate and thus tend to give short shrift to affirmative arguments. The traditionalist approach, then, often fails to substantively address biblical arguments advanced in favor of marriage innovation.

In part 3, accordingly, I will take up arguments for marriage innovation that draw analogies from or make appeals to Scripture in favor of sanctioning same-sex union. Chapter 7 considers arguments to the effect that the church, due to historical precedents of changing views and reinterpreting Scripture about other matters, may again change view and reinterpret Scripture to affirm same-sex union. Chapter 8 considers arguments to the effect that the church, on strength of warrants within Scripture, may override or set aside the teaching of Scripture on sex and marriage in order to bless same-sex union. In critically examining these innovationist analogies and appeals to Scripture, I will consider the hermeneutical, theological, and ethical issues at stake.

Third, whether approached from the innovationist side or the traditionalist side, the debate often falls short of offering the church wisdom to guide discernment and lessons to inform practice regarding sex and marriage. Along the way in parts 2 and 3, accordingly, I will glean insights and lessons for discernment and practice from the biblical, theological, and historical discussions. Part 4 concludes the book by considering proposals and precedents for discernment drawn from the early church that might help guide the church today. Chapter 9 tests paths of discernment that have been proposed to lead the church toward sanctioning same-sex union. Chapter 10 looks to the Jerusalem Council as a guiding precedent for the church today.

Discernment must go beyond theology, ethics, and hermeneutics to consider the calling and character of the church. Discerning with integrity carries a commitment to enact our convictions within communities whose character corresponds to what we've discerned. It is one thing to discern a direction; it is another thing to cast a vision for *how* we will walk this way *as the church*. God calls the church to be a people whose common life in the Holy Spirit makes walking the way of Jesus both plausible for believers and visible to the world. What does it look like when a community of believers—male and female, married and single, straight and gay—embodies a vision of chastity in which celibacy and marriage are credible and desirable on distinctively Christian terms? How can congregations become communities in which costly sacrifices of discipleship are viable for all believers, especially believers who forgo marriage for the sake of God's kingdom? I have invited Wesley Hill to address this vital question in the afterword.

There is much at stake in this matter: not only whether same-sex intercourse is sin but also what marriage is and how sanctioning same-sex union would alter marriage—and, beyond that, how it implicates how we read the biblical narrative, reflect on salvation history, think about Jesus Christ, recognize the Holy Spirit, and live together as the church. As we will see, this matter poses questions and presents challenges for both traditionalists and innovationists— and thus calls for discernment by the whole church.

I reference several appendixes (labeled *A* through *J*) in footnotes throughout this book. These appendixes, which address specific texts and topics, are subordinate to and supportive of the main argument of this book. I have published them separately as a supplement to this book. The supplement is freely accessible online as a downloadable document at https://onu.academia .edu/DarrinSnyderBelousek.

PART 1

SURVEYING
THE
SITUATION

WHERE WE ARE

1

Stand at the Crossroads

TAKING A BEARING

Thus says the LORD:
Stand at the crossroads, and look.
Jeremiah 6:16

The Way We've Come

The main question this book addresses is whether the church should sanction same-sex union as true marriage, and thus extend its rite of nuptial blessing to same-sex couples, or not.[1] The church has traditionally taught that sexual intercourse belongs within the monogamous union of man and woman. This traditional teaching contains two interrelated norms: sexual intercourse belongs to the marriage bond, and marriage is man-woman monogamy. With respect to traditional teaching, to advocate sanction of same-sex union could, logically, be to advocate one or other of two things: revise the definition of marriage to include same-sex union or rescind the restriction of sexual intercourse to allow sex outside monogamous marriage for sexual minorities. The church's debate over same-sex union, for the most part, has concerned

1. Questions of civil law and public policy lie outside the scope of this book.

the definition of marriage. As I will show, however, the church's debate also implicates the restriction of sex to marriage.

In the matter of same-sex union, cultural winds in Western society have shifted sharply in a short span. Political and legal changes have followed in step with cultural shifts. Recognition of same-sex union is now the legal norm in the United States, Canada, England, Australia, and other Western nations. These changes have not come all of a sudden. Same-sex union ascended to social approval and legal status in a single generation. Yet more fundamental shifts lie behind and beneath this latest in a series of changes concerning sex and marriage. Such changes—contraception, pornography, sexual liberation, sex education, divorce, cohabitation, abortion—have been working their way through society over a century.[2]

As Western society has been altering its law, and image, of marriage, Christians in every quarter have been caught up in those cultural shifts. Different denominations have followed varied strategies in response to the sexual-social upheaval of the 1960s onward. Protestant mainline denominations have tended to pursue a strategy of accommodating Christianity to the shifting culture to maintain the intellectual respectability of Christian belief and social relevance of Christian institutions, while evangelical and Anabaptist groups have tended to follow a strategy of nonconformist resistance to cultural forces to preserve orthodox doctrine and distinctive witness.[3] Despite differing responses, however, Protestant groups off the mainline have found themselves replicating the same debates over sex and marriage that have played out in mainline denominations. Cultural changes in sex and marriage have put pressure on Christian practice and reshaped Christian understanding of sex and marriage.[4]

Because the cultural and ecclesial shift on same-sex union is the latest chapter in a century-long story of sexual-social change, the church cannot adequately address the question of same-sex union in isolation from the several shifts on sex and marriage that have preceded it. Discerning the question of same-sex union in the church will implicate the ways in which Christians have already become accommodating in practice, if not affirming in principle, of pornography, cohabitation, contraception, divorce, and so on.

The debate over same-sex union in North America is not new. Protestant mainline denominations, especially, have been dealing with this matter for decades. As this debate courses through the denominations, Protestant mainline groups tend to be about a generation ahead of evangelical and Anabaptist

2. See Griffith, *Moral Combat*.
3. See Douthat, *Bad Religion*.
4. See Ash, *Marriage*, 34–59; Grant, *Divine Sex*, 15–130; S. Holmes, "Listening to the Past," 176–86.

groups in both debating and deciding on this matter. The debate also finds different denominations following diverging paths—and even differing factions within denominations diverging into distinct groups.

Some Protestant denominations have already resolved debate and officially moved to redefine marriage and approve blessing of same-sex couples. Other denominations, while formally maintaining a traditional teaching, have continued in dispute over the matter without resolution. And still other denominations, whether because of lack of consensus or on account of church polity, have resolved debate by leaving the matter to local decision by congregations and clergy. My denomination maintains a traditional teaching as its confessional position, but differences in belief and dynamics of polity are moving it toward resolving dispute by local decision. For those North American denominations that belong to worldwide communions, denominational disputes have threatened global division. Many evangelical and Anabaptist groups, along with the worldwide communions of Catholicism and Orthodoxy, maintain a traditional teaching on sex and marriage. Yet winds of change are blowing in conservative camps, as some prominent evangelical leaders and Catholic theologians have changed minds and advocated publicly for blessing same-sex couples.

To take a bearing in the present situation, let's look back to see the way we've come over the last few decades. I won't attempt to rehearse the whole history of this debate. Charting a few data points will show an overall trend. In 1983, Robin Scroggs began his landmark book, *The New Testament and Homosexuality*, with a brief survey of debates among three Protestant mainline denominations that were underway in the late 1970s and early 1980s. At that time, the disputed question within denominational bodies was whether "practicing homosexual" persons could be ordained, which was connected to another disputed question of whether same-sex intercourse is intrinsically immoral. Blessing of same-sex couples in marriage was not (yet) up for formal discussion by denominational bodies. About twenty years later, C. Norman Kraus made a contribution to the ongoing debate among Mennonites. He framed the question for discussion in terms of justifying same-sex union as an exceptional situation: "Even if its [i.e., same-sex erotic attraction] expression in a monogamous covenanted context is recognized as moral, it can only be justified as an exception for a small minority."[5] Another twenty years later, the question for debate has shifted again. Now, while some mainline denominations have decided to sanction same-sex union, even some off-mainline denominations have moved beyond debating whether to justify same-sex couples

---

5. Kraus, "Making Theological and Ethical Decisions," 257.

as an exceptional situation and into debating whether to sanction same-sex union as marriage. The debated question has thus evolved: from whether same-sex intercourse should be judged as intrinsically immoral, to whether same-sex union may be justified as exceptionally moral, to whether same-sex union should be blessed as true marriage.

The Way We're Going

Given this bearing, we may look ahead to see the way we might be going. What will be the next debate? I expect that the church will soon find itself debating whether to rescind restriction of sex to marriage and allow sex outside marriage. As observed above, the church's debate over same-sex union has, for the most part, challenged the definition of marriage as man-woman monogamy while keeping the restriction of sex to marriage. Cultural shifts in society and theological shifts within the church, however, have put pressure also on the traditional restriction of sex to marriage, especially concerning sexual minorities.

One rationale advanced for rescinding restriction of sex to marriage concerning sexual minorities is the claim that marriage is a "heteronormative" construct or a patriarchal institution that should not be required of sexual minorities who desire sexual relationships. This rationale has secular origins in the 1960s and 1970s among postmodern philosophers and political radicals who rejected monogamous marriage as an oppressive structure from which queer sexuality needs liberation.[6] This way of thinking has moved from the secular arena into the church. Elizabeth Stuart, taking a lesbian-liberationist stance, characterizes marriage as "an institution that was born, formed, and structured for and by patriarchy."[7] Accordingly, she rejects marriage as a normative model for sexual relationships because, she argues, it is both unacceptable from the perspective of women's experience of suffering and inappropriate to the way that lesbian and gay persons understand their relationships. She advocates friendship as an alternative model for sexual relationships, which would require relationships of justice and mutuality but would allow pursuit of passion beyond the bounds of marriage and monogamy.[8]

Other theologians also have advanced variations of this theme—that sexual minorities need not be constrained by the heterosexual norm, thus rescinding restriction of sexual relations to monogamous marriage—over decades of debate about same-sex union. In the 1970s Tom Driver argued that affirming

6. See Eskridge and Spedale, *Gay Marriage*, 17–19; N. Collins, *All but Invisible*, 137–39.
7. Stuart, *Just Good Friends*, 174.
8. See Stuart, *Just Good Friends*, xiv–xvi, 102–77; Stuart, "Dancing in the Spirit."

same-sex relationship "as a valid behavior and way of life" does not ask the church to abandon marriage. Yet it does ask the church to accept two things incompatible with tradition: the liberation of sex from marriage ("Life outside marriage is not necessarily or even normally virginal") and the liberation of marriage from monogamy ("Life inside marriage is not to be construed as forbidding sexual relations with other persons").[9] In the 1980s Raymond Lawrence argued that the restriction of sex to marriage should be rescinded. "Sexual expression," he claimed, "is limited only by the principles that delimit self-actualization. . . . Even within a lifelong heterosexual monogamous relationship sexual expression need not be limited to that relationship." Because "self-actualization is shaped by its own inherent polymorphous character," we should not require all sexual activity to conform to the single paradigm of man-woman monogamy.[10] In the 1990s Michael Vasey argued that the church may have one ethical standard for the sexual majority and another ethical standard for sexual minorities: "A general Christian ethic does not require . . . the same ethical evaluation of genital acts for those who are able and those who are not able to conform to the gender patterns prevailing in the culture."[11] According to Vasey, the church could judge sexual relations for the sexual majority by values that restrict sex to marriage and marriage to monogamy, while judging sexual relations for sexual minorities by different values that allow sex outside monogamous marriage.[12]

Rescinding restriction of sex to marriage for sexual minorities, once marginal, has become mainstream. To illustrate, let's consider my denomination, Mennonite Church USA. A survey of credentialed leaders (licensed and ordained ministers) in 2014 found that 53 percent of all leaders hold an innovationist view. Among innovationist leaders, 40 percent would accept sexual-minority members and sanction same-sex union with restricting sex to marriage—but 60 percent would accept sexual-minority members and sanction same-sex union without restricting sex to marriage. Among innovationist leaders, the *majority* would not restrict sex to marriage; only a minority would maintain restriction of sex to marriage. Of all credentialed leaders in my denomination, then, more than half affirm sanctioning same-sex union and nearly one-third would allow sex outside marriage for sexual minorities.[13]

What some advocate today, justifying sex outside marriage as an exception for sexual minorities, parallels what some advocated yesterday, justifying

9. Driver, "Homosexuality," 18, 19.
10. Lawrence, "Bench Marks for a New Sexual Ethics," 95, 99.
11. Vasey, "Travelling Together?," 69.
12. See also Vasey, *Strangers and Friends*, 212–37.
13. See Kanagy, "2014 Survey of Credentialed Leaders in Mennonite Church USA."

same-sex union as an exception for sexual minorities. What yesterday some advocated as exceptional (same-sex union) is today accepted by many as normative. Likewise, I expect, what today some advocate as exceptional (sex outside marriage) will tomorrow be accepted by many as normative. In fact, some who advocate sanctioning same-sex union have extended their revised understandings of sex and marriage to reject restricting sex to marriage and advocate sanctioning premarital sex and sexual friendships.[14] The same-sex-union question points, potentially, to wholesale revision of Christian doctrine and full-scale revolution of sexual practice: the sanction of sex beyond marriage and monogamy.[15]

Which Way to Walk?

The church stands at a crossroads and must discern which way to walk. This historical juncture is forcing the church—members, congregations, and denominations—to face a choice: Which way should we go? What this decision calls for, beyond debate, is discernment: Which way is God's will for the church today?

Historically, the church has relied upon scriptural revelation, doctrinal tradition,[16] rational wisdom,[17] and communal experience[18] to guide discernment of God's will. Throughout the generations, Christians have turned first to Scripture as the God-inspired guide for the faith and life of the church. "All scripture," Paul reminded Timothy, is "useful for teaching, for reproof, for correction, and for training in righteousness" (2 Tim. 3:16). My denomination's confession of faith, accordingly, acknowledges Scripture as the "fully reliable and trustworthy standard for Christian faith and life." Scripture is the "authoritative source and standard" for "distinguishing truth from error" and "discerning between good and evil." Scripture is thus the criterion against which other sources of wisdom and claims to truth must be "tested and corrected."[19]

14. See Thatcher, *Liberating Sex*.

15. See the "sexual reformation" of Bolz-Weber, *Shameless*.

16. On the Western (Catholic and Protestant) traditions, see Reynolds, *Marriage in the Western Church*; Witte, *From Sacrament to Contract*; Roberts, *Creation and Covenant*. On the Eastern (Orthodox) tradition, see Meyendorff, *Marriage*; Hopko, *Christian Faith and Same-Sex Attraction*.

17. For a recent argument favoring traditional marriage based in rational wisdom, see Girgis, Anderson, and George, *What Is Marriage?*

18. In addition to taking account of tested wisdom from past generations, Western Christians would do well to listen to voices from the global South. See Azumah, "Through African Eyes."

19. Mennonite Church USA, *Confession of Faith*, art. 4.

In order for Scripture to function authoritatively as the doctrinal standard, the church must interpret Scripture. Now Scripture does not simply interpret itself. And as mere mortals, we are not self-sufficient interpreters of Scripture. God speaks to us through Scripture, but we need God's help to understand God's word. Even the apostles, who had heard God's word from Jesus, the Word made flesh, needed the risen Jesus to show them how to interpret Scripture's testimony to himself as Messiah and Lord (Luke 24:25–27, 44–45). Thankfully, we have not been left on our own without divine help. The ascended Jesus has sent the Holy Spirit to teach us in all things, remind us of all that Jesus has taught us, and guide us "into all the truth" (John 14:16–17, 26; 16:13; 17:17; cf. 2:22; 12:16). Nor do we interpret Scripture once for all. As human interpreters, we are finite and fallible, and thus our interpretations of Scripture are limited in scope and liable to error. Thankfully, again, we have help that has been handed down through the church. We have the apostles' testimony to the gospel and teaching of the faith, which the church has preserved in the canon of Scripture and summarized in the "rule of faith," to guide our interpretation and keep us from error (Acts 2:42; 1 Tim. 3:14–15; 2 Tim. 1:13–14; 2:2). We may also consult interpretations and teachings of past generations of faithful Christians that have been tested over time, from which we might gain insight and glean wisdom to aid discernment. It is the church's task in every generation—entrusting ourselves to the faithfulness of the Father, committing ourselves to the way of the Son, invoking the help of the Holy Spirit, listening to the teaching of the apostles, gathering in the company of our forebears in faith, and hearing the testimonies of sisters and brothers—to interpret Scripture to discern God's will for God's people.[20]

Signposts for the Church

I call to mind three signposts to orient the church at this crossroads. First, a signpost from the prophets. Jeremiah addressed Jerusalem in a time of crisis: "Thus says the LORD: Stand at the crossroads, and look, and ask for the ancient paths, where the good way lies; and walk in it, and find rest for your souls. But they said, 'We will not walk in it'" (Jer. 6:16). Listening to the prophet, we are reminded of our tendency to refuse God's way and wisdom and instead seek our own path by our own understanding (cf. Prov. 3:5–6). And we are exhorted to ask for and walk in "the ancient paths, where the good way lies."

20. See also Verhey, *Remembering Jesus*, 14–76.

Second, a signpost from the apostles. The church today is debating various views that would entail substantial revision of traditional doctrine. Paul warned early Christians to not let themselves be "tossed to and fro and blown about by every wind of doctrine" (Eph. 4:14). We should not "despise the words of the prophets" among us, yet we should "test everything" so that we may "hold fast to what is good" and "abstain from every form of evil" (1 Thess. 5:20–21). John, alerting the church to "false prophets," charged the believers to not simply "believe every spirit" but "test the spirits to see whether they are from God" (1 John 4:1). Listening to the apostles, we are reminded that not every prophet, doctrine, or spirit comes from God. And we are exhorted to be spiritually transformed with renewed minds, "so that [we] may discern what is the will of God—what is good and acceptable and perfect" and thus distinguish God's will from schemes of the present age (Rom. 12:2).

Third, a signpost from Jesus. The church today, in order to discern well, should function like the household master of Jesus's parable. Jesus likened the "scribe who has been trained for the kingdom of heaven" to "the master of a household" who exercises discretion over the household's storeroom: he "brings out of his treasure what is new and what is old" (Matt. 13:52). Speaking to his disciples, Jesus was referring to his proclamation of God's kingdom by sermon and parable ("what is new") and to Scripture's testimony to God's will in the law and the prophets ("what is old"). The "scribe trained for the kingdom" draws from both "old" and "new" in discerning and doing God's will, neither spurning Scripture in favor of Jesus nor rejecting Jesus in favor of Scripture. The wise scribe recognizes that Jesus, who teaches with God's authority, has come to fulfill, not to abolish, the law and the prophets. While Jesus has inaugurated the new age of God's kingdom, no part of God's will from of old will cease until "all is accomplished"—until God's purpose comes to be on earth as in heaven (5:17–19; 6:10).

The gospel of Jesus and the teaching of the apostles have been added to the law and the prophets—these compose, for the church, "what is old." This canon of Scripture is the "good treasure" that is "entrusted" to the church, which the church is charged to "guard" and according to which the church is to judge "sound teaching" by "the help of the Holy Spirit" (2 Tim. 1:13–14). Today the church is also presented with new things—new theories about sexuality, new ideas about marriage, new ways of reading Scripture, and so on. As stewards of God's household, we should neither uncritically accept "what is new" nor casually discard "what is old." As wise stewards, we do well to soundly judge "what is new" in discerning whether to add to "what is old" in the household treasury—and then use the household assets, new and old, for the good of the household to the glory of God.

It is my aim in this book to serve the church in the role of a scribe trained for the kingdom, drawing discerningly from "what is old" and "what is new."[21] In doing so, I seek to test everything—every idea, every argument, every interpretation—according to Scripture. My hope is that, with the help of the Holy Spirit, we may be better able to discern where the good way lies for the church today.

21. A valuable contribution in this vein is O'Donovan, *Church in Crisis*.

2

Where I Start

APPROACH AND ASSUMPTIONS

> That which has been believed
> everywhere, always, and by all.
>
> Vincent of Lérins

My Approach to the Question

I am a confessing Christian, and I approach the question of same-sex union from that standpoint. The traditional doctrine that marriage is man-woman monogamy meets the classic criteria of catholic doctrine: it has been believed everywhere (universality), always (antiquity), and by all Christians (consensus). This is neither a local doctrine of a particular body nor a doctrinal distinctive of a peculiar group, neither a doctrine recently invented and not fully vetted nor a doctrine subject to perennial or even occasional dispute. The traditional doctrine that marriage is man-woman monogamy, one could argue, has greater claim to catholicity than some dogmas defined by the ecumenical councils of the patristic era. I begin discernment within this doctrinal consensus of the church catholic.

Vincent of Lérins, facing errors and schisms in the fifth-century church, counseled that Scripture, interpreted according to "that which has been believed everywhere, always, and by all," would guide the church in "distinguishing the true Catholic faith from the degraded falsehoods of heresy."[1] The church today, facing novel claims about sex and marriage, also needs to discern truth from falsehood. I do not assert, however, that the doctrinal consensus of Christian tradition is necessarily infallible or irreformable. Due to human fallibility, to which the church in a fallen world does not enjoy immunity, a doctrine could be catholic yet be in error or need reform. The possibility of error, and the potential for reform, cannot be ruled out from the start.

The doctrinal consensus on sex and marriage—sex within marriage only, marriage is man-woman monogamy only—could be in error or need reform. If that is clearly the case, by no means do I wish to stand in the way of reforming the Christian doctrine of sex and marriage in accord with truth. Yet if that is clearly the case, it should be possible for advocates of innovation to exhibit that error or justify that reform.

I approach the same-sex-union question by asking innovationists to justify this reform to the church. By "justify" I mean give reasoned arguments that sufficiently explain why the church should substantially revise doctrine, robust arguments that can withstand careful scrutiny according to Christian convictions. I recognize that my request for reason and rigor in argument sets a high bar for justification; and I acknowledge that other Christians might be satisfied with a lower bar. Yet I think that substantially reforming a Scripture-based doctrine, and doing so in a way that contradicts what the church has always taught and two millennia of faithful Christians have firmly believed, demands no less of those that advocate reformation.

The Assumptions of My Approach

Having stated my approach to the question, I will elaborate the major assumptions of my approach. I acknowledge that some Christians will disagree with these assumptions and may decline to proceed in discernment using these assumptions.

Primacy and Relevance of Scripture

Traditionally, the church has authorized its doctrine of marriage primarily by Scripture, secondarily by appeals to nature, law, and custom. I thus assume that Scripture is a necessary source of a rationale sufficient to justify substantially revising this traditional doctrine. If the doctrine of marriage is

---

1. Vincent of Lérins, *Commonitorium* 2.1, in Bettenson and Maunder, *Documents of the Christian Church*, 88–89.

to be reformed, it must be reformed in accord with Scripture. Luke Timothy Johnson, a biblical scholar advocating sanction of same-sex union, sets the bar for an innovationist position: "The task demands intellectual honesty. . . . We must state our grounds for standing in tension with the clear commands of Scripture, and include in those grounds some basis in Scripture itself. To avoid this task is to put ourselves in the very position that others insist we already occupy—that of liberal despisers of the tradition and of the church's sacred writings, people who have no care for the shared symbols that define us as Christian."[2] Dan Via, also a biblical scholar advocating an innovationist position, emphasizes the necessity of a biblical justification for marriage innovation: "The evidence of reason—science—and experience is relevant and important; but Christians who want to take an open, nontraditional position on this should be able to find biblical support for it."[3] I will thus consider only innovationist arguments that make some positive appeal to Scripture.

As Johnson's comment implies, to approach this matter candidly we must acknowledge the obvious: there is no direct support in Scripture for sanctioning same-sex union. At the same time, we should also acknowledge that relatively few biblical texts pertain directly to same-sex intercourse. These observations prompt a question: Is Scripture even relevant to our debate over same-sex union? I approach the question of same-sex union with the assumption that Scripture is relevant to the church's discernment of this matter.[4] Not all agree on this. I will survey a spectrum of views.

Some say that cultural conditions of Scripture, textual tensions within Scripture, and historical distances between Scripture and us render Scripture ethically inapplicable to sexual matters in the church today. Scripture describes what some humans have believed about sex and marriage or practiced at certain times or decided in certain events. But Scripture does not provide an authoritative source or coherent basis from which we might discern God's will for sex and marriage. Those who view Scripture this way would not likely engage the same-sex-union debate in positive relation to Scripture in the first place. Yet while I have not read (nearly) everything written on this matter, I have found that even advocates of radical revolution in sexual ethics make positive appeals to Scripture—such as wisdom's celebration of sex or Jesus's practice of friendship.

Others say that Scripture has ethical relevance to sexual matters in the church today—but due to cultural, contextual, and historical factors, the

---

2. L. Johnson, "Scripture and Experience," 15. See also Johnson, *Scripture and Discernment*, 43.

3. Via, "Bible, the Church, and Homosexuality," 29.

4. Concerning biblical texts in church debates, see Moberly, "Use of Scripture."

particular stories and specific teachings in Scripture are not ethically applicable to the church today. Biblical texts on sex and marriage, some say, presume patriarchy and encode misogyny. Consequently, applying "the surface meaning of biblical texts to contemporary sexual problems is both naïve and dangerous."[5] Thus we cannot translate the creation story of Genesis, the holiness laws in Leviticus, the divorce ruling of Jesus, or the vice lists of Paul into ethical directives for the church today. Yet, goes this view, major themes and general principles of Scripture are ethically applicable to the church today. So we can apply biblical themes of liberation and mercy and biblical principles of love and justice to our questions of sex and marriage. Walter Wink, citing the range of sex laws and marriage customs across the biblical canon, claimed that "the Bible has no sexual ethic" but "knows only a love ethic" that may be applied to sexual conduct in various eras and cultures.[6] Such a claim, plausible at first glance, looks less convincing when held to careful scrutiny.[7]

Others say that the stories and teachings in Scripture are ethically applicable to sexual matters in the church today. The creation story in Genesis sets forth God's ideal for sex and marriage, which is upheld across the biblical canon: the Decalogue upholds the ideal of fidelity ("You shall not commit adultery"; Exod. 20:14); Song of Songs upholds the ideal of mutuality ("My beloved is mine and I am his"; Song 2:16); the Gospels uphold the ideal of permanence ("What God has joined together, let no one separate"; Matt. 19:6). But, goes this view, biblical texts that condemn same-sex intercourse—holiness laws in Leviticus and vice lists of Paul—are not ethically applicable to the church today. These texts, in their cultural backgrounds and historical circumstances, could have referred to only coercive, exploitive, or hierarchical sexual practices that advocates of innovation would condemn. These texts are thus irrelevant to the question of whether the church today should sanction same-sex partnerships that are mutual and faithful, loving and just. Although popular among innovationists, this view has been seriously challenged by scholarly research. Historical evidence shows that consensual, mutual same-sex practices—even loving, lifelong same-sex partnerships—existed in the Greco-Roman world alongside the abusive practices of pederasty, prostitution, and master-slave sex. Textual evidence also suggests that Paul had in mind such partnerships, as well as abusive practices, when he condemned same-sex intercourse.[8]

5. Thatcher, *Liberating Sex*, 21.
6. Wink, "Homosexuality and the Bible."
7. See Gagnon, *Bible and Homosexual Practice*, 448–51; Fortson and Grams, *Unchanging Witness*, 169–81.
8. I discuss and assess this view in appendixes D, E, F, and G in the online supplement.

Still others say that while Scripture is relevant to sexual ethics in the church today, same-sex intercourse is peripheral to the concern of Scripture and thus should be peripheral to the concern of the church. William Countryman has argued that because the Old Testament prohibition of male-male sexual intercourse occurs only twice and "only in the Holiness Code" (Lev. 18:22; 20:13), this law is "a relatively peripheral aspect" of Israel's purity system. He thus infers that "the issue of same-gender sexual acts in ancient Israel was much less central" to Israel's purity system than the position that issue "occupies in certain modern purity systems."[9] We might observe, however, that the Old Testament commandment to "love your neighbor" also occurs only twice and only in the Holiness Code (19:18, 34). Yet we would be unwise to conclude that loving neighbors was a peripheral aspect of Israel's ethical system. Indeed, Jesus cited this commandment, with the commandment to love God (Deut. 6:5), as the two commandments on which depend "all the law and the prophets" (Matt. 22:40). Similarly, Robin Scroggs has averred that because the New Testament proscription of same-sex intercourse appears explicitly in "only" three texts (Rom. 1:26–27; 1 Cor. 6:9; 1 Tim. 1:10), the New Testament is "virtually silent" on the question. He thus infers that the early church was hardly interested in the matter.[10] We might observe, however, that the New Testament commandment to "love your enemies" appears explicitly in only three texts (Matt. 5:43–48; Luke 6:27–36; Rom. 12:17–21). Yet we should not say that the New Testament is virtually silent on, and that the early church was hardly interested in, loving enemies.

The rhetorical thrust of such arguments is that the church's debate over same-sex union is out of proportion to, and grants the matter relevance unwarranted by, Scripture.[11] Yet I doubt that many Christians would say that the church's concern for loving neighbors and enemies is disproportional to and unwarranted by Scripture. The importance of a matter in Scripture and the relevance of that matter for the church today cannot be gauged simply by its numerical frequency in the biblical canon.[12]

Because the same-sex-union question is a marriage matter, moreover, Scripture bears on the question by much more than only texts about same-sex intercourse. The biblical witness to marriage extends from Genesis to Revelation. Ephraim Radner observes: "For, clearly, there is much in Scripture bearing on the issue of homosexual conduct that does not explicitly treat it. Primarily,

---

9. Countryman, *Dirt, Greed, and Sex*, 24, 26.

10. Scroggs, *New Testament and Homosexuality*, 99–101.

11. Even some traditionalist scholars have made comments in this vein—see Hays, *Moral Vision of the New Testament*, 381; Lamb, *Prostitutes and Polygamists*, 161–64.

12. See also Gagnon, *Bible and Homosexual Practice*, 432–39.

we have scriptural teaching on marriage as the primordial (that is, the first in God's purpose) union of male and female from the beginning of creation (Gen. 2:24), which is made the supreme enacted symbol of God's love (cf. Hosea), upheld by Jesus (Mark 10:6–9), and then proclaimed as the divinely effective image of Christ's own self-giving for the world through the Church (Eph. 5:29–33)."[13] Setting the question of same-sex union within the extensive and consistent witness of Scripture to marriage as male-female union, a traditionalist could argue that Scripture's witness to marriage rules out the church's sanction of same-sex union, without even citing texts about same-sex intercourse.[14] To discern this matter, we will need to consider arguments for sanctioning same-sex union in relation to the entire witness of Scripture concerning sex and marriage.

Responsibility of Justification

Because sanctioning same-sex union would require substantially revising catholic doctrine, I assume that advocates of innovation bear the responsibility of justification. This responsibility of justification is implicit in Johnson's comment quoted above: innovationists must state their case to the church, on biblical grounds, or else occupy the position of "liberal despisers" of Scripture and tradition. In this assumption I concur with Kathryn Greene-McCreight: "I would reject the assertion that the burden of proof (regarding the failing of homoerotic activity to attain covenant righteousness) rests on the church, even while I affirm the clear obligation of the church to repent for any and all participation in hostility and cruelty toward homosexuals throughout the ages. My point here is that the 'burden of proof' always rests on those who propose something novel."[15] I would add that the proposition we are considering concerns not merely "something novel" but something actually contrary to the universal consensus of the church. I thus find insufficient the assertion that "the church's default position" in discernment "should be in favor of inclusion" of same-sex union.[16] Insofar as one advocates fundamentally altering church teaching, one is responsible to justify that alteration.[17]

As Greene-McCreight's comment indicates, some have argued that due to the experiences of sexual minorities, especially painful experiences of mistreatment within the church, "the burden of proof has shifted" from advocates

---

13. Radner, *Hope among the Fragments*, 150.
14. See Schmidt, *Straight and Narrow?*, 39–63.
15. Greene-McCreight, "Logic of the Interpretation of Scripture," 246.
16. Grimsrud, "Toward a Theology of Welcome," 132–33.
17. See also O'Donovan, *Church in Crisis*, 52–53.

for innovation to defenders of tradition.[18] The church's regrettable legacy of unkindness toward sexual minorities and the injury of indignity borne by sexual minorities do entail a moral burden. That burden calls for repenting from uncharitable attitudes and actions, supporting healing for and seeking reconciliation with those mistreated, and adopting postures that welcome and practices that include all those desiring to know God and follow Jesus.

The argument that this shifts the burden of proof regarding revising church doctrine is misplaced. Loving one another as Jesus loved us is a mark of true witnesses of Jesus. Maltreatment of sexual minorities is a failure to "love one another" as Jesus loved us and taught us (John 13:34–35; 15:12–14; 1 John 3:11–24). Failures to love prove that we fall short as Jesus's disciples, not necessarily that the church's teaching is flawed or false. Some Christians have misused the traditional doctrine of sex and marriage, and biblical texts supporting that doctrine, to denigrate sexual minorities in both church and society. Such abuse of brothers and sisters and neighbors by means of Scripture and doctrine is contrary to the gospel. Yet the age-old wisdom still holds true: misuse does not remove proper use. The fact that something can be or has been misused neither negates its proper use nor precludes its being used properly. Scripture and doctrine can be and have been misused. Yet that does not prove that fault lies with the abused Scripture or doctrine rather than the abuser of Scripture or doctrine.

David Gushee indicts the church across the centuries for transmitting a "teaching of contempt" toward sexual minorities, akin to anti-Semitic and racist views of Christians past.[19] Some Christians have expressed contempt for sexual minorities. The church ought to disavow, because of the gospel, any view that licenses contempt toward any group of persons. A "teaching of contempt" toward sexual minorities is distinct from the traditional doctrine that marriage is man-woman monogamy: one can affirm traditional doctrine without endorsing a "teaching of contempt." Many Christians, including some gay believers, adhere to traditional doctrine while repudiating contempt toward sexual minorities. Disavowing a "teaching of contempt" toward sexual minorities does not shift the burden of proof regarding the doctrine of marriage. It shifts the burden of proof only if one begs the question by asserting that traditional doctrine inherently encodes contempt toward, or necessarily entails exclusion of, sexual minorities.

Gushee acknowledges that Christians can adhere to traditional doctrine without endorsing a "teaching of contempt" but then claims that pastoral

---

18. Martin, *Sex and the Single Savior*, 50.
19. Gushee, *Changing Our Mind*, 132–35. See also E. Rogers, "Sanctification, Homosexuality, and God's Triune Life," 225–30; J. Rogers, *Jesus, the Bible, and Homosexuality*, 17–34.

concern without doctrinal change treats sexual minorities as "second-class Christians." Gushee assumes that maintaining traditional doctrine allows welcoming sexual minorities but "not on equal terms" and leads to excluding sexual minorities from "serving and leading the Church."[20] Ken Wilson also ties traditional doctrine to exclusionary practices.[21] Sadly, some traditionalist congregations have excluded gay believers from membership or leadership. Were it true that maintaining traditional doctrine on marriage necessarily entailed categorical exclusion of gay believers from membership or leadership in the church, then that in my mind would weigh heavily against the traditional view. Yet that should not, and need not, be true. In fact, there are many gay believers who are sincerely convinced by and faithfully adhere to traditional doctrine—and serve openly in church leadership.[22]

Consistency and Charity in Interpretation

Insofar as innovationists have responsibility to justify revising doctrine on the ground of Scripture, I assume an expectation of consistency in biblical interpretation. Whatever path through Scripture innovationists might take to justify marriage innovation, the rationale of that path should cohere with rules of biblical interpretation that the church has followed on previous questions—and that innovationists would agree to follow on further questions. Otherwise, if one thinks that advocating innovation warrants a novel interpretive approach, then one should explain why traditional rules are not appropriate to the present case and be willing to apply the novel approach to further questions. Greene-McCreight writes, "In order for traditional readers to be convinced of the righteousness before God of homoerotic relationships, they would need to be convinced on 'traditionalist' grounds. This will mean that if we are to offer a revisionist interpretation of Scripture, either the revisionist interpretation must follow the same 'rules' as the traditional interpretation or the revisionist side must convincingly show how and why the rules must be changed. Otherwise, both sides will continue to talk past each other."[23] To put it succinctly: arguments that invent reasons convenient to the case but lacking warrant in Scripture or tradition are insufficient for justification. Unless I see reason otherwise, therefore, I will follow traditional rules of biblical interpretation when assessing arguments for revising

20. Gushee, *Changing Our Mind*, 169, 171.
21. See K. Wilson, *Letter to My Congregation*, 34, 47, 58, 88.
22. See the writings by David Bennett, Gregory Coles, Nate Collins, Rachel Gilson, Martin Hallett, Wesley Hill, Greg Johnson, Ed Shaw, Eve Tushnet, Pieter Valk, and Christopher Yuan listed in the bibliography.
23. Greene-McCreight, "Logic of the Interpretation of Scripture," 246–47.

doctrine.[24] And when considering novel interpretive approaches, I will test such approaches by applying them to similar questions.

While advocates of innovation have the responsibility of justification, defenders of tradition have an obligation concerning interpretation. Confessing failures to love, all Christians must resolve to do all things in love: we must "[speak] the truth in love" (Eph. 4:15) and "love . . . in truth and action" (1 John 3:18). This includes how we interpret Scripture. Dale Martin rightly reminds us that, according to Christian tradition, love of God and neighbor is not only the rule of Christian life but also a criterion of interpreting Scripture.[25] Augustine instructed the church, "When someone has learnt that the aim of the commandment is 'love from a pure heart, and good conscience and genuine faith' [1 Tim. 1:5], he will be ready to relate every interpretation of the holy scriptures to these three things and may approach the task of handling these books with confidence." The "commandment" to which Augustine refers is the double commandment to love God and neighbor, which Augustine made a basic condition of sound interpretation: "So anyone who thinks that he has understood the divine scriptures or any part of them, but cannot by his understanding build up this double love of God and neighbour, has not yet succeeded in understanding them."[26] Where interpretation of Scripture fails to support love of God and neighbor, it falls short of the intention of the Holy Spirit. Traditionalists are responsible for interpreting Scripture with a view toward love of God and neighbor—and demonstrating how traditional interpretations of Scripture concerning sex and marriage can support loving practices toward sexual minorities, within the church and in society.

Relevance and Insufficiency of Experience

I assume that personal experience is relevant to the church's discernment. Listening to and reflecting on personal experiences can raise awareness, prompt questions, challenge assumptions, inform discussions, and even lead the church to research Scripture. Yet personal experience cannot be decisive in doctrinal matters.[27]

Sexuate bodies and sexual desires are God-created goods. Some have argued that because God created human bodies good, "our perception of the creation through our bodily experiences," including "our experiences of attraction and desire," give us "knowledge of God." We can thus read God's

24. See Greene-McCreight, "Logic of the Interpretation of Scripture," 249–52.

25. Martin, *Sex and the Single Savior*, 49, 168. See also J. Rogers, *Jesus, the Bible, and Homosexuality*, 62.

26. Augustine, *On Christian Teaching* 1.39–44.

27. I will consider the relevance of scientific research to ethical discernment in chapter 7.

design for human sexuality from bodily experience of attraction and desire. This argument assumes that our perceptions and experiences reveal "our bodies" and "our desires" simply "as God created them."[28] That assumption is dubious. And that is due to the one Christian doctrine that, as G. K. Chesterton observed, can be and has been corroborated by experience: the stubborn persistence of, and our persisting susceptibility to, the power of sin in the world and in ourselves. Perception and experience reveal not only God's design but also sin's distortions of God's design—and we must learn to discern the difference.

Lauren Winner has stated this point well: "A Christian ethic may, in cases, take experience into account, but Christians ground their ethics—their behavior—foremost in scripture and tradition. There are, to be sure, some instances where experience—the church's experience of living the church's narrative in a fallen world—significantly informs a Christian ethic. . . . In the main, however, experience considered apart from scripture and church tradition is not a very firm basis for ethics, for the simple reason of original sin."[29] Due to our fallen condition, all human perceptions and experiences are subject to the distortive effects of sin. Due to sin, all my loves—my affections and attractions, my desires and devotions—are susceptible to deviations from God's design. Experience might confirm my desires as good, yet it also might mislead me into mistaking what pleases me for what pleases God. Scripture warns repeatedly that our sin-twisted desires might deceive us about God and mislead us into wrong (Gen. 6:5–6; 8:21; Prov. 6:23–29; Jer. 17:9–10; Matt. 5:27–30; 15:19; Rom. 1:24–25; Eph. 4:22–24; James 1:14–16). Scripture warns also of our tendency to self-deception and self-justification concerning sin (Prov. 12:15; 14:12; 16:25; 30:12; 1 John 1:5–10). Consequently, Matthew Lee Anderson writes, "our experiences . . . are an inadequate guide for determining how we should live in the body."[30]

What is true generally of human experience is true specifically of human sexuality. Concerning sexual experience, Winner writes, "The experience of sex that I can describe and name and talk about is an experience of the natural. . . . But sex must be read as an experience of a fallen person—and, when sex is rightly ordered, an experience of nature infused by grace. This is why our record of experience is insufficient. My experience of sex is not bad data, but it is incomplete."[31] Due to our fallen condition, sex can go wrong—deviate from God's design—in either of two basic ways. Beth Felker Jones explains:

28. Mast and Mast, *Human Sexuality in Biblical Perspective*, 23–26.
29. Winner, *Real Sex*, 20.
30. M. Anderson, *Earthen Vessels*, 29.
31. Winner, *Real Sex*, 90.

"Sex—in a fallen world—happens in hurtful ways and in ways that fail to tell the good truth about who God is."[32] Sin's distortion in human sexuality is manifest in abused intimacies, betrayed trusts, coerced activities, and exploited vulnerabilities. Even if I experience my sexual activity as being true to myself and doing right by others, I can still demean myself or harm others. Sin's distortion in human sexuality is manifest also in disordered desires and idolatrous immorality. Even if I perceive my sexual activity as related rightly to God's will, I can still twist the truth about God and even substitute sex for God.[33]

The fact that everyone experiences sexuality within a self and a world distorted by sin is relevant whether one is male or female, married or celibate, straight or gay. Within each of us rages the "war" between the "law of God" and the "law of sin" at work in the "members" of our bodies, which urges us to obey the flesh rather than God (Rom. 7:21–25). Within each of us are "desires of the flesh" that are "opposed" to the Spirit and urge us to do "works of the flesh" rather than be "led by the Spirit" (Gal. 5:16–26). Consequently, Nate Collins writes, "there are no gay desires, or straight desires, for that matter, that are morally neutral in their entirety because *all* people experience desire in the context of their sinful flesh and first-creation bodies."[34] Sin-induced disorientation of sexual desire has affected all human beings, not just gay people; being straight, or married, does not exempt one's sexuality from the effects of sin. Although opposite-sex desires align generically with the creational pattern ("male and female"), many straight, married Christians are disposed to crooked desires that veer from the specific directionality of the marital bond (e.g., sexual desires for anyone not one's spouse). As Collins observes, "The world simply isn't divided into straight people and sexual deviants."[35] Because all human beings are susceptible to sin in their sexuality, we cannot read personal experience of sexuality, whether straight or gay, as indicative of God's design and thus as normative for our discernment.

This point—how sex can go wrong and how experience of sex can mislead—is illustrated by a disordered form of sexuality with which I have had personal experience: pornography. Some Christians say that sexual pleasure from erotic imagery is a God-given good (as long as no one is harmed in its production or gets addicted by its use), or that it is compatible with marital fidelity (as long as both spouses consent and benefit), or that it can promote

32. B. Jones, *Faithful*, 37.
33. See Ash, *Marriage*, 133–56.
34. N. Collins, *All but Invisible*, 114 (emphasis original).
35. N. Collins, *All but Invisible*, 155; cf. 146.

healthy sexuality for single persons (as a professional Christian counselor once told me).[36] But these, I've learned, are lies.

Pornography reveals not God's design but disordered desires, distorted relationships, and degraded bodies. Pornography appeals to my God-made-good desire to unite as "one flesh" with another, but it twists that desire back on itself and unites me only with myself, inducing me to perceive sex as a self-directed activity for self-gratification. Pornography appeals to my God-made-good need for companionship, but it relates me to another person not as an image of God but as an object of lust. Pornography appeals to my God-made-good body, but it degrades my body into an instrument of use and degrades another's body into something to grasp for my gratification. Pornography exchanges virtue for vice—even if I experience it as good, even if everyone said yes, even while society says it's healthy, even though some Christians say God approves.[37]

Some innovationists have appealed to experience to justify revising the church's doctrine of sex and marriage. Luke Timothy Johnson claims that personal and social experience of sexual orientation authorizes the church to countermand Scripture and sanction same-sex union: "I think it important to state clearly that we do, in fact, reject the straightforward commands of Scripture, and appeal instead to another authority when we declare that same-sex unions can be holy and good. . . . We appeal explicitly to the weight of our own experience and the experience thousands of others have witnessed to, which tells us that to claim our own sexual orientation is in fact to accept the way in which God created us."[38] Other innovationists have argued that spiritual fruit exhibited by gay believers in committed same-sex partnerships is evidence that God blesses same-sex union.[39] Our discernment should consider personal testimonies of gay believers, acknowledge moral virtues (charity, fidelity, etc.) manifested by committed same-sex couples, and recognize spiritual gifts and honor fruitful labors of gay believers for God's kingdom.

Arguments from experience of sexual orientation or from evidence of spiritual fruit are problematic, however. The argument from experience of sexual orientation assumes that such experience reveals "the way God created us." This argument neglects the Christian doctrine of a fallen creation. Due to sin's distortion of God's creation, to which every person and every inclination is susceptible, human appraisal of sexual experience is not self-certifying as

36. For example, see Bolz-Weber, *Shameless*, 135–48.
37. For critical views, on lust, see R. DeYoung, *Glittering Vices*, 159–79; on pornography, see Hollinger, *Meaning of Sex*, 141–43, 156–59; M. Anderson, *Earthen Vessels*, 133–35.
38. L. Johnson, "Scripture and Experience," 15.
39. See Keen, *Scripture, Ethics, and the Possibility of Same-Sex Relationships*, 57.

divine revelation and thus cannot suffice for overriding Scripture and revising doctrine. This has been acknowledged even by some gay believers who advocate innovation, including Michael Vasey: "Any use of [social and personal experience] must allow for the possibility that people's self-understanding may be distorted and should be brought to the bar of Scripture."[40]

The argument from spiritual evidence assumes two things: that sexual immorality obstructs the Holy Spirit's activity, such that a believer can't bear spiritual fruit despite sexual sin, and that God's spiritual gift indicates God's moral approval, such that spiritual fruit vindicates sexual relationship. Yet Scripture supplies examples of those whom God gifted spiritually for leading God's people—yet who sinned, sometimes sexually, even grievously. So it was with Israel's two greatest kings, David and Solomon, and with the church's two greatest apostles, Peter ("sinful man" [Luke 5:8] and "stumbling block" [Matt. 16:23]) and Paul ("chief" of sinners [1 Tim. 1:15 KJV] and "least" of apostles [1 Cor. 15:9]). God may produce spiritual fruit in one's life through the Holy Spirit—and yet one's life might still involve sinful conduct, including sexual sin. According to Scripture, our lives bearing fruit of God's Spirit testifies to God's grace, not our righteousness.

All this considered, I concur with Winner: "Our individual experience is corrupted; thus it must be interpreted by and refined by Christian scripture and tradition."[41]

40. Vasey, "Travelling Together?," 62.
41. Winner, *Real Sex*, 20.

PART 2

FRAMING
THE
QUESTION

A MATTER OF MARRIAGE

3

A Great Mystery

MARRIAGE IN SCRIPTURE AND TRADITION

"For this reason a man will leave his father and mother and be joined to his wife, and the two will become one flesh." This is a great mystery, and I am applying it to Christ and the church.

Ephesians 5:31–32 (quoting Gen. 2:24)

The First Matter: Marriage

It is crucial to properly frame a question for discernment. If the way we pose a question doesn't direct us to the heart of the matter, our discernment may miss the mark of truth and misdirect the church. We need to say what the matter is that we are to discern and why it matters to the church. Doing this for the question of same-sex union is the aim of part 2.

The question we are discerning is whether the church should sanction same-sex union. What, fundamentally, is this question for the church? One might say that it concerns primarily sexuality—sexual activity, or sexual relationship, or sexual identity. Or one might say that it concerns primarily ethics—love, or justice, or inclusion. These are aspects of the matter. Yet they don't direct us to the heart of the matter, as I see it.

Pharisees once asked Jesus whether divorce is ever permissible—and, if so, for what cause (Matt. 19:3–9; Mark 10:2–9). This question drew Jesus into a debate. What, basically, was this question? One might say it was a legal matter, parsing and applying what Moses wrote in the law. Or one might say it was a justice matter, balancing rights and responsibilities between men and women in household and city. Those were aspects of the matter. Yet they didn't get to the heart of the matter, as Jesus saw it.

While Pharisees asked about divorce, citing the law code, Jesus answered about marriage, citing the creation story. Jesus shifted the question, from legality of divorce to theology of marriage. Jesus's redirection of the question indicated that the divorce debate had become misdirected because it had lost sight of marriage. The matter of divorce, as Jesus saw it, concerns first of all God's design of marriage: to judge properly what the law says about divorce we must first ask what God intended for marriage.

Likewise, I suggest, we should address the question of same-sex union as, first of all, a matter of marriage. The church's debate typically begins with and centers on a question much like that of the Pharisees: whether same-sex intercourse is ever permissible—and, if so, under what conditions. That ethical question is easily detached from the theological frame within which the church has traditionally viewed sex—namely, marriage. Consequently, the church's debate about same-sex union can become misdirected when it loses sight of marriage. To judge properly whether the church might sanction same-sex union, then, we must first ask what God has willed for marriage. Stanley Hauerwas comments on the import of Jesus's reply:

> Jesus . . . reminds the Pharisees that marriage is not just about marriage, but is about the very character of Israel's faithfulness to the one who has been faithful to it. Marriage, and the question of divorce, cannot be abstracted from the purpose of marriage for the people of God.
>
> The grammar of the Pharisees' question to Jesus is very similar to discussion about marriage and sex by contemporary Christians. We ask about "any cause" before we know what we are talking about. We ask about homosexuality before we know what or how we should think about marriage. To begin the conversation this way, however, is a deep mistake. . . .
>
> Jesus's appeal to God's creative purpose to try to bring the Pharisees back to the story is necessary if we are to understand and practice rightly the gift of one another in marriage.[1]

The question the church must discern is not only, or primarily, an ethical matter, concerning right conduct in sexual activity. The question is also, and more so, a theological matter, concerning God's intention for sex and marriage.

1. Hauerwas, *Matthew*, 169–70.

The first matter we must consider, therefore, is Scripture's witness, and the church's tradition, concerning what marriage is, what marriage is for, and what marriage signifies.

I do not intend in this chapter to say anything essentially new about marriage. I will not attempt a comprehensive review of the biblical witness to marriage, much less develop a systematic theology of marriage. The discussion in this chapter is presented by way of reminder. My intent is to elaborate a traditional interpretation of Scripture and teaching on marriage as a baseline for discerning the question of same-sex union.

Marriage: Scripture and Tradition

Scripture and tradition witness to marriage as a God-ordained, three-faceted, interlocking reality: form, function, and figure (or pattern, purpose, and symbol). God designed marriage to inscribe the fidelity of covenant within the form of creation: marriage is unitive of the sexes, mutual between the spouses, exclusive of all others, and enduring throughout life.[2] God ordained and blessed marriage to serve God's purpose in creation and covenant: marriage is for the companionship-partnership of man and woman to generate, nurture, and instruct children, rule creation, cultivate virtue, solidify society, and remedy sin.[3] And God designated marriage to signify God's promise of salvation: the union of husband and wife figures or symbolizes God's covenant with Israel and Christ's union with the church, pointing to the consummation of creation and covenant.[4]

Preserving and developing the biblical witness, major theologians of the early church, East and West, acknowledged and articulated this three-faceted reality of marriage. The leading authority of the Eastern church concerning marriage is John Chrysostom, a presbyter of the Syrian church at Antioch and then archbishop of Constantinople in the late fourth and early fifth centuries.[5] Chrysostom cited all three aspects of marriage in a single paragraph of one homily: "Marriage is a bond ordained by God. . . . You are marrying your wife for the procreation of children and for moderation of life. . . . It is a mystery, an image of something far greater. . . . It is an image of the Church, and of

2. See Gen. 1:26–28; 2:23–25; Exod. 20:14; Deut. 5:18; Prov. 2:16–19; Song 2:16; 6:3; 8:6–7; Mal. 2:14–16; Matt. 19:3–9; Mark 10:2–9; Rom. 7:2; 1 Cor. 7:2–5, 10–11, 39; Eph. 5:21, 25–30.
3. See Gen. 1:26–28; 2:15–18; Pss. 127; 128; Prov. 5; 18:22; Eccles. 9:9; 1 Cor. 7:2, 9; Eph. 6:1–4; Heb. 13:4. Cf. Tob. 6:18; 8:5–8.
4. See Isa. 54:4–8; 61:10; 62:4–5; Jer. 2:2; 3:6–9; Ezek. 16; Hosea 1–3; 1 Cor. 6:15–17; 2 Cor. 11:2; Eph. 5:21–33; Rev. 19:6–9; 21:1–7.
5. On Chrysostom's views of sex and marriage, see Ford, *Women and Men in the Early Church*; Trenham, *Marriage and Virginity in St. John Chrysostom*.

Christ."[6] In Chrysostom's view, the fundamental truth of marriage is the unity in love of husband and wife, which is the foundation for both the function and symbol of marriage. The union of man and woman in marriage fulfills God's intention in creation: "From the beginning God in His providence has planned this union of man and woman." The love uniting man and woman in marriage was "deeply planted within our inmost being" at creation and is "the force that welds society together." The sexual union of man and woman as "one flesh" in marriage, further, symbolizes the spiritual union of believers with Christ in salvation: "Our relationship to Christ is the same; we become one flesh with him through communion, . . . because this has been His plan from the beginning."[7]

The leading authority of the Western church concerning marriage is Augustine, a bishop of the North African church in the late fourth and early fifth centuries.[8] Augustine famously characterized marriage in terms of several "goods" toward which marriage is ordered: charity, children, fidelity, and chastity. When a couple is united in the church, there is in their marriage a sacred bond between the spouses and a sacred sign of the union of Christ and the church.[9] Thomas Aquinas, a major theologian of Western Christianity in the medieval era, presented marriage as form, function, and figure: "Matrimony, then, as consisting in the union of male and female, intending to beget offspring to the worship of God, is a Sacrament of the Church. . . . By the union of male and female, there is figuratively represented the union of Christ with His Church."[10]

This three-faceted view of marriage has been transmitted across centuries through liturgical rites. Christians in early centuries typically adopted the wedding customs of their native cultures, while church leaders sought to moderate the excesses and sanctify the occasions with piety, prayer, and priestly blessing.[11] While there is evidence of a Christian rite of blessing marriage at the altar from the late fourth to early fifth century,[12] the oldest surviving Christian marriage rites date from the seventh and eighth centuries.[13] The following prayer

6. Chrysostom, *Homily 12 on Colossians*, in *On Marriage and Family Life*, 74–75.
7. Chrysostom, *Homily 20 on Ephesians*, in *On Marriage and Family Life*, 43–44, 51–52. See also Ford, *Women and Men in the Early Church*, 53–55; Guroian, *Orthodox Reality*, 111–14.
8. Concerning Augustine's theology of sex and marriage, see Reynolds, *Marriage in the Western Church*, 241–311; Roberts, *Creation and Covenant*, 39–72; Schafer, *Marriage, Sex, and Procreation*, 22–75; Witte, *From Sacrament to Contract*, 65–75.
9. Augustine, *On the Good of Marriage*.
10. Aquinas, *Summa Contra Gentiles* IV.78.
11. See Ignatius, *To Polycarp 5*, in M. Holmes, *Apostolic Fathers*, 197–99; Tertullian, *To His Wife* 2.8, in Hunter, *Marriage in the Early Church*, 38; Chrysostom, *Homily 12 on Colossians*, in *On Marriage and Family Life*, 77–80; Chrysostom, *How to Choose a Wife*, in *On Marriage and Family Life*, 113–14.
12. See Paulinus of Nola, *Carmen 25*, 199–233, in Hunter, *Marriage in the Early Church*, 138–39.
13. See Reynolds, *Marriage in the Western Church*, 318–23, 362–85.

of nuptial blessing invokes God as the one who created man and woman for inseparable partnership, blessed their union for generating children and ordering society, and sanctified their union to symbolize Christ and the church:

> O God, you who made all things out of nothing by the power of your goodness, at the beginning of the creation of the universe you established for man, made in the image of God, the inseparable assistance of woman. Out of the man you gave to the woman the origin of her flesh, thereby teaching that what had been created out of one ought never to be separated. O God, you have consecrated the conjugal union with so excellent a mystery in order to signify the sacrament of Christ and the church in the bond of married persons. O God, by your agency woman is united to man, and society is ordered from the beginning by the gift of that blessing, which is the only decree that was not removed by either the penalty of original sin or by the flood.[14]

The three-faceted reality of marriage is witnessed also, nearly a millennium later, by the rite for the solemnization of matrimony in the Book of Common Prayer. The rite begins by invoking God's ordination of marriage between man and woman and designation of marriage as a symbol of Christ and the church: "Dearly beloved, we are gathered together in the sight of God, and in the face of this congregation, to joyn together this man and this woman in holy Matrimony; which is an honourable estate, instituted of God in the time of mans innocency, signifying unto us the mystical union that is betwixt Christ and his Church." The rite continues by calling the couple and the congregation to give due consideration to "the causes for which matrimony was ordained." "First, it was ordained for the procreation of children, to be brought up in the fear and nurture of the Lord, and to the praise of his holy Name. Secondly, it was ordained for a remedy against sin, and to avoid fornication. . . . Thirdly, it was ordained for the mutual society, help and comfort, that the one ought to have of the other, both in prosperity and in adversity."[15] These nuptial rites, spanning centuries of tradition, acknowledge the pattern or form ("man and woman," "conjugal union," "never to be separated"), purpose or function (partnership, procreation, ordering society, preventing sin), and symbol or figure (Christ and the church) of marriage.

This three-faceted reality of marriage is evident also in the marriage rite of the Orthodox Church, with roots reaching back ten centuries. The full rite

---

14. *Hadrianum* 838a, in Hunter, *Marriage in the Early Church*, 152.

15. Cited from Cummings, *Book of Common Prayer*, 434–35. I cite the 1662 revision of the marriage rite, which became the liturgical norm for global Anglicanism—see Varcoe, "Marriage," 510–11.

comprises a service of betrothal, by which husband and wife are joined in wedlock, and a service of crowning, by which the spouses are blessed at the altar, crowned for the kingdom, and united with Christ in the Eucharist. The betrothal service, affirming that God ordained marriage to be "an indissoluble bond of love," acknowledges in prayer for the spouses the form and function of marriage that God ordained at creation: "Establish in them the holy union which is from Thee. For in the beginning Thou didst make them male and female, and by Thee the woman is joined unto the man as a helper and for the procreation of the human race." The crowning service recounts salvation history from Adam to Christ, placing God's ordination of marriage within God's purpose of creation and promise of covenant, and prays God's blessing on the spouses for "chastity, mutual love in the bond of peace, long-lived off-spring, . . . [and] a crown of glory that shall not fade away." After the couple is crowned, Ephesians 5 is read, culminating in the proclamation that the union of husband and wife reveals "a great mystery" of "Christ and the church."[16]

Over the centuries, the major branches of Christianity—Orthodox, Catholic, and Protestant—have recognized this three-faceted reality of marriage. Within that common framework, these branches have articulated diverse views of marriage.[17] One difference concerns which purpose—partnership of spouses, promotion of virtue, procreation of offspring, or protection from sin—receives primary emphasis. All three branches, while recognizing all these purposes, have variously prioritized them. Orthodoxy has tended to put first emphasis on the ascetic discipline of marriage in promoting virtue; Catholicism has tended to put first emphasis on the generative purpose of marriage in procreating children; and Protestantism has generally tended to put first emphasis on either partnership of spouses or protection from sin. Another difference concerns the symbol of marriage: the Orthodox, Catholic, and Protestant branches have agreed that Christian marriage presents a figure of Christ and the church, but they have differed on whether marriage solemnized by the church at the altar is a sacrament (analogous to baptism and Eucharist) and whether the sacred bond between spouses is temporal or eternal. Protestantism has generally not considered marriage a sacrament; Catholicism holds that the sacred bond endures until death, and Orthodoxy holds that the sacred bond endures into eternity.

Nonetheless, all branches of Christian tradition share an ecumenical consensus on the creational-covenantal form of marriage: one man and one

16. Meyendorff, *Marriage*, 29–42, 113–31. See also Schmemann, *For the Life of the World*, 107–11.

17. For the Eastern (Orthodox) tradition, see Meyendorff, *Marriage*; Schmemann, *For the Life of the World*, 99–114. For the Western (Catholic and Protestant) traditions, see Reynolds, *Marriage in the Western Church*; Witte, *From Sacrament to Contract*.

woman, joined in sexual-social unity, promised in exclusive-enduring fidelity.[18] The creational and covenantal aspects of marriage are correlated: God's creation of humankind as male and female, man and woman, establishes the fundamental form of marriage; and God's ordination of marriage inscribes the fidelity of covenant within this form of creation. In the traditional understanding of marriage, this form fits marriage for its function and figure, so that form, function, and figure compose an integrated reality.[19] God, having created humankind "male and female," ordained the "one flesh" union of man and woman in marriage to serve God's purpose in creation and promise in covenant and, further, designated the union of husband and wife to signify God's work of salvation fulfilled in the union of Christ and the church. Marriage is founded on the God-created sexuate correspondence of human embodiment—male and female, man and woman—which is the fundamental feature that underlies the form, function, and figure of marriage.[20]

The Purpose of Marriage according to Scripture: Creation and Covenant

The church has traditionally taught, based on Scripture, that God designed marriage to be both unitive and generative. A traditional perspective sees God's design of marriage, which fits form to function, in the Genesis account of creation. Genesis 1–2 has been interpreted traditionally as implying an intentional ordering: God creates man and woman as corresponding counterparts and ordains their union by marriage for the sake of partnership and procreation, which indicates the place of marriage in God's purpose of creation and promise of salvation. I will unfold these in turn.

Marriage in God's Creation

God creates humankind "in the image of God" and "male and female." These are fundamental facts of biblical-theological anthropology. Genesis puts "in the image of God" and "male and female" in parallel:

> God created humankind in his own image,
> *in the image of God* he created them;
> *male and female* he created them. (Gen. 1:27 NET,
>   emphasis added; cf. 5:1–2)

18. For a recent reaffirmation of this ecumenical consensus, see Evangelicals and Catholics Together, "The Two Shall Become One Flesh."

19. See B. Jones, *Faithful*, 68–71. Consequently, as Jones observes, "sex gone wrong" violates the God-ordained reality of marriage in all three aspects—see *Faithful*, 36–50.

20. See T. Wilson, *Mere Sexuality*, 33–36.

This parallel is important. Both "in the image of God" and "male and female" name the God-created being and point to the God-intended responsibility of humankind; both "in the image of God" and "male and female" state God's design of, and relate to God's purpose for, humankind. God created male and female in the image of God—and God intended male and female to work together as the image of God in the service of God.

Before proceeding, I will make two comments. First, a clarification. Many writers refer to "male and female" or "man and woman" by the term "sex(ual) difference." This term is accurate but incomplete. Sex in humankind is a God-created difference: God creates sex in humankind; and sex differentiates human beings. Yet "difference" falls short of what Genesis says about sex: God's creation of sex not only differentiates male and female but also correlates male and female for God's commission to procreation and dominion (Gen. 1); God makes woman by making a difference from man but God makes woman to correspond to man so that they can be united as partners (Gen. 2). In Genesis, sex is a difference that correlates, unites, and generates.[21] Nate Collins uses the term "sexuate" to express the fundamental fact of biblical-theological anthropology that God creates humankind as "male and female" such that humankind is "characterized by sex difference."[22] I use the term "sexuate correspondence" to indicate the correlative, unitive, and generative aspects of "male and female" or "man and woman."

Second, a qualification. I do not suggest that the following discussion exhausts the significance of "image of God" or "male and female" for being human or human responsibility. Nothing I say here should be taken to imply that humankind as "image of God" and "male and female" participates in God's purpose only by marriage and procreation. Genesis does not simply equate being human and being married such that to become fully human is to get married and beget children.[23] In the following discussion, the word "includes" is used advisedly to emphasize this point.

God's purpose for humankind as the image of God includes representing God's way of wisdom in the order of creation. God creates all other living creatures "according to their kinds / its kind" (Gen. 1:12, 21, 25 NET) but creates humankind "in the image of God" (1:27), which indicates that God creates humankind with a unique status and for a special role. God creates humankind in God's image so that, alone among God's creatures, humankind might relate to God in personal terms, receive God's instruction, and

21. See also Davidson, *Flame of Yahweh*, 15–54.
22. N. Collins, *All but Invisible*, 146.
23. See Callaway, *Breaking the Marriage Idol*, 109–17.

thus serve God as vice-regent in creation. God creates humankind, male and female, for the royal responsibility of ruling the earth in the wisdom by which God created all things: "Let us make humankind in our image, . . . so they may rule . . . over all the earth, and over all the creatures that move on the earth" (Gen. 1:26 NET; cf. Gen. 2:19; Ps. 8; Prov. 8). Humankind's responsibility as God's vice-regent includes acting as caretaker of the earth, by cultivating and maintaining the goodness of God's garden (Gen. 2:15), and acting as custodian of worship, by leading the choir of all creatures in praise of their Creator (Ps. 148).

God's purpose for humankind as male and female also includes participating in God's creative purpose; and humankind's participation in God's creative purpose includes procreation. God makes, blesses, and commissions humankind: "Male and female he created them. God blessed them and said to them, 'Be fruitful and multiply!'" (Gen. 1:27–28 NET). God creates "male and female," blesses male and female ("them"), and directs their blessed union toward procreation. "In Genesis sex was created for the sake of procreation."[24] Procreation is thus humankind's cooperation with God's purpose in creation; human begetting is the fruition of divine blessing.

God intends these two aspects of humankind—"in the image of God" and "male and female"—to work together for God's purpose. Whereas God blesses and commissions other creature kinds for procreation (Gen. 1:22), God blesses and commissions "male and female" to "be fruitful and multiply" with a view toward humankind's special role as "image of God." Humankind, by begetting and nurturing offspring through male-female union, propagates the image of God throughout the earth. The goal toward which God has ordered the making, blessing, and commissioning of humankind is evident by the ordering in the text:

> Then God said, "Let us make humankind in our image, . . . so they may rule. . . . "
>
> God created humankind in his own image, . . .
> male and female he created them.
>
> God blessed them and said to them, "Be fruitful and multiply! Fill the earth and subdue it! Rule over . . ." (Gen. 1:26–28 NET)

God creates humankind in the image of God and as male and female, blesses male and female, and commissions them to procreate, so that humankind

---

24. Goldingay, *Old Testament Theology*, 3:388.

might propagate God's image and administer God's rule throughout God's earth.[25]

Genesis 1 presents an orderly account of God's creating and blessing male and female with a view toward procreation of humankind and propagation of God's image. Genesis 2 presents a narrative account of God's creating man and woman as gendered counterparts for the sake of joining them in sexual-social partnership. God, because there was not yet any creature to serve the earth God made, makes the human being from the soil, infuses the human being with life breath, plants a garden, places the human being in the garden, and gives the human being the task of cultivating and maintaining the garden (2:5–8, 15). God, judging that "it is not good that the man should be alone" in executing this task, resolves to "make him a helper as his partner" (2:18). Not finding a suitable helper-partner among the animals that God has made from the ground, God makes a helper-partner corresponding to the man by making a woman—not from earth's soil, but from the man's side—and brings the woman to the man. The man rejoices in the woman: "This one at last is bone of my bones and flesh of my flesh" (2:23 NET). The narrative culminates by God joining man and woman in marriage: the man separates from his parents and unites to the woman; "They become one flesh"—sexually, as one body, and socially, as one family—and live together "naked" but "not ashamed" (2:24–25). Reading together Genesis 1 and Genesis 2: God creates humankind male and female and ordains marriage as the sexual-social union of man and woman, to be unitive ("They become one flesh"; 2:24) and generative ("Be fruitful and multiply"; 1:28)—and both unitive and generative for the sake of humankind's responsibility as God's vice-regent ("rule over"; 1:28) on earth and God's caretaker ("till and keep"; 2:15) of earth.[26]

Marriage in God's Covenant

God designs marriage with its purposes of partnership and procreation, furthermore, as fit for serving God's plan of salvation.[27] God's creation of humankind in the image of God and as male and female is designed not only for humankind to be participants in God's purpose of creation but also for humankind to become recipients of God's promise in covenant. God remains committed to God's purpose in creation and pattern of marriage, despite

---

25. See B. Anderson, *From Creation to New Creation*, 128–29; Bauckham, *Bible and Ecology*, 16–19; Dearman, "Marriage in the Old Testament," 54–55; Fretheim, *God and World in the Old Testament*, 48–50; Goldingay, *Old Testament Theology*, 3:518–21; Walton, *Lost World of Genesis One*, 68–69.

26. See also Ash, *Marriage*, 112–22.

27. See also Reno, *Genesis*, 29–76.

humankind's disobedience and even despite God's knowing the evil inclination of the human heart (Gen. 6:5–6; 8:21–22). God renews the blessing of marriage and commission to procreation beyond God's expulsion of human beings from the garden and destruction of living beings on earth (4:1; 5:1–2; 9:1–7).

Humankind's cooperation with God's commission—begetting and nurturing offspring by sexual-social one-flesh man-woman union—generates a people with whom God relates by covenant. God's blessing of marriage thus prepares for God's blessing through covenant: from the fecund union of man and woman come generations of God's people to whom God's promises will be made and fulfilled. God's blessing marriage and commissioning procreation in creation (Gen. 1:28; 5:1–3) thus correspond to God's promising blessing and giving commandment in covenant (Exod. 23:25–26; Deut. 6:1–9; 7:12–14; 28:1–30:20). God sustains this blessing and commission among God's people even while they dwell in foreign lands, oppressed by foreign powers, and while fulfillment of God's promise lies in the future (Gen. 35:10–12; Exod. 1:1–21; Ps. 105:23–25; Jer. 29:4–14).

The connection between God's blessing marriage in creation and God's promising blessing in covenant is evident in both God's covenant with Noah (Gen. 6:17–19; 8:15–17; 9:1–17) and God's covenant with Abraham, Isaac, and Jacob (12:1–3; 13:14–17; 15:1–6; 17:1–22; 22:16–18; 26:2–5, 24; 28:13–15; 35:10–12). Through covenant with Noah, God will bless all creatures on earth; through covenant with Abraham, God will bless all nations of humankind. God blesses and commissions male and female to be fruitful and multiply, and from among the families of humankind generated by marriage, God chooses and blesses the families of Noah and Abraham, with a view toward and for the sake of God's creational purpose and covenantal promise, which God works through successive generations of God's people to bless all nations and the whole creation.

So God fit pattern to purpose in marriage in order to serve God's purpose in creation and promise in covenant. "From the beginning, then, a marriage was designed to generate a household, initially to make it possible to fill the earth and serve the garden, then to make it possible to fulfill Yhwh's purpose to make Abraham a great nation such as will attract the world to Yhwh."[28] God's purpose in creating, blessing, and commissioning "male and female" to "be fruitful and multiply" is not merely to "fill the earth" with humankind (Gen. 1:26–28). According to prophets, God's purpose and promise will be fulfilled when through God's people, and through the messianic king descended from God's people, all nations will be ruled by justice and all creatures will

---

28. Goldingay, *Old Testament Theology*, 3:387.

dwell in peace, "for the earth will be full of the knowledge of the LORD" (Isa. 11:1–9; cf. Isa. 27:6; Hab. 2:14).

The biblical narrative shows that the generative purpose of marriage proceeds from God's creation and is ordered toward humankind's dominion—but, in a fallen creation, succeeds by God's providence.[29] Recurring circumstances of child loss or childlessness in Genesis, especially, amplify the message that God's creational purpose and covenantal promise, worked through marriage and procreation, are accomplished with God's help and as God's gift.[30] Accordingly, biblical genealogies attest to humankind's cooperation with God's creational purpose and covenantal promise—and to God's provision in sustaining humankind's part in God's purpose and promise. Biblical genealogies are thus theological testimonies as well as human histories: they testify to God's faithfulness to God's creational purpose and covenantal promise, worked by God's providence—despite infertility and maternal mortality, infidelity and incest, conflict and deceit, fratricide and famine—through humankind's generations by marriage.[31]

Marriage in God's Wisdom

Song of Songs, a book of poems celebrating love, sex, and marriage, emphasizes intimacy between spouses and the delights of sex but does not mention generation of offspring. Some innovationists have inferred from this that Scripture considers companionship as integral but procreation as incidental to God's purpose for marriage.[32] We might observe also that Proverbs 31:10–31, an ode honoring the "capable wife" (NRSV) or "wife of noble character" (NET), highlights her works of provision and words of prudence as household partner but mentions intimacy between spouses ("The heart of her husband trusts in her"; 31:11) and the blessing of children ("Her children rise up and call her happy"; 31:28) each only once. We might infer from this, likewise, that Scripture considers both companionship and procreation as incidental to God's purpose for marriage. The former inference seems no more probable than the latter inference.

---

29. Goldingay, *Old Testament Theology*, 3:388, comments concerning procreation: "God does not make it an invariable consequence of being married (that is, some people cannot have children), so we might not have to regard it as a categorical obligation." Fulfilling the commission of procreation in a fallen creation depends on factors that couples cannot control (infertility, physical frailty, infant and maternal mortality, etc.) but that in some cases God intervenes to overcome. Accordingly, although "Be fruitful and multiply" is formed grammatically in the imperative mood (in both Hebrew and Greek), I refer to procreation as "commission" rather than "command" or "mandate."

30. See Danylak, *Redeeming Singleness*, 25–53; Davidson, *Flame of Yahweh*, 447–57.

31. See Fretheim, *God and World in the Old Testament*, 60–61, 106–8; Goldingay, *Old Testament Theology*, 3:285–87.

32. See Brownson, *Bible, Gender, Sexuality*, 116; Vines, *God and the Gay Christian*, 141; Song, *Covenant and Calling*, 55.

Rather than reading these texts as depreciating procreation, I suggest, we do better to read them as appreciating further aspects of married love and domestic life. These texts belong to the wisdom writings, which paint a whole picture of marriage. Biblical wisdom, which esteems marriage as "a good thing" (Prov. 18:22), affirms the mutual enjoyment of marital companionship in a toilsome life (Eccles. 9:9) and approves the pleasure of sex between husband and wife (Prov. 5:18–19). At the same time, biblical wisdom sees children as the fruition of divine blessing in marriage: children are the fruit of sex and a gift of God (Pss. 127; 128). So, sex in marriage is for more than procreation: it bonds spouses and brings joy as well as begets children.[33] And a "capable wife" is worth more than her birthing and mothering of children: she herself, like Lady Wisdom, is much more valuable than gold and jewels (Prov. 31:10; cf. 3:14–15); she is praiseworthy, above all, because she is "a woman who fears the LORD" (31:30).[34] Procreation is not the sole purpose of sex in marriage; yet neither is procreation peripheral to God's purpose for marriage. Biblical wisdom esteems marriage as "a good thing" for reasons exceeding, yet including, procreation.

These observations beget questions of marriage and happiness: Is promoting happiness a purpose of marriage? Is being married necessary to being happy? The wisdom writings associate marriage with happiness, but not directly: children by marriage make a household happy (Ps. 127), but blessedness by fruit of the womb is secondary to happiness by fear of the Lord (128). Biblical wisdom maintains that fearing God—reverencing God's name, studying God's law, walking God's way—is the primary duty of humankind and true source of blessedness or happiness (Ps. 1; Prov. 1–4). According to biblical wisdom, while marriage is blessed of God and children by marriage are blessings from God, marriage is neither prerequisite of blessedness nor guarantor of happiness. Just as the creation story does not simply equate being human with being married, the wisdom writings do not simply equate blessedness or happiness with marriage and children.

The Purpose of Marriage according to Tradition: The Good of Marriage

God's fitting of pattern to purpose in marriage, evident in Scripture, has been emphasized by tradition. This is especially so with Augustine, whose marriage theology has been formative for the Western church. In the late

---

33. See also Hollinger, *Meaning of Sex*, 93–115, 146–55.

34. On Song of Songs, see Davidson, *Flame of Yahweh*, 545–632; Goldingay, *Old Testament Theology*, 3:357–63; B. Jones, *Faithful*, 51–60; Miles, *Redemption of Love*, 137–65. On Prov. 31, see Davidson, *Flame of Yahweh*, 283–86; Ash, *Marriage*, 168–69.

fourth century, an intense debate raged over the relative value of celibacy and marriage. Jovinian, a monk, taught that marriage and celibacy do not differ inherently in sanctity; Jerome, against Jovinian, defended celibacy at cost of denigrating marriage. In his treatise *On the Good of Marriage*, Augustine articulated a moderate view that affirmed marriage as a God-ordained good while maintaining the superiority of celibacy.[35] He answered the question "What is marriage for?" in terms of several "goods" or "ends" toward which God has ordered marriage: charity, procreation, fidelity, and chastity.

First, in marriage well lived, "the natural association . . . between the sexes" develops into an "order of charity between husband and wife." Second, through marriage "carnal or youthful incontinence . . . is directed toward . . . procreating children." Third, by fulfilling their conjugal obligations, husband and wife maintain a "mutual fidelity," which is "a great good of the spirit." Together, these goods of marriage enable husband and wife to maintain chastity by providing the "mutual service" of protection from "illicit intercourse." Augustine thus summarized the good of marriage: "The glory of marriage, therefore, is the chastity . . . of procreation and fidelity . . . in rendering the duty of the flesh."[36] Later in his treatise, Augustine added the good of "sacramental bond" to marriage entered within the church: marriage in Christ is a symbol of stability and thus is indissoluble.[37] When summarizing, Augustine drops charity and chastity, enumerating the famous triad often cited by tradition: procreation, fidelity, and sacrament.[38]

Augustine elaborated the relations among the goods of charity, fidelity, and procreation. He did not maintain that procreation is the only good of marriage, the unintended absence of which would justify dissolving marriage. Thus, the death of children before maturity or the aging of spouses beyond normal potential for procreation does not warrant abandoning the charitable society of husband and wife, which remains good even if a marriage happens not to result in offspring.[39] Augustine, moreover, did not maintain that procreation is the ultimate good of marriage, the pursuit of which would justify sacrificing the other goods of marriage. Thus, a lack of fertility cannot justify violating conjugal fidelity between husband and wife, by adultery or polygamy or divorce-remarriage, for the sake of generating offspring.[40]

---

35. See Brown, *Body and Society*, 359–60; Hunter, *Marriage in the Early Church*, 20–21; Reynolds, *Marriage in the Western Church*, 259; Schafer, *Marriage, Sex, and Procreation*, 11–21.

36. Augustine, *On the Good of Marriage* 3–4, 6, 12.

37. Augustine, *On the Good of Marriage* 17.

38. Augustine, *On the Good of Marriage* 32. Peter Lombard, *Sentences, Book 4*, dist. 31, simply assumes the Augustinian triad; Aquinas, *Summa Contra Gentiles* IV.78, follows suit.

39. Augustine, *On the Good of Marriage* 3.

40. Augustine, *On the Good of Marriage* 7, 17–18, 32.

Augustine, however, did maintain that, while not every couple will generate offspring or even engage in sexual intercourse throughout married life, procreation is an integral good of God's design of marriage. Thus, an open disposition of both spouses toward procreation is necessary to marriage.[41]

In Augustine's view, then, the goods of marriage are distinct but not separable or exchangeable. While each of charity, fidelity, and procreation is good, one good cannot be sought exclusive of the other goods: charity between spouses is its own good, but seeking companionship while violating fidelity or avoiding procreation does not make a marriage. Also, one good cannot be sought at the expense of another good: building charity or keeping fidelity cannot substitute for pursuing procreation; nor can charity or fidelity be sacrificed for the sake of procreation. The goods of marriage are not a menu of options among which couples might make elective choices or trade-offs. Couples entering marriage should be properly disposed toward each good, intending marriage in full. The goods of marriage are "integrated, interacting, and reinforcing goods. They are all important individually, and they are all important to each other."[42] According to Augustine, and the Western church after him, the goods of marriage are cooperative, divinely designed to function together as an integral whole.[43]

The Nuptial Figure in Scripture: A Summary of the Story

As presented in Scripture, marriage summarizes the overarching story of creation, fall, redemption, and new creation. The biblical canon is bookended by marriage: marriage is a canonical *inclusio* that correlates the beginning and end of Scripture and frames the entire story between.[44] The biblical story of God's providential dealing with humankind unfolds under the nuptial figure.[45] The story of salvation is depicted in the image of marriage.[46]

---

41. Augustine, *On the Good of Marriage* 5.

42. Witte, *From Sacrament to Contract*, 74.

43. See also Schafer, *Marriage, Sex, and Procreation*, 22–51; Levering, "Thomas Aquinas on Sexual Ethics," 175–80.

44. Marriage is one of (at least) six images or motifs that interconnect the biblical canon from creation through Christ to new creation: heaven and earth (Gen. 1:1; 2:1, 4; Matt. 5:18; 6:10; 24:35; Rev. 21:1); light (Gen. 1:3; John 1:1–9; 8:12; Rev. 21:23–24; 22:5); tree of life (Gen. 2:9; 3:22–24; John 15:1–6; Rev. 2:7; 22:2, 14, 19); river of life (Gen. 2:10; John 4:13–14; 7:37–38; Rev. 21:6; 22:1, 17); God-human communion (Gen. 3:8–9; Matt. 1:23; 28:20; John 1:14; 14:3; Rev. 21:3); and man-woman union (Gen. 1:27–28; 2:23–24; Matt. 19:4–6; 22:1–14; 25:1–13; John 2:1–11; Rev. 21:2). See also Driggers, "New Testament Appropriations of Genesis 1–2," 70–73.

45. On the nuptial figure in Scripture and tradition, see Radner, *Hope among the Fragments*, 121–38.

46. See also N. T. Wright, "From Genesis to Revelation"; O'Reilly, "What Makes Sex Beautiful?"

Marriage: Positive Image

At the beginning of the story, in a crowning act of creation, God designs humankind "in the image of God" and differentiates humankind as "male and female" and then joins them into "one flesh." God initiates relation with humankind through marriage of man and woman, whom God blesses to participate in God's purpose of creation, to propagate God's image and represent God's rule throughout God's earth (Gen. 1–2). At the center of the story, joining creation to salvation by incarnation, God sends Jesus. The Gospels present Jesus's messianic mission to inaugurate God's kingdom in nuptial figure: Jesus comes as the "bridegroom" to seek his "bride" (Mark 2:19–20; John 3:29); Jesus calls us to quickly accept the invitation to, and come prepared in proper clothing for, his "wedding banquet" (Matt. 22:1–14); Jesus admonishes us to eagerly anticipate and vigilantly await his coming as the "bridegroom" to his "wedding banquet" (25:1–13). At the end of the story, in a culminating act of salvation, God dwells personally with humankind in an eternal union of covenantal fidelity: they will be God's peoples, and God will be with them and be their God. God finalizes the covenant with humankind in the renewal of creation through the union of Christ and the church: the new Jerusalem, coming from God, descends from heaven "prepared as a bride adorned for her husband" (Rev. 21:2). God consummates relation with humankind, reuniting heaven and earth, through Christ's marriage to the church (Rev. 21–22).

From a canonical perspective, God blesses union of man and woman in monogamous marriage at the beginning as a sign, which God fulfills by the union of God with humankind in faithful covenant at the end. The nuptial of Adam and Eve at the beginning of the story prefigures the nuptial of Christ and the church at the end of the story: Christ is the "Last Adam" and the church is the "New Eve" betrothed to Christ (cf. 1 Cor. 15:45–49; 2 Cor. 11:2–3). The nuptial of Christ and the church, which culminates God's plan of salvation, fulfills God's creational purpose and covenantal promise initiated through the nuptial of Adam and Eve.[47]

Between beginning and end, prophets and apostles depict God's work of salvation in the image of marriage. Prophetic visions depict God's covenant with Israel in nuptial figure.[48] Isaiah envisions YHWH's redemption of Jerusalem in the image of a royal wedding, in which Jerusalem becomes YHWH's queen. In Isaiah's vision, YHWH and Jerusalem are as a

---

47. See also Guroian, *Orthodox Reality*, 135–36.

48. On nuptial imagery in the Prophets, see Dearman, "Marriage in the Old Testament," 60–63. A nuptial motif is also implicit in the Torah's depiction of YHWH as "a jealous God"— see Davidson, *Flame of Yahweh*, 113–17.

"bridegroom" decked "with a garland" and a "bride" adorned "with her jewels" (Isa. 61:10). Betrothed to YHWH, the once-forsaken Jerusalem is now to be called "Married," and YHWH will rejoice over Jerusalem "as the bridegroom rejoices over the bride" (62:4–5). Isaiah employs the nuptial figure as the core image of an allegory of salvation (61:1–62:12). The prophet's announcement that YHWH will wed Jerusalem in an "everlasting covenant" signifies that YHWH will redeem Jerusalem from the shame of exile and restore Jerusalem to honor in YHWH's service. It signals to all those that had once called Jerusalem "Forsaken" and "Desolate" that YHWH will vindicate Jerusalem as YHWH's crown jewel among the nations. Thus Jerusalem's wedding clothes are the "garments of salvation" and "robe of righteousness." And Jerusalem's "new name" as the betrothed of YHWH—"Married" and "My Delight Is in Her"—indicates YHWH's renewal of and rejoicing over Jerusalem as the city of God. Isaiah's allegory of the royal wedding of YHWH and Jerusalem, which proclaims the good news of Jerusalem's redemption, prefigures the eschatological renewal of heaven and earth and the eternal union of God and God's people, the new Jerusalem.

In apostolic testimony, marriage images God's plan of salvation, which God consummates through the union of Christ and the church. Paul, citing Genesis, sees Christ and the church, united by the sacrifice of Christ, figured in husband and wife, united in the bond of marriage: "'For this reason a man will leave his father and mother and be joined to his wife, and the two will become one flesh.' This is a great mystery, and I am applying it to Christ and the church" (Eph. 5:31–32; cf. Gen. 2:24). The "this" that is "a great mystery" is God's instituting marriage in the "one flesh" union of man and woman. By calling marriage "a great mystery" referring to "Christ and the church," Paul connects God's instituting marriage at the beginning to the "mystery" of God's "plan for the fullness of time" (Eph. 1:10) that is revealed and fulfilled in "the mystery of Christ" (3:3–4). This "plan" concerns the "eternal purpose that [God] has carried out in Christ," a "mystery" formerly hidden but now "revealed to his holy prophets and apostles by the Spirit" and made known to all creation through the church (3:1–12). In Paul's vision, the "mystery" of marriage refers to God's redemptive plan to reconcile all humankind—Jew and gentile—in Christ through the church: God's uniting the "two" of man and woman in the bond of marriage, through which God creates a new human family, the "one flesh" of husband-wife-children, figures Christ's reconciling the "two" of Jew and gentile by the sacrifice of the cross, through which Christ creates "one new humanity," the "one body" of Christ that is the church (2:11–22). God's creation of a new humanity in Christ, further, is the crucial stage in God's cosmic plan to "gather up all things"—"things in heaven and things on earth"—into Christ: God's uniting husband and wife in marriage in the order of creation, which brings forth new life, figures God's uniting heaven and earth in Christ in the economy of redemption, which brings forth new creation (1:9–10).[49] In Paul's vision, marriage is a "mystery" because marriage is a revelation of God's plan of salvation in Christ.[50]

John, recalling Jesus's words, witnesses the wedding that will fully and finally unite Christ the Lamb with the church his bride in the royal court of the heavenly city. The multitude of heaven, gathered around God's throne, rejoices and exults because "the marriage of the Lamb has come" and "his bride has made herself ready," so that the "marriage supper of the Lamb" may commence (Rev. 19:5–9). The "bride" who is "ready" to wed the Lamb is the church, comprising the gathered "saints" properly "clothed" in the "fine linen" of "righteous deeds" (19:7–8; cf. Matt. 22:11–14). In John's vision, which reprises Isaiah's vision, marriage figures the fulfillment of salvation: the economy of salvation, the coming of Jesus the "bridegroom" to seek his "bride" the church, culminates in the reunion of heaven and earth, God's final renewal of all things and eternal union with God's people (Rev. 21:1–7). The marriage of the Lamb unites Christ with the church, the new Jerusalem, "the bride adorned for her husband" (21:2). And this marriage of Christ and the church begets a renewed creation in which God will dwell with mortals and "death will be no more" (21:4).[51]

Seen from John's vision of the new Jerusalem, God's blessing to humankind in creation at the beginning—"God blessed them, and God said to them . . ." (Gen. 1:28)—is a prophecy that God fulfills through God's blessing to humankind in Christ at the end: "Blessed are those who are invited to the marriage supper of the Lamb" (Rev. 19:9). Seen from Paul's revelation of the "mystery" of Christ, God's joining man and woman in the earthly garden—"They become one flesh" (Gen. 2:24; cf. Matt. 19:4–5)—is a prophecy that God fulfills through Christ and the church in the heavenly city (Eph. 5:31–32; Rev. 21:1–2). The purpose that God initiates in creation through the marriage of Adam and Eve, God completes in new creation through the marriage of Christ and the church, so that God's instituting marriage at the beginning is a sign pointing to God's finishing salvation at the end: "It is done!" (Rev. 21:6). Marriage is a prophecy of salvation, from Adam and Eve in creation to Christ and the church in new creation.

---

49. Paul's terms "mystery" (*mystērion*) and "plan" (*oikonomia*), "body" (*sōma*) and "flesh" (*sarx*), "two" and "one," interlink these four passages (Eph. 1:3–14; 2:11–22; 3:1–12; 5:21–33) across the epistle. See Yoder Neufeld, *Ephesians*, 263–64; Verhey and Harvard, *Ephesians*, 238–39, 241.

50. See also Jeal, "Visions of Marriage in Ephesians 5," 123–26.

51. See also Mangina, *Revelation*, 219, 237–43.

Marriage: Negative Image

Prophets and apostles use the nuptial figure also with a negative significance, to depict the infidelity of Israel and the church toward God. The antifigure of marriage is adultery and harlotry. In the writings of the prophets, adultery and harlotry figure humans breaking faith with God, turning from God's ways by idolatry and immorality (Jer. 2:2; 3:6–9; Ezek. 16; 23; Mal. 2:10–12; cf. Matt. 12:39; 16:4; James 4:4). Marriage figures God's fidelity in keeping covenant; adultery and harlotry figure human infidelity in breaking covenant. Marriage and adultery/harlotry thus jointly figure the mystery of God's persistent fidelity despite repeated infidelities of God's people—and God's constant will to faithfully reconcile the unfaithful covenant partner, to be forever reunited "in righteousness and in justice, in steadfast love and in mercy" (Hosea 2:19; see chaps. 1–3; cf. Isa. 54:4–8).[52]

In the writings of the apostles, infidelity figures the temptation of the church to stray from the truth and from Christ. Paul, writing to believers in Corinth, expresses a "divine jealousy" for them: "I promised you in marriage to one husband, to present you as a chaste virgin to Christ" (2 Cor. 11:2). Although they are betrothed to Christ by their confession and baptism, whenever someone comes to them proclaiming "another Jesus" of a "different spirit" and a "different gospel" than Paul has proclaimed and they have received, they "submit to it readily enough" (11:4). Paul fears that they will be "led astray from a sincere and pure devotion to Christ" (11:3). In teaching concerning sexual conduct, Paul applies the nuptial figure to the believer's relationship to Christ. The believer, by baptism in the name of Christ, is joined bodily to Christ. Paul characterizes this baptismal union in nuptial terms—"The body is meant . . . for the Lord, and the Lord for the body"—and states the ethical implication of baptismal union: "The body is meant not for fornication" (1 Cor. 6:13; cf. 7:2–4). The baptized believer engaging sexually with a prostitute "becomes one body with her"—and, because his body is joined to Christ, he effectively unites Christ to a prostitute. By his sexual immorality, the baptized believer violates his bond to Christ and pollutes the body of Christ (6:14–17). Paul's exhortation to sexual chastity—"Flee sexual immorality! . . . Glorify God with your body" (6:18–20 NET)—is a call to honor baptismal fidelity to Christ, a fidelity depicted in the nuptial figure.

John, conveying the message of Jesus to the church at Thyatira (Rev. 2:18–23), approves them for their good works and patient endurance but then reproves them for tolerating the teaching of a false prophet, symbolically

---

52. See Goldingay, *Old Testament Theology*, 3:282–85, 369–70. On these prophetic texts and their marital imagery, see Davidson, *Flame of Yahweh*, 364–69.

called "Jezebel" (2:20; cf. 1 Kings 16:29–34; 2 Kings 9:22). This false prophet is teaching believers to practice sexual immorality and participate in idolatry. By following these teachings and doing such things, the believers "commit adultery" with the false prophet, betraying their fidelity to Jesus. The false prophet has refused to heed Jesus's call to repentance, so now Jesus is bringing the false prophet to judgment—and is warning the believers that, "unless they repent of her doings" (Rev. 2:22), they will receive the same judgment.

As Paul presented his exhortations to spurn false gospels and flee sexual immorality in the figure of marital fidelity to Jesus, so John presented Jesus's warnings to spurn false prophets and repent of sexual immorality in the figure of marital fidelity to Jesus. This ethical parallel has an eschatological correlate: infidelity to Jesus will be judged by exclusion from Jesus. As Paul listed idolaters and the sexually immoral (*pornoi*) among those who "will not inherit the kingdom of God" (1 Cor. 6:9; cf. Gal. 5:16–21; Eph. 5:3–5), so John saw that idolaters and the sexually immoral (*pornoi*) are among those "outside" the holy city (Rev. 22:14–15; cf. 21:8).

The Nuptial Figure in Tradition: A Symbol of Salvation

Early theologians used the nuptial figure from Scripture to present the Christian doctrine of salvation. I will not attempt a comprehensive review of the nuptial figure in Christian tradition but will only exhibit a few examples from the fourth century.[53] While not representing the entire tradition, these examples show how this scriptural figure has shaped theological imagination. The common theme is that marriage, interpreted christologically, is a vision of God's work in Christ: marriage is a symbol of salvation.

Methodius cast the creation of the church in the figure of marriage. Methodius developed the nuptial figure by seeing in the marriage of Adam and Eve an image of the marriage of Christ and the church. As God created Eve from Adam's side while Adam slept, so God created the church from the side of Christ while Christ slept between his passion and his resurrection. Thus, just as Eve was Adam's "bone" and "flesh" (Gen. 2:23), so also the church is formed from the bone and flesh of Christ, the Last Adam, such that the church is the "body of Christ." As a man leaves father and mother to be joined to a woman (2:24), so Christ left his Father in heaven to be joined to the church his bride. Methodius identified the water of baptism as preparing for and

---

53. For a classic study of the nuptial figure in Christian tradition, see Chevasse, *Bride of Christ*. In addition to the nuptial figure of Christ and the church, there is also a tradition of interpreting Song of Songs as an allegory of the spiritual relationship between Christ and the soul, from Origen of Alexandria (third century) to Bernard of Clairvaux (twelfth century).

pointing to Christ and the church united in marriage: Christ prepares the church for marriage to Christ by cleansing the church through baptism (Eph. 5:25–27); and by recapitulating Christ's dying and rising through baptism, the church is born to new life and united to the risen Christ (Rom. 6:3–5). Believers betrothed to Christ in baptism, "promised . . . in marriage" as a "chaste virgin" to "one husband" (2 Cor. 11:2), are as one body the helper-partner of Christ (see Gen. 2:18). In their marriage partnership, Christ and the church fulfill God's commission to "be fruitful and multiply" (1:28) by generating spiritual offspring: the church, receiving the "seed" of Christ's teaching, gives "birth" to "children" that are "born to salvation" by faith through the Word of Christ and the water of baptism.[54]

Chrysostom also cast the creation and salvation of the church in the figure of marriage. Chrysostom commented several times in his homilies on Paul's reference to marriage as a "mystery" of "Christ and the church" (Eph. 5:31–32). Chrysostom, like Methodius, elaborated the nuptial figure by seeing Adam and Eve becoming "one flesh" as an image of Christ and the church:

> How is marriage a mystery? The two have become one. This is not an empty symbol. . . . They come to be made into one body. . . . From one man, Adam, He made Eve; then He reunited these two into one. . . . How do they become one flesh? . . . Their intercourse effects the joining of their bodies, and they are made one. . . . Shall I also tell you how marriage is a mystery of the Church? The Church was made from the side of Christ, and He united Himself to her in a spiritual intercourse.[55]

In Chrysostom's elaboration of Paul's symbol, the sexual-bodily union of man and woman in marriage figures the spiritual-bodily union of Christ and the church in salvation. God created Eve from the flesh taken from Adam's opened side and then joined Adam and Eve into "one flesh" in marriage (Gen. 2:21–24). Likewise, God created the church from the blood and water that poured forth from Christ's pierced side (John 19:34) and then joined Christ and the church into a mystical body through the sacred mysteries of baptism and communion.[56]

As did Methodius, Chrysostom identified the water of baptism as initiating the union of Christ and the church. He instructed catechumens to see their approaching baptism as anticipating the "sacred nuptials" of the church with

54. Methodius, *Symposium* 3.1–9 (ANF 6:316–20).

55. Chrysostom, *Homily 12 on Colossians*, in *On Marriage and Family Life*, 75–77.

56. Chrysostom, *Homily 20 on Ephesians*, in *On Marriage and Family Life*, 51–52. See also Ford, *Women and Men in the Early Church*, 67–73; Trenham, *Marriage and Virginity in St. John Chrysostom*, 149–53.

Christ to be consummated in heaven.[57] In this way, Chrysostom echoed Cyril of Jerusalem. Cyril's catechetical lectures elaborated the rite of baptism in the figure of marriage, drawing from Jesus's parable of the wedding banquet (Matt. 22:1–14): "And while the Heavenly Powers rejoice, let the souls that are to be united to the spiritual Bridegroom make themselves ready. . . . Begin at once to wash your robes in repentance, that when called to the bride-chamber ye may be found clean. For the Bridegroom calls all without distinction . . . but the same Bridegroom afterwards separates those who have come in to the figurative marriage."[58] Here the nuptial figure joins baptismal initiation to final judgment: believers who have entered the "figurative marriage" with Christ the "spiritual Bridegroom" through baptism will be saved on judgment day, when Christ will separate those who have been cleansed by repentance and welcome them into the heavenly wedding chamber.[59]

Augustine presented the incarnation of God the Son for our salvation in the image of marriage. Where Paul and John had depicted the union of Christ and the church in the figure of marriage, Augustine depicted the entirety of Christology—the union of divinity and humanity in the person of Christ, and the work of Christ for our salvation—in the figure of marriage. Augustine did so by joining the nuptial motif with a christological interpretation of Scripture: "First he came into the Virgin's womb where the human creation was married to him, so that mortal flesh should not for ever be mortal. Coming forth from thence 'as a bridegroom from his marriage bed, he bounded like a giant to run his course' (Ps. 18:6). He did not delay, but ran crying out loud by his words, deeds, death, life, descent, and ascent—calling us to return to him."[60] The incarnation is accomplished through a divine-human marriage: Mary's womb is the "marriage bed" where, by the Holy Spirit, the divine Son is "married" to "the human creation" in Jesus. This holy union of Creator with creation by incarnation gives birth to our salvation: Jesus comes forth from "the Virgin's womb" as the "bridegroom" seeking his bride, who runs the whole course of his ministry beckoning humankind to repent from sin, be reconciled to God, and receive new life in the bridegroom's embrace.[61]

57. Chrysostom, *Instructions to Catechumens* 1.1 (NPNF[1] 9:159–60).

58. Cyril of Jerusalem, *Catechetical Lectures: Lecture III on Baptism* 1–2 (NPNF[2] 7:14). Cyril goes on to cite Song of Songs and Isa. 61 to further elaborate baptism as spiritual marriage.

59. For further examples in Eastern Christianity, see Ephrem the Syrian, *Hymns on Faith* 14.5, in *Harp of the Spirit*, 24–25; Ephrem the Syrian, *Hymns on Virginity* 33.1–3, in *Harp of the Spirit*, 75–76.

60. Augustine, *Confessions* 4.19. The psalm citation follows the numbering in the Latin (Vulgate) and Greek (Septuagint); see Ps. 19:5 in English versions.

61. Augustine used this nuptial motif in Christmas sermons—see *Sermon 192*, 3, in *Sermons to the People*, 107; *Sermon 195*, 3, in *Sermons to the People*, 124. Paulinus of Nola,

Reflecting on the figure of marriage enables us to see marriage as an integral reality. Thomas Aquinas commented on the fit of form to figure in marriage: "By the union of male and female, there is figuratively represented the union of Christ with His Church. . . . Now the figure must correspond to the reality which it signifies." The figural correspondence of marriage to God's covenant with Israel and Christ's union with the church is not arbitrary: to be a true figure, the character of human marriage must correspond to the character of divine covenant. Aquinas argued that, on account of the figural correspondence of marriage to Christ and the church, marriage must be the exclusive-enduring fidelity of monogamous union: "But the union of Christ with His Church is of one Bridegroom with one Bride to be kept forever. . . . Matrimony, therefore, as a Sacrament of the Church, must be of one husband with one wife, to continue without separation: this is meant by the *faith* (or *troth*), whereby husband and wife are bound to one another."[62] The form and figure of marriage are integrated: the figure of marriage (Christ and the church) delimits the form of marriage (one husband and one wife, bound inseparably) so that there is a true fit between form and figure.

In Scripture and tradition, marriage summarizes the biblical narrative of salvation history and symbolizes God's work for humankind's salvation. The scriptural designation of the covenantal union of the created sexes to summarize and symbolize God's creational purpose and covenantal promise is not an arbitrary association. Marriage of man and woman reflects God's design in creation, serves God's creational purpose and covenantal promise, and signifies God's plan of salvation. As symbol, marriage condenses the interconnections between creation and covenant, incarnation and redemption into a revelation—a "mystery"—of salvation. Visibly inscribing the fidelity of covenant within the pattern of creation, thus inseparably uniting creational and covenantal, marriage presents an image of salvation.

Hermeneutically, the covenantal monogamy of man and woman is a focal image woven throughout Scripture that brings the biblical story into meaningful coherence—a biblical image by which we can read the Bible as a whole.[63] This suggests that our interpretation of Scripture is fragmented apart from seeing how the nuptial figure shapes and unifies the biblical story. Theologically, marriage is a living icon of the divine economy—an embodied and

---

Carmen 25, 159–97, in Hunter, *Marriage in the Early Church*, 136–38, makes a similar use of the nuptial figure.

62. Aquinas, *Summa Contra Gentiles* IV.78 (emphasis original).

63. On focal images, see Hays, *Moral Vision of the New Testament*, 193–204.

enacted reflection of God's design in creation and plan of salvation.[64] This suggests that our vision of God's purpose and promise is myopic apart from seeing how marriage of man and woman proceeds from the inception of God's purpose through creation of heaven and earth and points toward the completion of God's promise through union of Christ and the church. As both a focal image within Scripture and an iconic reflection of salvation, the nuptial figure draws us in faith toward Jesus Christ.

Consensus, Confession, and Discernment: Marriage as Confessional Matter

The creational-covenantal pattern of marriage—the common ground on which the major branches of Christian tradition have articulated particular understandings and emphases—is a consensus doctrine of the church catholic. Until the present generation, all Christians everywhere have believed, and every branch of Christian tradition always has taught, that marriage is man-woman monogamy. From the first century and throughout the succeeding centuries, the pastors and teachers of the church have agreed in acknowledging, whether by implicit assumption or explicit argument, that sexuate correspondence is integral to marital union. Marriage, the whole church has always confessed, is not only a monogamous union but also a man-woman union.

Prior to Augustine, theologians held diverse views concerning the theological significance of sexuate correspondence as well as the relative value of virginity and marriage. Yet amid such diversity all agreed, at least by assumption, that marriage is predicated on the sexuate correspondence of male and female.[65] Within the Western church, "from Augustine to the Reformation, there was a consensus that God created human beings in sexual differentiation, that Christian social life will affirm this difference through marriage and the regulation of erotic life, and that sexual difference will be redeemed in the eschaton."[66] Although the Western church was divided in the Reformation, and while Protestants diverged from Catholics regarding whether marriage

---

64. Chrysostom conjectured that the "one flesh" of marriage is an analogy of the oneness of God: "I say that the husband and wife are one body in the same way as Christ and the Father are one" (*Homily 20 on Ephesians*, in *On Marriage and Family Life*, 52). It must be observed that Scripture does not present any analogy of the marital relation between human spouses to the immanent relations among divine persons (i.e., marriage as image of Trinity). Scripture uses the nuptial figure only in reference to the divine economy, the cooperation of Father, Son, and Spirit in relation to and for the sake of creatures.

65. See Hunter, *Marriage in the Early Church*; Brown, *Body and Society*; Roberts, *Creation and Covenant*.

66. Roberts, *Creation and Covenant*, 8.

is a sacrament, all major branches of Western Christianity continued to affirm the traditional definition of marriage as man-woman monogamy.[67] The
church's teaching that marriage is man-woman monogamy, therefore, meets
the classic criteria of catholic doctrine: universality, antiquity, and consensus.

The continuity of consensus on marriage as man-woman monogamy is
evident in the confessions and catechisms of the Western church. In the Roman
Catholic tradition, the Catechism of the Council of Trent (1566) carried
forward the consensus teaching. Its section "The Sacrament of Matrimony"
defined marriage in traditional terms: "Matrimony, according to the general
opinion of theologians, is defined: The conjugal union of man and woman,
contracted between two qualified persons, which obliges them to live together
throughout life."

Because many Protestant reformers did not consider marriage to be a sacrament or ordinance of the church, as they did baptism and Lord's Supper,
Protestant Reformation–era catechisms and confessions do not always treat
marriage. Yet where marriage is treated, it is defined in traditional terms.
Below is a sample of these catechetical and confessional documents.[68]

Luther's Large Catechism of 1529 affirmed that "God honors and extols
this estate [of matrimony]," for "by His commandment He both sanctions
and guards it," and "also wishes us to honor it . . . as a divine and blessed
estate." Marriage is God's first institution in creation: God "created man
and woman . . . that they should live together, be fruitful, beget children,
and nourish and train them to the honor of God" (pars. 206 and 207, under
the Sixth Commandment).[69] The Second Helvetic Confession of 1564, a Reformed confession, affirmed that "marriage . . . was instituted by the Lord
God himself," who "willed man and woman to cleave one to the other inseparable, and to live together in complete love and concord" (art. 29). The
Westminster Confession of 1646, also a Reformed confession, affirmed that
"marriage is to be between one man and one woman" and "was ordained
for the mutual help of husband and wife, for the increase of mankind with a
legitimate issue, and of the Church with an holy seed, and for the preventing
of uncleanness" (chap. 24). From the Anabaptists, the Dordrecht Confession
of 1632 affirmed that "the church of God" recognizes "an honorable state of
matrimony," consisting of "two free, believing persons" joined together "in

---

67. See Witte, *From Sacrament to Contract*.

68. The catechisms and confessions cited here were accessed at The Book of Concord, http://
www.bookofconcord.org; Reformed.org, https://reformed.org; Global Anabaptist Mennonite
Encyclopedia Online (GAMEO), https://gameo.org.

69. See also the Augsburg Confession of 1530, art. 23, and Luther's Smalcald Articles of
1537, part 3, art. 11, both entitled "Of the Marriage of Priests."

accordance with the manner after which God originally ordained the same in Paradise . . . with Adam and Eve," which "original order" was restored by "the Lord Christ" (art. 12).[70]

The catechetical and confessional documents of the Reformation era state points of doctrinal disagreement, name abuses in practice needing correction, and even censure Christian groups espousing errors. The range of disagreement reflected in the documents includes certain points concerning marriage: whether marriage should be counted among the sacraments or ordinances of the church; whether church or state should administer marriage; whether priests may marry; whether divorce or second marriage is permissible; and so on. Amid the disagreement, however, one finds complete agreement that marriage is man-woman monogamy. The division of the Western church in the Reformation era, then, did not divide the doctrinal consensus of the whole church, that God designed marriage to be the monogamous union of man and woman.

Some innovationists question whether the doctrinal consensus transmitted through confessional traditions is relevant to our discernment. The question for us concerns same-sex union, but, some say, the catechisms and confessions of the traditions do not even mention same-sex union. Jack Rogers, writing from a Presbyterian perspective, affirms the "doctrinal consensus of the church" as a guide for the church's discernment. Yet he argues that, on account of the lack of any mention of same-sex union in the church's creeds and confessions, "opinions about homosexuality are not essential matters of faith."[71]

Although Rogers cites the Second Helvetic Confession and Westminster Confession, oddly he does not mention what these classic confessions of the Reformed tradition do state, explicitly and clearly, about marriage. The Second Helvetic Confession states that God willed "man and woman" to be joined in marriage. And the Westminster Confession, a century later, states, "Marriage is to be between one man and one woman." The fact that confessional statements from the Reformation era explicitly defined marriage as "man and woman" is important.

In the church today, when the definition of marriage is debated widely, a group issuing a formal statement emphasizing marriage as "man and woman" is likely reaffirming tradition in resistance to movements for innovation within the group—or declaring "where we stand" in contrast with shifting stances of other groups. When Reformation-era confessions were formulated in the

70. See also the Ris Confession of 1766, art. 31, "Of Marriage."
71. J. Rogers, *Jesus, the Bible, and Homosexuality*, 60–62.

sixteenth and seventeenth centuries, however, whether marriage is "man and woman" was not debated between Lutherans, Calvinists, and Anabaptists. Nor did it divide Protestants and Catholics: the Reformed confessions and the Roman catechism each defined marriage as "man and woman." That marriage is "man and woman" was the common confession of all Christians, such that there was no need to state as much to make a polemical point against ecclesial opponents. Reformation-era confessions do not state that marriage is "man and woman" to resist change or silence dissent or draw contrasts. Rather, Reformation-era confessional statements affirm that marriage is "man and woman" because, with the whole church, the Reformers confessed that "man and woman" is constitutive of marriage.

We should, I have argued, frame the question of same-sex union as a matter of marriage. We must, I will demonstrate (in chap. 6 below), acknowledge that sanctioning same-sex union would entail redefining marriage. Such redefinition would require removing, or at least qualifying, any mention of "man and woman" in reference to marriage within canonical, catechetical, and confessional documents. Because the canonical, catechetical, and confessional documents of our denominational traditions, Catholic and Protestant, have consistently defined marriage as "man and woman," therefore, the question of same-sex union is a confessional matter—and the confessional past bears on present discernment. The documentary heritages of our denominational traditions, which have transmitted the historical consensus of the church, founded on the canonical witness of Scripture, that marriage is "man and woman," condense the discernments of many generations of forebears in faith. We would do well in discerning the question of same-sex union to respectfully receive our doctrinal inheritance, together with its biblical source, and carefully consider this catholic consensus of church history.

4

From the Beginning

JESUS, MARRIAGE, AND GENESIS

> Have you not read that from the beginning the Creator "made them male and female," and said, ". . . The two will become one flesh"?
>
> Matthew 19:4–5 (NET)

Jesus, Confession, and Interpretation

In the previous chapter we encountered the christological aspect of marriage: marriage of man and woman figures union of Christ and the church, a symbol of God's saving work for us in Christ. In this chapter we encounter the christological aspect of interpretation and discernment: Jesus's authority over Scripture and teaching on marriage. This christological aspect has two dimensions, confessional and hermeneutical.

What we confess about who Jesus is matters to how we think about what marriage is. Some disagreement about marriage depends to some degree on disagreement about Jesus. This observation became evident to me in an exchange with a biblical scholar concerning Jesus's teaching on marriage and the question of same-sex union. We disagreed about not only how to interpret Jesus's teaching but also whether Jesus's teaching is relevant to sexual ethics and authoritative for the church. We also recognized that our disagreement about marriage reflected a deeper disagreement about Jesus. From his "low"

Christology perspective, Jesus's view of marriage and interpretation of Genesis was one view among others in the marriage debates of first-century Palestine. From my "high" Christology perspective, Jesus's teaching of marriage and interpretation of Genesis is God's word for God's people.

The church has long confessed that Jesus is fully human and fully divine, the incarnation of God the Son who is eternally and equally God with God the Father and God the Spirit. As the incarnate Son of God, Jesus uniquely embodies God's word for all humankind. Jesus's interpretation of Scripture and teaching on marriage thus bear God's authority. For the church Jesus is the chief authority for interpreting Scripture; Jesus's teaching is authoritative for the whole church at all times. The church's confession of Jesus thus makes a substantive difference for the church's interpretation of Scripture and discernment of marriage. Because Jesus's hermeneutical perspective and ethical teaching are uniquely and universally authoritative for the church, we must give Jesus's teaching on marriage and interpretation of Genesis central place in our discernment.[1]

The church also acknowledges Jesus as the focal point for reading the biblical canon. This matters for how we interpret Genesis concerning marriage. The creation account of Genesis 1–2 stands out as a key text for a biblical theology of marriage. The church does not read the Genesis account as a stand-alone story but as the beginning of the story of salvation that unfolds across the biblical canon. The church's teaching, then, must take stock of how the rest of Scripture cites and interprets the Genesis account concerning marriage. The church does not read Genesis only looking forward from "the beginning" into the rest of Scripture. The church also reads Genesis looking backward from vantage points of later stages of God's ongoing work of redemption. For the church, the key stage of salvation history from which we look back at "the beginning" of "heaven and earth" is the new beginning in Jesus Christ, through whom God is bringing forth "a new heaven and a new earth." God's presence and purpose in Jesus provides the prime vantage point from which the church reads Genesis concerning marriage.[2]

Jesus and a Marriage Debate

Matthew and Mark depict an exchange between Jesus and Pharisees about divorce (Matt. 19:3–9; Mark 10:2–9). In Mark's account, the Pharisees quiz

1. J. Rogers, *Jesus, the Bible, and Homosexuality*, 55–57, emphasizes "keeping Christ in the center" of interpretation and discernment concerning same-sex union—but, oddly, does not even discuss Jesus's teaching on marriage or interpretation of Genesis.
2. See Bontrager, Hershberger, and Sharp, *Bible as Story*, 325–29. A Christ-focused reading of Scripture took root in the early church—see Bouteneff, *Beginnings*.

Jesus whether divorce is permitted by the law: "Is it lawful for a man to divorce his wife?" (Mark 10:2). Jesus asks them what Moses commanded. The Pharisees answer by citing the law, where Moses allowed a man to divorce by issuing his wife "a certificate of dismissal" (10:4). In Matthew's account, the Pharisees, presupposing Moses's law allowing divorce, query Jesus concerning the causes for divorce: "Is it lawful for a man to divorce his wife for any cause?" (Matt. 19:3). That emphasis on legitimate cause situates this exchange within the divorce debate of Jesus's day. This debate revolved around competing interpretations of the "something objectionable" in Moses's law that could constitute cause for divorce (Deut. 24:1–4). Some rabbis took a strict view, allowing a husband to divorce his wife only for cause of sexual immorality (school of Shammai); other rabbis took a lax view, allowing a husband to divorce his wife for almost any reason (school of Hillel).[3] The Pharisees' question is thus a "test" for Jesus, to see which law school he favors (Matt. 19:3; Mark 10:2).[4]

Jesus, however, does not straightaway answer the Pharisees' question on their terms by offering his reading of Moses's law. Instead, Jesus cites the creation story as the ultimate precedent for reading the law code. Genesis 1–2, Jesus observes, testifies to God's intention "from the beginning of creation" that "male and female" joined by God into "one flesh" would be an inseparable union: "What God has joined together, let no one separate" (Mark 10:6–9; cf. Matt. 19:4–6). Divorce deviates from God's will, Jesus teaches, because divorce unmakes what God has made: whereas God joins "two" into "one flesh" by marriage, humans separate the "one flesh" into "two" by divorce. Jesus thus interprets Moses's law permitting divorce as God's concession to hardened hearts, which indicates that divorce is a human disordering of things out of joint with the divine ordering of things: "From the beginning it was not so" (Matt. 19:8; cf. Mark 10:5).

Jesus's response to this question has three immediate implications for the present matter. First, whereas the Pharisees ask about divorce, Jesus answers about marriage. Jesus shifts the question for discussion, from the legality of divorce to the theology of marriage.[5] Whether divorce is justifiable, as Jesus sees it, is fundamentally a question about what marriage is: "Jesus raises the discussion about divorce up to the level of marriage, focusing attention

---

3. The first-century Jewish historian Josephus illustrates the lax view: he commented that there are "many causes" for divorce (*Jewish Antiquities* 4.253) and that he divorced his wife because he was "not pleased" with her and married another woman of higher social status (*The Life* 426–27).

4. See Keener, *And Marries Another*, 38–40; Instone-Brewer, *Divorce and Remarriage in the Bible*, 85–132.

5. See Geddert, *Mark*, 230–31; Hays, *Moral Vision of the New Testament*, 351.

on the essence and nature of marriage."[6] Jesus's teaching here is primarily about marriage and secondarily about divorce—it is thus potentially relevant to any question of marriage. Whether to sanction same-sex union also, first and fundamentally, is a question of marriage. For this reason, this text about divorce cannot be set aside, due to supposed irrelevance, from our debate about same-sex union: divorce and same-sex union both are marriage matters.

Second, Jesus's response to this question exhibits Jesus's reading of Scripture, in two ways. It shows how Jesus reads the law codes: he subordinates the concession of divorce to the commandment against adultery, case law to apodictic law; the concession of divorce cannot be interpreted to sideline or circumvent the prohibition of adultery.[7] It shows also how Jesus reads the whole Torah: he reads the law of marriage in light of the story of creation; the creation account declares God's will for marriage and is thus the ultimate precedent for interpreting and applying marriage law. Jesus thus gives primacy to the creation account in setting the marriage standard: Jesus privileges what was so "at the beginning" (Matt. 19:4) over "from the beginning it was not so" (19:8).[8]

Third, Jesus affirms that marriage is a divine creation not subject to human alteration. As Jesus reads Genesis, God institutes marriage by creative act and word (Matt. 19:4–6): God made them male and female; God said, "For this reason . . . the two shall become one flesh"; God joined them together. Jesus thus grounds the moral norm of marriage in the original ordering of creation: "Jesus' judgment against divorce is not pegged to a superior morality, but to the divine verdict of creation."[9] God's purpose in original creation is not outmoded or overridden by subsequent eras of God's providence: God's concession of divorce does not replace or rescind God's intention for marriage. God's creation not only is the ground on which God passes judgment on human distortion (by divorce) of God's intention but also takes precedent over God's concession (by law) to human distortion. What God instituted marriage to be "from the beginning of creation," no human decision or historical evolution can alter: what God has done, we should not undo.

Now some might be inclined to downplay Jesus's reference to Genesis, because he is responding to a test question from Pharisees. Jesus's citation of

---

6. Trakatellis, *Authority and Passion*, 63.

7. On tension in the Torah between God's intention and God's concession, see Goldingay, *Old Testament Theology*, 3:337–39.

8. See Gardner, *Matthew*, 289; Keener, *And Marries Another*, 40–42; Hays, *Moral Vision of the New Testament*, 350; Bontrager, Hershberger, and Sharp, *Bible as Story*, 329–30. Likewise, in his rebuttals to Pharisees and scribes (Mark 7:1–13; cf. Matt. 23:23), Jesus emphasized (written) Torah over (oral) tradition and privileged the Decalogue over secondary and concessionary laws in the Torah—see Bockmuehl, *Jewish Law in Gentile Churches*, 3–14, 120.

9. Mauser, "Creation, Sexuality, and Homosexuality in the New Testament," 41.

Genesis, someone might say, is a rhetorical tactic chosen to fit a historical situation and thus carries no hermeneutical implication about Genesis or ethical consequence for marriage. This view of Jesus's citation of Genesis would empty it of import for not only the same-sex-union question we are addressing but also the divorce question he was addressing. This view, however, does not account for Jesus's conclusion from Genesis: "Therefore what God has joined together, let no one separate" (Matt. 19:6; Mark 10:9). Unless we are to read this as only a final flourish to silence Pharisees, Jesus's conclusion from Genesis indicates that Jesus's citation of Genesis is not mere rhetoric against opponents.[10]

By responding to the divorce debate with an authoritative teaching on marriage derived from Genesis, Jesus did two things at once. First, Jesus placed himself at the center of Scripture: his interpretation and teaching bear God's authority. Second, Jesus placed creation at the beginning of marriage: what is good in marriage originates in God's ordering of creation. "To remember Jesus in the world of our sexuality is to remember that story of creation."[11] How, then, might Jesus's interpretation of Genesis and teaching on marriage guide our discernment concerning same-sex union?

Jesus and the Genesis of Marriage

Jesus, citing Genesis as grounds that divorce is contrary to God's intention for marriage, interpreted the creation story as presenting a normative pattern for marriage. Preston Sprinkle takes this point further. Citing Mark, he argues that Jesus's citation of Genesis likely implies that Jesus believed sexual difference is essential for marriage:

> He only needed to quote Genesis 2:24 to make his point about divorce—married people have become "one flesh" and therefore shouldn't get divorced. Why, then, does Jesus start in Genesis 1:27—"God made them male and female"—which explicitly highlights sexual difference? Such difference is, in itself, irrelevant to the question of divorce. That is, it's irrelevant if one's sex makes no difference in marriage. If Jesus didn't think that sexual difference is essential for marriage, then his quotation of Genesis 1:27, which talks about sexual difference, is unnecessary and superfluous. But Jesus does quote it, so it would seem that male-female pairing is part of what marriage is according to Jesus.[12]

10. Those inclined to this view should consider also that Jesus's citation of the two "love" laws and declaration that these summarize "the law and the prophets" comes in response to the Pharisees' test question about the "greatest commandment" (Matt. 22:34–40).

11. Verhey, *Remembering Jesus*, 213.

12. Sprinkle, *People to Be Loved*, 35–36. See also Driggers, "New Testament Appropriations of Genesis 1–2," 61–62.

The key factor for our debate, according to Sprinkle, is Jesus's citation of this verse: "[God] made them male and female."

One might object here that, in historical context, Jesus's citation of this verse is a signal to his interlocutors that he is referencing the creation story. In an oral culture, one might argue, Jesus's reference to "male and female" is simply a shorthand way of saying, "As it is written in Genesis." As such, it contributes nothing substantive to Jesus's ruling on divorce and, therefore, reveals nothing concerning Jesus's interpretation of Genesis or his view of marriage.[13]

What should we make of Sprinkle's argument and this objection? Let's begin with the objection. Jesus says: "But from the beginning of creation, 'God made them male and female.' 'For this reason a man shall leave his father and mother and be joined to his wife, and the two shall become one flesh'" (Mark 10:6–8). Examining the Greek text, we see that Jesus does use an expression that would have been understood by his hearers as shorthand for "As it is written in Genesis"—but this expression comes *before* his citation of "[God] made them male and female." The initial phrase "from the beginning [*apo archēs*] of creation" recalls the Greek text of the first verse of Genesis: "In the beginning [LXX, *en archē*] God made the sky and the earth" (Gen. 1:1 NETS; cf. John 1:1). Jewish texts used the expression "from the beginning" to imply reference to the creation story (cf. Wis. 6:22).[14] This expression, then, is Jesus's oral signal that he is citing Genesis.

With this in mind, we can analyze Jesus's statement as follows. (a) Jesus signals reference to Genesis: "But from the beginning of creation . . ." (b) He then cites distinct texts from Genesis in immediate juxtaposition: "'God made them male and female.' 'For this reason . . . the two shall become one flesh'" (Mark 10:6–8, quoting Gen. 1:27; 2:24). (c) He then premises his ruling against divorce on these citations. With this textual analysis, we might restate Sprinkle's argument: Jesus premises his divorce ruling on two citations from the creation story; the first premise from Genesis ("[God] made them male and female") is logically unnecessary to the conclusion about divorce ("What God has joined together, let no one separate"); likely, then, Jesus includes the logically unnecessary premise because he sees the second premise (union into "one flesh") as grounded ontologically in the first premise (creation as "male and female").

Sprinkle's approach presents Jesus as delivering a legal brief, making his case in court. This approach has some merit. Jesus is tested with a legal

---

13. See Keen, *Scripture, Ethics, and the Possibility of Same-Sex Relationships*, 31.
14. See Keener, *And Marries Another*, 160n16; Davies and Allison, *Matthew 19–28*, 9–10.

question and renders the ruling that adultery cannot be made lawful by divorce.[15] As observed above, however, Jesus shifts the discussion from the legal dispute about divorce to God's design for marriage. Jesus thus shifts attention from the divorce law, which expresses God's concession, to the creation account, which reveals God's intention. This suggests a better approach to seeing how Jesus's citation of Genesis relates to Jesus's view of marriage: Jesus's legal brief is a story outline.

Biblical interpreters in Jesus's time tended to read Genesis 1–2 as a single, seamless story.[16] Modern scholars, using historical-critical and textual-critical methods, typically analyze the Genesis story into two distinct accounts (Gen. 1:1–2:3; 2:4–25), derived from disparate sources composed in different periods, and then interpret those accounts separately. Ordinary readers can detect differences in how the respective accounts depict the manner and sequence of God's creative acts. Ancient interpreters, while cognizant of the different features of the two accounts, understood the narrative "technique of placing two parallel accounts in dynamical complementary sequence."[17] They tended to read the whole story (1:1–2:25) as a unified narrative of God's creation and a normative account of humankind's vocation. With this in mind, when we look again at Jesus's citation of Genesis we can see that Jesus read the entire section of the Genesis account pertaining to humankind—from creation as "male and female" in "the image of God" (1:26–27) to union of "man and woman" into "one flesh" (2:23–24)—as a single story of God's creating humankind and instituting marriage.

Jesus cites Genesis to summarize a story. Jesus's citation comprises three elements: the beginning of the creation story (Mark 10:6a; Gen. 1:1) and the two bookends bracketing the portion of the story about humankind, creation as "male and female" (Mark 10:6b; Gen. 1:27) and union into "one flesh" (Mark 10:7–8; Gen. 2:24). Jesus's citation brings together Genesis 1:27 and 2:24 "into a virtually seamless whole."[18] Jesus does much more than merely "quote fragments of Genesis 1 and 2," as one scholar puts it.[19] Jesus cites the Genesis story to recall, and situate marriage with respect to, God's creative acts and intents. Jesus sets God's joining man and woman into "one flesh" in relation to God's creating humankind as "male and female," and he sets all that in relation to God's intention "from the beginning of creation."

15. See Geddert, *Mark*, 240–41.

16. See Loader, *Making Sense of Sex*, 9–11; Bouteneff, *Beginnings*, 12–32; Matlock, "Interpretation of Genesis 1–2," 32–37, 42.

17. Alter, *Art of Biblical Narrative*, 175–83.

18. Bouteneff, *Beginnings*, 51.

19. Gushee, *Changing Our Mind*, 153.

Even some scholars favoring an innovationist view recognize the import of Jesus's citation of Genesis for the question of same-sex union. William Loader comments:

> One of the most important texts underlying attitudes towards sexual behaviour is Jesus' encounter with the Pharisees when they test his views on divorce. . . . Mark depicts Jesus addressing the issue of marriage itself. . . . The appeal to 'the beginning of creation' is an appeal to what God originally created and how it therefore should remain. . . . The allusion to God's making human beings male and female in Genesis 1.27 is not an argument in itself, but rather a presupposition for the argument to follow. . . . The conclusion, 'So they are no longer two, but one flesh,' assumes Genesis 1.27, since it refers clearly to two, male and female.[20]

Loader observes that Jesus's citation of Genesis does not explicitly exclude same-sex union as contrary to God's intention "from the beginning of creation." But he adds: "This is not explicit, though likely to be the case when it is read in association with the Leviticus prohibitions."[21]

So Jesus likely did understand union into "one flesh" to be inseparable from creation as "male and female." He evidently read the Genesis account as a seamless story of humankind's creation that establishes the normative pattern for marriage. Jesus's citation of Genesis indicates how he views marriage: God's joining "two" into "one flesh" is founded on God's creation of "male and female," and God's joining "male and female" into "one flesh" fulfills God's intention "from the beginning." He interpreted God's creating humankind "male and female" as the precursor and presupposition of union into "one flesh"—and interpreted the reason for man and woman becoming "one flesh" in relation to God's creating humankind "male and female."[22]

Jesus and the Interpretation of Genesis

Some innovationists argue that the Genesis story presents what is *normal*, but not necessarily *normative*, in marriage. According to this view, the Genesis portrayal of marriage as man-woman monogamy is not (wholly) prescriptive of marriage—and thus not (necessarily) definitive of marriage. I'll consider two variations of this view.

20. Loader, *Sexuality in the New Testament*, 44.
21. Loader, *Sexuality in the New Testament*, 45.
22. See also Mauser, "Creation and Human Sexuality in the New Testament," 4–5; Mauser, "Creation, Sexuality, and Homosexuality," 40–41.

The Descriptive-Story Hermeneutic

Some innovationists argue that, concerning sex and marriage, the Genesis story only describes what *is*, not prescribes what *should* be. The creation accounts are meant only to explain the way things, normally, are but not to show how things, normatively, ought to be. Thus, "male and female" being fruitful and multiplying reflects what is typical of the human condition, and man and woman becoming "one flesh" in marriage reflects what is customary in human cultures. But neither "male and female" nor "one flesh" constitutes a God-ordained model for marriage.[23] Victor Paul Furnish argues that the creation accounts in Genesis 1–3 are merely etiological—they are "told to explain why things *are* as they are, not to prescribe what people *ought* to do."[24] As an etiological story, the creation account explains how it came to be that humans marry in the world that God created—and so it answers the question, "Why do man and woman marry?" But the creation account does not represent what God intended for human marrying—and so it does not answer the question, "May only man and woman marry?"

Read as a descriptive account of typical conditions and cultural customs in marriage practice and as an etiological explanation of the human tendency to marry, Genesis is neither here nor there regarding prescriptions for marriage. On this view, Genesis does not present any moral norm for marriage and thus does not speak normatively to any question about marriage—say, whether monogamy and fidelity are the standard of marriage, or whether same-sex union may be sanctioned as marriage. This view neutralizes the Genesis account in the marriage debate: as a descriptive account of typical conditions and cultural customs, Genesis tells us nothing about the moral norms of marriage; as an etiological explanation of the human tendency to marry, Genesis tells us nothing about God's will for marriage. The ethical implication of this hermeneutical view is evident: Genesis prescribes nothing for marriage and thus precludes nothing, including same-sex union, from marriage. The anthropological implication of this hermeneutical view should also be noted. If the Genesis creation account is merely descriptive, then that is true of both lines of the textual parallel, "image of God" / "male and female" (Gen. 1:27). As a descriptive account, Genesis no more makes "image of God" constitutive of humankind than it makes "male and female" normative for marriage.

23. See Furnish, "Bible and Homosexuality," 21–23; Bird, "Bible in Christian Ethical Deliberation," 165–68; Thatcher, *Liberating Sex*, 134.

24. Furnish, "Bible and Homosexuality," 21 (emphasis original). See also Countryman, *Dirt, Greed, and Sex*, 242–45.

It seems evident that the Genesis 2 account does serve an etiological purpose. Recounting God's making the man, placing him in the garden, and making the woman from the man to remedy the deficiency of the man's lacking a suitable partner for tending the garden (Gen. 2:15–23), the text says: "That is why a man leaves his father and mother and unites with his wife, and they become one family" (2:24 NET). Recounting God's acts in making man and woman serves to explain why a man and a woman marry and thereby become a new kinship unit. The descriptive-story hermeneutic, however, maintains that the creation account serves *only* an etiological purpose concerning sex and marriage. Yet a story could be *both* etiological, explaining how things came to be, *and* prescriptive, expressing how things ought to be—these two need not be divided. And the Genesis story, as Jesus read it, unites the etiological and the prescriptive.

Jesus cited three verses from the creation story (Matt. 19:4–6; Mark 10:6–9), ending with the etiological conclusion concerning marriage: "from the beginning of creation" (citing Gen. 1:1); "God made them male and female" (citing Gen. 1:27); "for this reason a man" is "joined to his wife" and they "become one flesh" (citing Gen. 2:24). From this etiological explanation of marriage, Jesus drew a prescriptive implication for marriage: let no one divide what God has joined. Jesus thus read the Genesis story as both etiological and prescriptive, prefacing the prescriptive with the etiological. Jesus derived the prescriptive import of the story from the etiological function of the story by a theological interpretation of the story: Jesus read the Genesis story to say that marriage originates by a divine act ("The Creator made them male and female" [Mark 10:6]) and culminates in human union ("The two shall become one flesh" [10:8]) through a divine act ("God has joined together" [10:9]). Because marriage originates by God's intention and action, the etiological explanation carries prescriptive implication: God created the two for the reason of joining the two into one, so we should not divide the one into two.

Genesis, as Jesus read it, is both etiological and prescriptive concerning marriage. It explains why marriage came to be and prescribes what marriage ought to be. Due to Jesus's authority over Scripture, therefore, we would do well to likewise interpret the Genesis story as revealing God's institution of and intention for marriage.

The Majority-Story Hermeneutic

Other innovationists maintain that Genesis sets forth a normative pattern for marriage—but the pattern presented is only the "majority pattern" of marriage. While Genesis prescribes a marriage pattern, it describes only the majority pattern of God's marriage prescription. The Genesis pattern of man-woman monogamy is thus the normative pattern for only the majority population. On this view, the church may sanction same-sex union as a "minority pattern" of marriage that is compatible with the Genesis description of the majority pattern. This view, which I will refer to as the majority-story hermeneutic, deserves extended treatment.

Mark Achtemeier, a Presbyterian pastor, agrees that "the union of male and female [presented in the Genesis story] is clearly established as the majority pattern for love and marriage across the whole span of human history." But, he argues, "the mere existence of a majority pattern does *not* mean that all departures from this pattern are automatically off-limits or condemned."[25] Achtemeier contends that the "majority pattern" in the Genesis account, while setting forth the normal mode for marital union, is not normative for all humankind. Similarly, Megan DeFranza, an evangelical theologian, maintains that, in the Genesis account, "Adam and Eve can be understood as the majority story rather than the exclusive model for what it means to be human. By extension, heterosexual marriage can be seen as the majority story, not the exclusive model."[26] DeFranza argues the church can bless forms of marriage that don't fit the "majority story," including same-sex union.

Assessing the Majority-Story Hermeneutic: Exegesis of Genesis

As I understand it, the majority-story hermeneutic affirms that what God willed marriage to be "from the beginning" is normative for marriage: God willed the monogamous union of man and woman. This view argues, however, that the Genesis pattern of man-woman monogamy is *not all* that God willed marriage to be: God actually willed marriage to be man-woman—and also man-man and woman-woman. Genesis, which presents only the majority pattern of man-woman monogamy, is an *incomplete description* of God's creation of humankind and thus provides only a *partial prescription* of God's intention for marriage.[27]

The majority-story hermeneutic, as a logical possibility, cannot be strictly ruled out exegetically. Genesis apparently presents male-female (or man-woman) as the God-ordained normative pattern for marital union, but the text itself does not say *explicitly* that male-female is the *only* pattern of marriage ordained by God. Even so, the majority-story view suffers from an obvious weakness. Although a logically possible reading of Genesis, this view finds

---

25. Achtemeier, *Bible's Yes to Same-Sex Marriage*, 63 (emphasis original).
26. DeFranza, "Journeying from the Bible to Christian Ethics," 90; cf. 70–71.
27. Vasey, *Strangers and Friends*, 115–18, and Seow, "Textual Orientation," 26–27, also suggest similar readings of Genesis.

no corroborating evidence anywhere in Scripture. There are no alternative examples to the majority pattern of male-female marriage, no minority pattern marriages of the relevant kind (i.e., same-sex union), to bolster the case. And Jesus's citation of Genesis concerning God's institution of and intention for marriage confirms the male-female pattern.

Achtemeier attempts to remedy this deficiency by making special appeals for scriptural support.[28] He asserts that God's blessing of married couples—Abraham and Sarah, or Zechariah and Elizabeth, or Mary and Joseph—with children outside the normal course indicates that God would also bless marital unions that are outside the majority pattern, including same-sex union. Yet each of these examples fits the Genesis pattern of male-female union. He also presses stories of fidelity and friendship in same-sex pairings—Ruth and Naomi, David and Jonathan—to imply that these couples may have been erotic lovers, or at least to suggest that God would bless same-sex couples. Yet such appeals to these cases, which strain the texts and stretch the evidence, fail to persuade even some scholars favorable to an innovationist view.[29]

Assessing the Majority-Story Hermeneutic: Gender-Marriage Analogy

DeFranza takes an alternative path to motivate her version of the majority-story hermeneutic. She begins by observing that a small percentage of human beings are born with chromosomally or anatomically indeterminate gender, which includes several conditions having various causes that are grouped under the general term "intersex."[30] Given this observation, she contends that the Genesis account of God's creation of humankind is merely the majority story because it leaves out a minority of persons (intersex) who do not fit the majority pattern (male and female). Based on this premise, she extends this majority-story hermeneutic from gender to marriage by analogy: Genesis leaves room for intersex persons in addition to male and female persons in God's original creation of humankind; likewise, Genesis leaves room for same-sex union in addition to male-female union in God's original intention for marriage.[31]

DeFranza's concern that the church show compassion toward and make room for sexual minorities is well placed, of course. Her argument, which deserves serious consideration, is susceptible to objections, however.

---

28. Achtemeier, *Bible's Yes to Same-Sex Marriage*, 65–68, 83–85.

29. See Nissinen, *Homoeroticism in the Biblical World*, 53–56, 121–22; Loader, "Homosexuality and the Bible," 23–24. For traditionalist perspectives on these stories, see Zehnder, "Observations on the Relationship between David and Jonathan"; Gagnon, *Bible and Homosexual Practice*, 146–53.

30. See Intersex Society of North America, "What Is Intersex?," http://www.isna.org/faq/what_is_intersex.

31. DeFranza, "Journeying from the Bible to Christian Ethics," 70–71.

Consider first DeFranza's analogy. The stated analogy is this: same-sex union is to marriage as intersex conditions are to gender. This analogy, to serve her argument, implicitly presupposes a further analogy: same-sex oriented persons are to sexual orientation as intersex persons are to bodily gender. To complete the analogy of same-sex union to intersex conditions and warrant the inference from gender to marriage, therefore, one would have to argue further that, just as some persons are born with intersex conditions, so also some persons are born with same-sex orientations. That some persons are simply born with intersex conditions is evident. Despite the popular slogan "born this way," whether any persons are simply born with same-sex orientations is scientifically questionable. Scientific research indicates that, probably, a mix of prenatal biological factors and postnatal environmental factors influence same-sex orientation, with a variable combination of factors operative in individual cases.[32]

Consider next the premise of DeFranza's argument—namely, the fact that some humans are born intersex entails that God designed some humans to be intersex. DeFranza points to Jesus's reference to "eunuchs who have been so from birth" (Matt. 19:12), who might (or might not) correspond to persons identified today as intersex, as biblical evidence for her premise. Even were that questionable correspondence correct, it would not follow that Jesus was positing a "third sex" of God's creation alongside male and female. At one point in his ministry, when Jesus heals "a man blind from birth," Jesus denies attribution of the man's blindness to personal sin. Yet Jesus does not attribute the man's blindness to God's creation but sees the man with God's compassion (John 9). Likewise, we should see persons born intersex with God's compassion. Yet it does not follow that we should attribute intersex conditions to God's creation.

Setting aside objections to DeFranza's premise, her extension of the majority-story hermeneutic from gender to marriage is also vulnerable to criticism. Genesis lacks the logical linkage or exegetical bridge needed to warrant extending the argument from gender to marriage.[33] Suppose, moreover, that we allow DeFranza's claim that Jesus's reference to "eunuchs from birth" identifies a "third sex" other than male and female—and thus corroborates the majority-story hermeneutic of Genesis concerning gender. Even so, there would be no analogous instance of a biblical text that identifies same-sex union as a "second way" of marriage in addition to male-female union. Other than a desire to see a connection between the two cases, there is no reason evident from Scripture why we should transfer the majority-story hermeneutic from gender to marriage.

---

32. See Bailey et al., "Sexual Orientation, Controversy, and Science"; Mayer and McHugh, "Sexuality and Gender."

33. See S. Holmes, "Response to Megan K. DeFranza," 113–14.

Assessing the Majority-Story Hermeneutic: Marriage and Monogamy

The majority-story hermeneutic, furthermore, prompts questions that go beyond same-sex union. How far, it is fair to ask, can the majority-story hermeneutic of Genesis be taken in regard to marriage? Suppose, for the sake of argument, that we adopt the view that Genesis presents only the majority pattern of male-female marriage. As observed above, Jesus cited Genesis as establishing that the fidelity of marriage is exclusive (the union of "two" into "one flesh" excludes all others) and enduring (the "one flesh" union should not be sundered). So, does Genesis present exclusive-enduring fidelity also as merely the majority pattern of marriage?

The phenomenon of nonmonogamy in Western society comprises several nonmajority practices, each of which deviates from the pattern of exclusive-enduring fidelity. In North America, open marriage—a mutual arrangement permitting external partners—has seen a small but steady incidence among opposite-sex couples in recent generations.[34] Open relationship is the preferred arrangement for many same-sex couples.[35] Polygamous marriage is practiced by small subcultures in North America, but public opinion shows a significant increase in the acceptability of polygamy.[36] And serial marriage (marriage, divorce, remarriage, divorce, remarriage, . . .) has become the accepted course for a small but growing portion of the population.[37] Perhaps these cultural variations of nonmonogamy, like the cultural variation of same-sex union, should also be seen as minority patterns that are nonnormal (divergences from the majority pattern) but not therefore immoral (deviations from God's intention). If same-sex union can be a minority pattern compatible with God's intention for marriage in Genesis, could nonmonogamy—whether open marriage, polygamous marriage, or serial marriage—also be a minority pattern compatible with God's intention? If not, why not?

This line of questioning may be reasonably extended. Were we to read Genesis as presenting merely a majority pattern for sexual relations, we might just as well see marriage itself as the majority pattern. Rather than presenting male-female union as merely the majority pattern of marriage, one might say, Genesis presents marriage as the normative pattern for only male-female sexual relations. Maybe marriage, as some innovationists maintain, is a

34. See Oppenheimer, "Married, with Infidelities"; Dominus, "Not Just Us."

35. See James, "Many Successful Gay Marriages Share an Open Secret"; Thrasher, "Master Bedroom, Extra Closet." The Gay Couples Study conducted by San Francisco State University found that nearly half (47%) of male-male couples have an open arrangement—see Hoff et al., "Relationship Characteristics."

36. See J. Jones, "Americans Hold Record Liberal Views on Most Moral Issues."

37. See Livingston, *Four in Ten Couples Are Saying "I Do," Again*, 15.

"heteronormative" pattern of sexual relations—and Genesis presents only this majority pattern. Marriage is appropriate especially for sexual relations likely to generate offspring: exclusive-enduring coupling is best suited for nurturing children. Because same-sex relations are not even suitable to generating off-spring, one might then say, it is not appropriate to restrict same-sex relations to exclusive-enduring couplings. Perhaps friendship, as some innovationists have argued, is a pattern for sexual relationships better suited to the experiences of sexual minorities.[38] Genesis, one might thus conclude, presents God's blessing of the majority "heteronormative" pattern of sexual relations within marriage, leaving open the possibility that God blesses minority patterns of same-sex relations outside marriage.

The majority-story hermeneutic, extended from male-female union to monogamy to marriage itself, thus cuts against both norms of traditional teaching: marriage only between man and woman, and sex only within monogamous marriage. Supposing a majority-story hermeneutic, therefore, it is fair to ask: Why see monogamy, or even marriage, as necessarily normative for same-sex relations?

DeFranza affirms monogamous fidelity as the necessarily normative pattern of marriage, "common ground" between traditionalists and innovationists.[39] Surely, such common ground can be sought in doctrinal tradition; but that same tradition weighs against the innovation DeFranza advocates. Some advocates of sanctioning same-sex union, moreover, regard monogamy and marriage as majority patterns not to be required of all sexual relationships, especially those of sexual minorities. So, were we to adopt the majority-story hermeneutic, why *biblically* should we regard male-female union as a merely majority pattern, but regard exclusive-enduring fidelity as a necessarily normative pattern, for marriage? Why should we even regard marriage itself as the necessarily normative pattern for all sexual relations? The majority-story hermeneutic generates serious questions that it cannot answer.[40]

Assessing the Majority-Story Hermeneutic: Marriage and Image

The majority-story hermeneutic carries anthropological implications also. DeFranza invokes "the biblical teaching of the image of God in all people" to motivate marriage innovation: sanctioning same-sex union would honor God's image in sexual minorities. She then applies the majority-story hermeneutic to

---

38. See Stuart, *Just Good Friends*.
39. DeFranza, "Journeying from the Bible to Christian Ethics," 94–95.
40. On Scripture and monogamy, see N. T. Wright, *Scripture and the Authority of God*, 175–95.

Genesis to loosen the link between "male and female" and marriage enough to make a case for same-sex union.[41]

Genesis puts "image of God" in parallel with "male and female" (Gen. 1:27). This parallel is important: it affirms that both male and female of humankind are created in, and enjoy the dignity of, the image of God. Unless we are to arbitrarily separate this textual parallel with an exegetical scalpel, we should apply the same hermeneutic to both "image of God" and "male and female." So if we apply the majority-story hermeneutic to "male and female" regarding gender and marriage, then for the sake of consistency we should apply it also to "image of God" regarding humankind.

Acknowledging this parallel, questions follow: If "male and female" is merely the majority pattern of gender and marriage, might "image of God" be merely the majority truth of humankind? If "male and female" is the marriage norm for only the heterosexual majority, might "image of God" be the human truth for only the heterosexual majority?

The majority-story hermeneutic implicitly destabilizes the biblical-theological truth that God created all humankind in the image of God—and, consequently, undermines appeal to this truth to motivate marriage innovation.

Assessing the Majority-Story Hermeneutic: Jesus and Genesis

In assessing interpretations of Genesis, finally, we should remember Jesus's authority over Scripture.[42] Jesus cites the Genesis story of God creating "male and female" and God joining them into "one flesh" as grounds for the normative pattern of exclusive-enduring fidelity in marriage. As read by Jesus, Genesis gives grounds for both patterns—male-female union and exclusive-enduring fidelity—of marriage. And there is no obvious reason to suppose that Genesis, as Jesus read it, gives different grounds to the two patterns: if Genesis prescribes a marriage pattern, then it prescribes male-female union and exclusive-enduring fidelity as equally normative. Accordingly, either both patterns are normative for only majority marriages or both patterns are normative for all marriages. So, by citing Genesis, either Jesus was appealing to a merely majority pattern or Jesus was appealing to a universally normative pattern. Jesus, evidently, was doing the latter: he interprets Genesis as standing in judgment over patterns of practice that deviate from God's intention "from the beginning of creation." Given that Jesus reads Genesis as prescribing the normative pattern of marriage, and that Genesis gives the same grounds to both patterns of marriage, therefore, it seems arbitrary to argue that Genesis presents exclusive-enduring fidelity as the universally

---

41. DeFranza, "Journeying from the Bible to Christian Ethics," 90.
42. See also Hill, "Response to Megan K. DeFranza."

normative pattern of marriage but presents male-female union as a merely majority pattern of marriage.

DeFranza correctly observes that how one understands the figures of Adam and Eve in Genesis depends on one's theological framework.[43] And in this regard, the perspectives of the Western and Eastern traditions do differ. Catholic and Reformed Christians, following Augustine, have tended to interpret Adam and Eve as being created initially mature in mind and perfect in will and as living, at first, fully according to God's will but then rebelling against God's will and falling into disobedience. From this perspective, we can look back to the prefall Adam and Eve as exemplifying God's intention for marital union.[44] Orthodox Christians, following Irenaeus, have tended to interpret Adam and Eve as being created initially immature in mind and imperfect in will and as being intended by God to grow toward perfection in obedience to God but instead disobeying God in the process. From this perspective, we cannot look back to Adam and Eve as having exemplified God's intention for marital union in a prefall perfection.[45]

This difference of perspectives between Western and Eastern understandings of human origins, I think, makes no difference regarding whether the Genesis story presents a normative pattern for marriage. For the church, the prescriptive status of the Genesis marriage pattern derives not from any particular understanding of human origins in Christian tradition but from Jesus's reading of Genesis. And Jesus's interpretation is neutral between these differing perspectives: both Western and Eastern understandings of human origins are compatible with how Jesus reads Genesis. Jesus's reading of Genesis as prescribing a normative pattern for marriage need not be taken to imply that Adam and Eve, as "first couple," perfectly exemplified that pattern in every respect. Rather, we can take Jesus's reading to imply only that Genesis sets forth the normative pattern for marriage according to God's intention "from the beginning of creation"—whether or not Adam and Eve (or any human couple) ever perfectly fulfilled God's intention. In Jesus's reading of Genesis, it is God's action and intention that sets the norm for marriage. Whether we understand Adam and Eve from a Western or Eastern perspective, therefore, makes no difference for whether we read Genesis as prescribing a normative pattern for marriage. The majority-story hermeneutic, I thus think, fails to adequately consider the hermeneutic import of Jesus's reading of Genesis concerning marriage.[46]

43. See DeFranza, "Rejoinder."
44. Augustine, *City of God* 13.15; 14.11.
45. Irenaeus, *On the Apostolic Preaching* 11–16. See also Bouteneff, *Beginnings*, 73–85. As Bouteneff shows, Eastern theologians in the patristic era held diverse views on Adam and Eve.
46. See also Hill, "Response to Megan K. DeFranza," 109–10.

Jesus and the Future of Marriage

Marriage, Creation, and New Creation

Christian ethicist David Gushee proposes that the church should "not rely . . . for sexual ethics" on "arguments from God's purported design in creation." Instead, "Christians should look forward rather than backward when thinking theologically-ethically about the LGBTQ issue."[47] Gushee goes on to argue that, due to various misuses of Genesis in church history, the church should, more or less, leave Genesis behind and look ahead to Jesus in its moral discernment: "I am not suggesting . . . that Genesis 1–11 can play no constructive role in Christian ethics. But I am suggesting the idea that *Christian theology does better leaning forward into Jesus Christ*, his person and his work, his way of doing ministry and advancing God's kingdom, the new creation he brings forth, rather than leaning backward to the primeval creation narratives, where we so often run into trouble."[48] I concur with Gushee that the church should orient its theology and ethics, including how we interpret Scripture and view marriage, according to Jesus. Gushee's proposal that the church "lean forward into Jesus" and away from Genesis—and then move toward affirming same-sex union—stumbles over the Jesus of the Gospels, however.

First, obviously and ironically, Jesus himself relied on an argument from creation design concerning sexual ethics (Mark 10:2–9; Matt. 19:3–9). When Pharisees questioned him about marriage and divorce, Jesus did precisely what Gushee proposes that we not do: Jesus "lean[ed] backward to the primeval creation narratives" and invoked "God's purported design in creation" to argue that God intends exclusive-enduring fidelity in marriage. Jesus cited the creation account to preface and premise his ruling that divorce-remarriage, except for unchastity, is tantamount to adultery. Because Jesus appealed to Genesis on marriage, were the church to "lean forward into Jesus" in its discernment concerning marriage, we would also look backward with Jesus to Genesis, contrary to the direction change that Gushee advocates.

Gushee's argument that misuse of Genesis by the church yesterday warrants disuse of Genesis by the church today neglects the classic axiom that misuse does not negate proper use. In the Gospels, Jesus shows us proper use of Genesis. Gushee does briefly discuss Jesus's citation of Genesis, and he sees Jesus's ruling on divorce as having continuing relevance concerning marriage practice. But he sets aside Jesus's citation of Genesis as of doubtful relevance

---

47. Gushee, *Changing Our Mind*, 93.
48. Gushee, *Changing Our Mind*, 95 (emphasis original). See also DeFranza, "Rejoinder," 122–23.

for the same-sex-union question.[49] Gushee's view thus fails to adequately consider the hermeneutic import of Jesus's interpretation of Genesis.

Second, ironically if not obviously, were the church to "lean forward into Jesus" in the direction of "the new creation he brings forth," as Gushee proposes, we would see, by Jesus's teaching about the coming age, that this points the church beyond all marrying, whether male-female or same-sex. In the exchange with Pharisees about divorce, Jesus looks back to the origin of marriage. In an exchange with Sadducees about resurrection, Jesus looks forward to the future of marriage.

Marriage and the Resurrection

As was divorce, the resurrection of the dead was a disputed matter between religious parties in Jesus's day: Pharisees affirmed it, Sadducees denied it. Pharisees had used the law of divorce to prompt Jesus to take a side in the divorce debate. Here Sadducees used the law of levirate marriage in an attempt to leverage Jesus to their side in the resurrection debate. They posed the following scenario (Matt. 22:23–28; Mark 12:18–23; Luke 20:27–33; cf. Tob. 6:11–15). Suppose the first of seven brothers marries a woman but dies childless, and the next brother marries her but also dies childless, and so on successively with all seven brothers, until the woman herself dies. Whose wife will she be, then, in the resurrection of the dead? Logically, there would seem to be three options: she is wife of only the first, or one of the other six, or all seven. Any option would seem to run afoul of the Torah: the situation is either adulterous, or incestuous, or polyandrous (one bride for seven brothers!). Jesus faced an apparent choice: either repudiate laws in the Torah or affirm the novelty of polyandry or deny the resurrection.

The ancient custom of levirate marriage functioned to generate descendants for deceased husbands. Within a patriarchal society, levirate marriage perpetuated family lines of descent, preserved inheritance rights within kinship groups, and protected widows from destitution (Gen. 38; Ruth 4). This pre-Israelite custom is assumed and regulated by Israelite case law to deal with particular circumstances (Deut. 25:5–10).[50] As a cultural custom, levirate marriage maintained patrilineal inheritance: a brother's duty is to "raise up offspring for [his] brother" so that the deceased brother's descendants may inherit his portion of familial land (Gen. 38:8). As an Israelite practice, levirate marriage served also to continue the man's family among God's people: "so that his name may not be blotted out of Israel" (Deut. 25:6). Both purposes

49. See Gushee, *Changing Our Mind*, 82–84, 153–54.
50. See Goldingay, *Old Testament Theology*, 3:376; Davidson, *Flame of Yahweh*, 461–76.

are evident in Ruth's story: Boaz pledges to marry Ruth "to maintain the dead man's name on his inheritance, in order that the name of the dead may not be cut off from his kindred" (Ruth 4:10). The witnesses hope that this marriage will generate descendants not only to inherit Elimelech's land but also to perpetuate Jacob's line: they call on God to bless Ruth so that she will be "like Rachel and Leah, who together built up the house of Israel" (4:12). The Sadducees' scenario reflects this concern for the perpetuation of God's people according to God's promise—and assumes that this depends on marriage and procreation.

Whereas Jesus rebutted the Pharisees by contrasting the divorce law with the creation story, Jesus rebutted the Sadducees by contrasting the present age with the future age. The premise of their scenario is the order of marriage and procreation in the present age; and the logic of their dilemma assumes that the present order will continue unchanged into the future age. Jesus accepted their premise but refuted their logic.

Jesus, importantly, confirmed God's ordering of marriage in the present age: "Those who belong to this age marry and are given in marriage" (Luke 20:34; cf. Matt. 24:37–39). Yet Jesus refuted the notion that the present order will continue unchanged into the future age. Jesus announced that, regarding marriage, the future age will differ markedly from the present age: "Those who are considered worthy of a place in that age and in the resurrection from the dead neither marry nor are given in marriage" (Luke 20:35; cf. Matt. 22:29–30). Jesus, contrasting "this age" and "that age," undercut the Sadducees' assumption: perpetuation of God's people into the future age will depend not on human work of procreation but on God's gift of resurrection.[51]

Jesus, implicitly, also confirmed God's procreative purpose of marriage and the continuing purpose of procreative marriage. In the future age, Jesus reveals, there will be no more marrying because there will be no more dying: when dying has been surpassed, begetting and thus marrying will no longer be necessary (Luke 20:35–36). In the present age, therefore, marrying is needed for the sake of begetting, which implies that procreation is integral to God's purpose for marriage. Procreative marriage continues serving God's purpose of multiplying humankind and propagating God's image—and will cease service of God's purpose only when death has been surpassed in resurrection.

Jesus's Revelation of the Future Age

In "that age" of resurrection, Jesus reveals, marrying and begetting will be surpassed because its God-ordained purpose in creation will have been fulfilled.

---

51. See Danylak, *Redeeming Singleness*, 163–66.

God's "children of the resurrection," having become immortal, like angels, will no longer need to conjugate and procreate to perpetuate God's people. In the resurrection, God's people will live perpetually in God's presence, sustained by God's eternal life (Luke 20:36–38). Jesus's revelation evidently revises Isaiah's vision, which seems to assume that marriage and procreation will continue in the new creation (Isa. 65:17–25).

Even now in "this age," Jesus affirms men "who have made themselves eunuchs for the sake of the kingdom of heaven" (Matt. 19:12). Eunuchs "who have been so from birth" or "have been made eunuchs by others" are men who are involuntarily incapable of either uniting sexually or generating offspring. Those "who have made themselves eunuchs" are men who, although capable of uniting sexually and generating offspring, have voluntarily, not cut off their genitals, but cut themselves off from marrying and begetting. Jesus thus honors men who choose to forgo marriage in order to devote their lives to God's royal service.[52]

Jesus affirms women who devote their lives to the teaching of Jesus and obedience to God. At the home of Martha and Mary, Martha demanded that Jesus dismiss Mary from sitting at the teacher's feet to assist with domestic duties. Jesus deflects Martha's demand and praises Mary's devotion: domestic duties are useful, but "there is need of only one thing," learning from Jesus; Martha has done a good thing, yet "Mary has chosen the better part," becoming Jesus's disciple (Luke 10:38–42). A woman in the crowd called out, praising Jesus's mother on account of Jesus's amazing deeds and wise words, "Blessed is the womb that bore you and the breasts that nursed you!" Jesus replies, "Blessed rather are those who hear the word of God and obey it!" (11:27–28; cf. 1:26–38). Jesus calls Mary blessed most of all—even more than for birthing and nursing him—because she heard God's word and responded obediently. Jesus declares women blessed, apart from domestic service and childbearing as wives and mothers, on account of devotion and action as God's servants and Jesus's disciples.[53]

By honoring men who forgo marriage and children for God's service, and by praising women who obey God and become disciples, Jesus fulfills the prophets' visions. Jesus's honoring "eunuchs for the kingdom" fulfills God's promise to make eunuchs fruitful by their faithfulness, to give them a "monument" in God's house and "a name better than sons and daughters" that "shall not be cut off" (Isa. 56:3–5). Jesus's blessing women for obeying God and following Jesus, apart from marrying husbands and bearing children, fulfills God's word of blessing to the "barren one who did not bear," the "desolate

---

52. See Loader, *Making Sense of Sex*, 123–25; Danylak, *Redeeming Singleness*, 150–63.
53. See Verhey, *Remembering Jesus*, 178–80.

woman" whose children "will be more than the children of her that is married" (54:1–3). Belonging to God's people and receiving God's promise, Isaiah envisioned and Jesus confirms, depends ultimately not on getting married and begetting children but solely on God's gracious provision.[54]

Jesus reveals a future age for God's people when marrying and begetting will be surpassed. Jesus honors disciples who forgo marrying and begetting for the sake of God's service in the present age. In light of Jesus's revelation, we may see Jesus's celibacy as a first sign of the future age and thus see celibacy among Jesus's disciples as prefiguring resurrection. It does not follow, however, that Jesus alters marriage, or authorizes his disciples to alter marriage, by subtracting begetting from marrying and sanctioning begettingless marrying (and so, possibly, same-sex or childless-by-choice marrying). Wesley Hill comments:

> The coming of Christ . . . opens up, for the first time in redemptive history, the possibility of viewing marriage as a *freely chosen* vocation. It is not necessary in the way that it once was, and singleness is now an equally . . . honorable calling. But, crucially, this does not alter the definition of marriage. Marriage remains what it has always been. . . . What is now available, in Christ, is the option of *not* marrying. This is different from [the] claim that what is now available is the option of marrying *in a different way* (i.e., nonprocreatively).[55]

What Jesus affirms is not-marrying, not marrying otherwise than God ordained from the beginning.

When Pharisees question him on divorce, Jesus looks to creation as a protological reference point for marriage, confirming God's original blessing of exclusive-enduring fidelity in the one-flesh union of male and female. When Sadducees question him on resurrection, Jesus looks to resurrection as an eschatological reference point for marriage, confirming God's continuing purpose for procreative marriage yet revealing God's future age beyond marrying and begetting. Jesus frames his teaching on marriage in reference to *both* horizons—beginning and end. When we look back with Jesus to creation, we see marriage established: God's purpose at creation's beginning for marriage as man-woman monogamy. And when we look forward with Jesus to resurrection, we see marriage surpassed: God's promise at creation's completion of life-beyond-marriage in life-beyond-death. When we look with the vision of Jesus in the Gospels—whether toward the beginning or toward the end—same-sex union does not appear on either horizon.

---

54. See Danylak, *Redeeming Singleness*, 101–7.
55. Hill, "Rejoinder," 164 (emphasis original).

Jesus's "Silence" on Same-Sex Union

Some observe that the Gospels do not report Jesus addressing the question of same-sex union. Jesus never mentioned, much less censured, same-sex relations. Had the matter of same-sex relations been of great importance to Jesus, or had Jesus believed that same-sex intercourse is contrary to God's will, one might argue, he would surely have spoken about or against it—and his disciples would surely have recorded him as saying such. Yet he did not. Jesus's silence, one might suggest, signals that the matter was at least unimportant to Jesus.[56] Jesus's silence, some might venture, leaves open the possibility that, were he to speak today, Jesus might affirm same-sex union.

Arguments from silence, however, contain a logical weakness: an inference from silence presumes a premise that nearly begs the question ("He surely would have said so, wouldn't he?"). This argument from silence, moreover, can be balanced by another argument from silence: Jesus's teaching on sex and marriage offers not even the merest suggestion of affirmation of same-sex union. Jesus's "silence" on same-sex intercourse, furthermore, has a plausible explanation that undercuts drawing any inference. In the Gospels, Jesus teaches on marriage in response to provocations by Pharisees and Sadducees amid current debates over divorce and resurrection. All parties to each debate would almost certainly have been in unanimous agreement on this question: all Jewish writers of the time rejected same-sex intercourse as "perversion."[57] There is no need to state what everyone already assumes or to debate that on which everyone already agrees. Had Jesus diverged from the Jewish consensus on same-sex intercourse, on the contrary, we might expect Jesus to have voiced his dissent, as he did on other matters—and expect his novel view to have been the subject of controversy.[58] I thus think that Jesus's "silence" cannot be leveraged to favor marriage innovation.

Does Jesus's "silence" on same-sex union leave us with no clue concerning what his view might have been? William Countryman thinks so: "Given that Jesus said nothing on the topic of same-gender sexual relationships, the most one can say is that we do not know whether he would have regarded them as contrary to the created order."[59] Countryman's reasoning seems sound. The claim that "Jesus said nothing on the topic," however, assumes that same-sex union is not a marriage matter. Recognizing that same-sex

56. See Verhey, *Remembering Jesus*, 232.
57. See Loader, *Making Sense of Sex*, 131–40.
58. See Gagnon, *Bible and Homosexual Practice*, 185–88; Gagnon, "Bible and Homosexual Practice," 73–74.
59. Countryman, *Dirt, Greed, and Sex*, 246.

union is a marriage matter, and remembering that Jesus taught about marriage, we have more than silence to go on concerning what might have been Jesus's view on same-sex union. When asked about divorce, Jesus answered about marriage, recalling the creation story. One may thus imagine that had Jesus been queried about same-sex union he might have replied, as he did on divorce, by citing Genesis: "Have you not read that from the beginning the Creator made them male and female and said, 'For this reason the two will become one flesh'?" Willard Swartley comments: "It seems to me that this answer, so typical of Jesus who does not engage in casuistry, would also have been his answer had the question of same-sex covenant union (unthinkable in Jewish culture) been posed to Jesus."[60] Jesus's reading of Genesis, then, may speak to the same-sex-union question as much as to the divorce question.

Jesus and Marriage in This Meantime

Jesus confirms God's blessing of marriage and God's commission to procreation and yet reveals that marrying and begetting do not define humankind's destiny in God's plan. While God ordained marriage for God's purpose "from the beginning of creation," marriage will be surpassed when God's promise is fulfilled "in the resurrection from the dead."[61] What, then, of marriage in this meantime, between Jesus's resurrection and our resurrection?

The church should be guided by *both* Jesus's confirmation of the protological pattern and procreative purpose of marriage *and* Jesus's revelation of the eschatological surpassing of marriage and procreation. Discerning by one apart from the other would misdirect the church. At the same time, the church should see both marriage and celibacy in relation to Jesus's proclamation of the kingdom and call to discipleship: Jesus's disciples, whether married or celibate, are to seek first God's kingdom and follow Jesus in the way of the cross (Matt. 6:25–33; 8:18–22; 10:34–39; 16:24–26; 19:16–30).

Jesus's revelation that marriage and procreation will be surpassed in the future age, therefore, does not entail, in this meantime, that the creational form of marriage is alterable or that the procreative purpose of marriage is obsolete. Yet Jesus's commendation of those who forgo marriage for the sake of God's service does indicate that, in this meantime, celibacy is a blessed vocation for Jesus's disciples. Jesus's teaching on marriage carries implications for both innovationist and traditionalist views.

60. Swartley, *Homosexuality*, 41.
61. See O'Donovan, *Resurrection and Moral Order*, 69–70.

Jesus and the Innovationist View

Some might see Jesus's emphasis on the coming kingdom as giving freedom to marriage innovation. Jesus's confirmation of protological order, however, tempers an innovationist impulse. Jesus reestablished marriage according to God's creational purpose and covenantal promise even while inaugurating the completion of God's purpose and promise. Jesus never proposed changing the sex-unitive pattern or neglecting the procreative purpose of marriage, much less encouraged inventing new forms of sexual union, on account of initiating the next stage in God's plan. Eschatological hope, then, does not license the church to revise marriage or devise novel unions.

Robert Song invokes Jesus's revelation to advocate innovation. Song agrees that, according to Genesis, marriage is man-woman monogamy and is ordered toward procreation. He agrees that Jesus and Paul affirmed the creational pattern of marriage and assumed the procreative purpose of marriage. He also agrees that Jesus and Paul commended celibacy as an alternative vocation to marriage. Yet Song argues that the surpassing of marriage and procreation in the resurrection makes possible sexual union surpassing procreative marriage in the meantime. The church may thus sanction a "third vocation" of "covenant partnership," a hybrid of marriage and celibacy: faithful and permanent, like marriage; but nonprocreative, like celibacy. Covenant partnerships would include deliberately childless male-female couples and same-sex couples. Song correlates hybrid union with in-between time: whereas marriage manifests continuing creation and celibacy points to coming resurrection, covenant partnership would witness to this meantime in which we wait for resurrection.[62]

Song is correct that Jesus's revelation revises expectations of the future age and reorders priorities in the present age. Jesus's revelation, however, does not warrant Song's innovation. Song claims that the eschatological surpassing of marriage creates an ethical opening, between marriage and celibacy, for covenantal partnership apart from creational purpose. Song's claim, in effect, uncouples Jesus's revelation of resurrection from Jesus's confirmation of creation, as if the former were independent of the latter. Yet, as observed above, Jesus holds these together, confirming God's creational ordering of marriage even while revealing humankind's resurrectional future beyond marriage. Jesus's revelation that marriage and procreation will be surpassed in the resurrection, therefore, does not imply that covenantal partnership may be separated from creational purpose in the meantime.

62. Song, *Covenant and Calling.*

Jesus and the Traditionalist View

Others might see Jesus's confirmation of the protological pattern as re-inforcing a traditional emphasis on marriage and family. Jesus's eschatological orientation, however, resists a simple traditionalism. Jesus, while confirming God's pattern and purpose of marriage "from the beginning of creation," directs marriage and family toward the coming of the kingdom. Jesus, while confirming that the way that leads to life still includes the old command-ment, "Honor your father and your mother" (Matt. 15:4; 19:16–19; Luke 18:18–20; Exod. 20:12; Deut. 5:15), recognizes the members of his family by obedience to God (Matt. 8:21–22; 12:46–50; Mark 3:31–35; Luke 8:19–21; 9:57–62). Jesus, while exhorting husbands to avoid adultery and keep fidel-ity (Matt. 5:27–30), insists that love for him comes before love for wife and children (Matt. 10:34–39; Luke 14:26–27). Jesus, born of a virgin and living as a celibate, praises women who obey God and follow Jesus and honors men who make themselves "eunuchs" for the kingdom. Jesus promises that those who leave homes, spouses, or families "for the sake of the kingdom of God" will be rewarded "in this age" and "in the age to come" (Luke 18:28–30; cf. Matt. 19:27–29).

A church true to Jesus should honor both celibacy and marriage as authen-tic modes of Christian life. In traditionalist congregations that have inherited an exclusive emphasis on marriage or a negative image of celibacy, honoring both celibacy and marriage will require recognizing celibacy, on par with marriage, as worthy of a place in the life of the church. We should beware seeing singleness as a deficient mode of Christian life, defined by absence of a spouse and having potential primarily in relation to marriage ("*un*married" or "*pre*married"). The church should see singleness as a sufficient mode of Christian life, patterned on the life of Jesus, sustained by the presence of the Spirit, and having potential primarily in relation to discipleship. Jesus's teach-ing calls the church to cast a theological vision for celibacy and to cultivate forms of community that affirm and support single Christians so that they may be faithful and fruitful as Jesus's disciples in God's service.[63]

Jesus's teaching also challenges the temptation to organize the church around marriage and family—to make marriage and children the goal of Christian life and place biological families at the center of congregational purpose. "The real sin of marriage today is not adultery. . . . It is the idolatry

63. See Beckett, "Desire in Singleness"; Conrad, "Gift and Celibacy"; Danylak, *Redeeming Singleness*; Eileen, *8 Essential Thoughts*; Gilliam, *Revelations of a Single Woman*; Hill, *Spiritual Friendship*; Hitchcock, *Significance of Singleness*; Grenz, *Sexual Ethics*, 181–99; Yuan, *Holy Sexuality and the Gospel*, 97–121.

of the family itself, the refusal to understand marriage as directed toward the Kingdom of God."[64] The church does not exist to promote marriage and family simply for its own sake. In this meantime, the church sanctions marriage because God ordained marriage as good from the beginning and because God designated marriage to figure the union of Christ and the church—and thus because marriage serves God's purpose in creation and testifies to God's promise of salvation. At the same time, because Jesus commissioned his disciples to make disciples of all nations, the church blesses couples and nurtures children so that families might walk faithfully and work fruitfully as Jesus's disciples in service to God's mission in the world. A church true to Jesus will organize congregational life around the family of believers and order domestic life toward God's kingdom.[65]

64. Schmemann, *For the Life of the World*, 110.
65. See Ash, *Marriage*, 122–32; J. Smith, *You Are What You Love*, 111–36; Callaway, *Breaking the Marriage Idol*.

5

Admiring Virginity,
Honoring Marriage

EARLY CHURCH DEBATE

Let marriage be held in honor by all, and let the marriage bed be
kept undefiled.

Hebrews 13:4

We admire virginity accompanied by humility; . . . we honor the
holy companionship of marriage.

Synod of Gangra (fourth century)

We are not the first Christians to debate questions about marriage. Within a
generation of Jesus's ascension, believers were espousing diverse views on sex
and marriage, prompting responses from the apostles. In the postapostolic era,
the church engaged in a protracted debate about sex and marriage, stretch-
ing from the second through the fourth centuries and involving bishops and
theologians from East and West. In this chapter I will revisit and reflect on
these marriage debates of the early church, with a view to garnering wisdom
for discernment in the church today.

Debating Marriage in the Apostolic Era

Paul's correspondence with the Corinthians exhibits a cross section of various views on sex and marriage that arose among early Christians. The congregation at Corinth was home to divisions along factional loyalties to human leaders (1 Cor. 1–4) and among social classes at communal meals (1 Cor. 11). It was home to disputes between those of "strong" and "weak" conscience concerning eating meat sacrificed in temples, sold in markets, and served at banquets (1 Cor. 8–10). It was also home to disagreements among disparate parties concerning sexual ethics (1 Cor. 5–7). The believers in Corinth held diverse and clashing attitudes about sex and marriage: there was no Corinthian consensus.

It Is Reported: Sex in Corinth

Some believers were espousing tolerance of deviant sexual relationships. This "toleration" party approved of church members living openly in such relationships, congratulating themselves for their tolerance. In the case reported to Paul, they approved a man living in sexual relationship with his stepmother (1 Cor. 5:1–2).[1] The toleration party sanctioned sexual partnerships beyond the bounds of licit marriage. Their approval of deviant sexual relationships transgressed biblical law and offended cultural sensibility.

Other believers were espousing license to pursue sexual activity according to personal appetite. This "liberation" party advocated sexual license as a species of freedom from law, advancing their antinomian agenda under the slogan, "All things are lawful for me" (1 Cor. 6:12). They argued that one could consume sex to sate desire just as one would consume food to fill hunger. The liberation party regarded bodily matters as morally indifferent and thus judged sexual chastity and sexual promiscuity as morally equivalent. Their license of extramarital sex fit the cultural norm permitting men, married or unmarried, to satisfy sexual urges with slaves in the household or prostitutes in the marketplace.

Still other believers were espousing abstinence from sexual relations. This "renunciation" party advocated avoiding sexual relations, maintaining that "it is well for a man not to touch [i.e., have sexual relations with] a woman [or, "a wife"]" (1 Cor. 7:1).[2] Apparently, inferring from Paul's response, they

---

1. The text indicates an ongoing relationship, but it is ambiguous whether the man was cohabitating with, or had officially married, his stepmother (who, presumably, had been divorced, or widowed, by his father). See Thiselton, *First Epistle to the Corinthians*, 384–87.

2. On the difficulties of translating and interpreting 1 Cor. 7:1, see Thiselton, *First Epistle to the Corinthians*, 497–501. I follow Thiselton and other scholars in reading this verse as Paul

exhorted Christians to practice abstinence within marriage (continence), or gain release from marriage (divorce), or remain unmarried (celibacy). Possibly, again inferring from Paul's response, their reasons for practicing abstinence included devotion to ascetic discipline (cf. 7:5) or reaction to a distressing situation (cf. 7:26) or presumption of spiritual superiority (a major theme of the letter). Their renunciation of sexual relations may have mimicked certain philosophical schools (e.g., Cynics and Epicureans) that doubted the wisdom of marriage and denied the need of sex for a good life.

Do You Not Know? Apostolic Responses

The attitudes of these Corinthian parties prompted responses from Paul. Paul rebukes the toleration party's complacency: they should have mourned rather than celebrated this man's relationship. Paul reminds them that God has redeemed them in Christ to be a community of new life characterized by holy living, which requires putting away old ways of wickedness. He urges them to purge their community of believers who persist unrepentantly in practicing sexual immorality, greed, and idolatry (1 Cor. 5:3–13).

Paul rebuts the liberation party's slogan: sexual freedom is slavery to desire. Paul reminds them that, although some of them used to practice sexual immorality, their bodies were freed from slavery to desire and cleansed of the impurity of sin in baptism so that now their bodies belong to the Lord. Bodies for the Lord should not be used for promiscuity; bodies united to Christ should not be united to prostitutes. He exhorts them to keep their bodies holy for God's glory (1 Cor. 6:9–20).

Paul counters the renunciation party by upholding the goodness of sex in marriage: sexual satisfaction with one's spouse is a good of marriage; marital conjugality guards against sexual immorality. Paul goes on to affirm monogamy in marriage: each man should have his own wife, each woman her own husband. He also affirms mutuality in marriage: husbands and wives have reciprocal obligations in conjugal fidelity; couples may abstain from sex for prayer but only by agreement. Paul restates Jesus's ruling against divorce: believing couples should not divorce; but if they separate, they should seek reconciliation; if that fails, they should not remarry. He also counsels singles and widows on the choice between celibacy and marriage: remaining

---

restating a view expressed by the Corinthians. K. Bailey, *Paul through Mediterranean Eyes*, 199–200, reads this verse as Paul answering a question asked by the Corinthians: "Is it well for a man not to touch a woman?" Danylak, *Redeeming Singleness*, 174–211, reads this verse as expressing Paul's own view and reconstructs 1 Cor. 7 as Paul's counsel to the Corinthians against the background of the Greco-Roman marriage debate, whether it is better to marry or remain unmarried.

unmarried is preferable in Paul's opinion; but marrying is better if one lacks self-control (1 Cor. 7:2–11).

The New Testament indicates that such attitudes toward sex as Paul addressed were not confined to Corinth. Hebrews was written likely by a Jewish believer, maybe a coworker of Paul, possibly Apollos or Priscilla. The author admonished the Christian community: "Let marriage be held in honor by all, and let the marriage bed be kept undefiled; for God will judge fornicators and adulterers" (Heb. 13:4). This admonition restated the warning against sexual immorality that was standard teaching in Hellenistic-Jewish synagogues and early Christian congregations. It might also have responded to views akin to the marriage-dishonoring or immorality-licensing attitudes found among the Corinthians.

First Timothy is a deposit of apostolic instruction concerning Christian faith and church order, possibly written by Paul and later redacted by a disciple of Paul, perhaps Timothy himself. It responded to false teachers in Ephesus of an apparently Gnostic-like sect, who were leading some believers to "renounce the faith."[3] These false teachers were advocating extreme asceticism: "They forbid marriage and demand abstinence from foods" (1 Tim. 4:3). Adherents of so-called knowledge (*gnōsis*) went beyond bridling desires for the sake of spiritual growth; they denied the body's goodness and held that human salvation demands extreme fasting from food and sex to free the spirit from evils of the flesh. Apostolic teaching responded by affirming that the body and marriage are God-created, God-given goods, which God intended "to be received with thanksgiving by those who believe and know the truth." Marriage is not "to be rejected" but "is sanctified by God's word and by prayer" (4:1–5; cf. 6:20–21).

Apostolic Wisdom for Present Discernment

The apostolic responses to aberrant attitudes on sex and marriage among early Christians are instructive for our discernment. I will briefly discuss three interrelated lessons.[4]

Distinguish Matters

First, Paul distinguished between matters concerning which the church must declare judgment and exercise discipline and matters concerning which the church may accommodate difference of opinion and allow freedom of

---

3. See Fairchild, *Christian Origins*, 81–86.

4. On Paul's responses and their pastoral implications, see Hays, *First Corinthians*, 80–134; Thiselton, *1 Corinthians*, 81–122; Elias, *Remember the Future*, 425–30.

choice. Paul judged the cases at Corinth involving the toleration and liberation parties with canonical strictness, issuing emphatic injunctions: "Drive out the wicked person from among you[!]" (1 Cor. 5:13); "Never!" (6:15); "Shun fornication!" (6:18). By contrast, Paul addressed some of the concerns raised by the renunciation party with flexibility, leaving room for adjusting counsel and exercising discretion in particular circumstances.

In parallel to distinguishing between matters of discipline and matters of discretion, Paul distinguished between matters concerning which Scripture has testified to God's will or Jesus has ruled with authority and matters concerning which the church does not have a word of God from Scripture or Jesus but which may be left to local decision or personal discretion. On whether Christian couples may divorce, Paul cited Jesus's ruling against divorce and, accordingly, instructed the community by command: Christian couples should not divorce; but if they separate, they should reconcile or not remarry (1 Cor. 7:10–11). On whether Christian singles and widows should marry or not, Paul acknowledged that Jesus had not ruled on this and so advised the community by concession rather than command: it is well whether one marries or remains unmarried; better to not marry than to marry, but better to marry than to burn with desire (7:6–9, 25–40). Paul also addressed matters in the middle, on which Jesus had not ruled but to which Jesus's ruling was relevant. On whether believers married to unbelievers may divorce, Paul acknowledged that Jesus had not ruled on this but devised a rule for the community in accord with the authority of Jesus: a believer whose wife or husband is an unbeliever yet consents to remain married should not divorce, for the sake of the spouse's salvation; but if the unbelieving spouse insists on separating, the believer may let the unbeliever go, for the sake of peace (7:12–16).[5]

Paul's response to the Corinthians suggests a set of parallel questions that the church today would do well to consider in discerning whether to sanction same-sex union: Is this a matter in which the church must be strict, declaring judgment and exercising discipline, or a matter in which the church may be flexible, accommodating difference and allowing freedom, or a middle matter in which the church needs to discern between what must be "bound" and what may be "loosed" (Matt. 16:19; 18:18)? Is this a matter on which Scripture has spoken clearly and consistently or on which Jesus has ruled authoritatively, or a matter that may be left to local decision or personal discretion, or a matter in which the church needs to discern how to apply the rule of Jesus under guidance of the Spirit? In concrete terms, is the matter of same-sex union akin to the case of the man living in sexual partnership with his stepmother, or to

5. See Good, *Bible Unwrapped*, 237–39.

the question of whether Christians should marry or not, or to the question of believers married to unbelievers?

Emphasize Theology

Second, the apostolic responses dealt with both ethical and theological aspects of attitudes toward sex. In the first case at Corinth, Paul named the moral conceit and exposed the ecclesiological danger of sexual tolerance: the sin of one implicates the holiness of the whole; accommodating immorality corrupts community. The toleration party had a deficient theology of the church as a holy people redeemed in Christ for God. In the second case at Corinth, Paul named the moral contradiction and elaborated the soteriological implication of sexual liberation: treating the body as disposable forgets the body's future with God in resurrection; license with the body neglects the body's belonging to the Lord by redemption; defiling the body by immorality corrupts the body's glory as the Spirit's temple. The liberation party had an errant theology of the body in relation to the economy of salvation.

The apostolic response to false teachers, likewise, dealt with the theological error in their doctrine. The Corinthian ascetics affirmed the superiority of celibacy but did not expressly deny the goodness of marriage. Paul's response to their view thus affirmed the ethical use of marriage and emphasized the practical advantage of celibacy but did not appeal directly to the theological basis for marriage. Gnostic-like asceticism, however, did deny the very validity of marriage, denigrating sex in marriage as participation in evil. Refuting false teaching, accordingly, called for a theological defense of marriage. The apostolic response thus exhibited the doctrinal stake in that debate: to reject the good of marriage is to refuse the gift of creation and thus to renounce faith in the Creator.

The cases in Corinth called for communal judgment and strict discipline, and the false teaching in Ephesus called for confrontation and refutation, precisely because of the theological implications of toleration, liberation, and extreme asceticism. The church today should acknowledge that discernment adequate to the present matter must go beyond questions of sexual ethics. In discerning the same-sex-union question, the church should consider the theological implications of altering marriage—and discern whether those theological implications warrant a similar response (see below and chap. 6).

Avoid Ditches

Third, diverse views on sex and marriage among early Christians pressed the church from two angles. From one angle, libertines were licensing sex outside marriage; from the opposite angle, ascetics were censuring sex inside marriage. The apostles sought to steer a steady course through these crosscurrents to avoid crashing the church into shoals on either side. In resisting error, apostolic teaching assumed a "neither-nor" posture: neither embracing liberation nor imposing asceticism; neither permitting immorality nor forbidding marriage. Between the extremes, the apostles delimited a range of freedom: one may marry or not marry, but sex only in marriage. In articulating truth, apostolic teaching assumed a "both-and" posture: defending the honor of marriage while commending a life of celibacy; affirming the sanctity of sex in marriage while affirming the sacrifice of sex for the kingdom. This middle course of apostolic teaching, however, was not a bland policy of broad tolerance: some sexual relationships and activities are simply sinful and thus warrant discipline rather than accommodation.

The church today, amid its debate on sex and marriage, also needs to steer a middle path between ditches on either side. Both traditionalists and innovationists would do well to learn from the apostolic approach. Traditionalists should beware arguing against same-sex union in ways that, in effect, distort Christian chastity into a Gnostic-like asceticism for gay believers: "You are forbidden marriage; you must destroy the desires of your flesh to ensure the salvation of your spirit." A defensible no to same-sex union must derive from an attractive biblical-theological vision of sex and marriage that reinvigorates the biblical-traditional yes to celibacy and singleness.[6] Innovationists should beware advocating for same-sex union in ways that, in effect, mimic the self-congratulatory tolerance or sloganeering license of the Corinthians—that forsake the moral integrity of the Christian community for the sake of inclusion, or that imply the moral equivalency of all consensual-mutual sexual relations under the banner of love ("Love is love"). A responsible yes to same-sex union must be accompanied by a clear commitment that recalls our baptismal yes to renouncing the ways of sin and death and thus respects the biblical-traditional no to all sex outside covenant.[7]

Debating Marriage in the Patristic Era

From the second through the fourth centuries, Christians from East to West conducted a protracted debate over the theological status of marriage, sex, and procreation in the age of Christ. All parties to this debate agreed on basic premises: marriage is man-woman monogamy; marriage and procreation are conjoined. This theological debate revolved principally around two sets of

6. See also Hitchcock, *Significance of Singleness*, 132–35.
7. See also Otto, *Oriented to Faith*, 105–8.

questions: First, whether marriage is a God-created good or a necessary evil, and, if a God-created good, whether procreation, and thus marriage, remain valid after Christ. Second, whether sex within marriage is inevitably tainted by sin, and, correlatively, whether the virgin state is superior to the married state, and if so, in what way.[8]

In what follows I do not attempt a comprehensive recounting of the patristic-era debate.[9] Nor will I advance a novel thesis about this debate. My aim is to outline main contours and summarize major viewpoints, with the hope that this will prove instructive for our discernment. My point is not to draw direct lines between past and present but rather to glean lessons to help us discern wisely.

Restricting and Rejecting Marriage: Tertullian and Tatian

The second century saw the emergence of aberrant views on sex and marriage, often associated with Christian movements that were deemed to have deviated from sound doctrine: Montanists, Encratites, and Gnostics. Some Gnostic schools spawned antinomian sects that affirmed sexual liberation. Typically, these movements begot ascetical sects that restricted or rejected marriage. I will consider two such movements, Montanists and Encratites, represented by Tertullian and Tatian, respectively.[10]

Tertullian: Prophetic Rigorism

Tertullian, a teacher of the North African church in the late second century and early third century, considered the implications of Christ's coming for marriage, particularly the question of second marriage for Christian widows. In his earlier writing, Tertullian maintained a view consistent with the consensus that would develop in the church over the next two centuries. He rejected ascetic arguments for abolishing marriage due to the filling of the earth and the coming of Christ. God's law sanctioned "the union of man and woman," which God "blessed to be the seedbed of the human race" and "devised to fill up the earth and set the world in order." Christ's teaching brought increased

8. The patristic-era church, of course, continued the divorce debate—see Instone-Brewer, *Divorce and Remarriage in the Bible*, 238–58; Reynolds, *Marriage in the Western Church*, 173–212. The patristic-era church was concerned also with the contrast and conflict between divine law and human laws—see Reynolds, *Marriage in the Western Church*, 121–55.

9. For overviews, see Hunter, *Marriage in the Early Church*, 9–25; Trenham, *Marriage and Virginity in St. John Chrysostom*, 20–82.

10. For overviews of early movements, see Pelikan, *Emergence of the Catholic Tradition*, 68–108; González, *Early Church to the Dawn of the Reformation*, 70–74; McGuckin, *Path of Christianity*, 4–48. On the range of views opposed to marriage or procreation, see Noonan, *Contraception*, 57–72.

rigor in sexual discipline, rescinding concessions allowed to earlier genera-tions and restoring marriage according to God's intention. Yet, Tertullian argued, the earth's filling and Christ's coming did not "dissolve marriage or abolish sexual relations." Those who say that we may now divorce spouses and abandon marriages violate God's intention and Christ's teaching. Mar-riage remains a good, and so second marriage is permissible, at least for the sake of chastity, but abstinence is preferable to second marriage on account of anticipation of resurrection (cf. 1 Cor. 7:1–2, 9, 26). He thus maintained, based on Paul's instruction, that widows may remarry "in the Lord" (7:39).[11]

Later, in his Montanist phase, Tertullian shifted stance, revoking the allow-ance of second marriage based on reappraisal of procreation. To the question whether the multiple marriages of our biblical ancestors might justify second marriages for us, Tertullian replied: "Certainly it will . . . if even now there is a place for that saying: *Increase and multiply* [Gen. 1:28], that is, if it has not yet been superseded by another saying, such as: *The time is short* and *Those who have wives should live as though they had none* [1 Cor. 7:29]." He then affirmed that the commission to procreation has in fact been superseded and set aside, drawing a prophetic conclusion from Paul's instruction: "For by enjoining continence and restricting intercourse, the seedbed of the human race, he [Paul] abolished that *Increase and multiply*." Both the commission to procreation and the cancellation of that commission "were the work of one and the same God." God sanctioned marriage and even allowed multiple marriage "in order to provide a seedbed for the human race, until the world should be filled, until there should be cause for a new way of life." Christ's coming, inaugurating the "last days," signals that God's procreative purpose in marriage has been fulfilled, such that God "has suppressed the seedbed and revoked" the allowance of multiple marriage to our biblical ancestors for the sake of procreation. Now that God's purpose in marriage has been fulfilled, God's commission to procreation has been rescinded by Jesus's commenda-tion of celibacy, and God's allowance of marriage has been restricted to exact monogamy (one marriage only).[12]

According to the Montanist Tertullian, God has abolished the old dispen-sation, in which procreation served God's purpose, and begun a new dispen-sation, in which procreation is obsolete. As the new law of nonretaliation had replaced the old law of retaliation (Matt. 5:38–39), so now celibacy has superseded marriage; thus second marriage is forbidden in this "new way of

11. Tertullian, *To His Wife* 1.1–3, in Hunter, *Marriage in the Early Church*, 33–35.
12. Tertullian, *Exhortation to Chastity* 6, in Hunter, *Marriage in the Early Church*, 39–40 (emphasis original).

life." Tertullian defended the rigorist stance of exact monogamy against the charge of novelty by claiming a new dispensation from the Holy Spirit, who had supposedly given the "spiritualists" a previously unrevealed prophecy. As the new dispensation of Christ had revoked the concession of divorce, so an even newer dispensation of the Spirit has revoked the concession of remarriage: "The New Law abrogated divorce, the New Prophecy abrogates second marriage."[13]

Tatian: New-Age Asceticism

Tertullian the Montanist argued that a new dispensation of the Holy Spirit entailed the rejection of second marriage and restriction to single marriage. Encratites in second- and third-century Syria, following Tatian's teaching, argued that Christ's coming entailed rejection of marriage and restriction to celibacy.[14] In their view, marriage and children are not good gifts from the God of creation and covenant. God, from the beginning, never intended for humankind to engage in sexual relations and generate offspring. Sex and procreation are evils necessary to humankind's preservation in its fallen condition. Procreation in marriage, while perpetuating humankind, only furthers separation from God. Christ, a virgin born of a virgin, has brought liberation from death, and thus from the evils of sex and procreation made necessary by death, which makes possible the restoration of humankind to the pristine life of its prefall, presex state.[15]

Christ's coming has already ended the evil age to which belonged sex and marriage, birth and death. Baptism into Christ means entering a new age, which entails renouncing sexual relations, even within marriage, and thus practicing strict continence (*enkrateia*). The third-century Syrian text Acts of Thomas proclaims that disciples "will become holy temples" if they "refrain from this filthy intercourse." The bride and groom who leave their marriage bed, even on their wedding night, and are betrothed to Christ in baptism will be "saved from destruction" and "freed from what is temporary" and will "enter into that bridal chamber" of the Bridegroom "full of immortality and light."[16]

Tertullian and Tatian each diverged, in different ways, from both the witness of Scripture and what would become the consensus view of church teaching.

---

13. Tertullian, *On Monogamy* 1–2, 14 (*ANF* 4:59–60, 70–71). See also Brown, *Body and Society*, 76–82. The Montanist emphasis on ethical rigorism, including rejection of second marriage, was motivated by eschatological expectation—see Pelikan, *Emergence of the Catholic Tradition*, 100–101; McGuckin, *Path of Christianity*, 17.

14. Tatian, *Fragments* 1–3 (*ANF* 2:82).

15. See Brown, *Body and Society*, 90–102.

16. Acts of Thomas 12–15, in Hunter, *Marriage in the Early Church*, 61–63.

Tertullian rejected second marriage, even though Christ did not forbid it and Paul allowed it. Tatian rejected marriage, even though Christ and Paul each affirmed it. Despite their differences, there are two parallels worth noting. Both Tertullian and Tatian reappraised marriage in light of Christ's coming; and both reappraised marriage in relation to procreation. In Tertullian's Montanist view, Christ's coming revealed that procreation is obsolete in God's purpose: the commission to procreation in marriage has been abolished. In Tatian's Encratite view, Christ's coming revealed that procreation in marriage was never sanctioned by God's plan: sex and birth have always been cooperation with sin and death. Tertullian and Tatian shared the common premise of early Christians that marriage and procreation are conjoined: reappraising procreation meant reappraising marriage. Their respective reappraisals of procreation thus led, logically, to either restriction of marriage to exact monogamy (Tertullian) or rejection of marriage in favor of celibacy (Tatian).

Refuting Error and Defending Marriage: Clement and Methodius

The rejection of procreation—whether as abolished by Christ (per Tertullian) or as evil from the beginning (per Tatian)—and the consequent restriction or rejection of marriage provoked responses in the early church. Here I will consider the teachings of Clement and Methodius.[17]

Clement: Marriage Sanctioned by Creation

Clement, a teacher of the church in Alexandria in the late second century, refuted the Encratite repudiation of marriage and procreation. To repudiate marriage and procreation as cooperation with sin and death, Clement asserted, is tantamount to blasphemy: those "who teach that marriage and childbearing should be rejected" effectively "blaspheme both the creation and the holy Creator" by means of "their supposedly sacred continence."[18] In support of marriage and procreation, Clement cited the creation story, arguing that God's commission to procreation (Gen. 1:28) is still operative in the age of Christ and that we fulfill our vocation as God's image by cooperating with God's purpose of procreation through marriage.[19] Clement also cited Jesus's witness to himself in the Gospel: Christ's coming has fulfilled the prophecies in the law but has not canceled the law (Matt. 5:17–18); accordingly, Christ condemned adultery but confirmed marriage (5:27–28; 19:3–9).[20]

---

17. See also Trenham, *Marriage and Virginity in St. John Chrysostom*, 21–28, 39–51, 58–67; Harper, *From Shame to Sin*, 80–83, 105–12.

18. Clement of Alexandria, *Miscellanies* 3.6.45, in Hunter, *Marriage in the Early Church*, 50.

19. Clement of Alexandria, *Christ the Educator* 2.10.83; 2.10.94–95.

20. Clement of Alexandria, *Miscellanies* 3.6.46.

Clement argued not only that God's blessing of marriage and commission of procreation continue in the new age of Christ but also that God's decree in creation has ordered marriage toward procreation. Marriage serves purposes besides procreation: it provides spouses with mutual help, promotes self-restraint in spouses, and protects spouses from sin.[21] Yet procreation is integral to the function of marriage. Clement even suggested that we might interpret the husband and wife joined in marriage and the child generated from their union as the "two or three . . . gathered in my name" among whom Christ dwells (Matt. 18:20).[22]

Methodius: Marriage Confirmed in Christ

Methodius, a bishop of the church in Asia Minor in the late third to early fourth century, also defended marriage against prophetic rigorism and new-age asceticism. In his *Symposium*, a banquet of dialogue among ten virgins in praise of virginity, Methodius addressed the argument that with the filling of the earth and the coming of Christ, Christians should renounce marriage and embrace virginity. In defending marriage, Methodius refuted the view that Christ's coming canceled the procreative commission and affirmed the view that the created order and procreative commission continue in the age of Christ according to the purpose of God.

Marcella, first to speak, draws a sharp before-and-after line in God's purpose. God had commissioned humankind to marry and procreate, but humankind has filled the earth as God intended. God has now sent Christ to reveal the perfection of humankind in the practice of virginity, which Christ commended by teaching and demonstrated by example. With the earth's filling and Christ's coming, God's commission of procreation in marriage has ended and Christ's call to celibacy has begun.[23]

Theophila, second to speak, agrees that Christ's coming means that virginity is preferable to marriage as Christian vocation, because virginity comes closer than marriage to final perfection in God's plan of salvation. Yet she argues that Christ's coming did not terminate God's purpose in creation: "[Marcella's] suggestion that it is no longer necessary to produce children is mistaken. It is very clear to me from Scripture that with the coming of virginity the Logos did not completely abolish procreation." Citing the witness of Scripture to God the Creator, she argues that God's blessing of marriage, with its commission to procreation, continues as God ordained from the beginning: "God's declaration and command regarding procreation, all agree, is

---

21. Clement of Alexandria, *Miscellanies* 2.23.
22. Clement of Alexandria, *Miscellanies* 3.10.68.
23. Methodius, *Symposium* 1.

still being accomplished even now, since the Creator is still fashioning human beings." Humankind will have fulfilled its procreative commission in marriage when God ceases to sustain the creation: "Only then must there be no procreation." God's purpose of procreation in marriage continues as long as God upholds the order of creation: "But now it is necessary that human beings cooperate in producing the image of God, since the universe continues to exist and to be created. *Increase and multiply*, Scripture says [Gen. 1:28]. We must not recoil from the commandment of the Creator." Human cooperation with God's blessing in marriage, moreover, now furthers God's mission in another way: generating the future martyrs of the church.[24]

As Marcella's speech illustrates, early Christians recognized that Christ's coming makes a significant difference for the human vocation within God's purpose. This recognition was rooted in Jesus's teaching and life: marriage and procreation will be surpassed in the resurrection, so that virginity—manifest by Jesus himself—is even now a possible vocation for God's people, serving as a visible sign of the coming kingdom. God's commission of procreation, while continuing under God's blessing of marriage, no longer has the same priority in God's plan. Eschatological anticipation thus gave rise to a vigorous asceticism among early Christians.[25]

At the same time, as Theophila's rebuttal demonstrates, we must be careful not to draw the wrong conclusion. Marcella errs by drawing a sharp line between "before Christ" and "after Christ." Theophila maintains, against Marcella, that the Creator's original blessing and procreative purpose of marriage are confirmed by Christ and thus continue in Christ: humankind's filling the earth does not entail God's withdrawing blessing of marriage; Christ's coming does not cancel God's commission of procreation. Procreation in marriage remains necessary to God's purpose in creation and useful to the mission of God's people.

Admiring Virginity, Honoring Marriage: Gangra and Gregory

The views of Clement and Methodius reflect the tenor of a consolidating consensus of patristic-era church teaching. This consensus view valued celibacy above marriage as the preferable vocation for God's people yet honored marriage alongside celibacy. It affirmed a new epoch in Christ's coming yet maintained the validity of God's design in creation, thus avoiding the errors of prophetic rigorism and new-age asceticism. This consensus view is evident in the Synod of Gangra and Gregory of Nazianzus.

---

24. Methodius, *Symposium* 2.1–2, in Hunter, *Marriage in the Early Church*, 64–65 (emphasis original).

25. See Brown, *Body and Society*.

Synod of Gangra: Defending Orthodoxy

New-age asceticism emerged mostly among Eastern Christians. The Synod of Gangra, a council of Eastern bishops held in Asia Minor in the mid-fourth century, formally censured new-age asceticism and articulated consensus teaching on celibacy and marriage.[26]

The synod's letter repudiated the doctrines of an ascetic movement, associated with Eustathius, bishop of Sebaste, for their "utter abhorrence of marriage" and "adoption of the proposition that no one living in a state of marriage has any hope towards God."[27] The synod's canons anathematized those who "condemn marriage as sinful" (first canon), or who refuse to receive communion from a married priest (fourth canon), or who practice celibacy but "treat arrogantly the married" (tenth canon); they also anathematized any man who "remain[s] virgin, or observe[s] continence, abstaining from marriage because he abhors it" (ninth canon) and any woman who "forsake[s] her husband, and resolve[s] to depart from him because she abhors marriage" (fourteenth canon).[28] The synod's epilogue affirmed the view evident in Clement and Methodius: "We do, assuredly, admire virginity accompanied by humility; and we have regard for continence, accompanied by godliness and gravity; . . . [but at the same time] we honour the holy companionship of marriage."[29]

Gregory of Nazianzus: Orthodox Asceticism

Gregory of Nazianzus, the great theologian of Cappadocia in the later fourth century, articulated an orthodox asceticism. In his poem *In Praise of Virginity*, Gregory reappraised marriage in the age of Christ, admiring the ascetic life as the preferable vocation while honoring marriage as a God-given good.

In Gregory's view, the importance of marriage in God's economy diminishes with Christ's coming even as marriage continues to serve the purposes—prevention of fornication and procreation of children—for which God ordained marriage. God created man and woman for one another, giving them license "to embrace each other" in sexual union, yet within limits: "not always, nor with everyone." God thus ordained monogamy in marriage as a restraint on passion, to differentiate humankind from mere beasts by regulation of sexual relations. Because "mother Earth was deficient in human beings," and

---

26. See McGuckin, *Path of Christianity*, 369n21.
27. *Synodical Letter of the Council of Gangra* (NPNF² 14:91).
28. *Canons of the Holy Fathers Assembled at Gangra* (NPNF² 14:92, 93, 95, 96, 98). The views of this synod are echoed in Chrysostom's critique of extreme asceticism in *On Virginity* 1–11.
29. *Epilogue* (NPNF² 14:101; the brackets of "[but at the same time]" appear in the source).

because humans became subject to death through the devil's envy and their choice to sin, God blessed "coupling and marriage" for the sake of "human generation" as a "defense against destruction." When Christ came by birth of the virgin, "radiant Virginity illuminated mankind," releasing us from the duty of marriage and revealing celibacy as "far superior to the married life." The law had sanctioned marriage and blessed children, but "the end of the law is Christ" and the coming of Christ "through a virginal womb" signaled "that marriage should decline toward the ground." Marriage gives way to a "better world" in which the cycle of sex, birth, and death has been conquered by virginity. Heeding "Christ's exhortation" and choosing "total chastity," the ascetic partakes of the angelic existence of heaven and anticipates return by resurrection to the paradisal garden. Although Christ will honor marriage and virginity in heaven, virginity receives the higher honor.[30]

Marriage in Salvation History: Chrysostom and Augustine

We come to the chief figures of Christian tradition on marriage, Chrysostom in the East and Augustine in the West. Chrysostom and Augustine each reappraised marriage and procreation in the light of the coming of Christ—and each defended marriage over against ascetical views that not only vaunted virginity but also devalued marriage almost to the point of denying its goodness.

Chrysostom: Marriage as Christian Discipleship

Chrysostom believed that the importance of procreation in the function of marriage diminished with the incarnation and resurrection of Jesus. In Chrysostom's view, God did not intend humankind to procreate in the garden: paradisal humankind is virginal humankind; humankind would not have engaged in sexual relations and generated offspring had humankind not fallen into sin. God blessed sexual intercourse and commissioned procreation at the beginning in anticipation of sin and death: procreation in marriage is God's provision to ensure humankind's preservation. Although God created man and woman for each other, to be helper-partners in coruling creation as God's vice-regents, marriage and procreation pertain to humankind in its fallen condition.[31] With the earth's filling and Christ's coming, the urgency and necessity

---

30. Gregory of Nazianzus, *In Praise of Virginity* (Poem 1.2.1) 100–127, 197–208, 409–28, 717–27, 730–32, in *On God and Man*, 92–93, 96, 104–5, 118. Likewise, Ephrem the Syrian, poet and ascetic, depicted "the celibate and chaste" among the baptized as the flowering fruits of the future paradise, where "virginity dances" and "the married state finds rest" (*Hymns on Paradise* 6.8–12 [pp. 111–13]; 7.5–8 [pp. 120–22]).

31. See Trenham, *Marriage and Virginity in St. John Chrysostom*, 99–112.

of marriage and procreation have been surpassed. Jesus's resurrection promises life beyond death, so that procreation is no longer necessary to humankind's preservation, and, therefore, marriage is no longer necessary to God's plan of salvation. Virginity thus becomes a possible, and preferable, path for God's people. Virginity, considered eschatologically, is superior to marriage because it better approximates the paradisal perfection and anticipates the angelic existence that we will regain in resurrection.[32]

While hope of resurrection has ended need for procreation and thus ended need for marriage in God's plan of salvation, marriage remains a blessed good in creation, and procreation remains an integral good of marriage. Chrysostom saw the generation of offspring as implied within, and a natural extension of, man and woman becoming "one flesh."[33] Chrysostom assumed that God originally ordained sexual intercourse for procreation and that this continues in Christ.[34] Chrysostom thus affirmed marriage and procreation, yet with a change of priority in purpose: "These are the two purposes for which marriage was instituted: to make us chaste, and to make us parents. Of these two, the reason of chastity takes precedence."[35] Christ's coming does not abolish marriage but does shift the priority in marriage: from leaving behind an earthly posterity by begetting children to preparing for our heavenly destiny by maintaining chastity. Chastity of the spouses, accordingly, comes before procreation of children: abstaining from sex during prescribed periods of fasting and prayer for the sake of spiritual fruit is more important than engaging in sex for the sake of physical offspring. Christ's coming subordinates procreation to chastity in the function of marriage—a change that does not terminate procreation but does reorient it: from perpetuating the secular city to promoting the Christian community, which anticipates the true city of God.[36]

32. See Chrysostom, *On Virginity* 9–11, 14–19, 73. See also Ford, *Women and Men in the Early Church*, 80–82.

33. See Chrysostom, *Homily 12 on Colossians*, in *On Marriage and Family Life*, 76.

34. See Trenham, *Marriage and Virginity in St. John Chrysostom*, 128–32, 154–62.

35. Chrysostom, *Sermon on Marriage*, in *On Marriage and Family Life*, 85–86; see also *How to Choose a Wife*, in *On Marriage and Family Life*, 99. Chrysostom may have moderated his view over time, or at least adjusted his emphasis to his audience. In his early treatise *On Virginity* 19.1, addressed to monks, he stated that the two reasons for marriage (chastity and children) have been reduced to the one (chastity). In his later sermon on marriage, preached to his congregation, he stated that the one reason (chastity) now took priority over the other reason (children). Also, in his *Homily 12 on Colossians*, Chrysostom named children before chastity in the purpose of marriage (*On Marriage and Family Life*, 74). Elsewhere, Chrysostom added further purposes of marriage: he affirmed partnership and procreation, as well as chastity, in his *Homily V on 1 Thessalonians* (NPNF[1] 13:346). Chrysostom's various statements on the purposes of marriage thus need to be taken together—see Ford, *Women and Men in the Early Church*, 55–67, 74–78.

36. See Trenham, *Marriage and Virginity in St. John Chrysostom*, 213.

In the age of Christ, Chrysostom maintained, marriage continues under the blessing of God, procreation remains integral to the purpose of marriage, and thus man-woman monogamy remains the pattern of marriage. The Christian household is to be a "little church"—a place of worship, school of discipleship, and center of mission. Chrysostom did not see monastery and marriage as opposite modes of Christian life: Jesus's teaching of perfection, in the Sermon on the Mount, makes the same demands of monk and married. Indeed, Chrysostom said, when husband and wife participate regularly in church; maintain chastity in sex; practice piety, hospitality, and charity at home; and instruct children in godly virtue, their "perfection will rival the holiest of monks," and their whole household "will be able to finish the course of this life without fear and to enter the kingdom of heaven."[37]

Augustine: Marriage for the City of God

Augustine's mature theological account of marriage integrated the form and function of marriage into God's purpose in creation and plan of salvation.[38] He maintained that God blessed marriage and commissioned procreation prior to the entry of sin and its consequence of death, such that the form and function of marriage belong to God's original design and creative purpose. Even had Adam and Eve not sinned and death not ensued, Augustine insisted, humankind would have enjoyed God's blessing in marriage and fulfilled God's purpose in the generation and nurture of children. Marriage continues in valid effect according to God's pattern and in service to God's purpose despite the distortions of sin and frustrations of death. In his view, God ordained marriage to serve God's plan of building a people of faith oriented by love of God—the "city of God." God designed marriage for the sake of cultivating and guarding the charity, fidelity, and chastity of spouses, as well as generating and nurturing children in faith, so that spouses and offspring might become godly citizens of the heavenly kingdom.

As the biblical narrative evidences, God's purpose for sex and marriage in creation and covenant is not immediately, or perfectly, realized. Humankind's disobedience and downfall (Gen. 3–6) succeeds God's creation and blessing (Gen. 1–2). Sex and marriage—under condition of sin, amid disordered relationships between humankind and God, man and woman, parents and

---

37. Chrysostom, *Homily 20 on Ephesians, Homily 21 on Ephesians,* and *How to Choose a Wife,* in *On Marriage and Family Life,* 57, 61–62, 69–71, 113–14; Chrysostom, *Against the Opponents of Monastic Life* 1.3. See also Ford, *Women and Men in the Early Church,* 82–88; Trenham, *Marriage and Virginity in St. John Chrysostom,* 168–203; Guroian, *Orthodox Reality,* 141–58.

38. Augustine *City of God* 14.21–23.

children, sibling and sibling—becomes deformed and dysfunctional, as evident in the families of Adam, Noah, and Abraham. Accordingly, Augustine was very aware that the function of marriage is often frustrated in a creation corrupted by sin and death. Many factors in a fallen world—infidelity, infertility, infant mortality, and so on—might prevent particular marriages from fully realizing the good God intended.[39] Nonetheless, Augustine saw marriage rightly ordered, amid a corrupted creation, as serving God's aim of renewed creation.

Augustine believed that the role of marriage in God's purpose changed with Christ's coming. In Augustine's view, God's prime purpose in procreation was to prepare for the Messiah, who would fulfill God's promise in covenant. The Messiah's coming means that marriage and procreation are no longer necessary to God's purpose and thus no longer duties for God's people—so that virginity is now a possible, and preferable, vocation for God's people.[40] With Christ's coming, God's people promote God's kingdom better by sowing the seed of faith than by sowing the seed of flesh—"by spiritual regeneration rather than sexual generation, by rebirth rather than birth."[41] Christ's coming did not divorce marrying from begetting, as if God's creational commission had ceased operation. Yet Christ's coming did shift the procreative priority in marriage: more than generating offspring for filling the city of God, now the priority in procreation is ordering sexual intercourse toward its proper moral end. In the age of Christ, Augustine maintained, God's plan of salvation still involves marriage, God's purpose for marriage still includes procreation, and thus God's design of marriage still entails the union of man and woman.[42]

Sexuate Bodies and the Resurrection

Patristic-era theologians, while agreed that there will be no marriage in the resurrection age, debated whether sexuate bodies will belong to the resurrection age. Will the eschatological surpassing of marriage in resurrection involve the eschatological undoing of "male and female" in creation?

A few theologians held that "male and female" would not belong to the resurrection age because, they believed, "male and female" did not belong to the original creation. Gregory of Nyssa in the fourth century, following Origen of Alexandria in the third century, maintained that sexuate bodies would be surpassed in resurrection. Gregory held that sexuate correspondence does not belong to humankind as created originally by God. Rather, humankind's differentiation

---

39. Augustine, *City of God* 22.13–14.
40. Augustine, *On the Good of Marriage* 8–10; *Sermon 51*, 25–26.
41. Reynolds, *Marriage in the Western Church*, 269–70.
42. See Roberts, *Creation and Covenant*, 205.

into sexuate counterparts belongs to God's postlapse provision for humankind after expulsion from the garden: sexuate bodies, allegorically represented by the "garments of skin" with which God clothed Adam and Eve (Gen. 3:21), are God's concession in the age of sin and death, allowing procreation for humankind's perpetuation against extinction. Sexuate correspondence is thus a provisional, not a proper, aspect of humankind. God's redemption of humankind through resurrection will erase sex from human bodies, reversing that provisional differentiation and restoring humankind to its original condition.[43] Gregory's view, however, had only a tenuous basis in the biblical creation account.[44]

In church history, Beth Felker Jones observes, depreciation of the sexuate correspondence of human embodiment as a created good has often implied denigration of the female in God's design.[45] Among Gnostic sects, female disciples could become Christlike only by becoming male-like, such that salvation in Christ entailed erasure of female sex.[46] Gnostic practice might involve extreme fasting to shrink breasts and stop menstruation, thus converting a female body into an outward approximation of a male body. Among early Christians, sex conversion was associated with doctrinal distortion.

It is with such views in mind that Augustine posed the question, "Will women retain their sex in the resurrected body?" Refuting such views, Augustine argued that "there will be both sexes in the resurrection."[47] Augustine argued on two grounds.

First, Augustine argued that sexuate bodies have an eschatological future because they have a creational origin. Based on the plain sense of Scripture, Augustine held that, because God originally created humankind "male and female," bodily sex belongs properly to the created goodness of the human being: "A woman's sex is not a defect, it is natural." Appealing to the doctrine of redemption, Augustine affirmed that, because in the end God will redeem the good that God created in the beginning, God will redeem human beings as sexuate bodies in the resurrection: "While all defects will be removed from those bodies, their essential nature will be preserved." The sexuate correspondence of male and female will be preserved in our perfected bodies—our "spiritual bodies" will be flesh-and-bone bodies sustained by and subject to the spirit, he says—even as God renews sexuate bodies and redirects them toward purposes yet to be revealed.[48]

43. See Brown, *Body and Society*, 160–77, 285–304; Roberts, *Creation and Covenant*, 24–28.
44. See Bouteneff, *Beginnings*, 157–66.
45. B. Jones, "Embodied from Creation through Redemption."
46. See the Gnostic text Gospel of Thomas 114, in Robinson, *Nag Hammadi Library*, 130.
47. Augustine, *City of God* 22.17.
48. See also Augustine, *Sermon 243*, in *Essential Sermons*, 302–6.

Second, Augustine argued that sexuate correspondence has an eschato-logical future because it has a figural relation to salvation. God's creating male and female and joining them into one flesh prefigures God's saving humankind through Christ's union with the church: "The woman . . . is the creation of God, just as the man; but her creation out of man emphasizes the idea of unity between them; and in the manner of that creation there is . . . a foreshadowing of Christ and his Church." Because the spiritual union of Christ and the church will endure eternally, therefore, the sexuate corre-spondence that is integral to the figural relation between marriage and salva-tion will also continue eschatologically. Augustine concluded: "Thus he who established the two sexes will restore them both. . . . Thus Christ denies the existence of marriage in the resurrected life; he does not deny the existence of women in heaven."[49]

Linking creation and salvation in the divine economy is Christ's incarna-tion. In a Christmas sermon, Augustine emphasized that Christ's incarna-tion affirms the goodness of both sexes and assures salvation to both sexes. Augustine offered two reasons why Christ's incarnation, while accomplished without sexual intercourse, does not erase sexual difference. First, salvation repairs the fall, which affects both sexes. Second, salvation honors creation, which includes both sexes. Christ's incarnation, a man born of a woman, vindicates the creation of humankind as male and female and indicates the salvation of male and female.[50]

Since the fourth century, Western and Eastern traditions of the church have generally maintained that sexuate bodies will belong to the resurrection age.[51]

Chrysostom and Augustine: Contrast and Consensus

Chrysostom and Augustine differed at certain points regarding sex and marriage.[52] They agreed that God had ordained marriage and blessed procre-ation, but they differed in their respective speculations on whether humankind would have united sexually and generated offspring in the garden had sin not occurred and death not ensued. Augustine, in his mature view, held that pro-creation in marriage was God's intention for humankind from the beginning.

---

49. Augustine, *City of God* 22.17.

50. Augustine, *Sermon 190*, 2, in *Essential Sermons*, 252. See also *Sermon 51*, 3.

51. See Augustine, *City of God* 13.20, 22; 22.17–21; Aquinas, *Summa Contra Gentiles* IV.88. On Augustine's view, see Roberts, *Creation and Covenant*, 233–34; B. Jones, "Embodied from Creation through Redemption." On the Eastern view, see Meyendorff, *Marriage*, 13–16; Ford, *Women and Men in the Early Church*, 148; Trenham, *Marriage and Virginity in St. John Chryso-stom*, 248–54.

52. Concerning the several differences between Western and Eastern views on sex and mar-riage in the patristic era, see Ford, *Women and Men in the Early Church*, 12–37.

Chrysostom maintained that procreation in marriage was God's provision to humankind after the fall.[53] They agreed that marriage is God's good gift to be kept holy, but they differed on whether sexual intercourse is inherently disordered after the fall. Augustine held that all sexual intercourse is now latent with lust; marriage chastens sex by redirecting sex from evil (satisfying lust) toward good (generating offspring).[54] Chrysostom did not regard sexual intercourse within marriage as a moral problem in itself; he even portrayed the sexual pleasure shared by husband and wife as an adhesive bond and thus a positive good, whether or not sex happens to issue in children.[55] They agreed that celibacy is superior to marriage, but they differed in emphasis on the reason. Augustine emphasized that celibacy is morally superior to marriage, because exercising self-mastery over desire by abstinence from sex removes one from the lust latent within marital sex even as keeping the fidelity of marriage removes one from the immorality of adultery and fornication.[56] Chrysostom emphasized that celibacy is eschatologically superior to marriage, because a celibate life moves one toward the marriageless age of resurrection in which all will return to paradisal perfection.[57] They agreed that procreation remains integral to the purpose of marriage, but they differed regarding the priority of

53. Their different views arose, in part, because they stressed different points in the creation account: Augustine's view stresses that God blessed procreation when creating humankind (Gen. 1:28); Chrysostom's view stresses that humankind procreated only after leaving the garden (Gen. 4:1). Augustine's early view was similar to Chrysostom's view—see Reynolds, *Marriage in the Western Church*, 241–51.

54. Augustine, *On the Good of Marriage* 3. Augustine's view, inherited from Tertullian and shared with Ambrose and Jerome, was common, but not universal, in the West; it was denied a few generations earlier by Lactantius and challenged during Augustine's time by Julian. See Brown, *Body and Society*, 408–15; Hunter, *Marriage in the Early Church*, 24–25.

55. See Chrysostom, *Homily 19 on 1 Corinthians*, in *On Marriage and Family Life*, 25–33; Chrysostom, *Homily 12 on Colossians*, in *On Marriage and Family Life*, 75–76. See also Ford, *Women and Men in the Early Church*, 47–50; Trenham, *Marriage and Virginity in St. John Chrysostom*, 157–58.

56. Augustine maintained a moral hierarchy of sexual chastity, from best to worst: celibacy, continence within marriage or widowhood, sex within marriage for procreation (no sin), sex within marriage to pay conjugal debt and control lust (venial sin), sex outside marriage (mortal sin). See Augustine, *On the Good of Marriage* 6–9; Augustine, *Sermon 51*, 21–22; Augustine, *Sermon 96*, 9–10. See Schafer, *Marriage, Sex, and Procreation*, 51–63. Gregory the Great, *Book of Pastoral Rule* 3.27, and Peter Lombard, *Sentences, Book 4*, dist. 31, chap. 5, each replicated Augustine's moral hierarchy. Although Augustine appealed to Paul, Paul did not judge marital sex as a lesser good than celibacy or as a lesser sin than adultery and fornication but rather commended conjugal fidelity as a chaste alternative to sexual immorality (1 Cor. 7:2–5).

57. Return-to-paradise eschatology, which Chrysostom shared with Methodius of Olympus, Gregory of Nazianzus, and Ephrem the Syrian, was a common view in the East. It can be found also in Augustine—see *Sermon 132, 3*, in *Essential Sermons*, 205. This view, while motivated by Jesus's revelation of a marriageless resurrection, does not quite square with John's vision of the new Jerusalem (Rev. 21–22), which does not simply reprise the garden of Eden.

procreation. Whereas Augustine held that procreation is no longer necessary for God's kingdom, he held that pursuing procreation in marriage is necessary to pardon sin and maintain chastity due to the lust latent in sex. Chrysostom held that chastity takes precedence over procreation in the purpose of marriage, because chastity points us toward and prepares us for the coming age.

Despite differences, Chrysostom and Augustine concurred that Christ's coming had diminished the import of marriage in God's plan of salvation and had reordered priorities in God's purpose for marriage. Accordingly, each advocated virginity and counseled widows against remarriage. Nonetheless, Chrysostom and Augustine did not conclude that marriage had become obsolete in God's plan of salvation, or that procreation had become incidental to God's purpose for marriage. Both envisioned Christian marriage as generating a "domestic church" for serving God and making disciples. They thus agreed that Christ's coming had not altered the form or annulled the function of marriage. Chrysostom and Augustine each maintained that the God-ordained unitive form of marriage remains man and woman—and that the God-blessed generative function of marriage continues serving God's purpose in creation and the plan of salvation.

Patristic Wisdom for Present Discernment

The patristic-era church engaged in protracted debate about the place and purpose of marriage and procreation in the plan of God at the coming of Christ. We would do well to glean lessons from our forebears' discernment to guide our discernment of God's will for marriage. I will discuss three interrelated lessons and their implications.

Marriage in God's Providence

A first lesson from the marriage debate of the patristic-era church concerns a proper vision of marriage in relation to God. Major theologians, East and West, envisioned marriage, according to the biblical narrative, as God's ordination for God's purposes. They understood human marriage in relation to the divine economy, God's working for humankind's salvation. In particular, they tended to see the successive stages of the divine economy—from creation of humankind, to covenant with Israel, to redemption through Christ—as God's providential plan to gradually reveal salvation and guide God's people toward perfection. They understood marriage as partaking of every stage of God's providence and pointing toward God's salvation and perfection in Christ.

Two aspects of the patristic view of marriage are particularly relevant to our discernment. First, patristic theologians viewed marriage always from the perspective of divine design and purpose and never regarded marriage as a merely human design or reduced marriage to a merely mundane purpose. They viewed marriage under God's providence from beginning to end—and, accordingly, referred discernment concerning marriage to God's purpose for marriage in God's design of creation and plan of salvation. Second, acknowledging that God's providential dealing with humankind has changed from one era to another era, patristic theologians were attentive to changes in how marriage participates in God's providence.

On this latter point, patristic theologians took their cues from Jesus, in two respects. First, reflecting on Jesus's incarnation, patristic theologians viewed the virgin birth not only as a manifestation of God's all-possible power but also as a sign that God has begun a new era in salvation history. God's purpose in creation and promise in covenant had proceeded by God's providence in marriage and procreation down the generations from Adam and Eve through Abraham and Sarah, with each generation preparing for the Messiah's coming (Matt. 1:1–17; Luke 3:23–38). The angel's message that Mary will conceive by the Holy Spirit and bear God's Son apart from the sexual union of marriage (Matt. 1:18–25; Luke 1:26–38) signals that God's plan is entering a new era: Jesus's birth recapitulates the history of God's people and the working of God's purpose—and inaugurates the future of God's people and the fulfilling of God's promise.[58] Jesus reveals, furthermore, that marriage and procreation will be surpassed in the resurrection future of God's people; Jesus's own resurrection is the firstfruits of that future. Jesus's celibacy and the celibate life he honors among his disciples correspond to this new era of God's plan.

Second, drawing from Jesus's teaching, especially Jesus's ruling on divorce, patristic theologians appraised marriage and applied discipline in relation to the progression of God's providence. They sought to discern the dynamic between God's intention and God's concession across successive eras of salvation history. Their writings suggest a general scheme, which one might represent as follows:

- God institutes and blesses marriage in creation: monogamy, fidelity
  - God promises to Abraham, Isaac, and Jacob, conceding their incest and polygamy
- God upholds marriage in covenant with Israel: no adultery, no coveting
  - God's law forbids incest, restricts polygamy, but concedes divorce-remarriage

58. See also Hauerwas, *Matthew*, 31.

- Jesus confirms marriage in creation and covenant: monogamy, fidelity
  □ Jesus judges divorce-remarriage as adultery and forbids lusting
- Jesus reveals humankind's destination in resurrection: no marrying
  □ Jesus initiates and honors celibacy

This providential scheme shaped pastoral practice concerning marriage matters in the patristic-era church: the church is to instill believers with God's intention in creation as confirmed by Christ (thus uphold marriage, restrict concession, discipline immorality, and exhort to chastity); at the same time, the church is to direct believers toward humankind's destination in resurrection as revealed by Christ (thus commend celibacy; support virgins, monks, and widows; and prioritize the coming kingdom).[59]

We might evaluate certain innovationist proposals from a patristic perspective. Some advocate for sanctioning same-sex union by appealing to humankind's postparadise situation. David Gushee writes: "Our task, if we are Christians, is to attempt to order the sexuality we have in as responsible a manner as we can. We can't get back to Genesis 1–2, a primal sinless world. But we can do the best we can with the Genesis 3 sexuality we have." Because everyone's sexuality has been affected by the fall, such that no one can live up to God's original intention, the church may adjust its ethical standard for sexual conduct to the fallen condition of human sexuality. Sanctioning same-sex union would allow gay Christians to "do the best [they] can" by ordering their fallen sexuality "in as responsible a manner as [anyone] can"—within the boundaries of enduring-exclusive partnership.[60]

Gushee's proposal raises a question that was at stake in the patristic debate: By which era of God's providence should the church calibrate its sexual discipline? Tertullian the Montanist forbade second marriage for all Christians.[61] Tertullian's rule, which effectively mandated celibacy to all widows, went beyond the teachings of Jesus and the apostles.[62] The Montanists claimed

59. The sexual discipline of the patristic-era church was expressed formally through church orders (e.g., Apostolic Tradition, Apostolic Constitutions, Testament of the Lord), canons issued by synods of bishops (e.g., Elvira, Ancyra, Neo-Caesarea, and Gangra), and canons issued by bishops (e.g., Basil's letters to Amphilochius) and was administered pastorally through a penitential system. See McGuckin, *Path of Christianity*, 361–75.

60. Gushee, *Changing Our Mind*, 95–97. Gushee's discussion implies that same-sex attraction/orientation is a postparadise phenomenon of fallen humankind.

61. Tertullian, *On Monogamy*. See Reynolds, *Marriage in the Western Church*, 195–200.

62. Jesus ruled that remarriage after divorce (except for unchastity) is adultery (Matt. 5:31–32; 19:3–9), but even the strictest reading of Jesus's ruling permits second marriage for widows. Paul ruled that widows may remarry without committing adultery (Rom. 7:2–3); he counseled widows that celibacy is preferable but allowed remarriage, "only in the Lord" (1 Cor.

that a new dispensation of the Holy Spirit gave the church a further restriction on marriage: whereas the New Law of Jesus had ended the concession to divorce, a New Prophecy of the Spirit has ended the allowance of second marriage. The church, having entered a new and final era of God's providence, surpassing even Jesus's teaching in the New Testament, should recalibrate its sexual discipline in light of a new era of restriction.

Montanists claimed a new revelation of the Spirit to warrant greater restriction in marriage. Gushee cites new information from science and experience concerning sexual orientation to warrant greater concession in marriage. Gushee's proposal invites comparison with concession in biblical law to the postparadise situation: case law conceded divorce-remarriage on account of the persisting reality of hardheartedness, even though it was not so from the beginning (Deut. 24:1–4; Matt. 19:7–8); Gushee proposes that the church allow same-sex union on account of the "stubborn facts" of "irresistibly attracted same-sex people," even though it was not so in paradise.[63] Gushee's proposal to sanction same-sex union, and thus adjust marriage to postparadise sexuality, would have the church recalibrate its sexual discipline in line with the past era of concession.

Now, Gushee also proposes that the church should look to Jesus rather than Genesis for its sexual ethics.[64] Jesus not only looked to Genesis on marriage but also took a stringent, rather than concessionary, approach to sexual discipline. Lust, we know by experience, is a stubborn fact of postparadise sexuality that persistently afflicts human hearts, especially men's. Yet Jesus, far from adjusting moral norms to fallen sexuality, summoned men to discipline themselves to deal with their hearts' bent toward lust. Not only does a man who divorces his wife (except for unchastity) and marries another wife commit adultery, Jesus ruled, but also a man who gazes to desire a woman (not his wife) commits adultery. The adultery consummated with the body is commenced in the heart; the adultery begotten by sexual act is conceived with lustful look (cf. James 1:12–16). Therefore, Jesus taught, it is better to chasten one's eyes by self-discipline than to lose one's life by God's judgment (Matt. 5:27–30). Jesus's teaching upholds the old wisdom: the man who turns his desire from "the wife of [his] youth" toward "another woman" will "die for lack of discipline" (Prov. 5:15–23).

7:8–9, 39–40). Apostolic rules of church order restricted bishops, elders, and deacons to single marriage ("husband of one wife" [1 Tim. 3:2 mg; 3:12 mg; Titus 1:6 mg]), along with older widows who were put on the official list for financial support (1 Tim. 5:9 mg), but encouraged younger widows to remarry and bear children (5:3–16). In the postapostolic era, Shepherd of Hermas maintained that widows may remarry without sinning (Mandates 4.4).

63. Gushee, *Changing Our Mind*, 91–93. The quoted phrases are Gushee's. The comparison is mine.

64. Gushee, *Changing Our Mind*, 93–95.

Jesus's stringent approach to sexual discipline, which intensified rather than relaxed the law, fits with his overall teaching of God's kingdom: anyone who sets aside even "the least of [God's] commandments, and teaches others to do the same, will be called least in the kingdom of heaven" (Matt. 5:17–19; cf. Luke 16:16–17). According to Jesus, God's concession to imperfection through the law does not in the least degree mitigate God's intention that we strive for perfection in righteousness (Matt. 5:20, 48; cf. 19:16–22; 22:34–40). Jesus thus confirmed God's intention for marriage ("the two" of "male and female" joined into "one flesh" [19:3–9]) and, at the same time, narrowed the law's concession to divorce (5:31–32).[65] Chrysostom commented that Jesus's sharpening the law of sexual discipline for the sake of our salvation and perfection, which seems severe from a human perspective, actually shows God's gentle love and tender care toward us.[66] From Chrysostom's perspective, our task as Christians is to order our sexual lives according to the rule of Christ by the help of the Spirit.

Tertullian argued for greater restriction in marriage than is provided in the New Testament; Gushee advocates for greater concession in marriage than is provided in the New Testament. Tertullian's restriction went beyond Jesus's teaching; Gushee's proposed concession falls short of Jesus's teaching. Tertullian's rule treated sexual discipline as if the church had entered a post-Jesus providential future; Gushee's proposal treats sexual discipline as if the church were still in a pre-Jesus providential past. Each misses the mark in calibrating the sexual discipline of the church.

Marriage between "Old" and "New"

A second lesson concerns the tension between "old" and "new." The patristic-era church debated marriage primarily in response to innovational movements of asceticism, extreme versions of which expressed doctrinal distortions. Jesus, patristic theologians believed, had not simply begun a new era in the divine plan. As the "new Adam," Jesus had, by his God-approved celibate life, initiated a revolutionary innovation in the human vocation. Christian ascetics sought to imitate Christ: resisting social pressures for familial reproduction and setting hope on resurrection, they renounced sex, embracing celibacy over marriage or practicing continence within marriage.[67] With

---

65. Likewise, Jesus restricted or rescinded other concessions in Israel's law (e.g., oath-taking, retaliation) by his teaching of God's kingdom (Matt. 5:33–42)—see McKnight, *Sermon on the Mount*, 118, 125.

66. Chrysostom, *Homily XVII on Matthew 3* (NPNF[1] 10:115).

67. See Brown, *Body and Society*; Fox, *Pagans and Christians*, 336–74; Harper, *From Shame to Sin*.

Christ's initiation of "this novel virgin lifestyle," as Gregory of Nazianzus put it, the "old law," which had sanctioned marriage and procreation, "has made way for the new."[68]

This practical innovation offered a theological temptation. In receiving what Christ has promised in resurrection, one might be tempted to reject what God had blessed in creation: one might see God's "new" work in Christ as rescinding, rather than completing, God's "old" work of creation—such that the "new Adam" replaces, rather than redeems, the "old Adam." Gnostic, Encratite, and Manichaean versions of asceticism surely did involve doctrinal errors. Extreme asceticism—embracing celibacy at the expense of denigrating marriage, rejecting sex and procreation as belonging to the realm of evil—is the corrupt fruit of distorted doctrines of creation and salvation. Such erroneous views supposed that God's purpose in Christ voids, rather than vindicates, creation, and that our redemption in Christ entails freedom from, rather than healing of, the God-made-good sexuate body.

Resisting this temptation, the patristic-era church maintained that the innovation of celibacy initiated by Christ does not entail that God's purpose in creation has now ceased, or that God's blessing of marriage has been rescinded, or that God's commission to procreation has been canceled. Ascetical innovators that remained within the orthodox consensus embraced the "new" without rejecting the "old." They admired celibacy above marriage in anticipation of resurrection in Christ, but they honored the continuing validity of marriage and procreation as the creation of God. In embracing the "novel lifestyle" of vowed celibacy, moreover, they affirmed the original form of marriage as man-woman monogamy. They thus never envisioned that, in the new age of Christ, the church might bless novel forms of marriage or liberate sex from marriage.

The church today remains susceptible to the theological temptation faced by the patristic-era church. In the present marriage debate, we encounter innovationist views that also see the "new" in Christ as against or beyond the "old" in creation. Here I will consider the views of Dale Martin and Robert Song, each of whom sees a radical break between the "old" in creation and the "new" in Christ regarding sex and marriage.

Dale Martin, citing Paul's formula that there is "no longer male and female" in Christ (Gal. 3:28), calls Christians to use the "queerness" of this text "to help us get along with the task of queering our Christian selves." We should, Martin contends, "dispense with the dichotomy, the dualism, the

---

68. Gregory of Nazianzus, *A Comparison of Lives* (Poem 1.2.8) 16–26, in *On God and Man*, 119–20.

dimorphism" of male and female and "admit the queer observation that gender is multiplex, not duplex." Baptism into Christ bursts the binary of male and female, Martin claims, so that Christians are free to invent novel forms of sexual relations unbound by the gender binary, including same-sex union and polyamory: "Once we destabilize this duality, all sorts of new ways of being human, not just two and not just combinations of two, may be invented. The gender made possible by the new creation in Christ opens as yet unknowable ways of gendering human experience, combinations of which we cannot foresee as long as we retain the dualistic male-female limitation."[69] Martin thus reads Paul to say, in effect, that what God did in creation (humankind made male and female) has been undone and outdone by what Christ has done in new creation (humankind becomes many genders).

First, Martin misreads Paul. Paul's gospel proclaims that salvation in Christ is not dependent on or differentiated by sex any more than by ethnicity or class: Jew and Greek, male and female, slave and free—in baptism—now "belong to Christ" and have become "one in Christ Jesus" and, as such, "are all children of God through faith" and "heirs according to the promise" (Gal. 3:26–29). Paul affirmed that neither ethnicity nor sex nor class matters with respect to grace: in Christ, Greek receives God's promise of salvation just as Jew does, female as male, slave as free. Yet Paul did not consider the created sexes as outmoded or overwritten by saving grace: Paul maintained "male and female" as the criterion of sexual relations (Rom. 1:18–32).

Second, Martin's innovation implies erroneous soteriology. Seeing "new creation in Christ" as surpassing "male and female" in sexual relations effectively envisions salvation by Christ as overcoming creation by God. Martin presents Christ's saving work as surmounting and supplanting God's creating work, freeing us to exchange what God creates for what we invent. Martin depicts salvation as overcoming creation by liberating us from the limits of "male and female." Paul, by contrast, depicted salvation as redeeming creation, including the created good of our sexuate bodies, by liberating us from slavery to sin and death (Rom. 5–8). New creation in Christ overcomes the old order of sin and death, not God's creation of male and female.

Third, Martin's innovation implies erroneous Christology. Seeing salvation as overcoming creation effectively pits Savior against Creator: if Christ delivers us from creation, then the Savior conquers the Creator. Yet, Paul attests, the Savior is the Creator. All things in creation—things in heaven and on earth, things visible and invisible, including humankind as "male and female"—have been created by and for Christ, in whom all things cohere (Col. 1:15–17).

---

69. Martin, *Sex and the Single Savior*, 89–90.

The Christ in whom we become "a new creation" through reconciliation with God (2 Cor. 5:17–19) is the same Christ through whom exist all things, including ourselves as sexuate beings (1 Cor. 8:6). Seeing the "new" in Christ as overcoming the "old" in creation sets Christ the Savior against Christ the Creator. Martin thus abandons a key axiom of the theological tradition: the coherence and consistency of creation and salvation, which are unified in the divine economy by their common author and agent, Christ.[70]

Martin's innovationism is, in effect, a new twist on old Gnosticism. According to Genesis, "God created humankind in his image" as "male and female" (Gen. 1:27). Gnostic ascetics, despising the *female* of "male and female," saw salvation as erasing the difference of sex and remaking the female in the image of the male. Martin, spurning the *and* of "male and female," sees salvation as dissolving the correspondence of sex and remaking humankind in the image of multiplexity. These respective doctrines of salvation lead to opposing conclusions about marriage: Gnostic ascetics refused sex and marriage; Martin embraces sex and marriage beyond man-woman monogamy. Despite differences, both see the "new" of salvation as liberation from the "old" of creation.

Robert Song advocates sanction of "covenant partnership," male-female and same-sex, as a "third vocation" alongside marriage and celibacy. The only rationale for the sexuate correspondence of male and female in God's purpose, Song claims, is procreation. Yet Christ's coming, Song says, has completed creation: "God's purposes for creation *have been* fulfilled in Christ."[71] In particular, Christ has completed God's purpose of procreation: "Just as creation has *now* been fulfilled in Christ, so the purpose of procreation has *now* been fulfilled."[72] In Christ, therefore, the sexuate correspondence of creation is no longer significant in God's economy of salvation. This eschatological surpassing of sexuate correspondence in Christ, Song says, is realized by baptism. Citing Paul's baptismal formula (Gal. 3:28), Song claims that to be baptized into Christ is to be beyond creation: "Baptism and the new identity in Christ take us beyond the creation categories of male and female in a way that renders them no longer of defining importance."[73] The baptismal correlates with the eschatological: baptismal renewal through Christ transports believers beyond creation, so the church may now sanction sexual union that leaves behind procreation; baptismal identity in Christ surpasses the sexual duality of creation, so the church may now sanction sexual union beyond

---

70. See Athanasius, *On the Incarnation* 1.
71. Song, *Covenant and Calling*, 50 (emphasis added).
72. Song, *Covenant and Calling*, 27–28 (emphasis added).
73. Song, *Covenant and Calling*, 49.

male and female. This opens the possibility of same-sex union—faithful and permanent but nonprocreative—while we wait for resurrection.

First, Song misreads Paul. That God's dispensation of grace in Christ is not defined by male and female does not imply that male and female are "no longer of defining importance" in moral matters. Paul surmised that "the present form of this world is passing away" and thus advised the married to live as though they were not (1 Cor. 7:29–31). Yet Paul did not suppose that baptismal renewal allows sexual union beyond creational order: Paul maintained man-woman monogamy as the sanctioned form of conjugal fidelity in Christ's body (7:2–5).

Second, Song's innovation suggests aberrant soteriology. Song claims that baptism into Christ transports believers "beyond creation"—in particular, beyond "male and female." Baptism symbolizes salvation: being baptized into Christ signifies dying to sin and rising to new life with Christ; union with Christ in death by baptism points to union with Christ in resurrection (Rom. 6:1–11). Symbolically, Song's claim implies that salvation in Christ delivers believers "beyond creation," which suggests that resurrection with Christ will leave behind "male and female." Song's innovation thus seems to veer from Augustine's view that resurrection will redeem "male and female"—and angle toward Gregory of Nyssa's view that resurrection will undo "male and female."[74]

Third, Song's innovation assumes deficient eschatology. Song acknowledges that God's covenantal promise, confirmed in Christ, is *not yet* fulfilled in Christ; this fulfillment awaits the eschaton, when we will be fully and finally united with God in Christ. But Song claims that God's creational purpose has *already* been fulfilled by Christ's incarnation and resurrection.[75] Song depicts Christ's coming as beginning a divergence of covenant from creation: creation has been completed; covenant is yet to be consummated. This divergence has consequence: whereas procreation participates in what "has been" in creation, faithfulness and permanence point to what is "yet to be" in covenant; whereas originally in creation the goods of faithfulness, permanence, and procreation were joined inseparably, now in Christ the covenantal goods of faithfulness and permanence are separable from the creational good of procreation.[76] It

74. I also contest Song's claim that the only rationale for sexual differentiation in marriage is procreation—see chapter 6.

75. Song appears inconsistent on this crucial point: at another place he writes that "Jesus Christ in whom creation *is being renewed* . . . points the way to a different order in which marriage is *to be fulfilled*" (*Covenant and Calling*, 18; emphasis added)—which suggests ongoing process toward future fulfillment.

76. Song, *Covenant and Calling*, 27–28. Song's view sits oddly with Jesus's testimony: "What God has joined together, let no one separate" (Matt. 19:6; Mark 10:9).

is this divergence of covenantal from creational in Christ that makes possible the new vocation of nonprocreative covenant partnership in the church. Song, recalling Marcella's view in Methodius's *Symposium*, draws a sharp line regarding marriage and procreation between "before Christ" and "after Christ."[77]

Song is correct that creation is fulfilled in Christ, the one by whom and for whom all things were created and in whom all things cohere.[78] Biblical testimony, however, counters Song's claim that God's purpose in creation has *already* been completed in Christ. God has done by Christ's flesh for our salvation what our sinful flesh could not do, freeing us from condemnation by the law of sin and death—yet creation still groans under the futility of decay and death, waiting for liberation from bonds and redemption of bodies (Rom. 8). Christ's resurrection is the "first fruits" of God's redemption of creation—yet the full harvest of life and final victory over death await our resurrection "at the last trumpet"; Christ has been raised and given authority to rule creation—yet Christ's reign must continue until "the end," when death is destroyed and God is "all in all" (1 Cor. 15:20–28, 51–57). The gospel proclaims that God has done in Christ what is needed for our salvation—and that God has yet to complete in Christ what God has purposed for all creation.

Song is correct that Scripture envisages not a simple return to or repetition of original creation but a renewing transformation of creation.[79] Biblical narrative, however, confounds Song's claim that Christ's coming begins a divergence of covenant from creation. Across Scripture, we see an eschatological convergence of God's creational purpose and covenantal promise in Christ. God's purpose and promise—for which God created humankind male and female, blessing them and commissioning them to procreation and dominion, and for which God called Israel, commissioning them to be a light to all peoples—aim to fill the earth with the image and knowledge of God so that all peoples of God's realm might worship God, walk in righteousness, and dwell in peace. God's purpose and promise are being fulfilled in Christ. God's "plan for the fullness of time," to "gather up all things" in Christ, is both creational and covenantal: God makes peace by Christ's cross to reconcile all things in creation to God through Christ (Eph. 1:9–10; Col. 1:15–20; cf. 2 Cor. 5:14–21). God's creational purpose and covenantal promise are consummated by the nuptial union of Christ and the church: God and humans dwell in holiness, and creation rests in wholeness; God is with us, and we are

77. Song, *Covenant and Calling*, x.
78. Song, *Covenant and Calling*, 8.
79. Song, *Covenant and Calling*, 13–14.

healed of pain and death; God's glory is our light, and all peoples walk by this light (Rev. 21–22).

Song is correct that Jesus reveals the surpassing of marriage and procreation in resurrection.[80] Jesus draws the line in a different place than does Song, however. Jesus's revelation of the future age implies that God's procreative purpose of marriage will have been fulfilled only once death has been surpassed (Matt. 22:23–33; Mark 12:18–27; Luke 20:27–40). Procreative marriage is not rendered redundant by Jesus's resurrection but continues serving God's purpose of multiplying humankind and propagating God's image until final resurrection. Regarding marriage and procreation, Jesus draws a sharp line not before and after *his* resurrection but before and after *our* resurrection, which is yet to come. All this bears out Theophila's view in Methodius's *Symposium*: God's purpose in creation, including marriage and procreation, continues while Christ sustains the order of creation by his word of power (Heb. 1:1–4)—and will be completed when God in Christ brings forth a new creation.[81]

Distinguishing Questions of Marriage

A third lesson is the need to make careful distinctions among the questions for discernment. When interpreting Scripture's witness and discerning God's will concerning marriage and procreation, patristic theologians distinguished two questions: whether procreation by marriage remains necessary to God's plan of salvation and whether procreation remains integral to God's purpose for marriage. The patristic-era consensus reached different conclusions on these distinct questions, answering no to the first but yes to the second. The patristic-era consensus reflects this distinction: Christ's coming reveals the temporary importance of marriage in God's plan of salvation, and procreation changes priority within God's purpose for marriage; yet marriage continues to serve God's plan of salvation, and procreation remains integral to God's purpose for marriage, such that sexuate correspondence remains integral to God's design of marriage.

We would do well in our discernment to mind this distinction between these questions. Whether procreation by marriage is still necessary to God's plan of salvation is distinct, logically and theologically, from whether procreation is still integral to God's purpose for marriage. Thus, whether marriage remains central or becomes peripheral to God's plan of salvation is distinct from whether sexuate correspondence remains integral or becomes incidental

---

80. Song, *Covenant and Calling*, 14–15.
81. See also Ash, *Marriage*, 170–75.

to God's design of marriage. This distinction of questions is not without a difference in conclusions for our discernment.

The significance of this distinction becomes evident when considering an argument by James Brownson in favor of sanctioning same-sex union. Brownson observes, as Chrysostom and Augustine observed, that Christ's coming effects a priority change in God's plan. Yet Brownson argues, as Chrysostom and Augustine did not argue, that this priority change shifts marriage and procreation to the periphery of God's people and thus shifts procreation to the periphery of God's purpose for marriage. He writes: "The New Testament church . . . did not understand itself any longer to be directed primarily by the mandate given in creation to 'be fruitful and multiply . . .' (Gen. 1:28). Rather, that community's call was to 'make disciples of all nations' (Matt. 28:19), even if that meant forgoing marriage and becoming 'eunuchs for the sake of the kingdom of heaven'" (19:12). This reappraisal of marriage and procreation in the purpose of God, he continues, was shaped by eschatological anticipation: "Paul insists that 'the appointed time has grown short; from now on, let even those who have wives live as if they had none' (1 Cor. 7:29). Soon the resurrection would come, in which the joining of male and female would be no more (Matt. 22:30; Luke 20:35; Gal. 3:28)." He concludes: "In this 'interim' period marriage continued to be valid, but procreation moved to the periphery of the meaning of life in general—and thus of marriage in particular."[82]

Brownson states that the church belongs to a new stage of God's plan in which the prime directive of God's people has shifted from begetting children to making disciples. From that premise he infers a three-part conclusion: "[a] Marriage continued to be valid, but [b] procreation moved to the periphery of the meaning of life in general—and thus [c] of marriage in particular." Parts a and b concern the question of marriage and procreation in the plan of God, while part c concerns the question of procreation in the purpose of marriage. The "and thus" in Brownson's conclusion assumes that an answer to the first question begets the same answer to the second question. Because these are distinct questions, however, c does not follow from a and b: from the premise that marriage and procreation become peripheral to God's plan after Christ's coming, it does not follow that procreation becomes peripheral to God's purpose for marriage. Brownson's argument, by shifting the question from marriage in the plan of God to procreation in the purpose of marriage, slides over the distinction between these questions. Brownson's conclusion, therefore, does not follow from his premise.

82. Brownson, *Bible, Gender, Sexuality*, 116–17.

Minding this distinction can also prevent making faulty inferences from historical evidence. James Nelson, advocating an innovationist view, discusses tradition concerning marriage and procreation in relation to same-sex union. He observes that Western Christians, until the Reformation, often valued celibacy above marriage—but then, after the Reformation, tended to value marriage above celibacy. This, he claims, shows that marriage and procreation is not the consistent norm for Christian sexuality. He then argues that our forebears' affirmation of nonprocreativity in celibacy is precedent for our affirming nonprocreativity in same-sex union. A yes to celibacy supports a yes—or, at least, undercuts a no—to same-sex union.[83]

Nelson's argument, in effect, conflates the questions distinguished within the marriage debate of the patristic-era church. He makes an observation relating to the question of celibacy versus marriage in the church (i.e., marriage in the plan of God) and then draws a conclusion relating to the question of procreation versus nonprocreation in marriage (i.e., procreation in the purpose of marriage), as if these questions were the same. Because these questions are distinct, however, one cannot simply infer an answer to the second question from an answer to the first question. The argument's conclusion, consequently, does not follow from its premise. The logic of Nelson's argument from Christian tradition thus falters on the distinction drawn by patristic theologians.

83. Nelson, "Sources for Body Theology," 82–84.

6

Coupled Together Otherwise

ALTERATIONS AND IMPLICATIONS

> For be ye well assured,
> that so many as are coupled together
> otherwise than Gods Word doth allow,
> are not joyned together by God.
>
> Book of Common Prayer (1662)

Redefining Marriage: Innovation Is Alteration

Mark Achtemeier prefaces his case for sanctioning same-sex union with this remark: "My goal has not been to overturn classical Christian teachings about marriage but to extend them so that their application to same-sex relationships becomes clear."[1] Achtemeier assumes that, were the church to sanction same-sex union as marriage, the church's marriage doctrine would remain unaltered even while the church's nuptial rite would extend to same-sex couples. It may be that some innovationists do not seek to alter church doctrine on marriage, yet sanctioning same-sex union would entail as much.

Sanctioning same-sex union as marriage would substantially alter the church's doctrine of what marriage is. To show that this is so, and what would

1. Achtemeier, *Bible's Yes to Same-Sex Marriage*, xiii.

follow from it, I will characterize same-sex union in relation to what the church has taught that marriage is—and consider how the church's traditional teaching bears upon the question of same-sex union. Sanctioning same-sex union as marriage would, from the first, require revising the creational-covenantal form of marriage.

This redefinition of marriage is evident in denominations that have formally decided to affirm blessing of same-sex couples. Episcopal Church USA and Presbyterian Church USA have each sanctioned same-sex union by changing their respective official definitions of marriage, but they have done so in different ways. The General Convention of Episcopal Church USA authorized a change to its canon law concerning marriage.[2] This change, in effect, excised the phrase "a man and a woman" from its canonical definition of marriage. A majority of presbyteries ratified a constitutional amendment passed by the General Assembly of Presbyterian Church USA that substituted new language for old language—"between a man and a woman" was replaced by "between two people, traditionally a man and a woman"—in its Book of Order.[3] This change, in effect, altered the sense of "man and woman" from prescriptive to descriptive and thus demoted the status of the traditional definition from doctrinal authority to historical artifact.

Such redefinition of marriage is evident also in some innovationist proposals and congregational policies for extending marriage to same-sex union. David Gushee cites the traditional creational-covenantal pattern of marriage: "God's plan . . . a man and a woman . . . fidelity and exclusivity, until one partner dies a natural death." Then, in order to extend "the covenantal-marital ethic of the Christian tradition" to same-sex union, he drops "a man and a woman" from "the covenantal-marital sexual ethical standard." Marriage thus becomes, in Gushee's redefinition, union with "one person, for life, faithful and exclusive."[4] A congregation of my denomination that has adopted a policy of "inclusive love" states that they accept our denominational confession of faith, except its limitation of marriage to "one man and one woman." They seek not to change marriage but to add celebration and recognition of unions between any two adults that intend lifelong fidelity. Yet to define is to limit; removing the limit of "man and woman," in effect, redefines marriage.

In each of these redefinitions, marriage does not have to do, constitutively, with "man and woman." Marriage is redefined irrespective of the sexes of the spouses. Now, one might ask: What does it matter? What difference

2. Episcopal Church USA, 78th General Convention (2015), resolution #2015-A036.
3. Presbyterian Church USA, 221st General Assembly (2014), amendment 14-F.
4. Gushee, *Changing Our Mind*, 101–4.

to marriage does the difference of sex make? After all, simply subtracting "man and woman" from the definition of marriage is inconsequential, isn't it? Everything else about marriage remains the same, doesn't it? No, it isn't, and it doesn't.

There is more at stake for marriage, and for the church, in altering the form of marriage than changing the wording of canonical definitions or confessional statements. Because the traditional view of marriage integrates form, function, and figure, altering the form of marriage might entail altering the function and figure of marriage. I will show this by considering recent innovations that have already altered marriage.

Altered Fidelity: No-Fault Divorce and Open Marriage

A traditional perspective sees God's ordination of marriage as inscribing the fidelity of covenant within the form of creation: marriage is unitive of the sexes, mutual between spouses, exclusive of all others, and enduring throughout life. This creational-covenantal form of marriage is evident in the traditional rite of nuptial blessing preserved in the Book of Common Prayer (1662). That marriage unites the created sexes is reflected in the opening words of the traditional rite: "Dearly beloved, we are gathered here in the sight of God, and in the face of this congregation, to joyn together this man and this woman in holy Matrimony." The exclusivity and endurance of covenantal fidelity are expressed in the familiar vows of the traditional rite: "forsaking all other" (exclusivity); "for better for worse" and "till death us do part" (endurance).[5] To draw out the implications of alterations, I will consider two innovations—no-fault divorce and open marriage—that alter the fidelity of marriage, and I will trace implications for the function and figure of marriage. Considering these innovations will illustrate how altering one facet of marriage implicates other facets of marriage.

No-Fault Divorce: Nonenduring Fidelity

No-fault divorce—that is, marriage dissolved by mutual consent without justifying cause (adultery, abuse, or abandonment)—is a practice now widely accepted, culturally and legally, in Western society. It has also been accepted, to some extent, among Christians. Obviously, the church could not affirm no-fault divorce and adhere to Jesus's teaching of God's intention for permanence in the marriage bond (Matt. 19:3–9; Mark 10:2–12). Yet there is more to consider.

5. Cummings, *Book of Common Prayer*, 434, 436.

The practice of no-fault divorce implies altering marriage from a covenantal union of spouses, founded on a noncontingent promise of enduring fidelity, into a contractual agreement, established and dissolvable by the concurring wills of the partners. Accepting no-fault divorce vitiates the vows of "for better for worse" and "till death us do part" in the traditional nuptial rite. Such an understanding of marriage as a contingent, transactional arrangement erodes the function of marriage. Without the reliability of partnership underwritten by stability of commitment, marriage is inadequate to sustain the conditions conducive to spouses growing in charity, nurturing children toward maturity, and building communal solidarity.[6]

Accepting no-fault divorce also renders marriage unfit as a figure of God's promise to Israel and Christ's love for the church. No-fault divorce, which mars the enduring fidelity of the marriage covenant, fractures the figural correspondence between human marriage and divine covenant that God intended. A fidelity that endures only as much as we choose, a tie that binds only as long as we want, could figure only our fickle selves and our fleeting loves. It could not image God's faithfulness, which endures despite our faithlessness (cf. Mal. 2:13–16), or present a figure of Christ, who in his undying love for us gave himself fully and endured suffering utterly for our sake. Only by being a fidelity that endures "for better for worse" can marriage signify the faithfulness of God, who is always loyal to the chosen covenant partner, Israel, even despite Israel's disloyalty. Only by being a tie that binds "till death us do part" can marriage figure the love of Christ, the messianic Bridegroom whose faithful love endures all, even unto death, for his chosen bride, the church. Were the church to accept no-fault divorce, therefore, it would not only alter marriage from its covenantal form but would also erode the function of marriage and empty the figure of marriage.

Open Marriage: Nonexclusive Fidelity

Open marriage—marriage that by mutual consent of the spouses permits spouses to engage sexually with other partners—is an emerging form of non-monogamy within Western society. It is already accepted within certain cultural subgroups, including the secular gay community.[7] Even some Christian ethicists have advocated for church acceptance of open marriage.[8]

Open marriage effectively alters the marriage covenant from an exclusive union into an inclusive arrangement: instead of "two become one flesh,"

---

6. On the contractual model in the Anglo-American context, see Witte, *From Sacrament to Contract*, 287–323.

7. See Oppenheimer, "Married, with Infidelities"; Dominus, "Not Just Us"; James, "Many Successful Gay Marriages Share an Open Secret"; Thrasher, "Master Bedroom, Extra Closet."

8. See Lawrence, "Bench Marks for a New Sexual Ethics."

the "one flesh" includes a third (or a fourth). It ostensibly respects the vow of "till death us do part" but vitiates the vow of "forsaking all other" in the traditional nuptial rite. Marriage as an open arrangement inclusive of other partners affects the function of marriage. Open marriage divides devotion between spouse and lover, creating conditions for conflict of loyalty, alienation of affection, and thus jealousy and rivalry between spouse and lover—all of which risks unraveling the charitable ties that bind spouses.

Open marriage, as no-fault divorce, also spoils the symbol of marriage: it renders marriage unfit to figure God's covenant with Israel and Christ's love for the church. Open marriage, which mars the exclusive fidelity of the marriage covenant, fractures the figural correspondence between human marriage and divine covenant that God intended.[9] A union of two inclusive of others, even consensually, cannot signify God's exclusive fidelity of covenant love with Israel, by which Israel becomes God's "treasured possession out of all the peoples" (Exod. 19:5–6) and which commits Israel to serve God only and forsake all other gods (20:1–3; Deut. 6:13–15; 7:1–11). Only by being an exclusive fidelity that entails "forsaking all other" can marriage image God's election of Israel and Israel's devotion to God: "You are my people" and "You are my God" (Hosea 2:23; cf. 1:9). Likewise, a marriage that allows each spouse to become "one flesh" with many partners cannot present a figure of Christ's love for the church. Because there is one Christ and one church, only an exclusive fidelity of "two become one flesh" can symbolize the union of Christ and the church. Were the church to bless open marriage, therefore, it would damage the function of marriage and corrupt the figure of marriage by altering marriage from its covenantal form.

Because the form, function, and figure of marriage compose an integrated reality, altering the form of marriage implicates marriage as function and figure. No-fault divorce and open marriage each alter the covenantal fidelity of marriage: no-fault divorce alters the endurance, and open marriage alters the exclusivity, of the marriage bond. Both alterations undermine the function and corrupt the figure of marriage.[10]

Altered Unity: Same-Sex Union

I now consider implications of sanctioning same-sex union. Whereas no-fault divorce and open marriage alter the fidelity of marriage, same-sex union alters the unity of marriage. This alteration might be elaborated in three interrelated ways.

9. This point applies to all forms of nonmonogamy.
10. See also T. Wilson, *Mere Sexuality*, 77–91.

First, sanctioning same-sex union would redefine marriage from sex-unitive to sex-neutral. In the traditional nuptial rite, the covenantal promises of exclusive and enduring fidelity are binding of not just a pair of persons but a couple reflecting the creational form of sexuate correspondence, whose marriage unites the sexes in which God created humankind. The vows "forsaking all other" and "till death us do part" join not generically "*this* one and *this* one" but specifically "this *man* and this *woman*" (emphasis added). Marriage as "man and woman" in the Book of Common Prayer is not a Reformation innovation but transmits an ancient tradition that marriage pairs persons and also unites the sexes.[11] The traditional nuptial rite presupposes that "man and woman" is constitutive of marriage as ordained by God: marriage *is* sex-unitive covenant. Blessing same-sex couples in marriage would alter the unity of marriage: marriage would not, inherently, unite "male and female"; "man and woman" would not be integral to "one flesh." Sanctioning same-sex union, that is, would *de*sexuate marriage: sexuate correspondence would not be constitutive of marriage.

Second, desexuating marriage would effectively disintegrate creational and covenantal in marriage. God's ordination of marriage, which joins "male and female" into "one flesh," inscribes covenantal fidelity within creational form. Sanctioning same-sex union would render covenantal fidelity in marriage (the exclusive-enduring union of "one flesh") separable from the creational form of humankind (the sexuate correspondence of "male and female"). Were the church to sanction same-sex union, uniting the sexes in fidelity, thus integrating creational and covenantal, would be incidental to marriage: whether a particular marriage happens to join the created sexes in faithful union would reflect not the will of God but the wills of the spouses.

Third, desexuating marriage would also effectively disembody marriage. To subtract "male and female" from marriage would be to abstract the "one flesh" of marriage from the sexuate form of human embodiment. Whereas sex-unitive marriage orders "male and female" toward fulfilling God's blessing and commission to "be fruitful" and "have dominion" (Gen. 1:27–28), thus directing sexuate embodiment toward God's purpose, desexuating marriage would disconnect sexuate embodiment from God's blessing and commission, leaving "male and female" an isolated fact of creation incidental to God's purpose. And whereas the "one flesh" of marriage (2:23–24) welcomes bodily kinship (they are of the same "bone and flesh") and affirms sexuate embodiment (they correspond as "man and woman"), desexuating marriage

11. See *Verona Sacramentary* 1110 (seventh century) and *Hadrianum* 838 (eighth century), in Hunter, *Marriage in the Early Church*, 150–53.

would render the one-ness of marriage indifferent to the two-ness of sexuate embodiment.

Now, there is more to marriage than man and woman, as innovationists correctly emphasize. The "one flesh" of marriage involves spiritual union of two persons and social union of new family as well as bodily union of two sexes. Same-sex couples can, and some do, commit to exclusive-enduring fidelity. The point here, however, is not to ignore the covenantal character of marriage; the point, rather, is to give due to the creational ordering of marriage.

Some proposals for sanctioning same-sex union emphasize the covenantal but deemphasize the creational. Gerald Schlabach claims that "marriage need not be redefined for gays and lesbians." He defines marriage in terms of covenantal commitment, communal context, and social purpose: "marriage is the communally sealed bond of lifelong intimate mutual care between two people that creates humanity's most basic unit of kinship, thus allowing human beings to build sustained networks of society."[12] There is much to affirm in this definition. Yet the alteration is evident in this definition: marriage remains a "sealed bond" but morphs into the neutered unity of "two people." Consequently, while marriage constitutes "humanity's most basic unit of kinship" and builds and sustains "networks of society," this definition leaves behind the origin of human kinship in God's joining man and woman into one flesh and thus obscures the root of social networks in the God-created sexuate correspondence of human embodiment.

Robert Song, while maintaining a traditional definition of marriage as man-woman monogamy, proposes that the church sanction "covenant partnership" as a "third vocation" alongside marriage and celibacy. Covenant partnership, which could be male-female or same-sex, would be faithful and permanent but not procreative. It would keep the covenantal character, but leave behind the creational purpose, of marriage. Whereas marriage is grounded protologically in creation, covenant partnership would be motivated eschatologically by resurrection.[13] Song's proposal is explicitly premised on separating the covenantal from the creational in sexual union.

Discerning the same-sex-union question requires acknowledging that sanctioning same-sex union would entail separating "one flesh" from "male and female," exclusive-enduring bond from sexuate-correspondent bodies, and thus disintegrating covenantal fidelity and creational pattern. In subsequent sections, I will trace the implications of that alteration regarding the purpose and symbol of marriage.

12. Schlabach, "What Is Marriage Now?," 24.
13. Song, *Covenant and Calling*.

Same-Sex Union and the Purpose of Marriage

According to Scripture and tradition, God's purpose in marriage is manifold: the companionship-partnership of man and woman to generate, nurture, and instruct children; rule creation; cultivate virtue; solidify society; and remedy sin. According to Scripture, God's blessing of sex in marriage is also manifold: sex bonds spouses and brings joy as well as begets children. According to tradition, these "goods" of marriage are interrelated and should not be intentionally separated. Marriage, and sex in marriage, is more than procreation. At the same time, the immediate implication of desexuating marriage concerns procreation. Altering the unitive alters the generative: fidelity that does not unite the sexes cannot generate offspring. I will thus give particular attention in this section to procreation in God's purpose for marriage. To focus here on procreation is not to reduce marriage and sex to procreation but rather to ask whether procreative purpose is integral to God's ordination of marriage and sex.

First I will present a traditionalist view that the good of procreation is integral to the purpose of marriage, and then I will consider innovationist arguments for regarding procreation as nonintegral to marriage. Next I will reassess same-sex union with respect to procreation by considering analogies of same-sex couples to male-female couples. Last I will draw out implications of the procreation question for marriage traditionalists.

Marriage and Procreation: Tradition and Innovation

Argument from Tradition

The God-blessed purpose of marriage, as presented in Scripture, includes the good of procreation, which serves God's purpose in creation and covenant. Augustine set the tenor for the Western church by characterizing marriage as a complex of goods: charity, fidelity, procreation, and chastity. Augustine recognized that procreation is not the only or ultimate good of marriage. He acknowledged that not every marriage will generate offspring, whether due to chances and circumstances in an imperfect world or even due to the sovereign choice of God. And he affirmed that a particular marriage that does not generate offspring nonetheless remains good on account of charity and fidelity between spouses. Yet Augustine also maintained that charity, fidelity, procreation, and chastity are interrelated goods composing an integral whole. The several goods of marriage, while distinct, should not be treated as separable from one another or interchangeable for each other: charity and fidelity may not serve as alternatives to or substitutes for procreation; procreation may not be pursued at the expense of charity and fidelity. He maintained that an open disposition toward the distinct good of procreation is necessary for a sexual coupling to constitute true marriage.[14]

That God's ordering of sex in marriage toward procreation is integral to God's purpose for marriage, traditionalists often argue, is ground for ruling out sanction of same-sex union.[15] One might elaborate this argument in Augustine's terms as follows. A same-sex couple could build charity and keep fidelity with each other; in fact, some lifelong same-sex partners have done so. A same-sex couple could, to that extent, fulfill the goods of marriage. A same-sex couple could not, however, fulfill the good of procreation. While a same-sex couple would not intervene to avoid offspring (say, by contraception), neither could they aim to generate offspring by their sexual union—for, obviously, same-sex intercourse lacks generative potential. This lack of generative potential is not due to some failure of sexual functioning or frailty of physical condition: even a fully healthy, sexually functional same-sex couple lacks generative potential. Nor is this lack of generative potential due to divine intervention: God has not disrupted the natural process to prevent same-sex couples from conceiving children. Lack of generative potential is a general feature of same-sex union, due to God's design of creation's operation. A same-sex couple, even were the partners desiring of children, could not enter marriage aiming to generate offspring by their sexual union, because same-sex intercourse is inherently unfit to that end. A same-sex couple, consequently, cannot actually embody in their partnership, and express in their sexual union, an open disposition toward the distinct good of procreation. Same-sex union cannot be ordered toward the goods of marriage as an integral whole and, therefore, cannot constitute true marriage.

Arguments for Innovation

Altering the form of marriage to sanction same-sex union would alter the function of marriage. Because the inherent lack of generative potential necessarily impedes same-sex union from fulfilling the procreative purpose of marriage, sanctioning same-sex union would require reappraising procreation within the purpose of marriage: the good of procreation would be incidental, rather than integral, to the purpose of marriage. Sanctioning same-sex union would thus implicate the purpose of marriage generally: pursuing procreation would become peripheral to the purpose of marriage and thus optional in the practice of marriage, for all couples.

14. Augustine, *On the Good of Marriage* 5.
15. See Hill, "Christ, Scripture, and Spiritual Friendship"; S. Holmes, "Listening to the Past"; Hollinger, *Meaning of Sex*, 194; Ash, *Marriage*, 247–48.

Sanctioning same-sex union requires reappraising procreation, which in turn requires reinterpreting Scripture. A traditional view interprets Genesis as giving marriage a twofold procreative function in relation to God's purpose. First, God ordered marriage toward procreation for the sake of God's creation: God created humankind "male and female," then blessed and commissioned them to "be fruitful and multiply" and "fill the earth" and "have dominion" (1:28), which serves to propagate God's image to administer God's rule throughout God's earth. Second, God ordered marriage toward procreation with a view toward God's covenant: God designed marrying and begetting to bring forth the future generations of God's people, who would inherit the covenant blessing that God had promised. Set against a traditional interpretation of Scripture, there are two possible hermeneutical routes for an innovational reappraisal of procreation.[16]

An innovationist might argue, first, that the traditional interpretation of Genesis is mistaken. While "God blessed them" and then commissioned them "Be fruitful and multiply" (1:28), one might argue, it does not follow that God blessed male and female for the sake of procreation: there is no necessary connection between God's blessing of marriage and God's commission to procreation. Genesis, one might argue further, weighs against the traditional view: the "one flesh" union of Adam and Eve, which remedies the "not good" of Adam's being "alone," does not mention procreation (2:18, 24). From the beginning, one might conclude, God has blessed marriage for companionship apart from procreation, such that procreation has never been integral to God's purpose for marriage.

Alternatively, an innovationist might argue that, although God blessed marriage for procreation in the beginning, the traditionalist view neglects that God's plan for humankind has entered a new era. The purpose for which God ordained procreation in marriage has already been surpassed in the fullness of time. There are two options on this alternative. Now that humankind has filled the earth, one might argue, procreation in marriage is no longer necessary for God's creational purpose: with humankind's success in propagation, God's commission to procreation ceases operation. Or now that Christ has completed the covenant, one might argue, procreation in marriage is no longer necessary for God's covenantal promise: with Christ's incarnation and resurrection, God's people need not generate further offspring; for God's people

---

16. Variations and combinations of the following arguments are evident in Brownson, *Bible, Gender, Sexuality*, 112–21; Countryman, *Dirt, Greed, and Sex*, 270; Mast and Mast, *Human Sexuality in Biblical Perspective*, 55; E. Rogers, "Sanctification, Homosexuality, and God's Triune Life," 220–25; Song, *Covenant and Calling*, x–xi, 27–28; Vines, *God and the Gay Christian*, 137–41. See also Keen, *Scripture, Ethics, and the Possibility of Same-Sex Relationships*, 30–35.

now receive the promise of life and propagate into the future by spiritual rebirth, not physical birth. Either way, the procreative purpose of marriage belongs to the periphery, or past, of God's plan for humankind, such that procreation is now incidental to God's purpose for marriage.

Jesus and Procreation

In arguing that procreation is now incidental to marriage, some innovationists observe that Jesus does not mention, much less emphasize, procreation in marriage.[17] Given that Jewish tradition regarded marrying and begetting as blessing and duty from God, the fact that Jesus talked about marrying without mentioning begetting seems telling. Jesus cited Genesis on marriage—but only the statements that God created "male and female" and that God joined them as "one flesh," not that God commissioned them to "be fruitful and multiply." Had Jesus interpreted Genesis to mean that God blessed marrying for begetting, surely he would have included begetting with marrying, wouldn't he? Jesus's silence suggests that, with his coming, procreation is no longer integral to God's purpose for marriage, even if it had been so from the beginning. From Jesus's silence we can infer that procreation is now incidental to God's purpose for marriage, so that marriage is now separable from procreation.

I have previously noted the logical weakness of arguments from silence. As before, this argument from silence can be balanced by another argument from silence: Jesus does not emphasize procreation in marriage, but Jesus does not in any way downplay procreation in marriage.[18] As before, Jesus's "silence" on procreation has a plausible explanation. All parties to the marriage debates of Jesus's day, on account of Genesis, would have agreed that marriage and procreation go hand in hand. That is an unstated assumption of the Sadducees' scenario of levirate marriage, which Jesus confirmed without comment (Matt. 22:23–33; Mark 12:18–27; Luke 20:27–40).

A version of this innovationist argument invokes Jesus's ruling on divorce (Matt. 5:31–32; 19:9).[19] Jesus conceded divorce as an exception in case of adultery, not infertility. Judging adultery but not infertility as exceptional cause for divorce suggests that adultery fundamentally violates marriage, while infertility does not necessarily invalidate marriage. Because Jesus appealed to God's intention "from the beginning of creation" (Mark 10:6) to premise his ruling, this suggests that Jesus understood fidelity, but not fertility,

---

17. See Brownson, *Bible, Gender, Sexuality*, 116–17; Countryman, *Dirt, Greed, and Sex*, 270; E. Rogers, "Sanctification, Homosexuality, and God's Triune Life," 221–22; Vines, *God and the Gay Christian*, 140–41; R. Williams, "Body's Grace," 319.

18. See Keen, *Scripture, Ethics, and the Possibility of Same-Sex Relationships*, 21.

19. See Brownson, *Bible, Gender, Sexuality*, 116; Vines, *God and the Gay Christian*, 140–41.

to be integral to God's original design of marriage: the unitive ("one flesh") is essential to marriage, but the generative ("Be fruitful and multiply") is not.

Making an argument from silence out of Jesus's ruling on divorce implicitly assumes that adultery and infertility are similarly related to the divorce question. For theological and legal reasons, however, adultery and infertility are not similarly related to the divorce question. First, a theological reason: adultery is a willful choice, sometimes abetted by hardened hearts, but (in)fertility is beyond voluntary control, often despite the heart's desires; whereas adultery is due to a spouse's transgression, (in)fertility depends on God's providence. One might thus see Jesus's ruling, by which adultery but not infertility is cause for divorce, not as indicating that faithful union but not procreative purpose is integral to marriage, but rather as differentiating between divine judgment on human sin and divine compassion on human frailty. Second, a legal reason: adultery is a deliberate transgression of a prohibitive commandment (Exod. 20:14; Deut. 5:18), but infertility is a suffered condition that prevents fulfilling a performative commission (Gen. 1:28; 9:1, 7); whereas committing adultery offends God's holiness and defiles both parties, requiring purgation by penalty (Lev. 18:20; Deut. 22:22; cf. Deut. 24:4), suffering infertility solicits God's attention, sometimes receiving reversal and blessing (Gen. 29:31–30:24; 1 Sam. 1; Ps. 113:5–9). One might thus see Jesus's ruling not as distinguishing what is essential from what is inessential to marriage but rather as distinguishing what defies God's commandment from what deserves God's kindness. There are plausible, biblical reasons why Jesus would judge adultery but not infertility as exceptional cause for divorce that do not correspond to the question of what is (in)essential to marriage. Therefore, one cannot infer from Jesus's divorce ruling that God intends faithful union ("one flesh") but not procreative purpose ("Be fruitful and multiply") to be integral to marriage.

We have more than silence to go on, moreover. Jesus revealed that marriage will be surpassed in the resurrection because death will be surpassed (Matt. 22:29–30; Mark 12:25; Luke 20:35–36). Jesus's revelation contains an implicit logic: immortality will render marriage unnecessary; so, marriage is necessary due to mortality. Marriage is necessary in this age because marriage preserves mortal humankind according to God's purpose, which marriage does by procreation, such that procreation is integral to God's purpose for marriage. Jesus's "silence" on procreation, therefore, does not imply that he saw procreation as incidental to marriage and marriage as separable from procreation.[20]

---

20. Jesus twice spoke of coming days of "great distress" in which women who are pregnant and nursing would experience "woe" and women without children would be called "blessed"

Augustine and Innovation

Some innovationists have sought to adapt Augustine's account of marriage to same-sex union. Augustine characterized "the good of marriage" by three main goods: sacred bond, conjugal fidelity, and procreation of children. Same-sex couples can be joined in bond and keep fidelity but cannot procreate children. Gerald Schlabach removes this barrier by generalizing the procreative good beyond children. He revises Augustine's trilogy as "permanence, faithfulness, and fruitfulness" to accommodate same-sex couples. We understand that faithfulness in marriage means more than spouses keeping exclusive and regular sexual relations; faithfulness is expressed through the many ways that spouses give and receive care and service to one another. Likewise, Schlabach argues, while bearing and rearing children may be "the prototypical expression of fruitfulness," we need not regard it as the only form of fruitfulness; fruitfulness in marriage is expressed in the many ways that spouses offer "hospitality and service to others." As "faithfulness" stands for all the ways that spouses might relate in mutual regard and support, so "fruitfulness" stands for all the ways that couples might "contribute to a still larger community."[21] By revising procreation as fruitfulness, same-sex couples as well as male-female couples can be fruitful in marriage.[22]

Schlabach's adaptation of Augustine's account prompts questions. First, in Augustine's account, procreation in marriage not only serves a social function through offspring but also participates in a moral economy between spouses: marriage redirects the evil of lust toward the good of procreation; and pursuing the good of procreation redeems the evil of lust in sex and pardons the couple of sin.[23] Augustine established a moral schema of sexual relations: sex outside marriage by adultery or fornication is a mortal sin; and sex within marriage to satisfy lust is a venial sin, excusable on account of marital fidelity; but sex within marriage for the sake of procreation is no sin.[24] Where would

---

(Luke 21:23; 23:29). Countryman, *Dirt, Greed, and Sex*, 179, reads this as Jesus announcing a reversal of God's blessing of marriage and procreation and of Scripture's declaration that children are a blessing from God; similarly, Brownson, *Bible, Gender, Sexuality*, 116, sees apocalyptic implications in Jesus's sayings. Considering the context of these sayings, it seems likely that Jesus was referring to the impending tribulation that would come with Jerusalem's destruction by the Romans (cf. Luke 19:41–44; 21:20–24; 23:28–31)—and thus was speaking of the suffering associated with a specific event, not making a general comment on the place of marriage and procreation in the plan of God.

21. Schlabach, "What Is Marriage Now?," 23.

22. Song, *Covenant and Calling*, 5–7, 27–29, also revises Augustine's goods of marriage as faithfulness, permanence, and fruitfulness in proposing sanction of "covenant partnership," including same-sex union.

23. Augustine, *On the Good of Marriage* 3.

24. Augustine, *On the Good of Marriage* 6.

the sexual relations of a same-sex couple fit in this moral schema: mortal sin, venial sin, or no sin? Augustine placed all same-sex relations under mortal sin, alongside adultery and fornication. Schlabach places same-sex relations of covenanted couples within marriage. So would a same-sex couple, inherently incapable of procreative sex, be perpetually guilty of venial sin? Or would intentionally nonprocreative sex in marriage be no sin? Schlabach evidently takes the latter view: he affirms "other-directed sexual pleasuring" in marriage because it "bonds a couple," which implies that marital sex is good for unitive benefit apart from a couple's procreative intent.[25] Augustine linked sex to procreation because, in his view, the fall linked sex to lust. Schlabach's proposal, in effect, breaks both links.

Second, Schlabach states that procreation has been and will continue to be seen as "the prototypical expression of fruitfulness" in marriage.[26] What makes procreation "prototypical"? Augustine cited the creation story: in the beginning God blessed humankind and commissioned them, "Be fruitful and multiply."[27] Yet Schlabach does not ground his marriage account in the creation story, and the theological status of procreation is left ambiguous. The ethical status of procreation is evident, however. Schlabach proposes "a single account with a single standard" such that what is good (and bad) in sex and marriage would be good (or bad) for all covenanted couples, male-female and same-sex.[28] If there is a single standard for male-female union and same-sex union, then the ethical status of procreation in marriage must be the same for both; because pursuing procreation cannot be standard for same-sex couples, therefore, pursuing procreation cannot be standard for male-female couples, either. Although "prototypical," procreation becomes one among many expressions of marital fruitfulness that couples might opt to pursue or opt to forgo. Schlabach's proposal, in effect, renders procreation optional in marriage, for all couples.

Schlabach hopes to move us "out of our impasse and toward a church-wide consensus on marriage" that strikes a "grand compromise" between conservatives and progressives.[29] Conservatives, for their part, would agree to substantial alteration of Augustine's account: separating procreation from the moral economy of marital sex and demoting procreation to an elective good of marriage. Whether Schlabach has persuaded conservatives who orient their view of marriage by an Augustinian compass to join his hoped-for consensus remains to be seen.

25. Schlabach, "What Is Marriage Now?," 24.
26. Schlabach, "What Is Marriage Now?"
27. Augustine, *City of God* 14.21–23.
28. Schlabach, "What Is Marriage Now?," 25.
29. Schlabach, "What Is Marriage Now?," 22, 27.

Tradition and Innovation in Question

A major question of the marriage debate in the early church—marriage and procreation in the purpose of God—is being rehashed by the same-sex-union debate in the church today. Innovationist arguments to the effect that procreation was incidental to marriage from creation's beginning, or that procreation becomes peripheral to marriage after Christ's coming, effectively replicate views advanced during the marriage debate in the patristic-era church—and are subject to similar criticisms (see chap. 5 above). Christ's coming does not leave behind or push aside God's purpose in creation any more than revoke or forsake God's promise in covenant. Christ's coming confirms, and inaugurates completion of, God's creational purpose and covenantal promise.

Whereas such innovationist arguments stumble theologically, the argument from tradition falls short logically. This argument observes that same-sex union is constitutionally incompatible with procreative function and concludes that a same-sex couple cannot be properly disposed to the procreative good of marriage. Yet this argument overlooks various ways that same-sex couples might be considered compatible with, or rendered capable of, procreative function.

So the question of same-sex union and procreation requires more of both innovationists and traditionalists. Unless the innovationist position is effectively rejection of God's creational commission, rationales for sanctioning same-sex union must be presented in positive relation to procreative function. Unless the traditionalist position is effectively repetition of doctrinal tradition, Augustine's view will need to be brought to bear on such rationales.

Justifying the innovation of same-sex union, then, requires arguing that same-sex union is analogous, in some relevant way, to male-female union with respect to procreative function. I see three possible avenues of innovationist argument: comparing same-sex couples to infertile male-female couples; making same-sex couples comparable to fertile male-female couples; or comparing same-sex couples to nonprocreative male-female couples.[30] I will discuss and assess each possibility.

Same-Sex Union and Procreation: Infertility

The first avenue of innovationist argument would be to compare same-sex couples to infertile male-female couples. Were we to recognize same-sex couples as procreative counterparts to infertile male-female couples, one might

---

30. Song, *Covenant and Calling*, 29–37, explores all three avenues in arguing for sanction of nonprocreative "covenant partnership," including same-sex union.

argue, same-sex couples could receive the blessing of the church—and then, if so inclined, adopt children as some infertile couples do.

This analogy could be approached from three angles. From a Scripture angle, one might appeal to examples from Scripture in which God blessed couples despite their infertility, or in which God intervened to prevent a couple from conceiving (by "closing" a woman's womb). Children are a blessing from God, but God does not withdraw the blessing of marriage on account of the absence of children; God's blessing of marriage thus does not depend on the presence of children. Such biblical examples, some innovationists argue, may serve as analogies for sanctioning same-sex union: God has blessed opposite-sex couples unable to bear children, so God blesses same-sex couples, who also are unable to bear children. From a tradition angle, one might appeal to Augustine's appraisal of infertile couples. Augustine held that a marriage that happens not to result in children remains a good on account of the charity and fidelity between the spouses: absence of children does not annul or warrant abandoning a marriage. The church could thus extend Augustine's appraisal of infertile couples to same-sex couples: a same-sex union is good on account of charity, fidelity, and stability, without need for procreation. Thus, as lack of actual children is not reason for an infertile couple to abandon their marriage, so lack of potential for children is not reason to not bless a same-sex couple in marriage. From a logic angle, one might argue that a same-sex couple is functionally equivalent to an infertile couple. As functional equivalents with respect to procreation, such couples deserve equivalent consideration with respect to marriage. The church blesses opposite-sex couples who cannot conceive children; so the church should bless same-sex couples who, likewise, cannot conceive children.[31]

The analogy fails from the Scripture angle because it begs the question. God's blessing of an infertile couple in their childlessness continues God's initial blessing to that couple in their marriage. God's continued blessing of an infertile couple thus presupposes God's blessing from the start. Each of the biblical examples involves an opposite-sex couple and thus presupposes God's initial blessing of male-female union. The analogy to same-sex couples requires an analogous presupposition. God's blessing of a same-sex couple in their childlessness would presuppose God's blessing of that couple's union— and so would presuppose God's blessing of same-sex union. An appeal to God's blessing infertile couples as analogy for God's blessing same-sex couples thus assumes that God would bless same-sex union. This appeal to biblical examples, then, begs the question.

31. See Brownson, *Bible, Gender, Sexuality*, 115–16; Vines, *God and the Gay Christian*, 140; Thatcher, *Liberating Sex*, 144–47.

The analogy fails from the tradition angle because an infertile couple and a same-sex couple are not comparable with respect to the good of procreation. Augustine held that while charity, fidelity, and procreation are distinct goods, and while marriage is good on account of each, the goods of marriage are interrelated, so that a couple should aim at these goods as an integral whole. With this in mind, consider the respective dispositions of two couples—an infertile couple and a same-sex couple—toward the goods of marriage. The first couple aims at each of charity, fidelity, and procreation, but their sexual union happens to not result in children because of infertility. The second couple aims at charity and fidelity but, from the start, cannot even aim at procreation because their sexual union is inherently unfit for that end. An infertile couple and a same-sex couple are thus not similarly disposed to the good of procreation: for the infertile couple, the absence of children is the absence of an aimed-at good; for the same-sex couple, the absence of children is the absence of aiming at a good. With respect to the good of procreation, then, a same-sex couple is not comparable to an infertile couple.

The analogy fails from the logic angle because the cases are incongruous. A same-sex couple's procreative incapacity is not due to failed sexual functioning or frail physical condition, nor because God has intervened to disrupt the natural process in their situation. A same-sex couple's procreative incapacity is due to God's design of creation's operation and the very constitution of a same-sex union: a same-sex couple lacks procreative potential because their sexual union is inherently incompatible with the creational conditions of procreative function. Comparing the cases involves a category mistake: the procreative incapacity of same-sex union is not infertility. Infertility presupposes the possibility of fertility: an infertile couple contingently lacks the actuality of fertility; a same-sex couple necessarily lacks the possibility of fertility. There is no "likewise" in conditions that would warrant similarity in conclusions.

This analogy fails from all three angles, therefore. Same-sex couples are not comparable to infertile male-female couples. This avenue of innovationist argument is a dead end.

Same-Sex Union and Procreation: Assisted Reproduction

A second avenue of innovationist argument would be to make same-sex couples comparable to fertile male-female couples. One might argue that same-sex couples could pursue the good of procreation as do male-female couples. A same-sex couple can, with technological assistance, seek to conceive and birth children by means of an engineered procreative capacity. Such pursuit would, necessarily, involve human partners beyond the couple's sexual union: artificial insemination (AI) or in vitro fertilization (IVF), using sperm (for female-female couples) or ovum (for male-male couples) from a third party, plus a gestational surrogate (for male-male couples). In this way, same-sex couples could become comparable to male-female couples with respect to the procreative function of marriage. Indeed, one might observe, some male-female couples, in various circumstances, elect to pursue procreation by such means. So, one might conclude, if the church blesses male-female couples who pursue procreation with technological assistance, then the church should bless same-sex couples, who, likewise, can pursue procreation with technological assistance.

This avenue of argument, however, generates ethical problems and theological implications. These problems and implications pertain to both male-female union and same-sex union.

Ethical Problems

The ethical problems generated by technologically assisted reproduction are many and well known, so I will discuss briefly only a few major issues. The IVF process, for any couple, presents ethical problems. Most acute among these is the dilemma of "disposing" of unused embryos—and the prospect of deliberately destroying one's own offspring—that commonly accompanies IVF. Conceiving children using third-party gametes, whether by AI or IVF, which is necessary for all same-sex couples, presents further ethical problems, for both couple and child. This process involves the deliberate creation of asymmetrical relations of couple to child: by design, only one spouse is procreative parent. This process also deliberately creates a confused identity and obscured lineage for the child: by design, the child is conceived with intent to separate it from one of its procreative parents.

Surrogacy, which is necessary for male-male couples, presents further ethical problems, for both surrogate and child. Surrogacy places the surrogate at the intersection of three transactional relationships: she enters a contract with the couple, which she has little freedom to renegotiate or exit once pregnant, leaving her vulnerable to abuse; she adopts a transactional relation to the child she carries, which impedes the natural process of emotional attachment between mother and child and thus may harm her psychologically or the child developmentally; and, in commercial surrogacy, she adopts a transactional relationship to her own body, the procreative capacity of which she treats as a tradable good. Surrogacy also compounds the ethical effects of using third-party gametes: by design, the child is conceived with intent to separate it from its birth mother.[32]

---

32. This intent to separate distinguishes third-party procreation from adoption.

Not all assisted reproduction technologies present all these ethical problems. Yet all assisted reproduction technologies do risk reductive thinking
and distorted perception about sex and children. We risk seeing sex as a
mere source of materials for a production process. We risk seeing children
as manufactured products rather than divine blessings: "mades" rather than
"begottens," "crafts" rather than "gifts." These ethical problems cast serious doubt on assisted reproduction technologies as appropriate practices for
Christian marriage, even apart from the question of same-sex union.[33]

Theological Implications

Beyond ethical problems are theological implications for marriage. A couple that conceives children with technological assistance using third-party
gametes, which is necessary for all same-sex couples, effectively alters their
marital union. Such an arrangement succeeds only by one partner of the
couple becoming united sexually with a third party. Because this sexual union
occurs with spousal consent, apart from bodily intercourse, it might not be
judged as adultery, strictly speaking. Acting to procreate by such means,
nonetheless, a couple expands their conjugal union to include a third party:
one partner consents to the other partner procreating with a third party.[34] The
"one flesh" of their marriage thus shifts from "two become one" into "three
become one," at least temporarily. This couple, then, conceives children in a
way that renders their conjugality inclusive of a third party, which effectively
alters the unity of their marriage: the couple's sexual union becomes a non-
exclusive union, for procreative purposes.

This alteration and its implication can also be analyzed in Augustine's
terms. This couple aims at the good of procreation but does so by means that
alter their unity: their conjugal union now includes a third party. Third-party
inclusive conjugality loosens the unitive-generative link in marriage. For this
reason, Augustine argued that lack of fertility cannot justify acting outside the
exclusive conjugality of husband and wife for the sake of generating offspring.[35]

These theological implications bear directly on the innovationist argument
that same-sex couples can be comparable to male-female couples with respect
to procreation. According to the analysis above, there is an apparent asymmetry
between the cases: same-sex couples, unlike male-female couples, could pursue
procreation only by means that would effectively loosen the unitive-generative
link and alter their sexual union. This asymmetry is apparent even when we

---

33. See Burtchaell, *Giving and Taking of Life*, 119–52; Grenz, *Sexual Ethics*, 174–77; Hollinger, *Meaning of Sex*, 199–222; Meilaender, *Bioethics*, 10–25.
   34. See Grenz, *Sexual Ethics*, 172–74.
   35. Augustine, *On the Good of Marriage* 7, 17.

compare same-sex couples to male-female couples who pursue procreation with technological assistance. Male-female couples, under certain conditions, could conceive children by means—using their own gametes—that would not separate the goods or alter the unity of marriage.[36] Same-sex couples, however, could conceive children only by means—using third-party gametes—that would separate the goods and alter the unity of marriage. Recognizing same-sex couples as comparable to male-female couples with respect to the procreative function of marriage, therefore, would imply accepting that the goods of marriage are separable and that the unity of marriage is alterable for the sake of procreation. This avenue of innovationist argument takes a wrong turn.

This conclusion does not settle the question, however. On account of the ethical problems and theological implications outlined above, many traditionalists would argue that assisted reproduction technologies, except under certain conditions, are not practices appropriate to Christian marriage. Some traditionalists would disagree, however.[37] Some traditionalists might even agree to assisted reproduction technologies for male-female couples that generate the theological implications discussed above. Traditionalists that would accept separating the goods of marriage and altering the unity of marriage, through third-party inclusive conjugality for procreative purposes, must accept the burden of argument at this juncture of the debate. If separating the goods of marriage and altering the unity of marriage are allowable for male-female couples, why not make the same allowance for same-sex couples? The question of same-sex union thus challenges traditionalists to critically examine their attitudes concerning technologically assisted reproduction in light of the tradition of marriage that they seek to uphold.

Same-Sex Union and Procreation: Nonprocreation

The third avenue of innovationist argument is to compare same-sex couples to male-female couples who have intentionally converted their sexual union into a nonprocreative union through habitual contraception or surgical sterilization. A same-sex couple, one might argue, is comparable to a male-female couple that deliberately intervenes to perpetually frustrate the procreative potential of their sexual union. If the church blesses male-female couples who render their sexual union devoid of procreative potential, then the church should bless same-sex couples who enter sexual unions devoid of procreative potential. This argument for sanctioning same-sex union, I think, demands serious attention from traditionalists.

36. See Hollinger, *Meaning of Sex*, 208.
37. See Shellnutt, "My Pregnancy, Not My Baby."

Same-Sex Union and Nonprocreation

Comparing same-sex couples to nonprocreative male-female couples requires identifying the appropriate analogue for comparison. That, further, requires distinguishing between couples who avoid procreation due to circumstantial constraints and couples who avoid procreation by intentional choice—that is, distinguishing between circumstantial nonprocreation and intentional nonprocreation. In the former case, a couple's procreative options are constrained by conditions external to their control—say, genetic, chronic, or debilitating conditions, physical or mental, or severe economic conditions or chaotic social conditions (such as famine or war)—that would make childbearing dangerous to the mother or child or childrearing onerous to the couple. In that case, the couple deems procreation inadvisable in their circumstance. In the latter case, a couple's procreative options are *not* constrained by circumstance—but, say, they lack desire for children, or prefer to avoid parental responsibility, or pursue some personal goal incompatible with bearing or rearing children. In this case, the couple deems procreation undesirable according to their decided preference or incompatible with their chosen pursuit.[38]

Comparing same-sex couples to circumstantially nonprocreative male-female couples would not make a suitable analogy: a same-sex couple's nonprocreativity is not circumstantial (see above on infertility). Comparing same-sex couples to intentionally nonprocreative male-female couples, it seems, would make a suitable analogy. The nonprocreativity of a same-sex couple seems relevantly similar to the nonprocreativity of an intentionally nonprocreative male-female couple: the male-female couple intentionally renders their sexual union functionally nonprocreative; a same-sex couple intentionally enters a sexual union that is functionally nonprocreative. A same-sex couple could desire children and welcome parental responsibility—and some same-sex couples do so. At the same time, they pursue a partnership whose sexual union is inherently incompatible with procreative potential. The sexual union of an intentionally nonprocreative male-female couple and the sexual union of an inherently nonprocreative same-sex couple relate to the good of procreation in a relevantly similar way: nonprocreation is not the unintended absence of an aimed-at good but the absence of intended aiming at a good. The intentionally nonprocreative male-female couple thus seems a suitable analogue to a same-sex couple with respect to procreation.

With the appropriate comparison identified, this innovationist argument can be restated: Insofar as the church blesses intentionally nonprocreative

---

38. Song, *Covenant and Calling*, 29–31, does not distinguish these cases when discussing "deliberate childlessness."

male-female couples, who intentionally render their sexual union nonprocreative, the church should bless also same-sex couples, who intentionally enter a nonprocreative sexual union. The intentionally nonprocreative male-female couple has rendered their sexual union, by means of habitual contraception or surgical sterilization, the procreative counterpart to a same-sex couple. If the church would bless intentionally nonprocreative couples, then why, because of the procreative purpose of marriage, deny blessing to same-sex couples?

Contraception and Same-Sex Union

Discerning the question of same-sex union implicates the practice of contraception, the most common method of rendering sexual union nonprocreative. Some Christians, from either side of the marriage debate, have argued that accepting *any* use of contraception in marriage leads ineluctably to sanctioning same-sex intercourse. They argue that deciding for or against contraception correlates directly with deciding for or against same-sex union.

On the traditionalist side, Elizabeth Anscombe, the late Catholic philosopher, famously defended the official Catholic teaching of absolute prohibition of artificial contraception. Contraceptive sex, she argued, changes the couple's intention in sexual union and thus alters the character of their sexual intercourse into a nonmarital act akin to fornication by closing off their sexual intercourse from its proper end of procreation. Accepting any use of contraception, even in exceptional circumstance, she argued further, undercuts every objection to same-sex union.[39] On the innovationist side, Rowan Williams, the former Anglican archbishop, has famously advocated openness of the church to same-sex union. He claims that any acceptance of contraception use renders indefensible the unconditional disapproval of same-sex union. Once the church has conceded contraception, he argues, any stance against same-sex union must resort to either biblical fundamentalism or biological naturalism.[40] Anscombe and Williams, while disagreeing on both contraception and same-sex union, agree that any justification for using contraception gives ground to sanctioning same-sex union.[41]

On the one hand, Christians can, consistently, allow contraception use and oppose same-sex union; for not every justification of contraception use in marriage gives ground to sanctioning same-sex union. Allowing provisional contraception in exceptional circumstance need not approve severing

---

39. Anscombe, *Contraception and Chastity*.
40. R. Williams, "Body's Grace."
41. Analyzing and assessing this argument require consideration of logical, moral, biblical, and historical issues beyond what space here allows. I have developed an extended discussion of the contraception question in appendix C of the online supplement. What follows is a summary of my main conclusions from that extended discussion.

marriage from procreation.[42] Because circumstantially nonprocreative male-female couples are not procreative counterparts to same-sex couples, allowing contraception use for circumstantial nonprocreation does not lead ineluctably to affirming same-sex union.

On the other hand, Christians can*not*, consistently, affirm intentionally nonprocreative marriage and then oppose same-sex union on account that God intended procreation as a good integral to marriage. Accepting habitual use of contraception, to the point of intentionally rendering marriage nonprocreative, approves severing marriage from procreation. Because intentionally nonprocreative male-female couples are procreative counterparts to same-sex couples, therefore, justifying intentionally nonprocreative marriage gives ground to sanctioning same-sex union.[43]

Therefore, the question of same-sex union and nonprocreation corresponds not simply to contraception, which does not necessarily sever marriage from procreation, but to intentional nonprocreation in marriage, which directly implicates the procreative purpose of marriage. Affirming intentionally nonprocreative marriage effectively reappraises procreation as incidental to the purpose of marriage and thus optional in the practice of marriage. Even more than third-party procreation, intentionally nonprocreative marriage disintegrates the goods of marriage: rather than pursuing procreation by problematic means, intentionally nonprocreative marriage neglects procreation as a good integral to God's design of marriage.[44]

Nonprocreation and Traditionalists

The church always has affirmed Christians who remain childfree voluntarily by celibacy for the sake of God's service. And the church today should support Christians who are childless involuntarily because of infertility or singleness or other circumstances. The question here concerns not choosing to remain childfree, nor childlessness without choice, but chosen childlessness in marriage. Many traditionalists still regard procreative purpose as integral to God's design of marriage and thus would regard intentional nonprocreation as falling short of God's intention for marriage. Yet some who affirm that marriage is man-woman monogamy also affirm childless-by-choice marriage.[45] Such traditionalists must accept the burden of argument at this juncture of the debate.

---

42. See also Grenz, *Sexual Ethics*, 147–53; Hollinger, *Meaning of Sex*, 161–66; Meilaender, *Bioethics*, 17–18.

43. See Payette-Bucci, "Voluntary Childlessness," whose arguments defending childless-by-choice marriage would readily lend themselves to advocating same-sex union.

44. For the full discussion, see appendix C in the online supplement.

45. See Timbol, "Fruitful Callings of the Childless by Choice," who cites Brownson, *Bible, Gender, Sexuality*, in support of a Christian choice for childless marriage.

The avenue of argument from intentionally nonprocreative marriage to same-sex union, ironically, has been paved by Christians who would affirm in principle a traditional definition of marriage but, amid cultural shifts on sex and marriage, have become acclimated in practice to contraceptive sex and sterilized bodies to the point of accepting intentionally nonprocreative marriage. The Protestant trend over the past century, including among evangelicals, has been increasingly toward expanding contraception in the practice of marriage[46]—and, correlatively, depreciating procreation in the purpose of marriage. In a few generations, Protestants have gone from accepting contraceptive sex to accepting intentional nonprocreation to debating, or even accepting, same-sex union. The Protestant acceptance of contraception has thus implicated the Protestant conception of marriage: the exceptional circumstance has become the intentional circumstance, and provisional contraception has morphed into habitual contraception, such that the practice of nonprocreation has reshaped the purpose of marriage.[47] Seen against the Protestant trend toward accepting intentionally nonprocreative marriage, sanctioning same-sex union as yet another form of nonprocreative marriage seems a minor shift in the same direction. Some Protestants have thus argued, reasonably, that acceptance of contraceptive sex and intentionally nonprocreative marriage weighs in favor of sanctioning same-sex union.[48]

Opposing same-sex union on account that procreative purpose is integral to God's design of marriage points a hard question back to traditionalists. For a traditional view that procreative purpose is integral to marriage challenges the Protestant acceptance of habitual contraception and intentional nonprocreation in marriage. Using contraception in a manner appropriate to marriage, as with other aspects of married life, carries the responsibility of moral discernment and spiritual discipline aided by pastoral counsel. The "anything goes" attitude toward contraception that has become the default setting for Protestant practice not only has reshaped the purpose of marriage but also has exposed a traditional view of marriage to skepticism and ridicule. The question of same-sex union and procreation thus challenges traditionalists to critically examine their attitudes toward procreation and practices of contraception in light of the tradition on marriage they seek to uphold.[49]

---

46. See Jones and Dreweke, *Countering Conventional Wisdom*.

47. See Thorne, "Friendship," 59–63; Ash, *Marriage*, 46–49.

48. See Song, *Covenant and Calling*, 32–33; see also, from a traditionalist perspective, T. Perry, "Forbid Them Not," 152–55.

49. See also Ash, *Marriage*, 175–83; Blanchard, "Gift of Contraception"; Lenow, "Protestants and Contraception."

Same-Sex Union and the Symbol of Marriage

Sanctioning same-sex union, which alters marriage from sex-unitive union to sex-neutral union, would require reinterpreting the symbol of marriage. Redefining what marriage is entails reinterpreting what marriage signifies. Reinterpreting what marriage signifies would implicate not only what Scripture means but also what salvation is.

First, because the figure of male-female union is a focal image that interweaves the biblical narrative, redefining marriage as a sex-neutral union would entail reappraising sex-unitive imagery in Scripture. I will consider two possibilities for reappraising sex-unitive imagery in Scripture: downplaying the importance of the nuptial figure in the biblical narrative and doubting the significance of sexuate correspondence in the nuptial figure.

Second, because male-female union is a figure of God's work in Christ for our salvation, desexuating marriage would alter the nuptial figure. Altering the nuptial figure carries theological implications for how we understand salvation, especially in relation to creation. I will consider three implications of altering the nuptial figure: correspondence of marriage to the divine economy, testimony of marriage to the God of creation and covenant, and affirmation of sexuate embodiment in creation and salvation.

Reappraising Sex-Unitive Imagery: Downplaying the Nuptial Figure

An innovationist might reappraise sex-unitive imagery in Scripture by downplaying the importance of the nuptial figure in the biblical story. One might say that the nuptial figure is accidental in the biblical text, a by-product of cultures and times in which Scripture was written: marital imagery is a local peculiarity that can be ignored in other cultures or later eras. Or one might say that the nuptial figure is incidental to the biblical story, a vehicle to be left behind once we've traversed the narrative: marital imagery aids us in visualizing the meaning of the biblical story, but once we grasp the meaning, we can let go of the image.

The nuptial figure, however, is found throughout the biblical canon—law and prophets, Gospels and epistles. And it serves as a sign of God's work across the major eras of biblical history and within diverse contexts of ancient cultures. The major uses of the nuptial figure appear in texts written centuries apart (Isaiah, sixth century BC or earlier; Hosea, eighth century BC; Ephesians and Revelation, first century AD) and in disparate cultures (Isaiah and Hosea, Near Eastern–Semitic; Ephesians and Revelation, Greco-Roman). Because the nuptial figure pervades all of Scripture, spanning eras and cultures, it hardly seems an accident of culture or time.

The nuptial figure, moreover, depicts both beginning and end of the biblical narrative: creation and consummation (Gen. 1–2; Rev. 21–22). And it signifies the two major acts of God's plan of salvation: covenant with Israel and redemption through Christ. Referencing Paul's declaration that marriage is "a great mystery" of "Christ and the church" (Eph. 5:29–32), Ephraim Radner comments: "Given its placement in the larger scriptural tradition concerning marriage, [this text] is hardly peripheral. Indeed, it forms the summit of a consistent scriptural teaching on the shape of divine redemption that explicitly describes it as bound to the logic incarnated within human heterosexual marriage."[50] Marriage bookends and interconnects the entire canon of Scripture. Because the nuptial figure shapes major motifs of the main story line of Scripture—creation of humankind, covenant with Israel, redemption through Christ, and consummation of creation—it hardly seems incidental to the coherence of Scripture. The nuptial figure appears to be a God-designated focal image integral to the biblical narrative of salvation.[51]

Reappraising Sex-Unitive Imagery: Doubting Sexuate Correspondence

Alternatively, an innovationist might grant that the nuptial figure is integral to the biblical narrative but doubt that sexuate correspondence is integral to the nuptial figure. The nuptial figure is a God-designated image, one might say, but sex-unitive imagery—male and female—reflects human understanding of marriage rather than divine design of marriage: sex-unitive imagery in the nuptial figure is a divine accommodation to human limitation and thus can be removed as human understanding evolves.

The high point of the nuptial figure in the biblical canon, as Radner observes, is Paul's declaration that the "one flesh" of husband and wife is a "mystery" of Christ and the church (Eph. 5:31–32), a declaration that cites the "one flesh" of the creation story (Gen. 2:24). One might doubt the significance of sexuate correspondence at either end of this cross-canonical connection, Genesis or Ephesians. One might say, regarding Genesis, that the "one flesh" of marriage does not require sexuate correspondence, such that same-sex union can be marriage just as male-female union can. Or one might say, regarding Ephesians, that same-sex union can fulfill the "one flesh" symbol of Christ and the church just as well as male-female union.

One Flesh: Social, but Not Sexual?

Regarding Genesis, some innovationists doubt that sexuate correspondence is integral to the "one flesh" of marriage. The man's becoming "one flesh" with

---

50. Radner, *Hope among the Fragments*, 150.
51. See also O'Reilly, "What Makes Sex Beautiful?"

the woman, some argue, signifies the man's union with a creature who is like in kind to himself (a human) not with a human different in sex from himself (a woman). The "one flesh" union of Adam and Eve thus refers not to physical conjugation of sexual union but to kinship unit forged by social union. Marriage creates a husband-wife bond distinct from the parent-child bond: the man leaves his parents and cleaves to his wife, so that "they become one flesh" (Gen. 2:24). Therefore, this argument goes, because the "one flesh" of marriage is social bond, not sexual union, becoming "one flesh" need not unite the sexes, such that same-sex union can be "one flesh" just as male-female union can.[52]

Genesis, however, emphasizes both likeness and difference in humankind and marriage. Genesis 1 emphasizes two aspects of God's creation of humankind—a likeness to God and a difference in humankind. God creates humankind "in the image of God," "in the likeness of God." And God creates human beings "male and female" (Gen. 1:26–27; cf. 5:1–2). God creates humankind not in sexless sameness (all alike) but in sexuate correspondence (male and female).[53]

Genesis 2 places dual emphasis on likeness and difference in humankind and marriage. When God creates a helper suitable (*'ezer kenegdo*) to the man to be the man's partner (Gen. 2:18–22), God creates a helper (*'ezer*) who is both "like" (*ke*) the man in kind (a human) and "opposite" (*neged*) the man in sex (a woman): the woman is a sexuate counterpart who corresponds to the man.[54] The depiction of man and woman as sexuate counterparts is elaborated in the paired lines of poetic lyric—by which the man celebrates the woman—that preface the joining of man and woman in marriage:

Then the man said,

> "This at last is bone of my bones
>   and flesh of my flesh;
> this one shall be called Woman,
>   for out of Man this one was taken."

Therefore a man leaves his father and his mother and clings to his wife, and they become one flesh. (Gen. 2:23–24)

---

52. See Achtemeier, *Bible's Yes to Same-Sex Marriage*, 44–46; Brownson, *Bible, Gender, Sexuality*, 29–30, 32–34, 86–90; Countryman, *Dirt, Greed, and Sex*, 242; Mast and Mast, *Human Sexuality in Biblical Perspective*, 55–56; Vines, *God and the Gay Christian*, 144–45; Whitaker, "Creation and Human Sexuality," 9.

53. See Davidson, *Flame of Yahweh*, 35–36; Goldingay, *Old Testament Theology*, 3:543.

54. See Davidson, *Flame of Yahweh*, 37–38; Goldingay, *Genesis for Everyone*, 39; Sprinkle, *People to Be Loved*, 32; Kass, "Man and Woman." Brownson, *Bible, Gender, Sexuality*, 30n27, acknowledges that *kenegdo* "allows for the notion of difference" but claims, incorrectly, that "this aspect of difference remains undeveloped in the remainder of the passage."

The poetry highlights human kinship ("This at last is bone of my bones and flesh of my flesh") and sexuate correspondence ("This one shall be called Woman, for out of Man this one was taken"), both of which are integral to man and woman becoming "one flesh." The textual sequence contains an implicit logic: the woman is human kin ("bone" and "flesh") to the man because ("for") the woman was taken out of the man; on account of this ("therefore"), the man and the woman unite in marriage ("become one flesh"). Reversing the sequence displays the logic. The man and woman becoming "one flesh" is premised on God having created woman out of man; and God's creating woman out of man involves two facts: that woman shares "bone" and "flesh" with man (human sameness); and that woman is different from but counterpart to man (sexuate correspondence). "The twin themes of similarity and difference wind their way through the story like a double helix."[55]

Genesis depicts the union of two creatures that are like in kind to one another (human and human) and sexuate counterparts to each other (man and woman).[56] The "one flesh" of marriage unites the sexes in which God created humankind (sexual union) and creates a new bond in the human family (social union).[57]

Citations of Genesis in the New Testament, moreover, reflect sexual and social aspects of "one flesh" union. Jesus's citation of Genesis in the divorce debate reflects both sexual and social aspects of "one flesh." Jesus conjoins two texts—"God made them male and female" (Mark 10:6, quoting Gen. 1:27; cf. Matt. 19:4) and "For this reason a man shall leave his father and mother and be joined to his wife, and the two shall become one flesh" (Mark 10:7 and Matt. 19:5, quoting Gen. 2:24)—in one quotation. Jesus thus draws the sexuate correspondence of "male and female" into connection with the "one flesh" of marriage, so that, as Wesley Hill observes, "sexual difference and the meaning of marriage are pulled together and intertwined."[58] Jesus then emphasizes the social bond sundered by divorce: where God joins two into one by marriage, humans should not sever one into two by divorce (Mark 10:9; cf. Matt. 19:6).[59]

Paul cites Genesis in his ethical exhortation against sexual immorality, by which he emphasizes the sexual aspect of "one flesh" (1 Cor. 6:15–17). Paul's thrust is that physical conjugation has spiritual consequences: a believer's

55. Paul, *Same-Sex Unions*, 8.
56. See Bauckham, *Bible and Ecology*, 129–32; Schmidt, *Straight and Narrow?*, 44.
57. See Dearman, "Marriage in the Old Testament," 55.
58. Hill, "How Should Gay Christians Love?," 39.
59. Brownson, *Bible, Gender, Sexuality*, 90–97, emphasizes the kinship bond of "one flesh" in Jesus's ruling on divorce but neglects Jesus's juxtaposition of "male and female" with "one flesh" in Jesus's citation of Genesis.

sexual intercourse with a prostitute, which joins their bodies into "one flesh," conjoins Christ's body with a prostitute's body. To draw the connection between sexual union and spiritual consequences, Paul puts the believer's sexual union to a prostitute in parallel with the believer's spiritual union to Christ, citing the "one flesh" union of husband and wife as the common term of the parallel:[60]

> Or do you not know that anyone who is united [*kollōmenos*] to a
>   prostitute is one body [*hen sōma*] with her?
>   For it is said, "The two will become one flesh."
> But the one united [*kollōmenos*] with the Lord is one spirit [*hen
>   pneuma*] with him." (1 Cor. 6:16–17 NET)[61]

Because "the two" become "one flesh" when man and woman unite sexually, a believer that unites himself sexually to a prostitute becomes "one body" with her. And because the believer has become "one spirit" with Christ by baptism, by uniting sexually with a prostitute he takes a "member of Christ" and makes it a "member of a prostitute." The man's "one body" union to a prostitute thus violates his "one spirit" union to Christ.[62]

Paul cites Genesis also in his use of the nuptial figure, by which he emphasizes the social aspect of "one flesh." The joining of husband and wife as "one flesh" in marriage entails that their bodies now belong exclusively to each other—the wife's body is for her husband, and the husband's body is for his wife (1 Cor. 7:4). This social fact of "one flesh" union, that the husband's body is exclusively for his wife (and vice versa), entails that the husband may not give his body to anyone other than his wife (and vice versa). This social fact of "one flesh" union, that the wife's body becomes "his own body," entails also that the husband has the covenantal obligation to love his wife "just as Christ loved the church and gave himself up for her" (Eph. 5:25–31). Such self-giving love in marriage honors the vow of fidelity and strengthens the bond of charity, which characterize marriage as covenantal union—and thus fit marriage to figure Christ and the church (5:32).

---

60. See Mauser, "Creation and Human Sexuality in the New Testament," 6.

61. I have reformatted the text to accentuate the parallelism. Paul here cites and echoes the Greek version of the Genesis account: "A man . . . will be joined [*proskollēthēsetai*] to his wife, and the two will become one flesh" (Gen. 2:24 NETS).

62. See Hays, *First Corinthians*, 101–7; Thiselton, *1 Corinthians*, 92–97. Brownson, *Bible, Gender, Sexuality*, 101–2, acknowledges that Paul's language of "one flesh" here refers to sexual intercourse, but he still tries to press Paul's language of sexual union entirely into the mold of kinship bond.

Genesis presents the "one flesh" of marriage as sexual and social. Jesus and Paul, citing Genesis, each interpret the "one flesh" of marriage as sexual and social. The "one flesh" of marriage, therefore, entails sexual union and social union, involving likeness (human kinship) and difference (sexuate correspondence). Marriage as "one flesh" unites the created sexes of male and female and creates the new society of husband and wife.[63]

Nuptial Figure: Social and Spiritual, but Not Sexual?

Regarding Ephesians, some innovationists doubt the importance of the sexual aspect of "one flesh" in Paul's use of the nuptial figure. Appealing to Paul's emphasis on covenant in the nuptial figure, one might argue that only social and spiritual aspects of "one flesh" are integral to the nuptial figure. Paul's focus in the nuptial figure is covenantal fidelity of husband and wife, which is a symbol of covenantal fidelity between Christ and the church (Eph. 5:31–32). And covenantal fidelity between Christ and the church is a spiritual bond that, apparently, does not concern sexual union or sexuate correspondence. One might thus argue that only social and spiritual aspects, not the sexual aspect, of "one flesh" are integral to the nuptial figure—and, therefore, that fidelity in same-sex union can fulfill the symbol of Christ and the church just as well as fidelity in male-female union. One might then infer that only covenantal fidelity, not sexuate correspondence, is integral to marriage—and, therefore, that same-sex union can be "one flesh" marriage just as male-female union can.[64] This innovationist argument, however, is too quick—logically, hermeneutically, and theologically.

Logically, this innovationist argument assumes that, in Paul's mind, the sexual aspect of "one flesh" is separable from social and spiritual aspects of "one flesh"—and that the sexual aspect of "one flesh" does not pertain to the spiritual relationship between Christ and the church. The argument then concludes that, because Paul's use of the nuptial figure in reference to Christ and the church emphasizes social and spiritual aspects of "one flesh," the sexual aspect of "one flesh" is absent from the nuptial figure (and thus may be absent from marriage). This argument's assumption begs the question.

Paul interpreted "one flesh" as sexual and social—and Paul emphasized the sexual aspect of "one flesh" precisely in relation to the spiritual union of Christ and the believer. Indeed, in his ethical exhortation on sexual conduct, Paul constructed a parallel between sexual union to a prostitute and spiritual

---

63. See also Dearman, "Marriage in the Old Testament," 55; Ash, *Marriage*, 348–55; Paul, *Same-Sex Unions*, 8–10; Hill, "How Should Gay Christians Love?," 41.

64. See E. Rogers, "Sanctification, Homosexuality, and God's Triune Life," 234–35; Vines, *God and the Gay Christian*, 146.

union to Christ (1 Cor. 6:16–17).[65] Paul's parallel implies that sexual correlates to spiritual: sexual relations contrary to God's intention violate the believer's spiritual relation to Jesus Christ; and the believer's spiritual relation to Jesus Christ calls for sexual relations that align with God's intention.

Paul, then, saw sexual and spiritual not as opposable or separable but as parallel and correlated. It could thus be that Paul's use of the nuptial figure in reference to Christ and the church (Eph. 5:31–32), while explicitly emphasizing social and spiritual aspects of "one flesh" (fidelity and love), implicitly involves the sexual aspect of "one flesh" also (joining of sexes).[66] Extending the sexual-spiritual parallel to the nuptial figure, we might say that the symbol of the covenantal fidelity and love of marriage, as a sign pointing to the spiritual union of Christ and the church, inherently includes reference to sexual union that aligns with God's intention in creation. It cannot be so quickly concluded, therefore, that the nuptial figure, in Paul's mind, involves only social and spiritual aspects, not the sexual aspect, of "one flesh." And thus it cannot be so easily inferred that Paul sees only covenantal fidelity, not sexuate correspondence, in marriage as a symbol of Christ and the church.

Hermeneutically, this innovationist argument considers only one instance of the nuptial figure. This biblical image is not generically of covenantal partnership but specifically of sexuate counterparts—man and woman, husband and wife, bridegroom and bride—joined in covenantal fidelity. Sex-unitive imagery in marital union is woven through the tapestry of Scripture. Judging from the whole of Scripture, it seems that the Holy Spirit has designated union of the created sexes in covenantal fidelity to signify God's plan of salvation to unite all creation in Christ.

N. T. Wright comments on the nuptial figure in the Genesis-to-Revelation narrative:

> And so, right there at the start of the whole Bible as we have it and at the start of the book of Genesis, we have this rich symbolic account of God's good creation in which, at its very heart, the coming together of male plus female is itself a signpost pointing to that greater complementarity of God's whole creation, of heaven and earth belonging together. . . .
>
> The whole point of the biblical revelation is that the God who made heaven and earth together in the first place is going to renew them, so that the end of the whole story will not be "heaven" by itself, but God's new heaven and

---

65. See Mauser, "Creation, Sexuality, and Homosexuality in the New Testament," 42.

66. Cf. Chrysostom, *Homily 20 on Ephesians*, in *On Marriage and Family Life*, 55: "See how he [Paul] does not despise physical unity, however, but uses spiritual unity to illustrate it!" See also Jeal, "Visions of Marriage in Ephesians 5," 122.

new earth. We shouldn't be surprised, then, that the symbol for that reality is again marriage, the coming together of the man and the woman, in this case, of Jesus Christ and of his church, as the sign and pointer that this is what God had in mind all along.[67]

God creates humankind "in the image of God" and "male and female" (Gen. 1:27)—and then God unites them into a new sexual-social unity ("They become one flesh"; 2:24) in creation. Seen from the vantage of God's "mystery" revealed through Christ, God's design of marriage in the order of creation figures God's "plan" in the economy of salvation. God works this plan through God's covenant with Israel and, fully and finally, Christ's union with the church. God's joining the two sexes (male and female) into "one flesh" figures God's plan to reconcile the two groups (Jew and gentile) in "one new humanity" in the church and, ultimately, to reconcile all things (things in heaven and things on earth) in a renewed creation through the union of Christ and the church (Eph. 1:10; 2:15–16; 3:2–11; 5:31–32). God's "new thing" in creation, male and female joined into "one flesh" by marriage, figures God's "new thing" in salvation, Jew and gentile reconciled into "one new humanity" by Christ, which is the first stage of God's last thing in salvation—heaven and earth, God and humankind, united in "new creation"—accomplished by the marriage of Christ and the church (Rev. 21:1–6).[68]

Theologically, this innovationist argument neglects Christian tradition, which has emphasized sexuate correspondence in the nuptial figure. Methodius, Chrysostom, and Augustine each saw God's creating the woman from the man and joining them in sexual union as prefiguring God's creating the church from Christ and joining them in spiritual union. Chrysostom particularly depicted the sexual union of man and woman in marriage as figuring the spiritual union of Christ and the church in salvation: "Shall I also tell you how marriage is a mystery of the church? The Church was made from the side of Christ, and He united Himself to her in a spiritual intercourse."[69]

In patristic theological imagination, moreover, the nuptial figure has not only a sex-unitive aspect but also, correlatively, a generative aspect. Methodius explicitly developed the generative aspect of the nuptial figure: the marriage of Christ and the church generates offspring in children of faith, who are given birth to salvation through the seed of the gospel implanted in the church by

---

67. N. T. Wright, "From Genesis to Revelation," 88–89. Wright wisely warns against misreading the nuptial figure: "Not that the man represents heaven and the woman represents earth. . . . The point, rather, is that the idea of these two being designed to go together . . . is a very profound reality at the heart of the whole story of God's good creation" (87–88).

68. See also N. T. Wright, *Surprised by Hope*, 104–6.

69. Chrysostom, *Homily 12 on Colossians*, in *On Marriage and Family Life*, 77.

Christ. This generative aspect, explicit in the patristic imagination, is implicit in the apostolic imagination: Paul's declaration that the "one flesh" of husband and wife is a "mystery" of "Christ and the church" (Eph. 5:31–32) is followed by instruction to "children," who are to keep God's commandment by obeying parents "in the Lord" and whom parents are to bring up "in the discipline and instruction of the Lord" (6:1–4).[70] One might thus elaborate: the "one flesh" of husband and wife, whose sexually generative union issues in children of flesh, whom parents are to nurture and teach to obey God, figures the "one body" union of Christ and the church, whose spiritually generative union issues in children of faith, whom the church nurtures and teaches to follow Christ. This generative aspect of the nuptial figure depends logically on the sex-unitive aspect.

Biblical use of the nuptial figure by prophets and apostles and theological reflection on the nuptial figure by patristic theologians suggest that sexuate correspondence and covenantal fidelity are integral to the nuptial figure. Throughout Scripture, the covenantal fidelity of sexuate counterparts—man and woman, husband and wife, bridegroom and bride—figures God's covenant with Israel and Christ's union with the church. For Paul and John, marriage of man and woman in creation figures the marriage of Christ and the church in new creation. For Methodius and Chrysostom, man and woman generating offspring of flesh by sexual intercourse figures Christ and the church generating offspring of faith by spiritual intercourse. The sexually unitive and generative union of man and woman in marriage seems uniquely suited to figure the spiritually unitive and generative union of Christ and the church in salvation. In the figural correspondence between marriage and salvation, therefore, the sexuate correspondence of male and female is neither arbitrary nor trivial.[71]

Same-Sex Union: Altered Figure, Altered Testimony, Altered Salvation

Sanctioning same-sex union would entail desexuating the unity of marriage such that uniting the sexes would not be constitutive of marriage. On account of the integral reality of marriage, altering the form of marriage would alter the figure of marriage; on account of the symbolic correspondence between marriage and God's work of salvation in Christ, altering marriage would

---

70. See Radner, "Nuptial Mystery."

71. All this considered, I cannot concur with Vines, *God and the Gay Christian*, 146: "The Bible gives us no reason to think *gender* difference is the specific difference that's necessary to illustrate Christ's covenantal love for the church" (emphasis original). Nor with Song, *Covenant and Calling*, 48–49: "There are no other grounds [than procreation] that can provide the theological weight to *require* that marriage be sexually differentiated" (emphasis original).

implicate marriage as testimony to God and symbol of salvation. I will draw out these interrelated implications.

Altered Figure

Marriage is an iconic reflection of the divine economy: marriage figures correspondence of creation and salvation in God's work. In the counterpart union of marriage, we see the correspondence of unions in God's plan: God's design of marriage in creation, uniting the two sexes of humankind (male and female) into "one flesh," is a visible image of God's plan of salvation in Christ, uniting the two divisions of humanity (Jew and gentile) into "one body" as the bride of Christ and, ultimately, uniting the two realms of creation (heaven and earth) with God through the nuptial of Christ and the church. In the procreative union of marriage, we see the cooperation of body and spirit, flesh and faith in God's purpose: God's purpose to generate by the sexual-bodily "one flesh" union of man and woman a people for God's covenant prepares and prefigures God's plan to generate by the spiritual-bodily "one body" communion of Christ and the church a people for God's new creation. Desexuating marriage would fracture the figural correspondence between marriage and salvation. Were uniting the sexes not constitutive of marriage, marriage would not fully reflect God's unitive plan of salvation.

Now, a theology of same-sex union would—as any theology of marriage should—emphasize the "image of God" in which God created humankind as making marriage fit to image God's plan of salvation.[72] Whereas God blessed the sexual union of nonhuman pairs for procreative purpose in creation (Gen. 1:22; 8:15–19), Scripture never designates nonhuman union to image God's plan of salvation. This suggests that humankind's creation in God's image uniquely fits human union to mediate and image God's salvation. A theology of same-sex union, however, would deemphasize the "male and female" by which God differentiated humankind—and by which God united humankind in the marriage bond for the sake of God's creational purpose and covenantal promise. A theology of same-sex union could emphasize other differences—personal, familial, cultural, and so on—that might be combined in same-sex partnership.[73] Nonetheless, when rendering the nuptial figure of God's covenant with Israel and Christ's union with the church, Scripture consistently favors the specific difference-correspondence of sex, which God created in humankind and united in marriage. The overarching biblical witness indicates

---

72. See Vines, *God and the Gay Christian*, 149–62.
73. See Vines, *God and the Gay Christian*, 147.

that it is humankind's creation "in the image of God" *and* "male and female" that fits marriage to reflect God's plan of salvation.

Altered Testimony

Marriage in the biblical story testifies to the one God of creation and salvation. By blessing male and female for fruitful union and wise dominion, by joining man and woman in sexual-social union, God ordains marriage by inscribing the fidelity of covenant within the pattern of creation. Marriage testifies to the God who ordains marriage: "male and female" becoming "one flesh" testifies to the one God who made "male and female" in "the image of God" and joined them into "one flesh." The biblical story reveals that both humankind and marriage originate not from two different gods but from one God who creates and covenants, makes and blesses, differentiates and unites: the God who makes "male and female" is the same God who blesses them to "be fruitful" and "have dominion"; the God who makes man from the ground and then the woman from the man is the same God who joins the two into "one flesh." Marriage of man and woman, by which God inscribes covenantal fidelity within creational form, is a visible testament to the one God of creation and covenant revealed in the biblical story.

God's relating to humankind through creation and covenant, made visible in marriage, is evident beyond the creation account. The intertwined themes of creation and covenant run throughout Scripture: in narratives of God's salvation by means of creation (Gen. 6–9; Exod. 1–24); visions that the one Creator is the one Savior, that God, who is constant in creation, is steadfast in covenant (Isa. 40–55; Jer. 31:35–37; 33:19–22); thanks and praises to the God who creates and saves, makes and blesses (Pss. 136; 145–48); announcement of the Word of creation becoming flesh for our salvation (John 1:1–18); and in confession of Christ, in and for whom all things are created and through whom all things are reconciled to God (Col. 1:15–19).[74] The biblical canon testifies to one God who creates and covenants; and marriage, God's inscription of covenant within creation, encapsulates that testimony to this God.

Desexuating marriage would render covenantal fidelity separable from creational form in marriage. Were uniting the sexes not integral to the bond of marriage, marriage would not bear visible testimony, by its very constitution, to the one God of creation and covenant. Disintegrating creational and covenantal in marriage would alter marriage as a testament to God.

---

74. Concerning creation and covenant in the Old Testament, see Fretheim, *God and World in the Old Testament*, 181–98; P. Miller, "Creation and Covenant"; Mann, "Stars, Sprouts, and Streams"; Ollenburger, "Isaiah's Creation Theology."

Now, altering marriage to sanction same-sex union would not leave us without any visible testament to the one God who creates and covenants. All God's acts of salvation—especially the incarnation, cross, and resurrection of Jesus—testify visibly that the God who is faithful and righteous in commitment is the God who creates in power and is powerful to save. Nor would altering marriage to sanction same-sex union empty marriage of all testimony: the exclusive-enduring fidelity of marriage would testify, "God is faithful"; the self-giving love of marriage would testify, "God is love."

Nonetheless, disintegrating creational and covenantal in marriage would alter the testimony of marriage. Sanctioning same-sex union would separate fidelity in marriage from unity of the sexes. This alteration could be interpreted theologically in alternate ways. Marriage that separates covenantal fidelity from creational form could suggest that God's faithfulness in covenant forsakes God's fashioning of creation—or even that God's love in salvation is indifferent to God's wisdom in creation. Alternatively, marriage that separates covenantal fidelity from creational form could suggest that God's purpose in blessing "one flesh" marriage is divorced from God's purpose in creating humankind "male and female"—or even that the God who blesses marriage is different than the God who forms humankind. Either way, marriage that separates covenantal fidelity from creational form is suggestive of a theological testimony more Gnostic than Christian.

Altered Salvation

Marriage mediates and images salvation. God initiates the plan of salvation by means of marriage and procreation—man and woman joined in body and bond, the flesh and blood of sex and birth—to generate God's people of covenant and prepare humankind's redemption in Christ by the gift of his flesh and blood, his body for our bodies, in order to reconcile us to God (cf. Matt. 1). God elects to work out the plan of salvation through marriage, such that the marriage God blesses signifies the salvation God works. The "one flesh" of marriage conjoins the covenantal promise of faithful bond to the creational gift of sexuate bodies; and marriage signifies salvation in both creational and covenantal facets of this "one flesh."

The soteriological significance of the marriage bond is familiar from the traditional nuptial rite. The binding promise exchanged between husband and wife signifies God's promise of salvation, which God, faithful and true, confirms in Christ and completes in the union of Christ and the church. The soteriological significance of the marriage bed is less appreciated but no less important. The bodily-sexual union of man and woman signifies God's plan of salvation, in which humankind participates by sexuate embodiment—a salvation for which God partakes of sexuate embodiment by Jesus's incarnation (a man born of a woman), a salvation by which God redeems humankind in sexuate embodiment (male and female). Marriage mediates and images an economy of salvation in which the sexuate form of human embodiment, and human beings as sexuate bodies, matter to and are redeemed by God.

Desexuating marriage would disembody marriage by abstracting the "one flesh" of marriage from the "male and female" of human embodiment. Were uniting the sexes not integral to the bond of marriage, marriage would not take up, by form and function, the sexuate correspondence of humankind's creation into God's plan for humankind's salvation—and thus marriage would not signify, by figure, God's redemption of human beings as sexuate bodies. Desexuating marriage would alter marriage as a symbol of salvation.

Now, a theology of same-sex union might seek to "take bodies seriously." Eugene Rogers acknowledges the significance of human embodiment in God's economy of salvation.[75] "Salvation itself is bodily," he writes: God saves us by taking a body in Jesus, and God sanctifies us in our bodies by the Holy Spirit. God's saving work by Jesus's body, he writes, gives human bodies a soteriological significance: "For Christians, bodies are no more or less than a means by which God catches hold of and sanctifies human beings."[76]

In portraying the body's part in God's plan of salvation, however, Rogers demotes and subordinates bodies: "Bodies are no more or less than a means." I agree with "no less" but not with "no more." Rogers's depiction of salvation characterizes bodies as merely a means by which God redeems human beings, which renders bodies inferior to the human beings whom God redeems: bodies are only instruments of the redemption of which human beings are recipients. Paul's depiction of salvation, by contrast, affirms that bodies are more than merely a means by which God redeems: those "who have the first fruits of the Spirit" wait in patient hope, in sympathy with "the whole creation," for "the redemption of our bodies" (Rom. 8:22–24). As Paul sees it, bodies are not only instruments but also recipients of God's redemption.

In arguing that same-sex union, like male-female union, can fulfill the symbol of marriage, moreover, Rogers downplays and sidelines bodies. He recognizes that the "male-female version of the one flesh is especially apt for representing the union of Christ with his bride the church." But what matters in marriage as symbol of salvation, he says, is not bodily union but covenantal bond: "What matters is mirroring the election and fidelity of God

75. E. Rogers, "Sanctification, Homosexuality, and God's Triune Life," 233–37.
76. E. Rogers, "Sanctification, Homosexuality, and God's Triune Life," 233.

to God's people."[77] Rogers's rendition of the marriage symbol moves bodies to the margins, such that bodily union becomes incidental to marriage as mirror of the divine economy. Paul's rendition of the marriage symbol, by contrast, emphasizes bodily union: Paul prefaces the revelation that the "one flesh" of husband and wife is "a great mystery" of "Christ and the church" by putting husband and wife united as one body in parallel with Christ and the church united as one body (Eph. 5:22–33). As Paul sees it, bodily union is integral to the marriage symbol.

To support his argument, Rogers appeals to salvation history. "Taking the body seriously"—he argues, and I agree—"must leave room for the way in which the Bible shows *God* taking the body seriously in the history of salvation." Rogers observes that the genealogy of Jesus shows God acting outside normative marriage—through Tamar, Ruth, Rahab, and Bathsheba, involving incest and infidelity—to bring about redemption of God's people.[78] Rogers's review of God's use of "irregular sexual unions" in salvation history, however, overlooks the obvious: each of these sexual unions is a male-female union. This observation is not trivial, because these examples could be taken to show the opposite of what Rogers claims: the biblical fact that God works human redemption through male-female sexual unions outside normative marriage, one might say, indicates that sexuate embodiment is more important than covenantal fidelity in God's plan of salvation and thus in marriage as symbolic of salvation.

Rogers's recounting of salvation history to justify sanctioning same-sex union obscures the sexuate correspondence of human embodiment coursing through Jesus's genealogy—and abstracts God's redeeming work from human bodies in their sexuate form. In this respect, Rogers's view recalls the view of Origen of Alexandria and Gregory of Nyssa. Origen and Gregory held that God's endowment of humankind with sexuate bodies was not God's original intention at creation but God's provisional accommodation to humankind's postlapse predicament—and thus they believed that God's final redemption in resurrection will denude human bodies of their sexuate form. Their view bears on our question: if "male and female" will not belong to resurrection because it did not belong to creation, then "male and female" need not belong to marriage, either as an ordering of creation or as a symbol of salvation. Now, Rogers does not simply reprise Origen and Gregory; he maintains that sexuate bodies belong to God's original creation. Nonetheless, Rogers does denude the "one flesh" of marriage of the "male and female" of human embodiment

77. E. Rogers, "Sanctification, Homosexuality, and God's Triune Life," 234–35.
78. E. Rogers, "Sanctification, Homosexuality, and God's Triune Life," 235 (emphasis original).

and thus, as Wesley Hill observes, separates rather than unites the doctrines of creation and redemption.[79] In this way, Rogers's view exhibits a pertinent parallel with the view of Origen and Gregory: although each view in its way acknowledges that human bodies are soteriologically significant, each view in its way distances the redemptive aim of the divine economy from the sexuate form of human embodiment.[80]

Desexuating marriage would at least downplay, if not deny, the soteriological significance of the sexuate correspondence of human embodiment. Sex-unitive marriage affirms the God-created sexuate correspondence of human embodiment and welcomes its procreative possibility, honors sexuate embodiment with the embrace of covenantal fidelity, and incorporates sexuate embodiment into the divine economy. The church's sanction of sex-unitive marriage for serving God's purpose and as signifying God's promise has distinguished Christian doctrine from its Gnostic distortion, which envisions salvation as liberation from the sexuate embodiment of humankind's creation. Sanctioning same-sex union would imply reforming the doctrine of marriage—and, symbolically, the doctrine of salvation—in a way more redolent of Gnostic distortion than coherent with Christian doctrine.[81]

Sundered Union: Divorce-Remarriage and Same-Sex Union

Discussion of the symbol of marriage cannot rest on simply noting the theological implications of sanctioning same-sex union, however. Same-sex union is not the only innovation that would alter the symbol of marriage. I doubt that any traditionalist would even consider accepting open marriage, but many traditionalists do accept, to one degree or another, divorce. Treating the question of divorce in its biblical, historical, and theological dimensions could occupy its own volume.[82] I will focus on a single case of divorce-remarriage and consider briefly its implications for the church's discernment on the question of same-sex union.

According to Matthew, when Pharisees asked Jesus whether the law permits a husband to divorce his wife "for any cause," Jesus issued this ruling: "Now I say to you that whoever divorces his wife, except for immorality [*porneia*], and marries another commits adultery" (Matt. 19:3–9 NET; cf. 5:31–32). Interpreting and applying this ruling prompts several questions, including whether the exceptive clause is original to Jesus, an editorial elaboration by

79. Hill, "How Should Gay Christians Love?," 40–42.
80. See also Roberts, *Creation and Covenant*, 209–19.
81. See also O'Donovan, *Transsexualism*, 5–7; Schmidt, *Straight and Narrow?*, 57; Wannenwetsch, "Old Docetism—New Moralism?," 354–55; Guroian, *Orthodox Reality*, 125, 135–36.
82. See Keener, *And Marries Another*; Instone-Brewer, *Divorce and Remarriage in the Bible*.

Matthew, or a later addition by the church (cf. Mark 10:10–12; Luke 16:18); whether the exceptive clause is intended to amend Moses's law or to specify the "something objectionable" in Moses's law (cf. Deut. 24:1); whether *porneia* refers generally to any sort of sexual immorality or refers specifically to certain violations such as incest or adultery; whether the exception allows the possibility of divorce or states the necessity of divorce under the law in cases of *porneia*;[83] whether the exception allows the possibility of remarriage without adultery; and whether the church may recognize only this exception or may discern other exceptions from biblical law or pastoral practice (cf. Exod. 21:10–11; 1 Cor. 7:10–16).

Catholic, Orthodox, and Protestant traditions have interpreted and applied Jesus's ruling in diverse ways: Catholic teaching does not allow divorce-remarriage;[84] Orthodox teaching makes a limited allowance of divorce-remarriage;[85] and Protestants have taken a variety of approaches.[86] Among Protestants, some traditionalists, while maintaining that marriage is man-woman monogamy, interpret Jesus's ruling, with the exceptive clause, as allowing divorce-remarriage in cases of infidelity or immorality. Some traditionalists argue also that the church—appealing to Jesus, taking counsel from Paul, and guided by the Holy Spirit—may discern further cases, such as abandonment or abuse, that warrant allowance of divorce-remarriage.[87] However one might answer the above questions, whichever approach one might think best, this much seems indisputable: Jesus's ruling implies that, in at least some cases, divorcing one's spouse and marrying another constitutes adultery; in such cases, remarriage is adulterous.

Such is the case I have in mind, which I present as a test for traditionalists. A couple, baptized believers whose union was blessed by the church, has been married faithfully many years. Over time, one or other of the spouses has become unhappy, wants to leave the marriage, and asks for divorce. The other spouse wishes to reconcile, but the unhappy spouse refuses; the other spouse relents and they divorce. Eventually, while the other spouse is still living, the divorcing spouse wants to marry another and asks the church to bless the new couple.

83. For discussion, see Derrett, *Law in the New Testament*, 372–81; Bockmuehl, *Jewish Law in Gentile Churches*, 17–21; Loader, *Making Sense of Sex*, 69–71; Loader, *Sexuality in the New Testament*, 88–89.

84. On the origin and logic of the Catholic view, see Reynolds, *Marriage in the Western Church*, 213–26.

85. See Meyendorff, *Marriage*, 54–58.

86. See House, *Divorce and Remarriage*.

87. See Hays, *Moral Vision of the New Testament*, 347–78; McKnight, *Sermon on the Mount*, 94–109; B. Jones, *Faithful*, 44.

Some traditionalists, at least, would not give the church's blessing to this couple. Jesus's ruling applies to this case and implies a clear verdict: if one has divorced a spouse without just cause, to remarry is to commit adultery. The new couple would constitute an adulterous coupling: in the words of the Book of Common Prayer, they would be "coupled together otherwise than Gods Word doth allow" and thus "not joyned together by God." Accordingly, to Jesus's maxim "What God has joined together, let no one separate" (Matt. 19:6; Mark 10:9), the traditionalist should add this corollary: the coupling that Jesus has ruled adulterous God has not joined together—and the church may not bless.

Yet some traditionalists, who ostensibly maintain that marriage is man-woman monogamy, would give the church's blessing to Christian couples in such cases. Some may believe that blessing the new couple is the way of grace; some may see new life in the couple's love as a sign of the Spirit. Whatever the reasons, traditionalists who would bless those "coupled together otherwise than Gods word doth allow" undercut their stance against same-sex union. A fair-minded innovationist could reasonably protest: If you would allow one coupling (adulterous remarriage) otherwise than God's word allows, then why not allow another coupling (same-sex union) otherwise than God's word allows? If you are willing to override the judgment of Jesus to bless Christians who divorce without just cause and remarry, whether for the sake of their happiness or as a show of grace or in the name of the Spirit, then why not set aside Scripture and tradition to bless Christians who enter same-sex partnerships, for the same reasons? If you would say yes in a case of divorce-remarriage when Jesus did say no, then why not say yes on the question of same-sex union even if Jesus would say no?[88]

Beyond causing scandal and soliciting charges of hypocrisy, giving the church's blessing to adulterous remarriage carries ethical and theological implications for the doctrine of marriage. Ethically, blessing couples in adulterous remarriage alters the traditional norm that sexual relations belong properly to man-woman monogamy. Blessing adulterous couplings, in effect, sanctions sexual relations beyond monogamy. Giving blessing to adulterous couplings but denying blessing to same-sex couplings, moreover, implies a double standard: straight believers are permitted opposite-sex intercourse beyond monogamy, but gay believers are prohibited same-sex intercourse even within monogamy.

Theologically, blessing adulterous remarriage alters marriage in relation to creation and salvation. Blessing adulterous remarriage dishonors marriage as

88. See K. Wilson, *Letter to My Congregation*, 133–46.

an ordering of creation. Jesus's ruling on divorce confirms God's judgment against adultery, ensconced in the Decalogue, which upholds God's ordination of marriage, established in creation. Indeed, Jesus cited the creation story as preface to and premise of his ruling on divorce and adultery: God created "male and female" and said that "the two shall become one flesh" (Matt. 19:4–6). Adulterous remarriage, no less than same-sex union, deviates from God's design: whereas same-sex union deviates from "male and female," adulterous remarriage deviates from "two become one flesh."

Blessing adulterous remarriage, furthermore, disfigures marriage as a symbol of salvation. The prophets represented Israel's covenantal fidelity to God in the figure of marriage—and infidelity to God in the figure of adultery. The apostles represented the believer's baptismal fidelity to Christ in the figure of marriage—and infidelity to Christ in the figure of adultery. In the nuptial vision of Scripture, adultery symbolizes the exchange of faith for unfaith, obedience for disobedience: adultery is an antisymbol of salvation. When the church blesses adulterous remarriage, it exchanges marriage for adultery in the sanction of marriage and, correlatively, exchanges fidelity for infidelity in the symbol of marriage: the church, in effect, erects an antisymbol of salvation.

Christians can, consistently, allow recognition of divorce-remarriage in certain cases in accord with Jesus's ruling and oppose sanction of same-sex union. Christians can*not*, consistently, approve blessing of adulterous couplings by divorce-remarriage despite Jesus's ruling and then oppose blessing of illicit couplings by same-sex union for the reason that such would despise God's word. Any traditionalist who would approve blessing of adulterous remarriage must accept the burden of argument at this juncture of the same-sex-union debate. Sanctioning adulterous remarriage carries implications for the doctrine of marriage parallel to those of sanctioning same-sex union. Discerning the question of same-sex union thus demands that traditionalists critically reexamine their views on divorce in light of the tradition on marriage that they seek to uphold.

Innovation Is Alteration: Implications for Discernment

Indispensability of the Theological

The discussions of this chapter demonstrate that, Achtemeier's claim notwithstanding, what innovationists envision with the sanction of same-sex union would, to a considerable extent, "overturn classical Christian teachings about marriage." Sanctioning same-sex union would imply altering marriage in every facet—form, function, and figure—and thus would require a thoroughgoing theological revision of marriage. The debate between traditionalist and innovationist views, then, involves substantive disagreements in the theology of sex and marriage—disagreements that implicate the doctrines of creation and salvation.

Across part 2, I have shown that Scripture and Christian tradition of theological reflection on Scripture, witnessed by the church's rites of nuptial blessing, pose questions that are part and parcel of addressing the matter of marriage in terms that are authentically Christian. Any proposal for revising the church's doctrine of marriage must offer answers to these questions that are adequate to the biblical witness and doctrinal tradition that have posed those questions to us. Scripture and tradition make substantive demands on both traditionalist and innovationist views.

In discerning the question of same-sex union, therefore, the church must discern in what ways the divine ordination and destination of marriage restricts the human redefinition of marriage and thereby precludes certain alterations in the church's sanction of marriage. The biblical-traditional view of the three-faceted reality of marriage—marriage is a God-originated creational-covenantal pattern specially fitted for God's purpose in creation and covenant and divinely designated as a symbol of salvation—restricts the redefinition of marriage in particular ways. This theological reality of marriage precludes approval of no-fault divorce and open marriage. Sanctioning those innovations would entail altering the covenantal fidelity of marriage in ways that undercut the function of marriage and debase the figure of marriage. Likewise, the church must discern whether the integrated form, function, and figure of marriage preclude sanctioning same-sex union. Redefining marriage to sanction same-sex union would entail altering the form, function, and figure of marriage. Any proposal for sanctioning same-sex union must show how marriage might be refashioned as an integral whole in terms adequate to Scripture and tradition. Several innovationists have offered serious proposals for refashioning marriage to suit same-sex union.[89] Such proposals have received substantive criticism from traditionalists.[90]

The discussion here, while not resolving the question, does carry an important implication: the indispensability of a theological vision of marriage in the church's discernment concerning same-sex union. I will illustrate with two examples.

89. See, for example, McCarthy, "Relationship of Bodies"; E. Rogers, "Sanctification, Homosexuality, and God's Triune Life"; Schlabach, "What Is Marriage Now?"; Song, *Covenant and Calling*; R. Williams, "Body's Grace."

90. See, for example, Farrow, "Beyond Nature"; Hill, "How Should Gay Christians Love?"; Radner, "Nuptial Mystery"; Roberts, *Creation and Covenant*, 185–227, 239–41; Thorne, "Friendship"; Wannenwetsch, "Old Docetism—New Moralism?"

Rowan Williams, in his famous address favoring affirmation of same-sex union, states three times what he deems to be the core question for the church: "How much do we want our sexual activity to communicate? . . . Decisions about sexual lifestyle . . . are . . . decisions about what we want our bodily life to say, how our bodies are to be brought into the whole project of 'making human sense' for ourselves and each other. . . . Decisions about sexual lifestyle, to repeat, are about how much we want our bodily selves to mean."[91] Williams's thrice-asked question, which emphasizes what "we want" our bodies and sex to mean, is theologically deficient as a guide for the church's discernment. From a Christian perspective, marriage is much more than the human project of making sense of our bodily selves and sexual lives. God ordained marriage to serve God's purpose and to signify God's promise. We cannot alter the pattern of marriage to suit ourselves, therefore, because we are not free to give marriage just any purpose or meaning that we want. God has already spoken to the pattern, purpose, and symbol of marriage—a word in creation confirmed in Christ, a word through prophets echoed by apostles. The church's definition and sanction of marriage must be receptive of, and responsive to, the reality that God has revealed.

Gerald Schlabach seeks to bring same-sex couples into the ethical discipline and social benefits of marriage. To that end, he defines marriage in terms of covenantal commitment, communal context, and social purpose. He argues that the goods of marriage—permanence, faithfulness, and fruitfulness—can be realized by, and should be available to, male-female and same-sex couples alike. From a Christian perspective, marriage is even more than the ethical discipline and social benefits of fidelity and stability. Schlabach's account of marriage and argument for same-sex union are noticeably nontheological: in a marriage account that is consciously Christian, "the civilizational story of marriage" features more prominently than the biblical story of creation and salvation;[92] in a marriage account that adapts Augustine, marriage stands oddly detached from its origin in the garden of God and its destiny in the city of God. As the church, we should frame the question of same-sex union by God's origination and destination of marriage and orient our discernment by the biblical story of God's work of creation and salvation.

Insufficiency of the Ethical

Respecting God's ordination and destination of marriage requires discerning with respect to the full reality of marriage—and thus resists a reductionist

91. R. Williams, "Body's Grace," 313–16.
92. Schlabach, "What Is Marriage Now?"

approach that would boil the matter down into something less than what marriage fully is. Certain proposals for revising the doctrine of sex and marriage, therefore, should be judged inadequate from the start. Such proposals consider marriage only, or primarily, in ethical perspective.

William Countryman advocates sanction of same-sex union by a dual argument. First, he considers marriage in terms of its social-ethical function, the "goods" that marriage serves. He observes that modern Western society deemphasizes the "external" goods of marriage sought by ancient societies—financial security, legitimate offspring, and so on—and instead places primary emphasis on the "interior" goods of marriage that are shared between the spouses: intimacy, friendship, and so on. It is the goods interior to the spousal relationship, he argues, that now define what it means to belong to one another in marriage: "For us, the heart of sexual property in marriage and in other lasting sexual relationships lies in the interior goods."[93] Defined essentially in terms of interior goods, marriage can include opposite-sex and same-sex union: "Heterosexual and homosexual couples are essentially seeking the same goals, and it is increasingly difficult to explain why marriage ought to be limited to heterosexual couples alone."[94]

Second, Countryman considers same-sex union from the perspective of the ethical standards of marital relationship in the New Testament. What Jesus and Paul teach that husbands and wives owe each other in marriage, he argues, can be satisfied by same-sex couples as well as by opposite-sex couples: "In terms of the ethic of property and relationship that we have been exploring, there is no reason why a same-gender relationship may not fall within the bounds of biblical ethics as easily as a heterosexual one."[95] Because both opposite-sex relationships and same-sex relationships can satisfy the same ethical standards, he concludes, Christian marriage can include opposite-sex and same-sex union: "The account that we have given here of Christian marriage . . . contains nothing that is not applicable to both same-gender and opposite-gender couples."[96]

Countryman is correct, given his premises. First, were marriage defined essentially in terms of interior goods, there would be no rational basis for sanctioning male-female union but not same-sex union. Second, were marriage understood only as a mutual sharing of sexual property, there would be no theological basis for sanctioning male-female union but not same-sex union. Countryman's first argument, however, begs an important question.

93. Countryman, *Dirt, Greed, and Sex*, 265.
94. Countryman, *Dirt, Greed, and Sex*, 267.
95. Countryman, *Dirt, Greed, and Sex*, 281.
96. Countryman, *Dirt, Greed, and Sex*, 281.

His argument uncritically assumes the modern mindset of Western society: marriage is primarily for the relational intimacy and sexual satisfaction of spouses. Although such a companionate view of marriage has become commonplace among Protestants, traditionalists would object to separating the interior goods from the external goods of marriage and supposing that the interior goods suffice for the real stuff of marriage. Countryman's second argument, moreover, rests on an inadequate account of marriage. Marriage, according to Scripture and tradition, is more than a mutual sharing of sexual property regulated by ethical standards: marriage is a creational-covenantal union blessed for theological purpose and significance.

Other innovationists also have advocated sanctioning same-sex union on ethical grounds. Some have proposed considering marriage as an ethical ideal of lifelong fidelity toward which all Christian couples are called to aspire—an ideal under which the church could sanction same-sex union just as it does male-female union.[97] Some have appealed to ethical principles of love and justice (or "just love"), or equality and mutuality, or love and commitment, as a common denominator for evaluating all sexual relationships. Such criteria would apply to both same-sex and male-female relationships—and would sanction both nonmarital and nonmonogamous sexual relationships.[98]

One could well question whether any of these proposed ethics is adequate as a Christian ethic.[99] My point here is that any ethic by itself is insufficient to discerning questions of Christian marriage. Such marriage proposals fall short of appreciating the full reality of marriage as form, function, and figure.[100] Innovationist views that advocate sanction of same-sex union solely, or primarily, on ethical terms are inadequate for the church's discernment. Even some innovationists have critiqued such views.[101] The question of same-sex union cannot be reduced to the ethics of right relationship.

Segue

Sanctioning same-sex union, I have demonstrated throughout part 2, would entail substantially altering the church's biblical-traditional doctrine of sex and marriage. Blessing same-sex union with the church's rite of marriage

97. See J. Rogers, *Jesus, the Bible, and Homosexuality*, 44.

98. See Pittenger, "Morality of Homosexual Acts"; Farley, *Just Love*; Stuart, *Just Good Friends*; Lawrence, "Bench Marks for a New Sexual Ethics"; Turner, "Sex and the Single Life."

99. Hauerwas, "Love's Not All You Need," famously refuted the reduction of Christian theology and ethics to love.

100. See also Hollinger, *Meaning of Sex*, 181–83.

101. See Cahill, "Homosexuality," 62; McCarthy, "Relationship of Bodies"; Brownson, *Bible, Gender, Sexuality*, 46–49; Gushee, *Changing Our Mind*, 101–4.

would entail altering the form, function, and figure of marriage. Such alterations would carry implications beyond the doctrine of marriage, especially the doctrines of creation and salvation.

At this point, I expect, most traditionalists would judge the biblical witness to male-female marriage as too strong and the theological consequences of sanctioning same-sex union as too great to consider the question further. At the same time, I have argued, traditionalists are not free of the implications of altering marriage, as the questions of nonprocreative marriage and adulterous remarriage illustrate. Traditionalists, too, have a stake and bear a responsibility in the ongoing debate.

Innovationists, I have maintained, have a responsibility to the church, to offer reasons sufficient to justify reforming marriage. In the face of Scripture and tradition, what reasons could justify sanctioning same-sex union? Substantially altering marriage, due to its theological consequences, demands the best of reasons. For the church, those reasons must find a solid basis in Scripture. Are there good biblical reasons that could justify reforming marriage for the sake of blessing same-sex couples?

Part 3 considers two varieties of affirmative arguments for marriage innovation. Some arguments appeal to historical precedents where the church has changed on other matters in ways that require reinterpreting Scripture (chap. 7). Other arguments appeal to biblical precedents within Scripture to provide warrant for inclusion or concession (chap. 8).

EVALUATING
THE
CASE

ASSESSING ARGUMENTS
FOR MARRIAGE INNOVATION

7

Hasn't the Church Changed Before?

CONSIDERING HISTORICAL PRECEDENTS

The reason produced for condemning the opinion that the earth moves and the sun stands still is that in many places in the Bible one may read that the sun moves and the earth stands still.

Galileo Galilei[1]

In part 3 I will analyze and assess affirmative arguments for marriage innovation. In this chapter I consider innovationist arguments that appeal to precedents of change in church history. Over centuries the church has changed its mind on many matters; and some changes have involved reinterpreting Scripture. Marriage, many innovationists argue, is another matter on which the church may change its mind, and reinterpret Scripture accordingly, to allow sanction of same-sex union. I will consider three such arguments, in chronological order: changes in marriage practices from ancient Israel to the medieval church; changes in cosmology during the Reformation era; and changes regarding slaves and women in recent centuries.

---

1. Galileo, *Letter to the Grand Duchess Christina*, in *Discoveries and Opinions*, 181.

Marriage Is Not What It Used to Be: Changes in Marriage Practices

The Argument: Marriage Is Variable

One might acknowledge the constant pattern of man-woman marriage in the biblical canon and Christian tradition but, appealing to historical change and cultural variation in marriage practices, still argue that the church may sanction same-sex union. The social institution of marriage is not static but dynamic: marriage practices have not been constant across eras and cultures but exhibit variations and have undergone changes. Such variations and changes are evident within the biblical canon: marriage practice among first-century Christians in the Roman Empire was different from what it was among ancient Israelites in the tribal society. Such changes have continued within Western society: marriage practice among North Americans in the modern era is different from what it was among Europeans in the medieval era. Within the Western church over the centuries, the Catholic and Protestant branches of Christian tradition have elaborated the core elements of the Christian doctrine of marriage within different theological models that have become embedded within different cultural environments, political systems, and legal frameworks.[2]

An innovationist, then, might argue as follows. Marriage as a social institution has undergone substantial change from the biblical era throughout church history. Because changes in laws and customs about who can marry whom and by what procedure and at what age are "par for the historical course," the church can now consider changes regarding the gender of spouses.[3] Scripture shows that marriage practices have adapted in response to cultural values and altered in pursuit of familial goals: secondary marriages with servants to remedy infertility and generate descendants (e.g., Gen. 16; 30); arranged marriages within kinship groups to avoid ethnic mixing and preserve religious fidelity (e.g., Gen. 24; cf. Tobit); levirate marriages between in-laws to guarantee sustenance for widows and generate descendants for kinsmen (e.g., Gen. 38; Deut. 25:5–10; Ruth). In the church today, the theological value of honoring the human dignity of sexual minorities and the ecclesial goal of including sexual minorities within the faith community present another occasion for changing marriage. Megan DeFranza writes: "Contemporary Christian marriage is not 'biblical marriage' of the Old or New Testament. The biblical teaching of the image of God in all people has come to supersede ancient patterns of marriage. The question before Christians today is whether 'biblical marriage' can be revised *yet again* to better honor the humanity of

---

2. See Witte, *From Sacrament to Contract*.
3. K. Wilson, *Letter to My Congregation*, 153–54.

gay, lesbian, and bisexual people."[4] An innovationist might even argue further that, on account of variation in practices within Scripture and tradition, there simply is no consistent ethic of sex or normative understanding of marriage to be found in either Scripture[5] or tradition.[6]

An innovationist might refine this argument by observing that egalitarian marriage—as ensconced in the customs and codes of contemporary Western societies, which form the cultural environment and legal framework within which most modern Christians in North America and Europe practice marriage—is no more evident in the biblical canon than is same-sex union.[7] Patriarchal marriage was the predominant practice in ancient Near Eastern and Greco-Roman cultures and is reflected throughout the biblical canon. An innovationist might thus argue as follows. Christians today in European and North American democracies practice marriage within the cultural milieu and legal matrix of egalitarianism. Yet there is no biblical text directly validating the modern egalitarian marriage of Western society. So if the church can sanction marriage practiced within an egalitarian model, which is not directly validated by Scripture, then it can also sanction same-sex union, which likewise is not directly validated by Scripture.

Not So from the Beginning: Marriage Variation, Culture, and Creation

Assessing appeals to changes in marriage practices requires distinguishing between the *creational* pattern of marriage, which God ordained from the beginning, and the *cultural* instantiations of marriage, which humankind has exhibited in diverse ways. Such distinction is based in Jesus's teaching. When ruling on divorce, Jesus distinguished between God's ordination of marriage at the beginning and Israel's practice of marriage in ways that were not so from the beginning—and he judged Israel's practice of marriage according to God's ordination of marriage. According to Jesus, citing Genesis, God originally designed marriage as "the two" of "male and female" joined into "one flesh."

The logic of Jesus's ruling may be extended to considering cultural variations in marriage practice. Human instantiations of marriage vary widely across cultures and eras. Cultural variations in marriage practice are evident within the biblical canon (e.g., arranged marriage, near-kin marriage, secondary marriage, levirate marriage). Jesus ruled that the creational pattern, as God's original intention for marriage, takes precedence over the cultural

---

4. DeFranza, "Journeying from the Bible to Christian Ethics," 90–93 (emphasis original). See also J. Rogers, *Jesus, the Bible, and Homosexuality*, 93–94.

5. See Wink, "Homosexuality and the Bible."

6. See Nelson, "Sources for Body Theology," 82–84.

7. See Grimsrud, "Toward a Theology of Welcome," 62–63.

instantiation. Accordingly, the church should judge cultural instantiations of marriage practice as conforming or nonconforming with respect to the creational pattern of marriage—and thus as aligning with or deviating from God's original intention for marriage.

Some cultural variations in marriage practice appear neutral with respect to the creational pattern. Whether marrying involves a wife joining her husband's household, or a husband joining his wife's household, or husband and wife establishing an independent household, each practice may be compatible with the creational pattern. Other cultural variations in marriage practice distort the creational pattern in fundamental aspects and thereby deviate from God's original intention for marriage. Cultural variants of nonmonogamy— say, polygamy, open marriage, or serial marriage—deviate from God's original intention for exclusive-enduring fidelity of husband and wife.[8]

Now, biblical narratives show that God sometimes accommodates variant marriage practices for the sake of God's purpose, such as the near-kin and secondary marriages of Abraham and Jacob. Israel's case laws even regulated variant marriage practices such as primary and secondary wives (Exod. 21:7–11; Deut. 21:15–17) and divorce-remarriage (Deut. 24:1–4). Nonetheless, that God accommodated or regulated variant marriage practices does not imply that God sanctioned such practices. First, biblical case laws deal with situations that arise and require regulation (e.g., "If a man takes a second wife . . ." or "Suppose a man writes her a certificate of divorce . . .") without endorsing such situations as righteous. Biblical case laws indicate what is the case and prescribe what should be done if such-and-such is the case; but they do not sanction the situation and may even implicitly express divine disapproval of a tolerated deviation from the creational pattern.[9] Case laws could be adapted to varying circumstances and altered for human needs (cf. Exod. 21:2–11; Deut. 15:12–18) without fundamental changes in moral principles. Second, the church views the providence of God from the perspective of Jesus: God's dealing with hardheartedness does not alter God's desire for righteousness; legal concession to divorce does not imply theological revision of marriage. Accordingly, we see God's accommodation and regulation of marriage variants as God's merciful dealing with fallen humankind; and we discern what is good and holy in marriage according to God's original

8. C. S. Lewis, *Mere Christianity*, 85–86, drew a similar distinction between the "rule of chastity"—namely, "Either marriage, with complete faithfulness to your partner, or else total abstinence"—which "is the same for all Christians at all times," and the "rule of propriety," which varies "according to the customs of a given social circle."

9. See Lamb, *Prostitutes and Polygamists*, 61–62, 146–48; Davidson, *Flame of Yahweh*, 186–89, 191–93, 389–405; Ash, *Marriage*, 249–52.

intention for marriage. One thus cannot argue that God's accommodation to our biblical ancestors licenses the church to sanction practices that deviate from God's original intention for marriage.

The distinction between creational pattern and cultural variation applies also to the analogy between egalitarian marriage and same-sex union. Both egalitarian marriage and same-sex union are contemporary cultural instantiations; neither is directly validated in Scripture. Yet arguing from acceptance of egalitarian marriage to sanction of same-sex union overlooks the evident fact that the two differ in a relevant respect: egalitarian marriage, as a variety of man-woman monogamy, aligns with the creational pattern; but same-sex union, by its very constitution, deviates from the creational pattern. Judging by the creational pattern of marriage, the church may, with reason, discern one way concerning egalitarian marriage and, for the same reason, discern the opposite way concerning same-sex union.

Advance in Civilized Standards: Marriage Variation, Scripture, and Tradition

Christian history of marriage practice evidences constancy and change. The major branches of Christian tradition across centuries and cultures have consistently maintained man-woman monogamy as the definition of marriage, despite differences in theology and variations in practice of marriage. Likewise, Christians have practiced celibacy in various ways across the centuries: as desert hermits and communal monks, consecrated virgins and continent widows, anchorites and anchoresses, and so on. The major branches of Christian tradition have also differed regarding the comparative valuation of virginity and marriage. Yet the moral norm reserving sex to marriage has been the constant baseline of varying practices and theologies of celibacy.

The phenomenon of historical change in marriage practice did not go unnoticed during the formative period of the doctrinal tradition within the Western church. Patristic-era bishops and theologians were aware of variations in marriage customs and changes in marriage laws, yet they consistently affirmed that marriage is man-woman monogamy. I will illustrate by two examples. Christian practice inherited and adapted from Roman law the notion of conditions for valid marriage.[10] One condition for valid marriage was the absence of impediment to marriage. Among impediments to marriage were boundaries preventing certain pairs from marrying because of an existing relationship and barriers preventing certain persons from marrying because

---

10. See Brundage, *Law, Sex, and Christian Society*, 32–38; Reynolds, *Marriage in the Western Church*, 18–22.

of social status. Both classes of impediment have changed over time in the Christian practice of marriage.

Boundaries of Marriage: Impediments of Relationship

One impediment preventing two persons from marrying is an existing relationship of either party to a third party, particularly if either party is already betrothed or married. Another impediment preventing two persons from marrying is an existing relationship between the two parties, particularly if they are near of kin to one another. Such impediments of relationship mark out boundaries of marriage within a family and community: they regulate who may marry whom by declaring off-limits couplings between certain pairs. Pious concern to observe such boundaries is reflected in the traditional practice of "publishing the banns" prior to a couple's nuptial: "If any of you know cause, or just impediment, why these two persons should not be joyned together in holy Matrimony, ye are to declare it."[11] I will consider the latter type of impediment, which prevents marrying within close degrees of kinship. Changes in customs and laws regarding near-kin marriage are apparent in Israelite history and Christian history.

Near-kin marriage was a common custom among ancient Near Eastern cultures, a custom that Israel's ancestors carried with them from Mesopotamia to Canaan. Abraham's wife, Sarah, was his half sister, his father's daughter (Gen. 11:29; 20:12); Isaac's wife, Rebekah, was his cousin, his uncle's granddaughter (24:15); Jacob's wives, Leah and Rachel, were sisters, his uncle's daughters (29:15–30). Some of Jacob's descendants practiced near-kin marriage in Egypt: Moses's father, Amram, married his father's sister, Jochebed (Exod. 6:20). After God had delivered Jacob's descendants from Egypt, covenanted with Israel at Sinai, and led the Israelites to Canaan, the Holiness Code for Israel's life expressly forbade several varieties of near-kin marriage, thus instituting impediments of relationship in Israel's law (Lev. 18:6–18; 20:17, 19–21). These laws prohibited couplings of the sort observed in the cases of Abraham, Jacob, and Amram: no sexual relations with a sister, whether father's daughter or mother's daughter (18:9; 20:17); no sexual relations with an aunt, whether father's sister or mother's sister (18:12–13; 20:19); no marrying "a woman as a rival to her sister" while the sister still lives (18:18). Deuteronomy even declares "cursed" anyone who, like Abraham, has sexual relations with a sister (27:22).[12]

God apparently accommodated these marriage practices of Israel's patriarchs for the sake of God's plan, but then God expressly prohibited such

---

11. Cummings, *Book of Common Prayer*, 434.
12. Israelite law did not prohibit cousin marriage (cf. Num. 36).

marriage practices in the land that God promised to their descendants. The Holiness Code presents two reasons for repudiating the incestuous practices of Israel's patriarchs and the land's inhabitants. First, incestuous marriage was associated with the Egyptians, whose land the Israelites had left, and with the Canaanites, whose land the Israelites were entering; Israel was to be a distinct people that obeyed God's laws rather than followed the ways of neighboring nations (Lev. 18:2–5). Second, the previous inhabitants of Canaan, including the Israelites' ancestors, had "committed all of these abominations" and thereby "defiled themselves" and the land; the Israelites and non-Israelite residents were to "commit none of these abominations" lest they also defile themselves and the land and so come under God's judgment (18:24–30).

The Holiness Code marks a change in Israel's history, a shift in the boundaries of marriage from those observed by Israel's patriarchs. These laws left a lasting legacy for God's people, invoked centuries later by John the prophet (Matt. 14:3–4; cf. Lev. 18:16) and Paul the apostle (1 Cor. 5:1–2; cf. Lev. 18:7–8; 20:21; Deut. 22:30; 27:20). Yet this historical change in marriage law maintained unaltered the creational pattern of marriage. God's institution of impediments of relationship in marriage honored God's ordination of the "one flesh" union of man and woman (Gen. 2:23–24). Forbidding sexual relations with anyone of one's "own flesh" (Lev. 18:6 NJPS) served to guard the kinship nexus created by and generated from the one flesh of husband and wife against sexual temptation as well as to shield vulnerable family members (especially women) from sexual predation.[13] Sexual holiness is both constitutive of the communal holiness of God's people (20:22–26) and protective of the relational integrity of the family.

Christian theologians in the patristic era commented on changes in marriage customs and laws, including impediments of relationship. In the fifth century, Augustine observed that laws forbidding near-kin marriage had changed over time. Biblical law initially did not proscribe sexual unions with offspring and between siblings, he surmised, in order to allow for populating the earth. When a sufficient population had been generated and such unions were no longer necessary, however, biblical law forbade incestuous unions, in order to prevent an ingrown society and promote wider extension of social ties. Roman custom had long censured marriage of siblings, but only recently under a Christian emperor had Roman law forbidden marriage of cousins. Regarding the latter change, Augustine remarked: "The modern prohibition of marriage between cousins is an advance in civilized standards." Nonetheless, in his view, such

---

13. See Goldingay, *Old Testament Theology*, 3:414–17; Davidson, *Flame of Yahweh*, 428–46; Ash, *Marriage*, 256–71.

changes in custom and law neither altered the pattern of marriage from male-female union nor shifted the purpose of marriage away from procreation.[14]

The development of canon law in the medieval church, from the Fourth Lateran Council (thirteenth century) to the Council of Trent (sixteenth century), also involved changes in impediments to marriage based on degrees of kinship.[15] Yet throughout this development, theologians and jurists continued to cite the classic definition that "marriage is the union of a man and a woman." This development culminated in the catechism of the Council of Trent, which defined marriage according to the "general opinion of the theologians" as "the conjugal union of man and woman."[16] The Protestant Reformers sought to reform marriage law by limiting impediments to only those clearly mandated by biblical law or grounded in natural law.[17] Yet they never considered that by reforming the law of marriage they were changing the fundamental form of marriage. Within Christian tradition, while laws and customs regarding near-kin marriage have changed, the fundamental form of marriage—man-woman monogamy—has remained constant.[18]

Barriers to Marriage: Impediments of Status

Under Roman law, a person could marry only if he or she had legal right to form a valid marriage. Some persons, due to social status, lacked legal right to marry, which prevented them from forming a valid marriage. Such impediments of status were barriers to marriage, either preventing marriages between persons of unequal status or preventing persons of certain status from marrying. One impediment of status prevented citizens from marrying noncitizens: a Roman could not marry a foreigner, unless the foreign party was granted legal right to marry. Another impediment of status prevented slaves, a sizable portion of the imperial population, from forming valid marriages: no slave could marry anyone, either a free person or another slave. Couples lacking legal right to marry could enter a monogamous relationship of cohabitation: a Roman and a foreigner, or a free person and a slave, or two slaves. Although not valid marriage, cohabitation was common practice in Roman society; while cohabiting couples were socially acknowledged, cohabitation enjoyed no legal standing and entailed none of the legal consequences of marriage (e.g., legitimacy of offspring and inheritance of property). Impediments of

14. Augustine *City of God* 15.16.
15. See Brundage, *Law, Sex, and Christian Society*, 140–41, 191–93, 355–57; Witte, *From Sacrament to Contract*, 99–103, 105–11.
16. Witte, *From Sacrament to Contract*, 80, 108.
17. See Witte, *From Sacrament to Contract*, 145–49, 172–74.
18. See also Meyendorff, *Marriage*, 47–50.

status in Roman law varied in different eras. A third-century Roman emperor granted citizenship to all free persons, implying a significant shift in the impediments to marriage: many persons previously barred from valid marriage gained legal right to marry. Although this change left in place the legal barrier between slaves and marriage, that impediment of status would eventually be eliminated in the Christian practice of marriage.[19]

There is no barrier to marriage of slaves in Scripture. In fact, biblical narrative depicts marriage of slaves (e.g., Abraham's secondary marriage to Hagar); and biblical law assumes marriage of slaves. The Holiness Code did not prohibit marriage to slaves, or between slaves, within a household; slaves did not belong to the kinship nexus of "one flesh" and thus were not off-limits to family members as sexual partners. Indentured servant girls acquired from another household in exchange for remitted debts, for example, could become secondary wives for masters or first wives for sons; and case law regulated situations involving marriages of household slaves (Exod. 21:2–11). The New Testament does not address the question: Paul's instruction about marriage does not deal with slaves, and Paul's instruction to slaves does not deal with marriage. This is not surprising: because Roman law barred slaves from marriage, likely there were few married slaves among early Christians.

For the most part, early Christians married according to the customs of their peoples and the laws of their lands. The early church in the Roman Empire was in no position to reform marriage laws or to create its own legal institution defined by Christian conditions of marriage. In this milieu, bishops debated whether the church should bless monogamous cohabitation of Christian couples unable to form valid marriages due to unequal status. This question elicited a range of opinions. In the third century, Callistus, bishop of Rome, favored doing so, citing pastoral reasons, holding that such couples should adhere to Christian standards of fidelity and permanence.[20] In the fourth century, Ambrose, bishop of Milan, objected, citing legal and social reasons, arguing that such couples would offend decency and their children would lack legitimacy. In the fifth century, Leo, bishop of Rome, objected, citing theological reasons, claiming that the Roman law restricting valid marriage to free persons of equal standing had been divinely instituted.

Christian emperors, while not removing the legal barrier between slaves and marriage (much less abolishing slavery), did provide legal protection to cohabitation between slaves. Constantine, citing humanitarian reasons, enacted a law to prevent families of slaves from being divided when an estate

19. My discussion in this section relies on Reynolds, *Marriage in the Western Church*, 156–72.

20. Callistus's opinion generated controversy within the Roman church—see Apostolic Tradition 16, in Stewart, *On the Apostolic Tradition*, 118–23.

is divided. Centuries later, during the Carolingian era of Christendom, the question of whether slave families may be divided prompted the first official recognition in the Western church of marriages between slaves on Christian terms. A council in the ninth century, citing Jesus's declaration that humans should not divide what God has joined (Matt. 19:4–6), ruled that a master may not separate married slaves, if their marriage was lawful and their master had consented. The council ruled, in effect, that marriages of slaves were to be treated equally to marriages of free persons under divine law. Canonists, theologians, and bishops in the twelfth and thirteenth centuries, citing Paul's proclamation that "there is no longer slave or free" because all baptized believers "are one in Christ Jesus" (Gal. 3:26–28), argued that slaves should not be denied marriage in the church. In Christ, there is no distinction between slave and free; in the church, therefore, enslaved persons and free persons should be equally free to marry just as they are equally free to be baptized and receive Eucharist. Medieval theologians reasoned that enslaved persons were circumstantially capable of marrying: an enslaved condition as such did not necessarily impede a person's consensual commitment to exclusive-enduring fidelity. Thus the church should bless marriages between slaves and between slaves and free persons apart from a master's consent, just as it blessed marriages between free persons.[21]

Christian views in the Western church concerning marriage of slaves changed significantly over centuries. In the patristic era, Christians appealed to pastoral and humanitarian reasons for giving ecclesial recognition and legal protection to cohabitation between slaves. In the medieval era, Christians appealed to biblical and theological reasons for giving ecclesial blessing to marriage between slaves. Despite changing views and despite shifting reasons for changing views, the church maintained unchanged that marriage, whether of slave or free, is man and woman joined in faithful bond.

Lessons for Discernment

Distinguish Theological from Historical

Across centuries of church history, marriage customs, practices, and laws have varied and changed. Some changes in marriage practices have been responses to changes in economic conditions or political systems.[22] At the same time, the church has *not* changed its definition of marriage from man-woman monogamy into anything else. The constancy of the church's marriage definition despite variation in marriage customs, practices, and laws is not a his-

---

21. Thomas Aquinas, *Summa Theologiae* III supplement, q. 52, arts. 1–2.
22. See Miles, *Redemption of Love*, 113–35.

torical accident, due to contingent factors—unusual circumstances or unasked questions or unknown facts—that could have been otherwise. The unchanging marriage definition throughout Christian tradition is due to the catholic conviction evidenced across centuries—in sermons and treatises, catechetical and confessional documents, ecclesial rules and nuptial rites—that man and woman is constitutive of marriage.

Therefore, there are no precedents from church history of "changing marriage" in the relevant sense—changes in what marriage is—to which one could appeal to advocate altering marriage for the sake of sanctioning same-sex union.[23] I thus concur with Stephen Holmes's assessment of DeFranza's argument:

> I do not accept that there has been a change in our understanding of marriage, just many and repeated changes in its cultural expression. We need to distinguish, I suggest, between the theological reality of marriage and its ever-changing cultural trappings. . . . For this reason, I do not accept the logic of DeFranza's claim that, having changed marriage once, we are free to change it again. . . . The force of her position relies on our accepting the claim that it has been "revised" before; as I have argued, she has not shown this to be true.[24]

The argument for sanctioning same-sex union by appeal to past changes in marriage practices fails to prove its point, because it neglects to distinguish between marriage as theological reality, ordained by God from the beginning of creation, and marriage as historical phenomenon, varied by humans across eras and cultures.

Remove Impediment to Marriage

Some traditionalists speak of a celibacy mandate for gay believers. Unless a gay believer can overcome same-sex attraction and change sexual orientation, he or she must commit to celibacy as a requirement of Christian chastity, some traditionalists say. Some traditionalists even suggest that gay persons, simply due to same-sex attraction/orientation, are constitutionally incompatible with genuine marriage. A celibacy mandate, strictly speaking, would prevent a gay believer from marrying even an opposite-sex partner. That seems unwarranted to me, even on traditionalist grounds.

The history of marriage impediments provides a perspective from which to consider this view. Mandating celibacy to gay believers, in effect, bars every

23. Some historians (e.g., Boswell, *Same-Sex Unions in Premodern Europe*) have claimed that the premodern church blessed same-sex unions. Such claims have been shown mistaken—see Milliner, "One Soul in Two Bodies."

24. S. Holmes, "Response to Megan K. DeFranza," 114–15.

gay believer from marrying anyone, even an opposite-sex partner, with the church's blessing. It is tantamount to instituting an impediment between gay believers and marriage. Without altering the definition of marriage, traditionalists could—and, I argue, should—remove this impediment to marriage. Maintaining a traditionalist view of marriage does not necessitate an impediment barring gay believers from marrying.

The traditional definition that marriage is man-woman monogamy forbids certain kinds of unions (no adulterous, polygamous, or same-sex unions). Biblical laws and ecclesial rules stipulate conditions for marriage (age, consent, etc.) and impede unions between certain pairs of persons (no incestuous unions). While specific conditions (e.g., celibacy vows) might preclude certain persons from marrying, the traditional definition of marriage does not outright preclude categories of persons from marrying. Contemporary experience shows that gay persons are constitutionally compatible with marrying: genuinely entering and faithfully continuing in marriage with an opposite-sex partner is possible, physically and psychologically, for persons with same-sex attraction/orientation.[25] Accordingly, the church should not categorize baptized believers into marriage-eligible and celibacy-mandated groups based on sexual attraction/orientation; there should be no such categorical exclusion from marriage. The church today, while maintaining that marriage is man-woman monogamy, should allow gay believers to marry with the church's blessing.

I would offer additional reasons against mandating celibacy to gay believers. First, it misstates the Christian standard of chastity. The church, Nate Collins observes, should "state that Christian doctrine mandates celibacy for *everybody* who isn't married, but that different classes of individuals can experience this mandate as burdensome in different ways."[26] Second, mandating celibacy to gay believers undercuts lifelong celibacy as a voluntary commitment. Jesus commends disciples who have "made themselves" lifelong celibates for the kingdom; he does not authorize the church to mandate any believer to lifelong celibacy. Both lifelong marriage and lifelong celibacy should be voluntary and available for all Christians, including gay believers.[27] Third, mandating celibacy to gay believers, and thereby restricting marriage to straight believers, is an innovation. It implicitly predicates marriage on

25. See Yarhouse, *Homosexuality and the Christian*, 137–53.

26. N. Collins, *All but Invisible*, 87 (emphasis original).

27. Some innovationists object to the traditional view on the grounds that a celibacy mandate puts an unfair burden on sexual minorities, creates a double standard of chastity, and undercuts celibacy as a voluntary commitment. See Vines, *God and the Gay Christian*, 43–57; J. Rogers, *Jesus, the Bible, and Homosexuality*, 93; K. Wilson, *Letter to My Congregation*, 146–53. See N. Collins, *All but Invisible*, 87n3, for a critique of Vines's arguments.

heterosexual orientation and effectively redefines marriage by contemporary sexuality categories. Biblically and traditionally, marriage is man and woman (based on sex), not heterosexual and heterosexual (based on sexuality).

I thus advise traditionalists to allow and affirm marriages of mixed-orientation couples, man-woman couples of differing sexual attraction/orientation: gay man and straight woman, straight man and bisexual woman, and so on.[28] Some such Christian couples who have discerned that marriage is God's will for them have shared their stories with the church.[29] Such couplings should be considered as normative marriage—conjugal, covenantal union—not an exception to the norm.

Marriages of mixed-orientation couples should be approached cautiously, considered carefully, and entered openly; they will face special challenges and will need special care. Such couplings should not be promoted as the "answer" for gay believers: pastors should never counsel getting married as a "cure" for same-sex attraction; believers should never get married as a "cover" for being gay.[30] Rachel Gilson, a same-sex-attracted Christian married to a man for over ten years, writes: "I would never insist that marriage is the normal or 'correct' road for every (or even most) same-sex-attracted Christians."[31] Some gay believers may be drawn toward lifelong intimacy with a specific person of the opposite sex (an orientation toward "this woman" or "this man"). For such believers, marriage should be an allowed and affirmed option in the church.

The Universe Is Not as It Appears to Be: Changes in Scientific Understanding

Shifting from the medieval era to the Reformation era, I turn next to changes in scientific understanding. Before considering such precedents of change, I will comment briefly on the relevance and limits of science in matters of discernment.

Scientific research is pertinent but insufficient for gaining moral wisdom. Science can study what habits of human conduct have been practiced in human

---

28. See N. Collins, *All but Invisible*, 92–98; Gilson, *Born Again This Way*, 85–98, 113–26; Otto, *Oriented to Faith*, 94–95; Sprinkle, *People to Be Loved*, 162–63; Yuan, *Holy Sexuality and the Gospel*, 49–50.

29. See Aidyn Sevilla, "I Walk Between"; Joy Sevilla, "We All Walk Between"; Mike Allen, "Wait a Minute, a Mixed What?"; Nate Collins and Sara Collins, "A Simple Reason to Get Married."

30. Here the story of Josh and Lolly Weed, a formerly married "mixed orientation" couple, may serve as a cautionary tale. See Weed and Weed, "Devoutly Mormon. Happily Married. Undeniably Gay"; Weed and Weed, "Turning a Unicorn into a Bat."

31. Gilson, "I Never Became Straight," 54.

societies and can determine what results they have produced in the past and then predict what results they are likely to produce in the future. But scientific method cannot evaluate results and consequences as better or worse in moral terms and thus alone cannot decide which habits and practices should be accepted or rejected in human conduct. Science can determine what's typical of human beings, but science alone cannot discern what's best for human beings. To gain such wisdom we need more than science. A biblical-theological understanding of human beings as God's creatures is necessary to fully know the ends toward which we should strive and the means by which we should live.

Scientific research, moreover, investigates a fallen world, a world already affected by evil. Scientific method can guide our investigation of things as we find them, but science itself cannot help us distinguish God's design in creation from evil's distortion of creation. Scientific concepts can enhance our description of the world through quantitative categories (space and time, mass and energy, etc.), but science itself cannot guide our evaluation of things in the world in qualitative terms (good and bad, right and wrong, etc.). Scientific theories can speak of human beings as they are, but science itself cannot tell of human beings as God created them from the beginning or as God intends them in the end. To draw such distinction, to ground such evaluation, and to gain such vision, we need more than science. A biblical-theological view of the world—creation, fall, redemption, and new creation—is needed to see the world aright and make full sense of the world as God designed it and desires it to be.

The current scientific understanding of human sexuality has a relevant role but limited import in the church's discernment. Scientific study of human beings can deliver factual, though fallible, knowledge of the biology, psychology, and sociology of human sex, sexual attraction, and sexual behavior. Such knowledge can be helpful in revising popular perceptions of sexual minorities and adjusting pastoral responses to personal situations. Yet scientific research is insufficient to settle moral matters, much less substitute for discernment of God's will. Science can study human conduct in sex and marriage but can neither define what marriage is nor discern what marriage is for.[32]

The Argument: Galileo Was Right

Scientific understanding is not a sufficient basis for Christian discernment. Nonetheless, one might think, the church could revise its interpretation of Scripture concerning same-sex union on account of scientific evidence

---

32. See Yarhouse, *Homosexuality and the Christian*; Jones and Yarhouse, *Homosexuality*.

concerning same-sex orientation. After all, there is precedent for such change in church history.

The church has at times reconsidered biblical interpretation on account of new empirical data. Archaeological discoveries in the Holy Land, for example, have enabled scholars to piece together a picture of social organization and economic conditions in ancient Israel. Biblical scholars have looked to evidence of major changes during the reign of the kings in order to better understand the preaching of the prophets.[33] The precedent to which some innovationists appeal is Galileo's debate with church authorities over Copernican cosmology in the 1600s. They draw a parallel between the present debate, which pits the traditional censure of same-sex intercourse against the innovational sanction of same-sex union, and the earlier debate, which featured the ancient hypothesis of a geocentric (earth-centered) cosmos versus the modern hypothesis of a heliocentric (sun-centered) cosmos.[34]

Using this parallel, an innovationist might argue as follows. Church authorities had decided against the truth of heliocentric cosmology on account of biblical interpretation—namely, certain texts whose plain sense implies the earth's immobility (e.g., Pss. 93:1; 96:10; 104:5; 119:90) and the sun's motion around the earth (e.g., Pss. 19:5–6; 113:3; Eccles. 1:5). Accepting Copernican cosmology—the earth rotates on its axis and revolves around an immobile sun—would require reinterpreting Scripture. Yet the church eventually revised its view of the cosmos to fit the Copernican view and reinterpreted Scripture as Galileo had advocated on account of new scientific evidence demonstrating the earth's motions. Likewise, the church has decided against the righteousness of same-sex union on account of biblical interpretation—namely, certain texts whose plain sense condemns same-sex intercourse (e.g., Lev. 18:22; Rom. 1:26–27). Yet the church should now revise its standards of sexual morality to sanction same-sex union, and reinterpret Scripture accordingly, on account of recent scientific evidence concerning same-sex orientation. As the church once acknowledged that it had misinterpreted Scripture regarding cosmology, so the church should now acknowledge that it has misinterpreted Scripture regarding sexuality.

The Galileo affair was as much about Scripture as it was about science. The proposed comparison between cosmology and sexuality should be analyzed from both angles. I will assess this parallel from the respective angles of hermeneutics of Scripture and history of science.

---

33. See King, *Amos, Hosea, Micah*.

34. See Vines, *God and the Gay Christian*, 21–25; Brownson, *Bible, Gender, Sexuality*, 10; Gushee, *Changing Our Mind*, 91; Loader, "Homosexuality and the Bible," 47; Nissinen, *Homoeroticism in the Biblical World*, 126.

The Heavens Are Telling: Hermeneutical Angle

Cosmology–Morality Parallel

Galileo and his contemporaries debated cosmological hypotheses about the earth and sun; we are debating moral norms concerning sex and marriage. Drawing a parallel between these debates depends on making two implicit assumptions pertaining to both sides of the relation between science and Scripture. The first assumption concerns the scope of science: science relates to morality in the same way it relates to cosmology. The second assumption concerns the sense of Scripture: Scripture speaks of morality in the same way it speaks of the cosmos. I will consider these assumptions in turn.

The parallel assumes, first, that science is equally competent with respect to both cosmology and morality. Accordingly, scientific evidence is equally relevant to both cosmological questions and moral matters—and thus is equally relevant to interpreting Scripture in relation to both cosmology and morality. That assumption is erroneous, however. Science is competent to decide which of two incompatible hypotheses pertaining to physical facts (whether the earth is immobile at the cosmic center or not) better fits empirical evidence. Science is competent also to study the consequences of different courses of human conduct. But science is not capable of asking, much less answering, which of two incompatible propositions pertaining to human conduct (whether sexual intercourse belongs properly within man-woman marriage or not) better fits God's will. Science by itself is not competent in moral matters because scientific method cannot distinguish empirically between creation and corruption and thus cannot discern morally between good and evil. The implied parallel, between cosmology and morality in the competency of science, thus fails.

The parallel assumes, second, that Scripture speaks in the same way about both the cosmos and morality. Accordingly, our approach to interpreting Scripture may take account of scientific evidence in the same way whether Scripture speaks of the cosmos or morality—and thus biblical interpretation may change in response to scientific advance for moral matters in the same way it changes for cosmological questions. That assumption is questionable, however. Galileo's own approach to Scripture and science casts doubt on the implied parallel between cosmology and morality in biblical interpretation.

Galileo on Scripture and Science[35]

In defending his view, Galileo, a devout Catholic, adhered to common principles of Christian tradition on biblical interpretation. First, a principle

---

35. See Galileo to Castelli, 1613, in Blackwell, *Galileo, Bellarmine, and the Bible*, 195–201; Galileo, *Letter to the Grand Duchess Christina* (1615), in Galileo, *Discoveries and Opinions*,

of unity of truth: the book of Scripture and the book of nature have a single author and teach one truth; truth does not contradict truth, such that the truths of Scripture and the truths of science, properly understood, cannot conflict. If science conflicts with Scripture, then logically either our knowledge of nature or our interpretation of Scripture is faulty. Second, a principle of priority of faith: in dogmatic matters of faith, unknowable by sense and reason, Scripture always takes priority over science. The theological dogmas taught by the church and accepted by faith—God originated all things, God is three-in-one, Jesus is fully divine and fully human—are infallible; no proposition of philosophy or hypothesis of science that conflicts with an infallible dogma of faith could be demonstrated as true, and thus any such proposition or hypothesis is false. If any philosophical proposition or scientific hypothesis states or implies that the cosmos is without origin or that God is one but not three or that Jesus is not fully divine or not fully human, then it is to be judged by faith as false.

In addition to common tradition, Galileo invoked three principles regarding interpreting Scripture in relation to science. First, a principle of intention: the Spirit's intent in Scripture is to teach us truths of salvation, not truths of science; the Spirit teaches in Scripture "how one goes to heaven" (doctrines of faith and morals), not "how the heavens go" (theories of cosmology). Second, a principle of accommodation: Scripture speaks of the cosmos in a manner accommodated to human perspective and experience; biblical descriptions of natural phenomena reflect the subjective appearances of things and do not necessarily represent the objective reality of things. Third, a principle of prudence: Holy Scripture is inspired, but human interpreters are fallible; in cases where the biblical text is difficult and scientific knowledge is uncertain, such that we might be mistaken either way, it would be unwise to commit dogmatically to a literal interpretation if scientific advance might disprove that interpretation, which could bring discredit on Scripture and disrepute on the church.

Applying these principles to the Copernican hypothesis, Galileo argued his case: Scripture intends to teach the way of salvation, not theories of science—and thus does not pertain to deciding the truth of propositions in astronomy, which are not dogmatic matters of faith and so are to be decided by sense experience and natural reason rather than divine revelation. Even so, Scripture speaks of the sun and earth using common modes of human speech and

---

175–216. For historical and theological studies, see Blackwell, *Galileo, Bellarmine, and the Bible*; McMullin, *Church and Galileo*; Fantoli, *Case of Galileo*; Sobel, *Galileo's Daughter*. In what follows, I rely especially on Blackwell, *Galileo, Bellarmine, and the Bible*, 53–85; McMullin, "Galileo's Theological Venture."

from the mundane perspective of human experience—and thus should not be taken as making absolute statements of physical reality. Moreover, prudence counsels that, in astronomical matters, the church should not commit to a dogmatic position that might be overturned by future observations, which could undermine the authority of Scripture and the church.

Galileo's Hermeneutic and Christian Tradition

Galileo's approach to Scripture and science was no innovation. His hermeneutical orientation accords with Scripture's profession concerning the Holy Spirit's intention in Scripture. According to the apostles, "all scripture is inspired by God" to "instruct you for salvation through faith in Jesus Christ" and "for training in righteousness" (2 Tim. 3:14–17). The Spirit's purpose in Scripture—namely, that we might receive salvation and live righteously—orients the church's interpretation of Scripture.

Galileo's approach was also consonant with the Christian tradition of biblical interpretation. The question of Scripture and science did not newly arise in the Reformation era. Major theologians of the patristic era were familiar with the theories of cosmic structure and natural history taught by the Greek philosophers. And they recognized that the spherical cosmos constructed by Greek astronomers differed from the three-level cosmos depicted in the Genesis account. The relation between Scripture and science was a common question of the fourth century.

Galileo appealed directly to Augustine's authority and relied on Augustine's view to support his hermeneutical approach. In his commentary on the "literal meaning" of Genesis, Augustine articulated ideas that Galileo later cited in his defense. First, the Spirit speaks through Scripture in a manner suited to human language and comprehension: "Sacred Scripture in its customary style is speaking within the limitations of human language in addressing men of limited understanding, while at the same time teaching a lesson to be understood by the reader who is able." Second, the Spirit's intent in Scripture is to teach the way of salvation, not the structure of the cosmos: "In the matter of the shape of the heavens . . . the Spirit of God, who spoke through [the sacred writers], did not wish to teach men such things as would be of no avail for their salvation." Third, when Scripture treats obscure matters beyond present knowledge, when it does not pertain to doctrines of faith, the church would be wise to withhold judgment and allow different interpretations: "In such a case we should not rush in headlong and so firmly take a stand on one side that, if further progress in the search for truth justly undermines this position, we too fall with it."[36]

---

36. Augustine, *Literal Meaning of Genesis*, quoted in McMullin, "Galileo's Theological Venture."

The Cappadocian theologians of the Eastern church—Basil of Caesarea, Gregory of Nazianzus, and Gregory of Nyssa—also addressed the relation of Scripture to science. They maintained that we should read the biblical creation accounts not as presenting a competing theory of cosmology but as primarily intended to testify to the glory of the Creator and teach us the way of righteousness and salvation. The creation accounts ultimately point us to Christ, through whom God created the cosmos and in whom God's providence in creation and salvation is worked and completed. The creation accounts, they emphasized, are not intended to be taken as scientific descriptions of cosmic structure or natural history: the creation accounts are intended to teach us not the structure and substance of the heavens and the earth but the truth of the God who made and ordered the heavens and the earth. While referring to the same world studied by science, the creation accounts narrate the world and its history with a distinctive theological perspective and moral purpose. Reading Scripture in this way allows a degree of freedom between Scripture and science: we are free to interpret Scripture without need to serve science, and we are free to inquire scientifically without need to sacrifice Scripture.[37]

Galileo's view was also comparable to the Reformation views of Luther and Calvin in response to Copernicus's heliocentric cosmology. Luther and Calvin maintained a geocentric cosmology and rejected the heliocentric hypothesis; both stressed the plain sense of Scripture and rejected allegorical interpretations of the creation accounts. Yet Luther and Calvin each recognized that the biblical accounts were not intended as scientific descriptions. Luther emphasized that Scripture and science take complementary, not competing, views of the cosmos: Scripture concerns the theological significance of the cosmos (the light from heavenly bodies witnesses to God's providence), while astronomy concerns the physical nature of the cosmos (how the heavenly bodies produce light). Calvin acknowledged that Scripture speaks of the cosmos in a manner accommodated to human experience and common understanding: Genesis depicts the cosmos not in a precise way according to astronomical theories but in a popular style according to common sense. Luther and Calvin thus interpreted Scripture with respect to science in ways that allowed accepting a new scientific theory without rejecting scriptural truth.[38]

Following this traditional approach, the church may reconsider common interpretations of Scripture in light of new knowledge of nature. Because it is not the Holy Spirit's intention in Scripture to teach natural science, and because Scripture speaks of natural phenomena in a manner accommodated

37. See Bouteneff, *Beginnings*, 118, 130, 133–40, 156, 170–71, 182–83.
38. See Dillenberger, *Protestant Thought and Natural Science*, 28–32.

to human perspective, the church may reinterpret texts in Scripture—say, shift from a literal to a figurative reading—when it is fitting to the biblical text and warranted by scientific advance. This traditional way of interpreting Scripture may be illustrated by example. We now recognize that when Scripture says, "From the rising of the sun to its setting the name of the Lord is to be praised" (Ps. 113:3), it does not intend to assert as physical fact that the sun circles the earth. Rather than looking at the heavens from God's all-encompassing perspective, which is beyond our comprehension, Scripture looks at the heavens from our earthbound perspective, within our scope of understanding. And rather than speaking of the heavens in order to teach us about the cosmos, Scripture points to the heavens for the purpose of calling us to prayer. Using a figure of speech drawn from daily experience (sunrise and sunset), Scripture points to the sun as God's sign that we are to praise God at all times (morning to evening) and from all places (east to west), which affirms God's sovereignty over all nations and all creation (Ps. 113:4; cf. Ps. 50:1; Mal. 1:11). "The heavens are telling the glory of God" (Ps. 19:1)—and Scripture tells of the heavens not to instruct us in cosmology but to call our attention to the God who created the heavens and whose glory is displayed in the heavens. We can thus acknowledge that the sun, according to science, does not actually "rise" or "set" and still see the sun's daily "motion," according to Scripture, as our summons to praise God. In this way, these two perspectives—science and Scripture, cosmology and doxology—are complementary, not competitive.

Galileo's Hermeneutic and Marriage Innovation

Galileo's traditional approach to Scripture and science allows the church—in accord with the Spirit's intent in Scripture, as human knowledge of the cosmos expands—to reinterpret texts that refer to the cosmos without endangering the church's dogmas of faith. Whether Galileo's hermeneutic can be used to advocate revising interpretation on moral matters, such as sex and marriage, is doubtful. First, it would not fit Galileo's own view. Galileo distinguished between matters of faith and morals, on the one hand, and matters of science and nature, on the other hand. While he advocated that interpretation of Scripture should be revisable in light of science in matters of nature, Galileo adhered to the Council of Trent, which had decreed that Scripture as interpreted by the church is an infallible authority in dogmatic matters of faith and morals. Galileo would not have recognized science as having any authority in biblical interpretation on moral matters.

Second, setting aside Trent, completing the comparison between cosmology and sexuality would require constructing a case on Scripture and sexuality analogous to Galileo's case on Scripture and cosmology. Constructing that analogous case would require positing premises analogous to Galileo's principles: it is the Spirit's intent in Scripture to teach salvation but not morality; Scripture speaks of moral matters in a manner that reflects human experience and perception, such that the moral messages of Scripture do not necessarily represent divine truth. From such premises an innovationist might argue as follows: it is not the Spirit's intent in Scripture to teach a normative view of sex and marriage any more than a definitive theory of cosmology; just as Scripture depicts the cosmos in a manner accommodated to the prescientific beliefs of earthbound humans, so Genesis depicts marriage and Leviticus regulates sex in a manner accommodated to the common understanding of ancient-era cultures; therefore, just as the church today need not believe in the cosmological picture of Scripture, so also the church today need not be bound by the male-female marriage pattern of Genesis or the same-sex intercourse prohibition of Leviticus.[39] I'll appraise this argument by considering its premises.

Consider first the premise that it is not the Spirit's intent in Scripture, generally, to teach moral matters—and, particularly, to teach a normative view of sex and marriage. The general claim, that it is not the Spirit's intent in Scripture to teach morality, is at odds with Paul's view. Paul taught that "all Scripture" (i.e., law, prophets, and writings) is "inspired by God" and thus is both "able to instruct [us] for salvation through faith" and "useful for teaching, for reproof, for correction, and for training in righteousness" (2 Tim. 3:14–17). Even historical narratives, Paul attested, were written to serve as examples for our instruction (Rom. 15:4; 1 Cor. 10:1–13). As Paul saw it, the Spirit's intent throughout Scripture is to teach both salvation and morality.

The particular claim, that it is not the Spirit's intent in Scripture to teach a normative view of sex and marriage, seems at odds with the witness of Scripture. Consider this message about marriage: honor marriage, keep fidelity, flee adultery. This message is conveyed throughout Scripture: by exemplary story, "[Joseph] fled and ran outside" (Gen. 39:6–18); by apodictic law, "You shall not commit adultery" (Exod. 20:14; Deut. 5:18); by wise proverb, "Drink water from your own cistern" (Prov. 5:15); by prophetic parable, "You are the man!" (2 Sam. 12:7); by apostolic exhortation, "Let marriage be held in honor by all, and let the marriage bed be kept undefiled" (Heb. 13:4). In all these ways, the Spirit throughout Scripture teaches a normative view of sex and marriage: God declares marriage honorable, decrees fidelity in marriage, and judges adultery as sin.

---

39. See Brownson, *Bible, Gender, Sexuality*, 105; Keen, *Scripture, Ethics, and the Possibility of Same-Sex Relationships*, 106.

Consider next the premise that Scripture speaks of moral matters in a manner accommodated to human experience and perception, such that the moral messages of Scripture do not necessarily represent divine truth. Scripture does convey its moral messages in many modes accommodated to human perspective. Scripture's accommodation to human perspective, however, does not necessarily empty its moral messages of divine truth. Consider again Scripture's message to honor marriage, keep fidelity, and flee adultery. Scripture conveys this message by modes accommodated to human perspective. Genesis apparently adapts a literary motif from Egyptian culture to tell the story of Joseph in Egypt; yet Joseph's fleeing from Potiphar's house exemplifies righteous response to sexual temptation. Exodus apparently adapts a covenantal form from Near Eastern cultures to articulate God's covenant with Israel at Sinai; yet the Decalogue's commandments express God's will. Proverbs uses analogies and figures drawn from everyday life and natural phenomena, giving counsel tested by common experience; yet its purpose is to impart divine wisdom and instill "the fear of the LORD" (e.g., Prov. 1:7). The prophets speak in sundry ways in particular circumstances; yet their words place human conduct under divine scrutiny, naming evildoing and declaring judgment. The Spirit uses Scripture's accommodation to human perspective to convey divine truth on moral matters. That Scripture conveys a moral message in a mode accommodated to human perspective, therefore, does not imply that this moral message reflects human perception rather than represents divine truth.

While Scripture does intend to teach fidelity in marriage, an innovationist might still argue, Scripture does not intend to teach a male-female pattern of marriage. The Genesis depiction of marriage as man and woman, one might say, accommodates the common perception of ancient cultures, reflecting a human understanding of marriage but not representing God's ordering of marriage. Such a view is logically, and exegetically, possible: nothing in the Genesis text necessarily, or explicitly, rules it out. Such a view might also be hermeneutically plausible, were Genesis 1–2 read by itself.

The church does not read Genesis 1–2 only by itself, however. The church reads Genesis also from the perspective of Jesus. Jesus read Genesis 1–2 as revealing God's institution of marriage "from the beginning" as "the two" of "male and female" joined into "one flesh" and revealing God's intention that the "one flesh" not be sundered (Matt. 19:3–9; Mark 10:2–9; see chap. 4 above). Considering how Jesus interpreted Genesis, arguing that the male-female marriage pattern in Genesis reflects human understanding but does not represent God's ordering requires making a further claim about Jesus.

Jesus, one might claim, shared the common view of marriage of his era and culture and read Genesis from that human-historical perspective. Like his contemporaries, Jesus interpreted the male-female pattern in Genesis as if it were God's design of marriage, mistaking textual accommodation for original creation (as have most Christians since). This claim, however, implies "low" Christology, a Jesus having merely human understanding, which severely weakens the argument in my estimation.

Alternatively, one might claim, Jesus knew very well that the male-female pattern in Genesis accommodates human understanding of marriage. Jesus interpreted the "male and female" pattern in Genesis as if it were God's design of marriage not because that's the Spirit's intent but because that's how his contemporaries interpreted Genesis and understood marriage. Jesus thus argued against his opponents on their interpretation of Genesis without agreeing to their understanding of marriage. This claim, however, does not cohere with what Jesus said about marriage on account of Genesis. It does not fit the contrast that Jesus draws between the divorce law, which he says reflects God's concession to humans, and the creation account, which he says reveals God's intention for marriage. Nor does it fit the emphatic and apodictic conclusion that Jesus drew from Genesis about marriage—"Therefore what God has joined together, let no one separate" (Matt. 19:6; Mark 10:9)—which summons humans to conform themselves to God's will rather than suggests God's accommodation to the human condition.[40]

Consistent application of the accommodation hermeneutic to Jesus's interpretation of Genesis, moreover, generates conflicting implications for Jesus's view of marriage. Jesus read the Genesis account as a seamless story, from God's creating humankind as "male and female" to God's joining "the two" into "one flesh." Jesus's interpretation of Genesis leaves no gap to insert a hermeneutical distinction between "male and female" and "one flesh" regarding marriage, the former reflecting human understanding but the latter representing God's ordering. Jesus's interpretation implies that he viewed "male and female" and "one flesh" the same way. If Jesus viewed "male and female" in Genesis as accommodating human understanding rather than representing God's ordering of marriage, then he viewed "one flesh" the same way. Yet Jesus's ruling on divorce regards the "one flesh" of Genesis as representing God's ordering of marriage.

Extending Galileo's hermeneutic of Scripture on cosmology to the male-female pattern of marriage in Genesis stumbles at Jesus's hermeneutic of Genesis on marriage. From a hermeneutical angle, therefore, drawing a parallel

---

40. This approach also does not fit how Jesus responds to the question "Who sinned?" regarding the man born blind: Jesus, rather than accommodating a common yet false belief about blindness, rebuts human error and then teaches God's truth and does God's work (John 9).

between cosmology and marriage is of doubtful import for the church's discernment.

How the Heavens Go: Historical Angle

From a historical angle, this parallel is instructive for the church in its present discernment. The history of science regarding cosmology is not as simple as "Galileo was right, the church was wrong." And the state of science regarding sexuality is not as simple as "This view is right, that view is wrong."

From Galileo's Debate to the Great Debate

The cosmological debate in the 1500s and 1600s revolved around two major competing hypotheses. Ancient consensus had favored the geocentric (earth-centered) cosmos of Aristotle and Ptolemy. Copernicus hypothesized a heliocentric (sun-centered) cosmos in the mid-1500s. These competing hypotheses were premised on a common assumption: the cosmos, finite and spherical, has a center point occupied by an immobile material body around which revolves all celestial motion. The central question for scientific debate was which celestial body—earth or sun—is the cosmic center.

In Galileo's day of the early 1600s, celestial observations alone could not determine which cosmology—geocentric or heliocentric—was correct. Each hypothesis, with suitable adjustments (e.g., eccentrics and epicycles), could account more or less for all motions in the heavens that had been previously observed. Nor could the question be decided simply by looking through one of the recently fabricated telescopes. Galileo's telescopic observations of the moons of Jupiter, which showed that the earth was not the unique center of cosmic motion, were suggestive of a heliocentric cosmos but not conclusive. Galileo's telescopic observations of the phases of Venus, which showed that Venus orbited the sun, were explained easily, but not uniquely, by the heliocentric hypothesis; although these observations were incompatible with the geocentric hypothesis, they were compatible with Brahe's hybrid geo-heliocentric hypothesis, in which the sun and moon orbit the earth but the other planets orbit the sun. The heliocentric hypothesis, furthermore, made astronomical predictions (e.g., stellar parallax) that could not be observed with existing telescopes.

The heliocentric hypothesis generated difficulties, moreover. Placing the sun at the cosmic center required positing the axial rotation of the earth, which was apparently at odds with sense experience because the expected physical effects of this motion were undetectable. To substantiate the heliocentric hypothesis, Galileo needed physical evidence of the earth's axial and orbital motions; but Galileo's experimental attempts to supply that evidence (e.g., the tides) fell short. A heliocentric cosmos without Ptolemaic epicycles also required elliptical planetary orbits, which were incompatible with Aristotelian physics but also unexplainable otherwise. The heliocentric hypothesis thus implied physical problems that could not be resolved until Newton developed new laws of motion and gravity in the late 1600s.

Due to these empirical and theoretical problems, those astronomers of Galileo's day that favored Copernicus's hypothesis did so mostly because it was a simpler scheme for calculating known data, not because new data necessitated it or because they were convinced it was a true account of the cosmos. It took more than a century to forge a coherent consensus in favor of the heliocentric hypothesis: the earth, other planets, and stars revolve around the sun, the center point of a finite, spherical cosmos. During the 1700s and 1800s, aided by improved telescopes and techniques, new celestial observations (stellar parallax) and terrestrial experiments (Foucault's pendulum) eventually confirmed that the earth revolves around the sun and rotates on its axis. Although this evidence conclusively disproved the geocentric hypothesis, an immobile earth at the cosmic center, it still did not conclusively prove the heliocentric hypothesis, a sun-centered cosmos. Further empirical observations and theoretical speculations from the late 1700s to the early 1900s engendered a "Great Debate" in cosmology. This debate eventuated in overturning two centuries of scientific consensus around the heliocentric hypothesis: the sun is not the immobile cosmic center; our solar system orbits one galaxy among many galaxies in a vast, expanding cosmos.[41]

From Galileo's Debate to Our Debate

Scientific advance over three centuries rejected *both* cosmological hypotheses debated in Galileo's day: *neither* earth *nor* sun is immobile at the cosmic center. The current scientific consensus is that the cosmos does not even have a center. Galileo was not nearly as right about the cosmos as he thought, or we tend to think, he was.

This complex history of hypotheses prompts an exercise in hypothetical history. Suppose that the church in the 1600s, facing a revolution in cosmology, rather than censuring belief in heliocentric cosmology as heresy and silencing Galileo as a heretic, had sided with Galileo and adopted heliocentric cosmology as official doctrine, reinterpreting Scripture accordingly. Then the church in the 1900s, facing a new revolution in cosmology, would have had to change doctrine and revise interpretation again to fit the newest hypothesis—or resist scientific advance to save its older view.

---

41. See Crowe, *Modern Theories of the Universe.*

At present, there is ongoing scientific debate concerning sexual orientation within the fields of biology and psychology. There is no conclusive evidence and no scientific consensus concerning the causes of same-sex orientation.[42] There are competing hypotheses of various causes and a common conjecture that some mix of biological factors and environmental influences likely contributes to same-sex orientation.[43] There is ample evidence that some gay persons, particularly women, experience variability in their sexuality across their lives.[44]

Scientific research into sexual orientation is a relatively recent endeavor, and studies have yielded varying and conflicting results. It is quite possible that, as happened in cosmology, further research could overturn current conjecture. Were the church today to interpret Scripture and discern doctrine according to one or another hypothesis about sexual orientation, the church tomorrow could find itself facing a choice: reverse course or resist science.

Lessons for Discernment

Historical perspective cautions the church against hitching biblical interpretation and doctrinal discernment to the current state of scientific research. It is prudent, as Augustine and Galileo counseled, for the church to interpret Scripture in a manner that avoids dogmatically deciding between competing scientific hypotheses, unless basic Christian doctrine—faith or morals—is at stake. The question of biology versus environment in human sexuality does not concern basic Christian doctrine any more than did the question of geocentric versus heliocentric in cosmic structure.

In his handbook on Christian doctrine, Augustine taught that scientific theories about natural phenomena, which are limited and tentative, are not the proper object of Christian faith.

> When, then, the question is asked what we are to believe in regard to religion, it is not necessary to probe into the nature of things, . . . nor need we be in alarm lest the Christian should be ignorant of the force and number of the elements—the motion, and order, and eclipses of the heavenly bodies; the form of the heavens; the species and natures of animals, plants, stones . . . and a thousand other things which those philosophers have found out, or think they have found out. . . . It is enough for the Christian to believe that the only cause

42. See American Psychological Association, "Sexual Orientation & Homosexuality."
43. For an accessible assessment of research up to 2010, see Yarhouse, *Homosexuality and the Christian*, 57–80. For two review articles of research up to 2016, see Bailey et al., "Sexual Orientation, Controversy, and Science"; Mayer and McHugh, "Sexuality and Gender."
44. See Diamond, *Sexual Fluidity*.

of all created things, whether heavenly or earthly, whether visible or invisible, is the goodness of the Creator, the one true God.[45]

Rather than knowing the causes of this effect or that phenomenon in nature, Augustine went on, what is essential to the Christian life is "to know the causes of good and evil as far as man may in this life know them, in order to avoid the mistakes and troubles of which this life is so full."[46]

Scientific theories, whether about cosmic structure or human sexuality, are not themselves matters of Christian faith (what we are to believe) or morals (how we are to live). Whether the sun orbits the earth or the earth orbits the sun is not itself a matter of faith. Christian faith concerns trust in the God who created the heavens and the earth, not theories of the structure of the heavens or the composition of the earth. Likewise, whether sexual orientation is caused by biological factors, environmental influences, or some combination thereof is not itself a matter of morals. Christian morals concern voluntary choice in sexual conduct, not involuntary experience of sexual attraction. As Augustine observed, the Christian life within this fallen world will always be attended by persisting propensities toward what is evil and unbidden desires for what is sinful (whether longings for revenge or yearnings for illicit sex). What matters for the moral life in this mortal body is whether we willingly yield our consent or, with God's help, refuse our consent to such propensities and desires, whatever their proximate cause.[47]

Because the causation question in sexual orientation does not concern faith or morals, it is unnecessary for the church to take sides in this scientific debate. Because this scientific debate is entangled in cultural and political dispute, it would be unwise for the church to adopt one among the competing hypotheses. Because scientific hypotheses on this question are susceptible to future shifts, it would be imprudent to reinterpret Scripture and revise doctrine according to this or that current hypothesis. This caution pertains to both traditionalists and innovationists.

Caution for Traditionalists

Some traditionalists seize on hypotheses about environmental influences on same-sex attraction (especially psychoanalytic theories about distant fathers, sexual abuse, etc.). On the premise that same-sex-attracted persons "become this way," they argue that such influences are reversible and advocate

45. Augustine, *Enchiridion* 9.
46. Augustine, *Enchiridion* 16.
47. Augustine, *City of God* 12.23.

orientation-change therapies.[48] Traditionalists should beware such thinking. Even if same-sex attractions were caused by environmental influences and are alterable by psychotherapeutic interventions, it would not follow that the church should favor orientation change for all same-sex-attracted believers.

Some participants in such therapies might experience some change in sexual attraction, in degree or direction; most participants experience little or no change. Many participants report emotional and spiritual harm, from frustration and disappointment to trauma, leading some to doubt God, deceive others, or even harm themselves.[49] Such evidence is reason enough to eschew orientation-change therapies as a matter of pastoral care and professional ethics.

The theological point I wish to emphasize here would stand even were such therapies generally effective and harmless. Making orientation change the favored course for same-sex-attracted believers would mistake heterosexuality for chastity. Heterosexuality is neither sufficient nor necessary for chastity. First, heterosexuality does not ensure chastity. As a generic category of human sexuality, heterosexuality is compatible with varieties of promiscuity. Second, chastity does not need heterosexuality. Rachel Gilson, a same-sex-attracted Christian, writes: "Slowly, I came to understand that 'making me straight' wasn't the answer. There is no biblical command to be heterosexual."[50] Consider the fact that some persons experience no sexual attraction, or even experience aversion to sexual relations, whether opposite-sex or same-sex, a phenomenon known as asexuality. Asexual persons, too, are called by the gospel to follow Jesus and be renewed by the Spirit. Yet the goal of an asexual person's conversion and reformation as a Christian is surely not to acquire a certain direction or degree of sexual attraction or to overcome aversion to sexual relations. "Heterosexuality is not the end goal," writes Gilson; rather, "faithfulness to God, and the joy that comes from relationship with him, is what we run for."[51]

Third, as Gilson indicates, the criterion of chastity is not attraction to humans but faithfulness to God and obedience to Jesus. Christopher Yuan, an evangelical theologian who experiences same-sex attraction, elaborates this point: "God never said, 'Be heterosexual, for I am heterosexual.' He said, 'Be holy, for I am holy.' . . . Holy sexuality is not focused on orientation change—becoming straight—but on obedience."[52] More important than one's

---

48. See Rueger, *Sexual Morality in a Christless World*, 135–48.
49. See Dehlin et al., "Sexual Orientation Change Efforts"; Jones and Yarhouse, *Ex-Gays?*
50. Gilson, "I Never Became Straight," 53.
51. Gilson, "I Never Became Straight," 54.
52. Yuan and Yuan, *Out of a Far Country*, 187. See also Yuan, *Holy Sexuality and the Gospel*, 43–52.

sexual orientation this way or that way is one's spiritual disposition toward, or away from, God. Greg Johnson, a Presbyterian pastor who still wages "a constant battle for sexual holiness" many years after coming to faith, testifies: "While sexuality has a degree of fluidity in some people, the real change for me has not been in my sexual orientation but in my life orientation. Jesus has rescued me. That's everything."[53] Traditionalists should beware preaching a "heterosexual gospel" that substitutes the misguided goal of orientation change for the good news of God's grace.[54]

Caution for Innovationists

Some innovationists emphasize evidence of biological factors in same-sex orientation. On the premise that same-sex-oriented persons are "born this way," they argue that same-sex orientation is God's good creation and thus advocate biblical reinterpretation and doctrinal revision.[55] Innovationists should beware such thinking. Even if same-sex orientation were entirely innate, it would not follow that the church should sanction same-sex union.

Consider another example. Some men, straight and gay, seem innately inclined to seek sex with multiple partners, serially or simultaneously. Innate inclination to multiple sexual partners appears to be a naturally occurring variation in male humans. Some researchers in sociobiology have claimed that male humans have a biological tendency toward promiscuity, a disposition derived from evolution and driven by genetics. Sociobiological explanations have received scientific criticism. Even were such explanations scientifically correct, it would not warrant changing moral norms of sexual conduct: it would not justify excusing infidelity or sanctioning nonmonogamy so that men might follow innate inclinations for multiple partners. The fact that some humans are born with certain dispositions does not prove that acting on such dispositions is deserving of moral approval.

More than scientific explanation, moral wisdom needs biblical-theological perspective. The gospel announces the hope of a creation liberated from sin and death. Yet the gospel acknowledges the reality of a creation in chains. All creation, including our sexuate bodies, was "subjected to futility" and will gain fully the "freedom of the glory of the children of God" when all creation is finally liberated by Christ. Until then, we "groan inwardly" and wait patiently for "the redemption of our bodies" (Rom. 8:18–25). Christ has died and risen—and we look for Christ's coming again, when we will be

---

53. G. Johnson, "I Used to Hide My Shame."
54. See J. Perry, *Gay Girl, Good God*, 177–90.
55. See Via, "Bible, the Church, and Homosexuality," 29–39; Keen, *Scripture, Ethics, and the Possibility of Same-Sex Relationships*, 83–100.

raised with glorified bodies and Christ will destroy death, when all things will be subjected to Christ and God is "all in all" (1 Cor. 15:20–57). Even among baptized believers, having an innate disposition does not, by itself, justify behaving as one is innately disposed. Although we have been washed in the waters, our mortal bodies await redemption by resurrection. The native dispositions of our unredeemed bodies are not perfect indicators of God's will and thus are not reliable guides for right conduct. Even if we diagnose a disposition as due to natural causes, therefore, we must discern whether acting on that disposition might be compatible with God's will.

Karen Keen advocates that we see same-sex orientation not as a fallen condition, evidence of the "futility" of creation, but as a naturally occurring human variation and thus as a diverse part of God's creation.[56] Keen appeals to Augustine's view of congenital deformities and abnormalities and applies it to same-sex orientation. Augustine argued that "monstrous births" (e.g., humans born with additional appendages or both male and female features) should be viewed not as mistakes in creation but as ordered by God's providence and woven into the whole by God's wisdom, even if we cannot comprehend it.[57] So we might see same-sex orientation, Keen suggests.

Augustine's view does not favor the perspective Keen advocates, however. Augustine acknowledged that those abnormally born are human beings, yet he distinguished congenital deformities from the created good of the sexuate body. Whereas congenital deformities evidence the "penal condition" of mortal life, Augustine maintained, the resurrection will restore the created body to perfection. This bodily perfection will preserve the essential nature of the created body, including bodily gender (male and female), but will remove every bodily defect and deformity, including "the rare and the monstrous," which are "utterly incongruous with the future felicity of the saints."[58] Applying Augustine's view, then, implies that same-sex orientation, unlike the created sexes, evidences the fallen condition of human bodies and thus will not be preserved in the resurrection age.

Some traditionalists, appealing to hypotheses about environmental influences, see same-sex attraction as subject to the will and changeable through choices.[59] Some innovationists, appealing to hypotheses about biological factors, see same-sex orientation as determined by the body and ordained of

56. Keen, *Scripture, Ethics, and the Possibility of Same-Sex Relationships*, 97–99.

57. Augustine, *City of God* 16.8.

58. Augustine, *City of God* 22.17, 19.

59. Some traditionalists eschew not only psychoanalytic explanations but all scientific explanations of same-sex attraction in favor of a purely theological diagnosis—see Yuan, *Holy Sexuality and the Gospel*, 35–38, 40–42.

God.[60] From a scientific perspective, neither position has conclusive support for its premise. From a theological perspective, both positions miss the mark: sexual orientation is not the defining criterion of sexual chastity; natural causation is not the decisive question for moral discernment.[61]

Our Thinking Is Not What It Used to Be: Cases of Slavery and Women's Ministry

The Argument: The Abolitionists and Liberationists Were Right

I now consider changes in Christian views and practices in recent centuries concerning slavery and women. In the case of slavery, during the eighteenth and nineteenth centuries, the Western church shifted from centuries of tolerating, even justifying, slavery to organized movements advocating abolition and official declarations condemning slavery. In the case of women, during the twentieth and twenty-first centuries, the Western church, in many denominations, has shifted from centuries of restricting women to certain roles, mainly domestic and monastic, toward greater recognition of women's gifts and participation of women in public ministry and, in some denominations, even ordination of women to church offices.

Considering such changes, some innovationists argue as follows: Scripture, everyone acknowledges, proscribes same-sex intercourse, which the church also has always forbidden. Yet Scripture also allows slavery and patriarchy, which the church also has allowed. The church today denying blessing to same-sex union for biblical reasons is akin to the church yesterday justifying slavery and patriarchy for biblical reasons. Just as the church yesterday was wrong on slavery and patriarchy, the argument continues, so likewise the church today is wrong on marriage. Just as the church had misinterpreted Scripture to justify and tolerate slavery and patriarchy, so the church has misinterpreted Scripture to judge and exclude same-sex union. Therefore, the argument concludes, just as the church yesterday was right to reinterpret Scripture and revise its views on race and gender in favor of liberating slaves and women, so likewise the church today would be right to reinterpret Scripture and revise its doctrine of marriage in favor of sanctioning same-sex union.[62] An innovationist might

---

60. Some innovationists emphasize cultural factors or social conditioning in sexuality—see Vasey, *Strangers and Friends*, 141–59; Stuart, *Just Good Friends*, 178–81. Other innovationists are skeptical of explanatory theorizing about sexual orientation—see Thatcher, *Liberating Sex*, 129–33.

61. See also N. Collins, *All but Invisible*, 184–86.

62. See Achtemeier, *Bible's Yes to Same-Sex Marriage*, 19–20; Brownson, *Bible, Gender, Sexuality*, 61–63, 105–6, 213–14, 251–52, 275–77; Gushee, *Changing Our Mind*, 160–62; L. Johnson,

make a further argument: the same pattern of biblical interpretation used to defend slavery was then used to justify patriarchy and is now being used to prevent sanction of same-sex union.[63]

The cases of slaves and women present the church with challenging hermeneutical issues as well as important theological and ethical questions. Scholars have examined the hermeneutical issues in these cases from canonical, historical, and cultural perspectives.[64] I will focus on comparisons between each of these cases and the question of same-sex union, taking them in turn.[65]

Comparison to Slavery

This comparison makes an appeal to marriage traditionalists: Because you oppose slavery on a biblical basis, you should accept same-sex union on a biblical basis. The Old Testament gives laws for regulating slavery and the New Testament gives rules for masters and slaves. So if you would condemn slavery despite biblical laws that allow slavery, then why not allow same-sex union despite biblical laws that condemn same-sex intercourse?

I will approach this case in three steps: first, a historical review that constructs a parallel between the patristic and abolition eras concerning slavery; second, a restatement of the innovationist argument comparing uses of Scripture in supporting slavery and opposing same-sex union; third, a critical evaluation of that comparison.

Case Reviewed

Early Christian theologians viewed slavery as a consequence of sin: it was not so from the beginning and is contrary to created order. While some saw slavery as God's just punishment on sinful humankind, others saw slavery as an undesirable but ineradicable part of human society.[66] Early church practice tended to assume the legal institution of slavery in Roman society and accommodate the social fact of slaves in Christian households.[67] Church

---

"Scripture and Experience"; Loader, "Homosexuality and the Bible," 47; Song, *Covenant and Calling*, 72–76; Thatcher, *Liberating Sex*, 15–16; Vines, *God and the Gay Christian*, 15.

63. See J. Rogers, *Jesus, the Bible, and Homosexuality*, 17–34.

64. See Swartley, *Slavery, Sabbath, War, and Women*; Webb, *Slaves, Women and Homosexuals*.

65. Song, *Covenant and Calling*, 76–80, appeals to the church's acceptance of just war, in apparent contradiction to gospel teaching, as precedent: if "love neighbor" can justify war, despite Jesus's command "love enemies," why can't love justify love? While I appreciate the irony, this appeal gains little traction with me: as an Anabaptist, I dissent from just war on account of Jesus's teaching, which also is a central reason I maintain a traditional view of marriage (see chap. 4).

66. See Augustine *City of God* 19.15; Chrysostom, *Sixth Sermon on Lazarus*, in *On Wealth and Poverty*, 112–15.

67. See Fox, *Pagans and Christians*, 295–99.

rules allowed both masters and slaves to be catechized and baptized. Masters were admonished to be mindful of God in how they treated slaves; but unlike pimps, prostitutes, idol makers, and gladiators, who were required to desist or be rejected as catechumens, masters were not mandated to manumit slaves as prerequisite to baptism. Slaves of believing masters were admitted for baptism only on their masters' approval.[68] A second-century bishop advised another bishop against using church funds to buy freedom for believing slaves because, he said, they might become "slaves of lust."[69] A fourth-century preacher rebuked Christian masters in his congregation not because slavery is inherently unjust but for excessive slaveholding and mistreating slaves.[70] A fourth-century synod of bishops anathematized Christians who would encourage slaves "under pretext of piety" to repudiate their masters and leave their service.[71] A sixth-century pope counseled pastors to give spiritual advice to masters and servants in ways appropriate to each: a master should recognize that he is fallen and subject to the Lord just as his servants are; a servant should remember his humble position before his master and the Lord.[72]

Early Christian sources that evidence accommodation of slavery cited Scripture in support of this practice. Church rules concerning masters and slaves quoted the New Testament, typically Paul's instructions that believing slaves, whether in pagan or Christian households, should "obey [their] earthly masters" (Eph. 6:5–8; Col. 3:22–25; cf. 1 Tim. 6:1–2; Titus 2:9–10).[73] Some Christian writers observed the tension between the practice of slavery and other New Testament texts, such as Jesus's command "Love your neighbor as yourself" (Matt. 22:39; Mark 12:31) and Paul's gospel that in Christ "there is no longer slave or free" (Gal. 3:26–28; cf. Col. 3:11), and argued that, were Christ obeyed and the gospel lived, slavery would be no more. Yet Jesus had not ruled on the matter; and Paul did not command believing masters, not even Philemon, to manumit slaves as their Christian duty. In practice, then, Paul's rule that believing slaves, like believers married to unbelievers, should "remain in the condition in which [they] were called" (1 Cor. 7:17–24), became the default rule of the early church.

The abolition debate of the eighteenth and nineteenth centuries evidences Christians on both sides citing Scripture to make either proslavery

68. See Didache 4.10–11; Apostolic Tradition 15–16; Testament of the Lord 2.1–2.
69. Ignatius, *To Polycarp* 4.3, in M. Holmes, *Apostolic Fathers*, 197.
70. See Kelly, *Golden Mouth*, 99–100.
71. *Canons of the Holy Fathers Assembled at Gangra*, canon 3 (*NPNF*[2] 14:93).
72. Gregory the Great, *Book of Pastoral Rule* 3.5.
73. On Paul's "household code," see appendix B in the online supplement.

or antislavery arguments.[74] The proslavery case followed three main lines of argument. First, the biblical patriarchs sanctioned slavery: Noah cursed Ham's son, Canaan, to be slave of his brothers (Gen. 9:25), thus prophesying the subjugation of Africans to Americans; and Abraham, our father in faith, owned slaves, circumcised slaves, received slaves, and bequeathed slaves (12:5; 15:3; etc.), all of which, Scripture says, was God's blessing. Second, biblical law permitted and regulated slavery: Israelites were permitted to acquire slaves from foreign peoples as permanent, inheritable property (Lev. 25:44–46); and Israelites were permitted to sell their service to fellow Israelites or resident aliens for limited times, subject to rules of proper treatment (Exod. 21:1–11; Lev. 25:39–43, 47–55; Deut. 15:12–18). Third, the New Testament upholds slavery: Jesus never spoke against slavery, a common reality of his time; the apostles exhorted slaves to remain in their station and obey their masters; they exhorted masters to not mistreat slaves but never ordered them to free slaves (1 Cor. 7:17–24; Eph. 6:5–9; Col. 3:22–4:1; 1 Tim. 6:1–2; Titus 2:9–10; Philemon; 1 Pet. 2:18–19).

The antislavery case also followed three main lines of argument. First, neither the patriarchal practice of slavery nor the biblical regulation of slavery can justify slavery in the United States: Africans are not descendants of Canaan, so Noah's curse is irrelevant (Gen. 10:15–20); Abraham's servants were respected members of the household, and voluntary servitude among Israelites was a merciful and benevolent institution; there is little similarity and much disparity between those ancient practices, which hardly deserve to be called slavery, and this cruel, inhumane system of chattel slavery. Second, the history of Israel points away from slavery and toward freedom: God's liberation of the Israelites from slavery in Egypt indicates God's will against slavery and reminds God's people why neither permanent servitude of Israelites nor oppression of resident aliens is permitted (Exod. 22:21; 23:8; Lev. 25:42–43, 55; Deut. 15:15); God's prophets called upon God's people "to loose the bonds of injustice, undo the thongs of the yoke, and let the oppressed go free" (Isa. 58:6) and prophesied about God's servant who would "bring good news to the oppressed" and "proclaim liberty to the captives" (61:1). Third, neither Jesus nor the apostles ever approved of slavery: Jesus's silence proves that he approved of slavery no more than it proves that he approved of gladiatorial games or Bacchanalian orgies; the apostles did not legislate in favor of slavery but devised rules for households that appealed to both masters and slaves as fellow Christians; moreover, the teachings of Jesus and the apostles would, if put fully into practice, lead to slavery's abolition.

---

74. The next two paragraphs summarize Swartley, *Slavery, Sabbath, War, and Women*, 31–46.

This historical review exhibits similarities between the patristic era and the abolition era as well as differences between proslavery and antislavery arguments in the abolition debate. A similarity: both patristic-era rules accommodating slavery and abolition-era arguments defending slavery relied extensively, if not exclusively, on several texts of the New Testament, in which the apostles instructed believing slaves to obey their masters and believing masters to be mindful of God, to support their respective positions. A difference: whereas church rules accommodating slavery and arguments defending slavery cited particular texts in Scripture concerning relations between masters and slaves, abolitionist arguments appealed to the big story and general message of Scripture. The abolitionist appeal to the big story of Scripture highlighted creation of humankind in God's image, deliverance of Israel from bondage, prophecy of freedom to captives, and the gospel of salvation in Christ. The abolitionist appeal to the general message of Scripture emphasized principles of justice and righteousness, love and equality. From the abolitionist perspective, the debate pitted the antislavery "spirit" of Scripture against the proslavery "letter" of Scripture.[75]

Comparison Restated

In light of this historical review, I will restate the innovationist argument comparing the cases of slavery and same-sex union, in two parts. First, by using Scripture to oppose same-sex union in the church today, traditionalist arguments assume that the same-sex relationships for which innovationists advocate are morally equivalent to the same-sex activities which Scripture condemns. The biblical sex laws and vice lists cited by traditionalist arguments are applicable to the same-sex-union question only if the kinds of sexual activities that those laws and lists condemned are comparable to the kind of sexual relationships for which same-sex couples are seeking blessing. However, the ancient worlds of Leviticus and Romans knew only of same-sex practices involving hierarchical, abusive, exploitive relationships that we would condemn today and knew nothing of the mutual, loving, committed same-sex partnerships that we see today—such that Leviticus and Romans do not apply to our question. Moreover, the stories of Sodom (Gen. 19) and Gibeah (Judg. 19) involve gang rape, not consensual sex, and thus bear no resemblance to committed same-sex partnerships. Because the sexual activities that Scripture condemns are not morally comparable to the same-sex relationships that innovationists affirm, traditionalist appeals to biblical texts concerning same-sex intercourse are inappropriate to discerning the question of same-sex union.

75. See Noll, *Civil War as a Theological Crisis*, 33–45.

Traditionalist arguments present same-sex union in relation to Scripture, therefore, in the same way that proslavery arguments presented slavery in relation to Scripture. Just as proslavery arguments presented the chattel slavery of the American South as comparable to the forms of slavery referred to in Scripture and thus justified by the slavery laws in Scripture, so also traditionalist arguments present the same-sex relationships that innovationists affirm as comparable to the forms of sexual activity referred to in Scripture and thus condemned by the sex laws and vice lists in Scripture. Yet just as the kind of slavery in the American South bore no resemblance to the forms of slavery referenced in Scripture, so also the kind of same-sex relationships in the church today bear no resemblance to the forms of same-sex practices referenced in Scripture. Biblical opponents of same-sex union, like biblical defenders of slavery, apply biblical texts directly to our question while ignoring the wide gap between the biblical world and our world.

Second, when constructing arguments against same-sex union, traditionalists mostly cite scattered texts from Scripture that specifically concern, or apparently concern, same-sex intercourse. These citations typically include Old Testament stories that depict same-sex intercourse as depraved (Gen. 19; Judg. 19) and laws that forbid same-sex intercourse as detestable (Lev. 18:22; 20:13) plus New Testament texts that list same-sex intercourse among the moral vices (Rom. 1:26–27; 1 Cor. 6:9; 1 Tim. 1:10). Traditionalists sometimes add citations from Old and New Testaments that present marriage as between a man and a woman (Gen. 1–2; Matt. 19:3–12; Mark 10:2–12; Eph. 5:22–33). David Gushee, reconstructing "how traditionalists connect the biblical dots," claims that "the most commonly cited texts on the issue from the traditionalist side . . . are derived from 11 of the 1,189 chapters in the Bible."[76]

Traditionalists use Scripture to condemn same-sex union, therefore, in the same way that Scripture was used to defend slavery. Just as proslavery arguments relied primarily on scattered texts that specifically concern masters and slaves, so also traditionalist arguments rely primarily on scattered texts that specifically concern same-sex intercourse. And just as proslavery arguments neglected the big story and general message of Scripture, which favors liberation and justice and thus counters oppression and slavery, so also traditionalist arguments neglect the big story and general message of Scripture that culminates in the gospel of Jesus, which favors love and inclusion and thus counters judgment and exclusion of same-sex relationships. Biblical opponents of same-sex union, like biblical defenders of slavery, connect the "biblical dots" while missing the "biblical picture."

76. Gushee, *Changing Our Mind*, 55–57.

Marriage traditionalists who oppose same-sex union on biblical grounds are thus in the same position, hermeneutically if not morally, as those who defended slavery on biblical grounds. Insofar as one opposes slavery on biblical grounds, therefore, one should also, for the sake of consistency, support same-sex union on biblical grounds.

Comparison Assessed

Comparing the cases of same-sex union and slavery is less compelling than it might seem. First, some scholars and various innovationists have made claims across decades that the same-sex partnerships seeking blessing in today's church do not in any way resemble same-sex practices found in the biblical world. In today's church, we are being asked to sanction the covenantal unions of committed partners. In the worlds of Leviticus and Romans, by contrast, same-sex intercourse occurred only in hierarchical relationships such as man-boy pairings or master-slave pairings, or only in exploitive practices such as cultic prostitution and market prostitution. From this historical claim these innovationists draw a hermeneutical conclusion: Scripture's scattered references to same-sex intercourse are irrelevant to our question of same-sex union.[77]

Such historical claims have received serious scholarly criticism. Historical research in recent decades has exhibited a variety of sources—Greek, Roman, and Jewish; literary and artistic—that evidence consensual, mutual same-sex practices, even loving, lifelong same-sex partnerships, existing in the Greco-Roman world alongside the hierarchical and exploitive practices of pederasty, prostitution, and master-slave sex. It is not only possible that Paul was aware of such relationships but also plausible that he had such relationships in mind, in addition to abusive practices, when he described same-sex relations as "unnatural" (Rom. 1:26–27). The hermeneutical argument that Scripture's references to same-sex intercourse are irrelevant to our question of same-sex union thus falls flat along with the historical claim by which it is buttressed.[78]

Second, a traditionalist view need not employ the hermeneutic strategy of the proslavery arguments. The hermeneutic strategy of the abolitionist argument, moreover, is not incompatible with a traditionalist view and thus does not necessarily favor an innovationist view. One could even argue that

---

77. Most famously, Scroggs, *New Testament and Homosexuality*, followed by Achtemeier, *Bible's Yes to Same-Sex Marriage*; Brownson, *Bible, Gender, Sexuality*; Helminiak, *What the Bible Really Says about Homosexuality*; Thatcher, *Liberating Sex*; K. Wilson, *Letter to My Congregation*; and others.

78. For discussion of same-sex love in Greco-Roman culture, see appendixes D and E in the online supplement.

the abolitionist hermeneutic applied to the same-sex-union question fits well with a traditionalist view.

The abolitionist hermeneutic looked to the big story and general message of Scripture and read the several texts about slavery in relation to the larger biblical frame. In the question of same-sex union, whereas the "biblical dots" are the several texts referring to same-sex intercourse, the "biblical picture" appropriate to the question is that of marriage. A traditionalist argument following the abolitionist hermeneutic would begin with the "biblical picture" of marriage and then consider how the "biblical dots" referring to same-sex intercourse fit within that larger frame. The big story of Scripture—creation, fall, redemption, and new creation—exhibits the biblical picture of marriage. From the marriage of man and woman in creation (Gen. 1–2) to the marriage of Christ and the church in new creation (Rev. 21–22), the big story of Scripture exhibits a single picture of marriage: male-female union.

Scripture's depiction of marriage sets the larger frame within which to see the "biblical dots" referencing same-sex intercourse. Richard Hays writes: "From Genesis 1 onward, Scripture affirms repeatedly that God has made man and woman for one another and that our sexual desires rightly find fulfillment within heterosexual marriage. . . . This normative canonical picture of marriage provides the positive backdrop against which the Bible's few emphatic negations of [homosexual practices] must be read."[79] Just as the biblical story exhibits a single, positive appraisal of male-female union, so also the biblical canon presents a single, negative appraisal of same-sex intercourse. Scripture's negative assessment of same-sex intercourse is sustained consistently

- across both Old Testament (Lev. 18:2–30; 20:13) and New Testament (Rom. 1:18–32; 1 Cor. 6:9–11; 1 Tim. 1:8–11) canonical contexts;
- against both ancient Near Eastern and Greco-Roman cultural backgrounds, each of which tolerated same-sex practices;[80]
- regarding both male-male (Leviticus; Romans; 1 Corinthians; 1 Timothy) and female-female (Romans) sexual intercourse; and
- regarding both possibly exploitive practices (1 Corinthians; 1 Timothy) and mutual relations (Leviticus; Romans).[81]

79. Hays, *Moral Vision of the New Testament*, 390.

80. On same-sex practices and the Old Testament, see Nissinen, *Homoeroticism in the Biblical World*, 19–56; Wold, *Out of Order*, 27–158. On same-sex practices in Greco-Roman culture, see Nissinen, *Homoeroticism in the Biblical World*, 57–88; Harper, *From Shame to Sin*, 22–37.

81. For detailed discussions of Romans, 1 Corinthians, and Leviticus, see appendixes E, F, and G, respectively, in the online supplement.

Just as the biblical witness to marriage as male-female union is uniformly positive, so also the biblical assessment of same-sex intercourse is univocally negative. The "biblical dots" referencing same-sex intercourse thus connect consistently to each other and fit coherently with the "biblical picture" of marriage.[82]

To conclude: First, there is a significant difference regarding the biblical evidence in the respective cases. In the case of slavery, we find texts accommodating slavery and texts advocating liberating captives; in the case of same-sex union, by contrast, we find only texts prohibiting same-sex intercourse. In the case of slavery, biblical texts that accommodate slavery stand in tension with the biblical story of redemption and biblical principles of justice; in the case of same-sex union, by contrast, biblical texts that prohibit same-sex intercourse stand together with the biblical picture of male-female union that is interwoven throughout the biblical story of salvation. Second, there is a surprising similarity between abolitionist and traditionalist views from a hermeneutical perspective. The abolitionist hermeneutic on slavery applied to the question of same-sex union fits well with a traditionalist view on marriage. That the abolitionists were on the right side of the slavery question thus does not imply that traditionalists are on the wrong side, or that innovationists are on the right side, of the same-sex-union question.

Comparison to Women's Ministry

Women and Scripture is a many-faceted issue that ranges across the biblical canon. To work with a manageable comparison suitable to our purpose, I will focus on the specific case of women's ministry.[83] I will again take a three-step approach.

While marriage traditionalists agree with the whole church in condemning slavery, the whole church does not agree on women's ministry. Nor are marriage traditionalists of one mind on this issue. Whereas the previous comparison appealed to all marriage traditionalists, this comparison appeals to those marriage traditionalists who support the ministry of women as equal to that of men in the church: if you would accept women's ministry, then you should accept same-sex union. The Bible says women should not exercise any authority over men or even speak in church. So if you would set aside biblical rules on women's roles and ordain women to serve equally with men in ministry, then why not set aside biblical laws on same-sex intercourse and bless

---

82. The consistent witness of Scripture is continued in the consistent teaching of tradition—see Fortson and Grams, *Unchanging Witness*.

83. On the relation of men and women in marriage and household, see appendix B in the online supplement.

same-sex couples equally with male-female couples? Because I am married to an ordained minister, this comparison appeals to me in a personal way.

Case Reviewed

Early church sources evidence rules and views that restricted women's roles in church ministry and forbade women's ordination to church offices.[84] Church orders of the third and fourth centuries, East and West, affirmed women in recognized roles—virgins and widows—and typically specified that virgins and widows were appointed but not ordained, either because they do not offer the Eucharist or because ordination is for men. Ordination (i.e., the laying on of hands) is typically reserved for offices of bishop, presbyter, and deacon, which were typically restricted to men. Church orders typically viewed virgins and widows as laypersons, distinguishing them from the clergy. They were supported by the church and approved for ministries of prayer for the church and service to the sick and poor, while the functions of teaching, preaching, baptizing, and offering the Eucharist were reserved to men.[85] A fourth-century synod of bishops forbade appointment of women as presbyters or presidents and ruled that "women may not go to the altar," which in effect prevented women from offering or assisting in the Eucharist.[86] Patristic-era theologians also argued that women were forbidden roles reserved to men. Tertullian, in the third century, stated his rule for a woman's role: "It is not permitted to a woman to speak in the church; but neither is it permitted her to teach, nor to baptize, nor to offer [the Eucharist], nor to claim to herself a lot in any manly function, not to say in any sacerdotal office."[87] Chrysostom, in the fourth century, argued that women should be excluded from the priesthood and episcopacy on the grounds that women could not prove capable of the role: "The other things I have mentioned [i.e., fasting and praying, defending victims, caring for orphans] could easily be carried out by many of those under authority, women as well as men. But when someone has to preside over the Church and be entrusted with the care of so many souls, then let all womankind give way before the magnitude of the task—and indeed most men."[88]

Early Christian sources that restricted women's roles in church ministries cited Scripture in support of such practices. Typically, these sources cite Paul's

---

84. See Gryson, *Ministry of Women in the Early Church*.

85. See Apostolic Tradition 10–14; *Didascalia apostolorum* 14–15; Apostolic Constitutions 3.1.

86. *Canons of the Synod Held in the City of Laodicea*, canons 11 and 44 (NPNF² 14:129, 153).

87. Tertullian, *On the Veiling of Virgins* 9 (ANF 4:33).

88. Chrysostom, *Six Books on the Priesthood* 2.2, 54. Chrysostom's high praises of Junia, Phoebe, and Prisca in his later homilies, it seems to me, belie this earlier judgment.

rules that women are not permitted to either speak or teach in the church (1 Cor. 14:34–35; 1 Tim. 2:11–12). The Apostolic Constitutions, which forbade women to teach or preach, cited Paul's rule—"We do not permit our 'women to teach in the church,' but only to pray and hear those that teach"— and added that Jesus "did nowhere send out women to preach."[89] Tertullian, quoted above, cited Paul's rule—"It is not permitted to a woman to speak in the church; but neither is it permitted her to teach"—and extended it to exclude women from all priestly functions of administering sacraments. Chrysostom stated, "The divine law excluded women from this ministry [i.e., presbyter and bishop]," and he cited Paul's rule: "But they are women, the very ones who are not even allowed to teach. Do I say 'teach'? St. Paul did not allow them even to speak in church."[90]

The contemporary debate over women's ministry, between hierarchical and liberationist views, evidences both sides citing Scripture. A hierarchical view maintains that women are restricted from teaching or preaching publicly and may exercise leadership in the church only under the authority of men. Defenders of hierarchy typically appeal to those texts in Paul's letters that address women's participation in the worship and leadership of the church (1 Cor. 11:2–16; 14:34–36; 1 Tim. 2:11–12; 3:1–13). A liberationist view argues that spiritual gifts should determine who exercises which ministry functions in the church and that all leadership roles in the church should be open to women and men. Advocates of liberation typically appeal to Paul's baptismal formula, that in Christ "there is no longer male and female" (Gal. 3:26–28), arguing that this gospel declaration removes barriers of gender (along with ethnicity and class) in the church and thus qualifies any rule concerning relations between men and women in the church.[91]

There are three parallels between patristic-era practices and twentieth-century hierarchy regarding women's ministry. First, both patristic-era practices and twentieth-century hierarchy rely extensively, if not exclusively, on Paul's rule that women are not permitted to speak or teach in the church. Second, both read Paul's rule as God's law. Whereas Chrysostom called Paul's rule "the divine law," contemporary defenders of a hierarchical view see Paul's rule as issuing from "the will of God" and stating a "universally normative regulation" that is binding on the whole church at all times and places.[92] Third, both apply Paul's rule to all ministries of the church. Whereas Tertullian extended Paul's rule from preaching and teaching to baptizing and offering,

---

89. Apostolic Constitutions 3.1.6 (*ANF* 7:427).
90. Chrysostom, *Six Books on the Priesthood* 3.9, 78.
91. See Swartley, *Slavery, Sabbath, War, and Women*, 151, 164–74, 178–82.
92. Swartley, *Slavery, Sabbath, War, and Women*, 167–69.

contemporary defenders of hierarchy magnify Paul's rule that women pray and prophesy under male authority to require male leadership over every ministry function in the church.

Comparison Restated

In light of this historical review, I will restate the innovationist argument comparing the cases of women's ministry and same-sex union. Defenders of hierarchy construct their arguments against women serving equally with men in the ministry of the church mainly on the biblical basis of Paul's rules that restrict women from teaching or preaching, which they take to apply to all ministry and leadership in the church and to absolutely bind the whole church. Likewise, traditionalists construct their arguments against sanctioning same-sex union mainly on the biblical basis of laws and lists that condemn same-sex intercourse, which they take to prohibit same-sex relationships of any kind and to absolutely bind the whole church. Traditionalists use Scripture against same-sex union, therefore, in the same way that defenders of hierarchy use Scripture against women's ministry.

Marriage traditionalists who oppose sanction of same-sex union but support ordination of women are thus guilty of at least hermeneutical inconsistency if not moral hypocrisy. Insofar as one supports ordaining women, one should also, for the sake of consistency, support sanctioning same-sex union.

Comparison Assessed

Comparing the cases of same-sex union and women's ministry, also, is less compelling than it might seem. The consistency question raised by this comparison is whether there are biblical grounds for distinguishing these cases: Why, hermeneutically, treat biblical rules about women's ministry differently from biblical laws about same-sex intercourse? I will approach this question in two parts, each addressed to one side of the comparison. First, are there good reasons to interpret the biblical laws and lists that condemn same-sex intercourse as including all forms of same-sex intercourse and thus applying generally to same-sex relationships? Second, are there good reasons to interpret biblical rules restricting women's participation in the worship and leadership of the church as addressing particular circumstances and thus *not* applying universally to women's roles?

How to interpret biblical laws and lists condemning same-sex intercourse has been the subject of much debate over many decades. Some scholars and various innovationists have argued that these texts (Lev. 18:2–30; Rom. 1:18–32; 1 Cor. 6:9–11; 1 Tim. 1:8–11) are too distant in history, or too different in culture, or too narrow in scope, or too obscure in meaning to be useful or

consequential in the ethical discernment of the church today. I have undertaken my own examinations of these texts and their scholarly discussions.[93]
Based on the particulars of these texts, considering their canonical contexts
and historical backgrounds, I have reached my own conclusions, the upshot
of which I summarize here:

- The Holiness Code in Leviticus proscribes all male-male sexual intercourse, whether cultic or erotic, coercive or consensual, hierarchical
  or mutual, regardless of the age, status, role, or relation of the sexual
  partners.
- Paul's argument in Romans regards all same-sex intercourse as sinful,
  whether female-female or male-male, hierarchical or mutual, regardless of the social relations between or the sexual roles played by the
  respective partners.
- Paul's vice list in 1 Corinthians regards same-sex intercourse as inherently wrong and the ongoing practice of same-sex intercourse as
  morally incompatible with a Christian habit of life.

Although some scholars and many innovationists disagree with my conclusions, I concur with conclusions reached by some prominent scholars who
favor an innovationist view.[94] In any case, the arguments I present in support
of these conclusions provide good reasons to interpret these biblical laws and
lists as including all forms of same-sex intercourse and thus applying generally to same-sex relationships.

How to interpret Paul's rules concerning women's participation in the
worship and leadership of the church has also been the subject of much debate over many decades. I will proceed into this dispute by following the old
hermeneutical rule: read Scripture with Scripture. I thus begin with Paul's
statements about the ministries of the church and New Testament references
to women in ministry. I then offer observations about interpreting Paul's rules
concerning women's roles in light of these other texts.

At one place Paul elaborated "varieties of gifts" dispensed by the Spirit
for the ministries of the church (1 Cor. 12:4–6). He included a list of ministries: "And God has appointed in the church first apostles, second prophets,
third teachers; then gifts of healing, forms of assistance, forms of leadership,
various kinds of tongues" (12:28). Elsewhere Paul gave another list of the
several "gifts" that Christ has given for the ministries of the church: "The gifts

93. See appendixes E, F, and G in the online supplement.
94. See Brooten, *Love between Women*, 215–66; Loader, *Sexuality in the New Testament*, 7–34.

he gave were that some would be apostles, some prophets, some evangelists, some pastors and teachers, to equip the saints for the work of ministry, for building up the body of Christ" (Eph. 4:11–12).

Surveying the New Testament with this latter list in mind, one finds women named or described as exercising each of these gifts of ministry, including several in Paul's letters: Junia, apostle ("prominent among the apostles") in Rome (Rom. 16:7);[95] Anna, prophet in Jerusalem (Luke 2:36–38); the four daughters of Philip, prophets in Caesarea (Acts 21:8–9; cf. 2:17–18); Euodia and Syntyche, evangelists ("co-workers" who "struggled beside" Paul "in the gospel [*euangelion*]") in Philippi (Phil. 4:2–3; cf. 2:22); Nympha, pastor (house church leader) in Laodicea (Col. 4:15); Prisca, pastor (house church leader) in Rome and Ephesus (Rom. 16:3–5; 1 Cor. 16:19) and teacher of Apollos (Acts 18:24–26);[96] Lois and Eunice, teachers of Timothy (2 Tim. 1:5; 3:14–15). Paul also named several women—Mary, Tryphaena, Tryphosa, and Persis—as "workers" who had "worked hard" for the church (Rom. 16:6, 12). Paul described the labors of these women using the same Greek verb (*kopiaō*) used elsewhere regarding Paul's own labor to support his ministry (Acts 20:34–35) and the ministry of elders "who labor [*kopiōntes*] in preaching and teaching" (1 Tim. 5:17).

The New Testament also identifies what would later be recognized as three offices in the church: deacon, elder, and overseer. Paul mentioned "deacon" or "servant" (*diakonos*) at several places in his letters (Phil. 1:1; 1 Tim. 3:8–13; cf. Acts 6:1–6). Here, again, one finds Paul naming a woman exercising that office: Phoebe, "a deacon [*diakonon*] of the church at Cenchreae" and patron of Paul (Rom. 16:1–2).[97] Paul named Phoebe's ministry using the same word that he used elsewhere to name his own ministry and the ministries of Apollos, Tychicus, and Timothy (1 Cor. 3:5; Eph. 6:21; Col. 4:7; 1 Tim. 4:6), which implies that Phoebe's ministry was equal in standing to their ministries. Apostolic rules for deacons, moreover, could be read to imply that women were serving as deacons or in an office parallel to that of deacons (1 Tim. 3:8–13). The offices of "overseer" (*episkopos*) and "elder" (*presbyteros*) are not clearly distinguished in the New Testament (cf. Acts 20:17, 28; Titus 1:5–9). The New Testament names Peter and John as "elder" (1 Pet. 5:1; 2 John 1; 3 John 1), but otherwise names no one, man or woman, as overseer or elder. So the office of deacon was open to women in the early church, and the New Testament does not restrict the office of elder or overseer, or ordination to office (i.e., the laying on of hands), to men.

95. See Epp, *Junia*.
96. See Keller, *Priscilla and Aquila*.
97. See Campbell, *Phoebe*.

In my estimation, these biblical references compose a compelling case of cumulative evidence that women actually did exercise many gifts of ministry, including preaching and teaching, in the early church. Especially important is Paul's greeting to the believers in Rome: one-third (nine of twenty-seven) of those named are women, and Paul greeted them on account of their labor for the gospel and leadership among the house churches of Rome (Rom. 16:3–16).[98] Taken together, Paul's approving references to women exercising gifts of ministry establish a hermeneutical context within which I read Paul's rules about women's roles in the church (1 Cor. 11:2–16; 14:34–35; 1 Tim. 2:11–12; 3:11–13).[99]

I would argue that our interpretation of apostolic rules about the possible ministries of women in the church must recognize the full range of actual ministries of women in the New Testament. Because Scripture testifies that women actually did exercise many gifts of ministry in the early church and that Paul approved and praised these women, it was possible under Paul's rules of order for women to minister and lead in the church. Paul's rule concerning propriety in worship assumes that women were already and would continue praying and prophesying in parallel with men: "Any man who prays or prophesies . . . , but any woman who prays or prophesies . . ." (1 Cor. 11:4). To avoid reading Paul against Paul, interpretation of Paul's rules must account for the biblical facts of women's ministries. I thus conclude: Paul's rules should be read not as general prohibitions or universal regulations of women's ministry and leadership but as specific counsels addressing particular circumstances.[100]

This way of reading Paul's rules is not a hermeneutical innovation. It finds a fourth-century precedent in John Chrysostom, who acknowledged and honored women's ministries in the early church. In a homily on Romans, he said approvingly of Prisca's role as church leader: "For she had been so estimable as to make their house a Church, both by making all in it believers, and because they opened it to all strangers."[101] In a subsequent homily on Romans, Chrysostom elaborated Prisca's ministries of teaching and administration and then commented, remarkably, that many women in Paul's day shared the work of the apostles for the gospel and "performed all other ministries" in the church. Further on, Chrysostom gave due honor to Junia, the one woman Paul named as apostle: "Oh! how great is the devotion of this woman, that she should be even counted worthy of the appellation of apostle!"[102] In a

---

98. See Toews, *Romans*, 357–61.
99. See Verhey, *Remembering Jesus*, 193–206.
100. See also Keener, *Paul, Women, and Wives*, 17–132, 235–57.
101. Chrysostom, *Homily XXX on Romans* (NPNF[1] 11:550).
102. Chrysostom, *Homily XXXI on Romans* (NPNF[1] 11:554, 555).

homily while archbishop of Constantinople, moreover, Chrysostom praised Phoebe and Prisca and then commented: "And there was another large band of women at that time who shared in the apostolic life."[103] Chrysostom, apparently, attested that there were many women apostles in the early church.

Chrysostom, accordingly, took account of women's ministries in the early church when reading Paul's rules of church order. In light of Prisca's role as teacher, Chrysostom argued that we cannot read Paul's rule "I permit no woman to teach or to have authority over a man" (1 Tim. 2:12) as absolutely forbidding women from "the word of teaching," or even from teaching men—else, "How came Priscilla to instruct even Apollos?" Chrysostom thus read Paul's rule, in the ecclesiastical context of the fourth century, not generally to exclude women from the teaching ministry of the church, but specifically to prevent women teaching a public assembly from the seat on the bema.[104] The bema of a Byzantine basilica was the raised platform in the main apse, at the eastern end of the naos, on which the holy table stood and where the clergy sat during the divine liturgy.[105]

Now, Chrysostom did not reverse his view on women's ordination on account of women's ministries in the early church. By distinguishing public teaching (priest to assembly) from private instruction (Priscilla to Apollos), and by distinguishing female teachers from male clergy, Chrysostom interpreted Paul's rule so as to preserve his earlier view that women are excluded from the priesthood and episcopacy.[106] Nonetheless, Chrysostom did revise his interpretation of Paul's rule on account of women's ministries in the early church. Whereas he had earlier cited Paul's rule as absolutely prohibiting women speaking in the church, Chrysostom later read Paul's rule as a specific counsel applying to a particular circumstance and thus allowing women teachers.

Chrysostom's reading of Paul's rule confirms my previous conclusion that Paul's rules should be interpreted contextually and circumstantially, not as absolute prohibitions of women ministers or categorical exclusions from church offices.[107] There are good reasons to interpret biblical rules restricting

---

103. Chrysostom, *Homily after the Remains of Martyrs Etc.*, in Mayer and Allen, *Early Church Fathers*, 90.

104. Chrysostom, *Homily XXXI on Romans* (NPNF[1] 11:554).

105. See Patricios, *Sacred Architecture of Byzantium*, 64–81.

106. See Gryson, *Ministry of Women in the Early Church*, 80–85.

107. Eastern church orders of the third and fourth centuries approved the ordination of women as deacons, in parallel to men, and also counted women deacons among the clergy. See *Didascalia apostolorum* 16; Apostolic Constitutions 8.3.19–20; Testament of the Lord 1.23. See also Madigan and Osiek, *Ordained Women in the Early Church*; Eisen, *Women Officeholders in Early Christianity*.

women's roles in the worship and leadership of the church as specific counsels addressing particular circumstances and thus *not* as general regulations applying universally to women's ministries.

Putting the parts together, one can argue cogently that there are hermeneutical grounds for treating biblical rules about women's roles differently from biblical laws and lists about same-sex intercourse. In the case of women's ministry, there are good reasons—biblical testimonies to women's ministries in the early church—that warrant interpreting biblical rules about women's roles as applying contextually or circumstantially. In the question of same-sex union, by contrast, there are good reasons to interpret biblical laws and lists as condemning all forms of same-sex intercourse. Even if one disagrees about the biblical laws and lists, there are no analogous testimonies—no approving biblical references to actual same-sex relationships—that would warrant interpreting those laws and lists as applying to only specific kinds of relationships, much less suggesting the equal standing of same-sex union with man-woman marriage. Some innovationists appeal to certain stories—David and Jonathan, or Naomi and Ruth, or even Jesus and John ("the beloved disciple")—as biblical evidence of divine approval (or, at least, absence of divine disapproval) of same-sex relationships.[108] But such appeals strain the texts too much and stretch the evidence too far to persuade even some scholars favorable to an innovationist view.[109]

Lessons for Discernment

The cases of slavery and women's ministry prove to be weak hermeneutical analogies for the case of same-sex union. In the cases of slavery and women's ministry, the biblical canon exhibits various texts that could be lined up on either side of the question. In the case of same-sex union, the biblical canon exhibits consistent texts that line up on only one side of the question. Richard Hays summarizes: "Though only a few biblical texts speak of homoerotic activity, all that do mention it express unqualified disapproval. Thus, on this issue, there is no synthetic problem for New Testament ethics. In this respect, the issue of homosexuality differs significantly from matters such as slavery or the subordination of women, concerning which the Bible

108. See Helminiak, *What the Bible Really Says about Homosexuality*, 123–26; Achtemeier, *Bible's Yes to Same-Sex Marriage*, 84–85; Thatcher, *Liberating Sex*, 137.

109. For critiques of such appeals by innovationist scholars, see Nissinen, *Homoeroticism in the Biblical World*, 53–56, 121–22; Loader, "Homosexuality and the Bible," 23–24; for critiques by traditionalist scholars, see Zehnder, "Observations on the Relationship between David and Jonathan"; Gagnon, *Bible and Homosexual Practice*, 146–54.

contains internal tensions and counterposed witnesses. The biblical witness against homosexual practices is univocal."[110] This difference between cases diminishes the import of these comparisons for the church's discernment of the same-sex-union question.[111]

Historical comparisons to cases of cosmology, slavery, and women's ministry fall short of providing hermeneutical support for marriage innovation. Yet consideration of these comparisons does carry implications for the church's discernment, for both traditionalists and innovationists.

Some innovationists portray traditionalists as engaging in an exercise of "connecting the biblical dots." This caricature fails to take seriously prominent defenders of a traditionalist view who interpret biblical texts in relation to canonical contexts, hermeneutical principles, and historical particulars.[112] Still, some traditionalists do argue against same-sex union by lining up biblical texts in a logical syllogism: "Leviticus says . . . ; Romans says . . . ; therefore . . ." Simply citing selected texts does not establish the "biblical position" on any issue. After all, it is possible to select texts to support a "biblical position" in favor of polytheism or polygamy, flat-earth geology or heretical Christology. Traditionalists should eschew such simplistic arguments. Responsible defense of a traditionalist view requires robust development of the biblical picture of marriage as the theological frame and hermeneutical perspective by which to address the question of same-sex union and interpret the relevant biblical texts.

Some innovationists claim that affirming same-sex union puts them on the "right side of history." As history has judged that Galileo, abolitionists, and liberationists were in the right, it is claimed, so history will judge that marriage innovationists are in the right. Revolution in science, abolition of slavery, liberation of women, and affirmation of same-sex union are movements that chart the "arc of history" toward truth, freedom, and justice. Seen from a "progressive" perspective, the "right sides" of these cases align historically. Examined closely, however, these cases do not align hermeneutically. Hermeneutical rigor does not necessarily validate "historical progress." Human judgments of historical progress are fallible and variable, moreover. During the nineteenth and twentieth centuries, proponents of scientifically respectable theories of human heredity combined with proponents of politically

110. Hays, *Moral Vision of the New Testament*, 389.
111. See also Swartley, *Homosexuality*, 16–19; Gagnon, *Bible and Homosexual Practice*, 443–48; Gagnon, "Bible and Homosexual Practice," 44–46.
112. See, for example, K. DeYoung, *What Does the Bible Really Teach about Homosexuality?*; Gagnon, *Bible and Homosexual Practice*; Grenz, *Welcoming but Not Affirming*; Hays, *Moral Vision of the New Testament*; Schmidt, *Straight and Narrow?*; Swartley, *Homosexuality*.

progressive ideas of human improvement to advance racial views of intelligence and promote public policies of eugenics.[113] What was yesterday seen as human progress is today judged as so much scientific error and social evil.[114] For hermeneutical and historical reasons, innovationists would do well to beware the "right side of history" claim.[115]

113. See Gould, *Mismeasure of Man*; Kevles, *In the Name of Eugenics*.
114. See also K. DeYoung, *What Does the Bible Really Teach about Homosexuality?*, 103–8.
115. Even some innovationists are wary of such claims—see Song, *Covenant and Calling*, 98.

8

Might Scripture
Provide Support?

CONSIDERING BIBLICAL WARRANTS

My brothers, listen to me. Simeon has related how God first looked
favorably on the Gentiles, to take from among them a people for
his name.

Acts 15:13–14

In chapter 7 I considered innovationist arguments that appeal to previous
changes across church history that could serve as analogies for revising biblical
interpretation in favor of sanctioning same-sex union. In each case I found
that the historical precedent provides only weak support for marriage innovation. These appeals to precedent fall short primarily on account of Scripture's
consistency, and tradition's continuity, regarding man-woman marriage and
same-sex intercourse. Innovationists seeking biblical support for sanctioning
same-sex union, therefore, must find in Scripture a reason that warrants overriding Scripture's consistent witness. In this chapter I consider innovationist
arguments that appeal to precedents and principles within Scripture to provide
warrant for overriding the consistent biblical pattern of male-female union
and the consistent biblical prohibition of same-sex intercourse.

God Looked Favorably: Analogies to Eunuchs and Gentiles

Luke Timothy Johnson, a biblical scholar who favors sanctioning same-sex union, acknowledges the high bar for the innovationist side but claims that it can be met: "The burden of proof required to overturn scriptural precedents is heavy, but it is a burden of proof borne before."[1] The "before" that Johnson references is the Jerusalem Council, where the early church discerned that God was gathering gentile believers into God's people. The gentile analogy, in my estimation, is the most robust attempt at a biblical argument for sanctioning same-sex union and deserves serious consideration.

Precedents of Inclusion

The biblical story is threaded through with God's plan to draw "outsiders" into God's people. The prime precedent of inclusion is God's creation of a new nation and God's promise of blessing to all nations through the call of and covenant with Abraham and Sarah (Gen. 12–17). The prophet Isaiah envisioned a coming day when "the word of the LORD" would go forth from Jerusalem and "all the nations" would come to God's temple and God would "judge between the nations" (Isa. 2:2–4). Isaiah also envisioned God promising blessing to all those "who keep the sabbath . . . and hold fast [the LORD's] covenant," including "foreigners who join themselves to the LORD" and "eunuchs . . . who choose the things that please [the LORD]"; the God "who gathers the outcasts of Israel" will "gather others to them besides those already gathered" (56:3–8). Jesus said that his death on the cross would "draw all people to [him]" (John 12:32). The risen Jesus appointed the apostles as his "witnesses . . . to the ends of the earth" (Acts 1:8) and commissioned them to "make disciples of all nations" (Matt. 28:19). By the Spirit's power through the apostles' preaching, Samaritans, eunuchs, and gentiles come to believe and receive baptism in the name of Jesus (Acts 8; 10). By the grace of the cross, gentiles, who were formerly "aliens" to God's people and "strangers" to God's promise, have been incorporated into the body of Christ and reconciled to God (Eph. 2:11–22).

Innovationist arguments often appeal to analogies of inclusion to advocate sanction of same-sex union. Some innovationists appeal to the early church's baptism of eunuchs—whom they characterize as an ancient analogue of modern sexual minorities—as a precedent for sanctioning same-sex union.[2] Biblical law had excluded eunuchs from entering the sanctuary to offer sacrifice and joining the assembly to worship (Lev. 21:16–24; Deut. 23:1); likewise,

---

1. L. Johnson, "Disputed Questions," 372. See also L. Johnson, *Scripture and Discernment*, 148.
2. See DeFranza, "Journeying from the Bible to Christian Ethics."

biblical law has excluded same-sex couples from marriage (Lev. 18:22; 20:13). Innovationists thus argue that baptizing believing eunuchs, which overrode biblical law to fully include eunuchs in the worshiping assembly of God's people, is a precedent for blessing same-sex couples, which would likewise override biblical law to fully include sexual minorities in the communal life of God's people. Many innovationists appeal to the precedent of gentile inclusion in the early church.[3] They argue that the church today should redefine marriage as sex-neutral, in order to bless same-sex couples, by analogy to how the early church redefined membership as ethnicity-neutral, in order to baptize gentile believers. Eugene Rogers concisely states the gentile analogy: "As God grafts gentiles . . . onto the domestic covenant of God's household with Israel, . . . so God grafts gay and lesbian couples . . . onto the domestic, married covenants of straight men and women."[4]

Assessing the Analogies

Precedents of inclusion, if they are to provide biblical warrant for sanctioning same-sex union, must provide a clear biblical reason for overriding the consistent biblical witness to the contrary. In order to do that, the precedents of inclusion must satisfy three criteria: first, the groups included by those precedents must be apt analogues for gay believers; second, the precedents of inclusion and the question of same-sex union must relate to the witness of Scripture in similar ways; third, the matters at stake in those precedents of inclusion must be directly relevant to the question of same-sex union. Assessing analogies of inclusion thus involves addressing three questions: Are eunuchs or gentiles in the early church apt analogues of sexual minorities and same-sex couples in the church today? Do the inclusion of eunuchs and gentiles and the question of same-sex union relate to the witness of Scripture in similar ways? Is the inclusion of eunuchs or gentiles materially relevant to the question of same-sex union?

In assessing these analogies, I will bypass the first question and proceed to the second and third questions. Even granting the contestable claim that eunuchs and gentiles in the early church are apt analogues of sexual minorities

---

3. See Achtemeier, *Bible's Yes to Same-Sex Marriage*, 68–70; Blosser, "Why Does the Bible Divide Us?," 142–44; Brownson, *Bible, Gender, Sexuality*, 9–10; Grimsrud, "Toward a Theology of Welcome"; Gushee, *Changing Our Mind*, 105–15; L. Johnson, "Disputed Questions"; Johnson, "Scripture and Experience"; Kirk, "Embracing the Gentiles"; Loader, "Homosexuality and the Bible," 46; Otto, *Oriented to Faith*, 100–101; E. Rogers, "Sanctification, Homosexuality, and God's Triune Life," 225–30; J. Rogers, *Jesus, the Bible, and Homosexuality*, 89–90; Siker, "Homosexual Christians, the Bible, and Gentile Inclusion," 187–90; Siker, "Gentile Wheat and Homosexual Christians," 145–46; Vines, *God and the Gay Christian*, 14–15.
4. E. Rogers, "Sanctification, Homosexuality, and God's Triune Life," 230.

and same-sex couples in the church today,[5] if the precedents of inclusion and the question of same-sex union do not relate to the witness of Scripture in similar ways, or if the matters at stake in those precedents of inclusion are not directly relevant to the question of same-sex union, then the precedents of inclusion prove to be weak warrants for overriding the consistent biblical witness in the present matter.

Analogy to Eunuchs

The prophet Isaiah declared that God promises blessing for "the eunuchs who keep [the Lord's] sabbaths, who choose the things that please [the Lord]" and "hold fast [the Lord's] covenant"; even though they lack off-spring to perpetuate their names in Israel, God says, "I will give [them], in my house and within my walls, a monument and a name better than sons and daughters" (Isa. 56:4–5). Likely, Isaiah is declaring the promise of God's blessing to exiled Israelites that had been made eunuchs in the courts of Babylon. To argue that including eunuchs in God's covenant and blessing same-sex couples in marriage are analogous with respect to Scripture, the innovationist would need to show that a biblical prophecy points to God blessing same-sex couples. There are biblical laws prohibiting same-sex intercourse, but there is no prophecy found anywhere in Scripture that would in any way indicate God's favor extending to same-sex union. The inclusion of eunuchs and the blessing of same-sex couples, therefore, do not relate to the witness of Scripture in similar ways.

To argue that including eunuchs and blessing same-sex couples are analogous questions, the innovationist would further need to show that the eunuch question bears directly on the same-sex-union question. The eunuch question in biblical law concerned the holiness of Israel's worship in YHWH's presence. A descendent of Aaron with "crushed testicles"—or having a physical disability, bodily deformity, crippling injury, or visible affliction—was not permitted to present sacrifice or serve as priest in the sanctuary, so that he would not "profane [God's] sanctuary" (Lev. 21:16–24). This paralleled the law that an animal designated for sacrifice must be "perfect" because an animal having a "blemish" is not "acceptable" as an offering to God (22:17–25). Both priest offering the sacrifice and animal offered for sacrifice were to be "without blemish." These restrictions, which allowed eunuchs among Aaron's descendants to eat the priestly share of the holy food but forbade

---

5. The question of whether eunuchs or gentiles are apt analogues of sexual minorities and same-sex couples involves debates over whether these categories are biologically determined or socially constructed and whether the ancient categories and modern categories are so in similar ways.

them to approach the altar or enter the sanctuary, imply that the presence of eunuchs in the sanctuary was incompatible with God's sanctifying presence. In addition to the holiness law pertaining to priests, no common man among the Israelites "whose testicles are crushed or whose penis is cut off shall be admitted to the assembly of the LORD" (Deut. 23:1). Isaiah's prophecy of God's blessing to eunuchized Israelites among the returning exiles implies at least that God would honor faithful eunuchs as full members of God's people and welcome faithful eunuchs in the worshiping assembly at God's house. The Ethiopian eunuch baptized by Philip fits the prophet's depiction of the faithful eunuch to whom God promises blessing: having undertaken a pilgrimage to Jerusalem "to worship," he is reading Scripture and requesting interpretation (Acts 8:26–35).[6] With the words "in my house and within my walls" Isaiah's prophecy may also suggest God ordaining faithful eunuchs to serve in the priestly function.

Isaiah's prophecy about eunuchized exiles, one might argue, took precedence over Levitical law restricting eunuchs among God's people. Even absent a prophecy of God's favoring same-sex union, might an analogy to eunuchs warrant overriding Levitical law prohibiting same-sex intercourse? The material relevance of eunuch inclusion to same-sex union is doubtful, however. These questions concern different matters not obviously related: the eunuch question concerned what God intended for worship and, consequently, which people may join the worshiping assembly in God's house (cf. Deut. 23:2–8); the same-sex-union question concerns what God intended for marriage and, consequently, which sexual relations are permitted among God's people. There is no biblical evidence that including eunuchs in the Israelite assembly or baptizing eunuchs into the Christian community entailed any changes in which sexual relations are permitted among God's people—no evidence that Isaiah's prophecy was understood as overriding Levitical laws against incest, adultery, same-sex intercourse, or bestiality (Lev. 18:6–23). Jesus did commend "eunuchs who have made themselves eunuchs for the sake of the kingdom of heaven"—that is, men who forgo marrying for God's service. This saying may indicate also that Jesus welcomed both "eunuchs who have been so from birth" and "eunuchs who have been made eunuchs by others" among his disciples (Matt. 19:12). Jesus's teaching, however, implies approval of *not* marrying, not approval of novel forms of marrying.

Baptizing eunuchs did not implicitly approve sexual relations previously forbidden or make available novel forms of marrying. That nothing prevented the believing eunuch from being baptized (Acts 8:36–38) does not imply that

---

6. See L. Johnson, *Acts of the Apostles*, 158–60.

nothing now prevents a believing same-sex couple from being blessed. The baptism of believing eunuchs, therefore, is not materially relevant to the blessing of same-sex couples.

The baptism of believing eunuchs as full members of God's people, a work of the Holy Spirit that fulfilled a prophetic oracle, removed a legal barrier to worshiping God and enlarged the social boundary of the worshiping assembly. If eunuchs are apt analogues of sexual minorities, then baptismal inclusion of believing eunuchs in the early church augurs in favor of baptismal inclusion of gay believers in the church today. Baptizing believing eunuchs, however, did not in any way either shift the boundaries of sex or alter the form of marriage. The baptism of believing eunuchs, therefore, is neither biblically analogous nor materially relevant to the blessing of same-sex couples. The eunuch analogy provides only weak warrant for overriding the consistent biblical witness in the matter of same-sex union.

Analogy to Gentiles

God's plan to gather gentiles into God's people is proclaimed repeatedly by Israel's prophets. Isaiah envisions "all the nations" coming to Jerusalem to receive God's teaching and convert to God's way (Isa. 2:2–4); the "servant" of YHWH will "bring forth justice to the nations" and be "a light to the nations" (42:1–4; 49:1–6); God's promise of blessing extends to "foreigners who join themselves to the LORD," so that God's "house shall be called a house of prayer for all peoples" (56:3–8; cf. 14:1). Jeremiah declares that those among Israel's neighboring nations who "learn the ways of [God's] people" and "swear by [the Lord's] name" will "be built up in the midst of [God's] people" (Jer. 12:14–17). Amos envisions YHWH rebuilding the dynasty of David so that "all the nations upon whom [God's] name has been called" might seek out YHWH (Amos 9:11–12 NETS). In God's promise to Abraham and Abraham's faith in God, Paul wrote, Scripture foresaw God's justification and blessing of gentiles (Gal. 3:6–9). Does Scripture likewise foresee God's justification and blessing of same-sex union?

To argue that the ingathering of gentiles into God's people and the blessing of same-sex couples in marriage are analogous with respect to Scripture, the innovationist would need to show that a biblical prophecy points to God blessing same-sex couples. Again, there are biblical laws prohibiting same-sex intercourse, but there is no biblical prophecy indicating God's favor extending to same-sex union. The ingathering of gentiles and the blessing of same-sex couples, therefore, do not relate to the witness of Scripture in similar ways.

To argue that the ingathering of gentiles and the blessing of same-sex couples are analogous questions, the innovationist would further need to show that the gentile question bears directly on the same-sex-union question. Now, the question of baptizing gentiles is materially relevant to the question of blessing same-sex couples in this way: baptizing gentiles (and Samaritans) implicitly shifted the intermarriage boundary for God's people from Israelite/non-Israelite or Jew/gentile to believer/nonbeliever. Scripture warns Israelites against marrying non-Israelites: Israelites marrying Moabites provoked God's wrath, resulting in a plague upon the Israelite camp (Num. 25:1–9); the Torah banned, and Joshua warned against, marriage between Israelites and non-Israelites in the promised land (Exod. 34:11–16; Deut. 7:1–4; Josh. 23:6–13); Ezra exhorted the Israelite remnant returned from exile to abandon marriages to non-Israelites (Ezra 9–10). Yet Scripture's prime concern with intermarriage is not ethnic purity but cultic fidelity: Israelite men who married Moabite women "bowed down to their gods" (Num. 25:2); intermarrying "would turn away your children from following [God], to serve other gods" (Deut. 7:4; cf. Exod. 34:16; 1 Kings 11:1–8) and divert the people from obedience to God's law (Josh. 23:6–8; Judg. 3:5–6); by intermarriage the Israelites have aligned with "the peoples who practice these abominations" and "broken faith with [their] God" (Ezra 9:14; 10:2). In fact, Scripture affirms marriages of Israelites to non-Israelites who have declared commitment to YHWH, including Rahab and Ruth (Josh. 2:8–14; 6:22–25; Ruth; Matt. 1:5). So "the Torah does not ban intermarriage as such," but rather insists "that Israelites should not marry people who worship other deities."[7] According to Scripture, an Israelite man need not marry a descendant of Jacob, but he must marry a worshiper of YHWH.

This concern about intermarriage continued into the early church. Paul, unlike Ezra, did not mandate divorce for believers already married to nonbelievers when baptized. In accord with Jesus's teaching, Paul counseled them to remain married in hope that their spouses might become believers (1 Cor. 7:12–16). At the same time, Paul, like Ezra, exhorted baptized believers to not marry unbelievers. Paul was concerned that believers might become defiled with idol worship, a common practice in Greco-Roman households (2 Cor. 6:14–7:1; cf. 1 Cor. 7:39, "only in the Lord"). So, baptizing gentiles shifted the intermarriage boundary while apostolic teaching preserved the theological rationale for avoiding intermarriage. Further, the now-permitted Jew-gentile union among baptized believers was still presumed to be a male-female union: "A Jewish-Christian woman need not marry a circumcised Jewish man, but, if she marries, she must marry a man."[8]

7. Goldingay, *Old Testament Theology*, 3:365. See also Davidson, *Flame of Yahweh*, 315–24.
8. Brooten, *Love between Women*, 264.

The gentile question, as a matter of marriage, is relevant to the same-sex-union question. Baptizing gentiles and Samaritans shifted the intermarriage boundary and thereby allowed marriage of mixed-ethnicity couples in the church. One might thus argue that gentile inclusion, by analogy, provides rationale for shifting the "intermarriage" boundary again to allow blessing of mixed-orientation couples in the church, for which I argued on other grounds in chapter 7. Yet baptizing gentiles did not alter the male-female form of marriage and thus does not provide rationale for blessing same-sex couples. The analogy to gentiles provides only weak warrant for overriding the consistent biblical pattern of male-female union and sanctioning same-sex union.

Membership and Marriage: Belonging and Behaving

Innovationists argue that the church today should redefine marriage as sex-neutral, blessing same-sex couples, by analogy to how the early church redefined membership as ethnicity-neutral, baptizing Samaritans and gentiles. Baptizing Samaritans and gentiles expanded the worshiping assembly of God's people and shifted the intermarriage boundary for God's people. Baptizing those who were formerly "aliens" and "outsiders" to Israel, however, did not alter the male-female marriage pattern. Such precedents of inclusion could provide warrant for sanctioning same-sex union only if there is a logical link between membership and marriage such that expanding who belongs to God's people warrants redefining what marriage is among God's people. Redefining marriage in analogy to membership, however, would obscure the biblical link between belonging (God's accepting "aliens" and "outsiders" into God's people) and behaving (God's people living in ways befitting God's people). This belonging-behaving link is evident and operative in a key episode concerning the gentile question in the early church that innovationists often cite as precedent for sanctioning same-sex union: the Jerusalem Council (Acts 15).

At the Jerusalem Council, the apostles and elders discerned that the church should baptize gentile believers *as gentiles* into God's people. Gentiles who repented from sin and confessed Jesus were baptized without requirement of circumcision and the obligation to observe the whole Torah that went with circumcision (Acts 2:38–39; 15:1–29; cf. Rom. 2:25; Gal. 5:3). The council's discernment was guided by Peter's testimony to the decision of God manifest through the dispensing of the Holy Spirit: "God . . . testified to them by giving [gentiles] the Holy Spirit . . . ; and in cleansing their hearts by faith [God] has made no distinction between [gentiles] and [Jews]" (Acts 15:8–9; cf. 10:44–48). The apostles and elders discerned, accordingly, that the church should baptize and recognize gentile believers as belonging to God's people just as it baptized and recognized Jewish believers; for God had dispensed grace without distinction between circumcised and uncircumcised.

At the same time, the Jerusalem Council distinguished between baptized gentiles who now belonged to God's people and certain practices from which baptized gentiles were required to abstain as befits God's people (Acts 15:19–21). In doing so, the Jerusalem Council carried forward Peter's declaration at Cornelius's house: "I truly understand that God shows no partiality, but in every nation anyone who fears him and does what is right is acceptable to him" (10:34–35). "God shows no partiality" between Jew and gentile, for God's grace has dispensed the promise of salvation to "every nation." Even so, being "acceptable to [God]," even for gentiles, entails fearing God and doing right. The Jerusalem Council also followed the prophetic pattern. Isaiah foresaw that "many peoples" of "all nations" will "stream" to "the mountain of the LORD's house," saying, "Come, let us go up to the mountain of the LORD, to the house of the God of Jacob; that he may teach us his ways and that we may walk in his paths" (Isa. 2:2–3). Those "days to come" (2:2), we may imagine, had begun with the Holy Spirit's drawing gentile believers toward God's people. According to the prophet, however, *inclusion* of all nations among God's people involves the *instruction* of the nations in God's ways ("that he may teach us his ways") and the *conversion* of the nations to God's ways ("that we may walk in his paths"). Following the prophetic pattern, the Jerusalem Council discerned that baptizing gentile believers into God's people entailed gentiles learning God's ways and exchanging their ways for God's ways.

Consistent with both Isaiah's visions of God gathering many nations into God's house and Peter's vision of God welcoming all peoples into God's people, the Jerusalem Council discerned a "restrictive inclusion" for the church. The apostles and elders discerned that God's grace extends to all persons without distinction: gentiles belong to God's people by believing in Jesus and receiving baptism (without circumcision). At the same time, baptizing gentiles into God's people entails behavioral restrictions for gentile believers: gentile believers should adhere to ethical requirements and thus abstain from certain practices. The Jerusalem Council discerned that the Jew-gentile distinction has been dissolved in God's economy of salvation: God will save both Jew and gentile by grace through Jesus (Acts 15:11). At the same time, the Jerusalem Council discerned that the belonging-behaving link remains operative for God's people: all those belonging to God's people, Jew or gentile, must live by God's ways.

The innovationist appeal to the gentile analogy moves from expanding membership to redefining marriage. This argument would move the church in the direction opposite to the discernment of the Jerusalem Council: whereas the innovationist argument advocates altering marriage for the sake of including gay believers among God's people, the Jerusalem Council discerned that baptizing gentiles entailed gentile believers changing behaviors as befits belonging to God's people.

Gentile Baptism and the Circumcision Requirement

Still, some innovationists appeal to the Jerusalem Council's decision to baptize gentiles without circumcision, which the Torah had made a criterion of belonging to God's covenant people (cf. Gen. 17; Exod. 12:43–49; Josh. 5:2–9). The Jerusalem Council's decision on the circumcision question, some innovationists argue, serves as precedent for the church today on the same-sex-union question.[9] Here, again, one could propose an analogy: including gentiles in God's people meant setting aside the biblical requirement of circumcision for God's people; likewise, sanctioning same-sex union means overriding the biblical prohibition of same-sex intercourse for God's people. One might thus argue: just as the early church with the Holy Spirit's approval set aside the circumcision requirement and thereby redefined covenant membership for the sake of including gentile believers among God's people, so also the church today with the Holy Spirit's approval can override the same-sex-intercourse prohibition and redefine marital union for the sake of including gay believers among God's people.

The gentile-circumcision question and the same-sex-union question are not precisely parallel with respect to Scripture: the former involved a "must do" (circumcision) for Israelites; the latter involves a "must never do" (same-sex intercourse) for both Israelites and non-Israelites. This difference matters to the Torah, which distinguishes performative commandments ("must do") and prohibitive commandments ("must never do"). Neglecting a performative commandment (e.g., festal observance or firstfruit offering) implicated the individual sinner (cf. Num. 9:13); but transgressing a prohibitive commandment (e.g., idol worship or illicit sex) generated consequences for the whole community (cf. Lev. 18), such that even unintentional transgression required atoning sacrifice (cf. Lev. 4). While the Torah makes performative commandments binding only on Israelites, the Torah makes prohibitive commandments binding also on non-Israelite residents of Israel.[10] This difference matters also to the gentile analogy: baptizing gentiles without circumcision set aside a

---

9. See Blosser, "Why Does the Bible Divide Us?," 142–44; Gushee, *Changing Our Mind*, 107–8; Kirk, "Embracing the Gentiles"; Kraus, "The 'H' Words," 36–37.

10. See Milgrom, *Leviticus*, 42, 185–87.

performative commandment ("must do") not binding on non-Israelites; blessing same-sex couples, by contrast, would override a prohibitive commandment ("must never do") binding on both Israelites and non-Israelites.

The apostles and elders discerned that, by God's action through the Holy Spirit, God's people had surpassed the circumcision boundary. Baptizing gentiles without circumcision marked a major shift in the dispensation of God's grace and the composition of God's people. One should pause before concluding that this shift altered everything at once, however. The innovationist might be tempted to argue that the Jerusalem Council, by not requiring circumcision for baptized gentiles, decided that gentile believers were not required to observe biblical law. Matthew Vines claims, "Gentiles were included in the church, and the church recognized that the old law was no longer binding."[11] Achtemeier, similarly, claims that doing "an end run around the requirements of biblical law" in the matter of same-sex union "would be utterly consistent with this biblical precedent" of gentile inclusion.[12]

The Jerusalem Council, to the contrary, did not do "an end run around biblical law" or decide that "the old law" for God's people was simply "no longer binding." For the apostles and elders went on to discern not *whether* biblical law should apply to gentile believers but rather *which* biblical laws were appropriate for gentile observance. And the biblical laws that they discerned were required of gentile believers in the church were prohibitive commandments binding on non-Israelite residents of Israel.

Gentile Believers and the Apostolic Decree

The Jerusalem Council issued its decision regarding gentile believers in a decree. This decree, transmitted by letter from the apostles and elders in Jerusalem to gentile believers in Antioch, states in part, "For it has seemed good to the Holy Spirit and to us to impose on you no further burden than these essentials: that you abstain from what has been sacrificed to idols and from blood and from what is strangled and from fornication [*porneias*, sexual immorality]. If you keep yourselves from these, you will do well" (Acts 15:28–29). These "essentials" or "necessities" for gentile believers were neither arbitrary impositions nor novel inventions. These ethical mandates were derived from biblical laws given by God to Israel for observance by gentiles.

The Jerusalem Council addressed two questions together: whether gentile believers could belong as gentiles to God's people and whether gentile believers among God's people should observe God's Torah. The apostles and

11. Vines, *God and the Gay Christian*, 15.
12. Achtemeier, *God's Yes to Same-Sex Marriage*, 70.

elders, in agreement with the Holy Spirit, concluded yes on *both* questions. The church decided that gentile believers who now belonged to God's people as gentiles—baptized without circumcision—were obliged to observe those holiness laws that God had provided in Torah for observance by gentiles. The Jerusalem Council, far from simply setting aside biblical law, discerned by the Holy Spirit the continuing validity and appropriate applicability of biblical law for gentile believers among God's people.[13]

The Jerusalem Council, therefore, reaffirmed biblical norms of sexual holiness at the same time that it affirmed baptizing gentiles as equal members of God's people. The apostolic decree issued by the council condensed those biblical norms into the mandate that gentile believers "abstain" (*apechesthai*) from "sexual immorality" (*porneias*). In the New Testament, the generic term "sexual immorality" (*porneia*) covered various forms of illicit sex (e.g., prostitution, incest, adultery) and effectively encompassed all sexual intercourse outside marriage (including same-sex intercourse). Likely, this mandate meant to include all forms of illicit sex named in the Holiness Code of Leviticus as forbidden to both Israelites and non-Israelites: incest, adultery, marital sex during the menstrual period, male-male sexual intercourse, and bestiality.[14]

The Jerusalem Council's decision—at a crucial juncture in salvation history, in agreement with the Holy Spirit—that biblical law forbidding sexual immorality remains binding on gentile believers was not a minor matter. The apostles and elders discerned that abstaining from sexual immorality is an "essential" or "necessity" of belonging to God's people, a practical consequent to saving grace. Nor was sexual holiness a peripheral concern to the early church. In communicating an injunction against sexual immorality to gentile believers, the apostles and elders continued both Jewish tradition and Jesus's teaching (Matt. 5:27–30; 15:10–20).[15] Paul reiterated this injunction in the same terms as the apostolic decree: "For this is God's will: . . . that you keep away [*apechesthai*] from sexual immorality [*porneias*]" (1 Thess. 4:3 NET). He summarized instruction on sexual conduct with this injunction: "Flee sexual immorality [*porneian*]!" (1 Cor. 6:18 NET). And he repeatedly admonished believers that those who habitually practice sexual immorality "will not inherit the kingdom of God" (6:9–10; Gal. 5:16–21; Eph. 5:3–5).[16]

---

13. For further discussion, see chap. 10.

14. See Bauckham, "James and the Gentiles," 173–74; Hays, *Moral Vision of the New Testament*, 383. See also appendixes G, H, and I in the online supplement.

15. See Verhey, *Remembering Jesus*, 223–24.

16. See also Rom. 13:11–14; 1 Cor. 5:1–2, 9–13; 6:9–20; 7:2; 10:8; 2 Cor. 12:19–21; Col. 3:1–11; 1 Thess. 4:1–8. Concerning sexual ethics in the Pauline churches, see Meeks, *First Urban Christians*, 100–102; K. Bailey, *Paul through Mediterranean Eyes*, 153–226; Fortson and Grams, *Unchanging Witness*, 183–89.

The first-century Didache, a discipleship training for gentile believers, commanded, "You will not have illicit sex [*ou porneuseis*]," warned against the lust that leads to "illicit sex" (*porneian*), and listed "illicit sexual acts" (*porneiai*) under the "Way of Death."[17] An injunction to abstain from sexual immorality belonged to the deposit of instruction that the church transmitted and taught consistently during the postapostolic era—in apologetic writings, catechetical manuals, and church orders—throughout the second, third, and fourth centuries.[18] Cyril, bishop of Jerusalem in the fourth century, repeated this injunction in his oration to catechumens at the beginning of their Lenten preparation for baptism.[19] An injunction against sexual immorality, coupled with an exhortation to sexual chastity, characterized the early Christian lifestyle of sexual discipline, which was both distinctive of the Christian community and attractive to curious outsiders.[20]

Innovationist appeals to the gentile analogy typically fail to cite or discuss the apostolic decree. Jeffrey Siker's appeal to the gentile analogy obscures the belonging-behaving link. He claims that we might see the "case for the acceptance of 'nonabstaining' homosexual Christians as analogous to how early Jewish Christians accepted 'nonabstaining' Gentile Christians."[21] He ignores the apostolic decree's mandate that gentile Christians "abstain" (Acts 15:29) from unclean practices prohibited by biblical law. Jack Rogers states simply, and mistakenly, "These gentiles did not have to meet any of the former Jewish requirements."[22] He also ignores the apostolic decree, which spells out ethical "requirements" (15:28 NIV) from Jewish law for gentile Christians. Similarly, Mark Achtemeier states, mistakenly, "These new believers . . . continue to live outside traditional understandings of biblical law, as they always have."[23] He neglects the fact that the apostolic decree obligated gentile believers to observe laws God had provided in Torah for gentiles. James Brownson does cite a key phrase from the apostolic decree, "It seemed good to the Holy Spirit and to us."[24] But he does not mention, much less discuss, what did seem good to the

17. Didache 2.2; 3.3; 5.1. Milavec, *Didache*, 170: "It is quite probable that the *Didache* wished to include all these prohibited unions [Lev. 18:7–23] when it communicates to gentiles that the Lord commands, 'do not have illicit sex' (*ou porneuseis*) (*Did.* 2.2)."

18. See Shepherd of Hermas, Mandates 4.1.1; 8.1.3; Epistle of Barnabas 19.4; Aristides, *Apology* 9; 15; Theophilus, *To Autolycus* 1.14; 3.15; Apostolic Tradition 15.6–7; 16.2, 13–14; Apostolic Constitutions 6.5.28.

19. Cyril of Jerusalem, *Procatechesis* 4, in *Lectures on the Christian Sacraments*, loc. 985 of 2456, Kindle.

20. See Kreider, *Patient Ferment of the Early Church*, 101–2. Sexual discipline as integral to the peculiar lifestyle of early Christians is evident in Epistle to Diognetus 5.

21. Siker, "Homosexual Christians, the Bible, and Gentile Inclusion," 188.

22. J. Rogers, *Jesus, the Bible, and Homosexuality*, 89.

23. Achtemeier, *Bible's Yes to Same-Sex Marriage*, 69.

24. Brownson, *Bible, Gender, Sexuality*, 10.

Holy Spirit and to the church: namely, the requirement that gentiles in the church abstain from practices that Torah had already prohibited for gentiles in Israel, including sexual immorality.[25]

Luke Timothy Johnson is the only innovationist, as far as I've read, who deals substantively with the apostolic decree. He acknowledges the apostles' injunction against *porneia* and maintains that the church today cannot approve what Scripture calls *porneia*. Yet he reconciles the apostolic injunction against *porneia* with church sanction of same-sex union by redefining *porneia* in terms compatible with covenanted same-sex couples—*porneia*, he says, is sex that violates covenantal fidelity—but narrower than the New Testament: *porneia*, Paul says, violates baptismal fidelity to Christ and desecrates one's body as the Spirit's temple (1 Cor. 6:15–20).[26] In Johnson's version of the gentile analogy, this precedent of inclusion bears the burden of proof if we lower the bar.[27]

Conclusion

The apostolic decree undercuts an appeal to baptizing gentiles in favor of sanctioning same-sex union. If baptized gentiles are apt analogues of gay believers, then gay believers are bound by the biblical laws of sexual holiness, including the Levitical prohibition of same-sex intercourse. I concur with Willard Swartley: "Almost I am persuaded, until I read Acts 15:20, and realize that the included Gentiles are now expected to conform to the Jewish sexual codes that forbid *unchastity* (*porneia*), a generic term matching our popular word (sexual) *immorality*. The New Testament texts . . . leave no doubt whether same-sex intercourse is included as one expression of immorality."[28] The apostolic decree substantially qualifies the import of the Jerusalem Council. The Jerusalem Council, in setting aside the circumcision requirement and thus widening membership boundaries, did not override biblical sexual norms or redefine marriage or deviate from the consistent biblical pattern of male-female union and prohibition of same-sex intercourse. In widening membership boundaries, they reinforced moral boundaries.

The precedents of inclusion—eunuchs and gentiles—provide only weak warrants for overriding the consistent biblical pattern of male-female union and prohibition of same-sex intercourse in order to redefine marriage and sanction same-sex union. The baptism of eunuchs lacks material relevance

---

25. Several other innovationist appeals to the gentile analogy—by Blosser, Kirk, Kraus, Otto, E. Rogers, and Vines (each cited above)—also neglect the apostolic decree of the Jerusalem Council.

26. L. Johnson, "Disputed Questions," 370–71.

27. For further discussion, see appendix I in the online supplement.

28. Swartley, *Homosexuality*, 72 (emphasis original).

to the same-sex-union question and thus does not support marriage innovation. The baptism of gentiles relates to the same-sex-union question via the intermarriage question, but the gentile analogy, on account of the apostolic decree, actually counters marriage innovation.[29]

Come to Me All: Appeal to Hospitality

Some innovationists would argue that, the apostolic decree notwithstanding, the church today is warranted in privileging biblical precedents of inclusion over the biblical prohibition of same-sex intercourse and redefining marriage to sanction same-sex union. There is good reason, some would say, for the church today to follow the Jerusalem Council's discernment regarding membership inclusion but revise the council's discernment regarding moral restriction. That reason, some have claimed, is ethically grounded in a biblically derived imperative of hospitality: welcoming the stranger.

Appeal to Hospitality: Jesus and Gentiles

An innovationist appeal to hospitality is typically presented as an appeal to Jesus. Ted Grimsrud appeals to the premise that "Jesus modeled inclusiveness" and "Jesus models welcome" as biblical warrant for privileging an inclusive practice of hospitality toward sexual minorities over restrictive laws that prohibit same-sex intercourse.[30] David Gushee appeals to a "Hebraic-prophetic-kingdom-of-God-love-justice-mercy-compassion Jesus" as the "hermeneutical center" by which we should interpret Scripture and discern doctrine.[31] Such appeals claim that Jesus's practice of hospitality, or Jesus's exercise of love and compassion, provides a biblical precedent that warrants the church to override the consistent biblical witness and sanction same-sex union.

The appeal to hospitality might also be presented as an extension of the analogy to gentiles. On the one hand, to be inclusive concerning marriage (blessing same-sex couples) would, like being inclusive concerning membership (baptizing gentiles), accord with the hospitality imperative. On the other hand, to be restrictive concerning marriage (blessing male-female couples only) would, like being restrictive concerning membership (baptizing Jews

---

29. For further critique of the gentile analogy, see Gagnon, *Bible and Homosexual Practice*, 460–66; Gagnon, "Bible and Homosexual Practice," 43–44; Goddard, *God, Gentiles, and Gay Christians*; Greene-McCreight, "Logic of the Interpretation of Scripture," 253–58; Hays, *Moral Vision of the New Testament*, 399; Roberts, *Creation and Covenant*, 217–18; Farrow, "Beyond Nature," 261–67.

30. Grimsrud, "Toward a Theology of Welcome," 133, 139.

31. Gushee, *Changing Our Mind*, 158.

only), be contrary to the hospitality imperative. Just as the church yesterday was warranted in baptizing gentiles as a way of practicing hospitality toward ethnic outsiders, so also the church today is warranted in blessing same-sex couples as a way of practicing hospitality toward sexual minorities.[32] One might state the argument in stronger terms: in order for the church to truly welcome sexual minorities, welcome must go beyond membership inclusion to doctrinal revision; demonstrating genuine pastoral concern for sexual minorities requires sanctioning same-sex union.[33]

The church should extend Jesus's love and compassion to all those who desire to follow Jesus and seek God's kingdom. The church should practice hospitality by welcoming sexual minorities as baptized believers into Christian fellowship. Genuine pastoral concern includes willingness to listen to sexual minorities tell of their experiences with the church and acknowledge any pain the church may have caused. Making the church a hospitable place that welcomes sexual minorities requires repenting from ways in which the church has mistreated sexual minorities and seeking reconciliation with those mistreated.

I will examine the Jesus version of the appeal to hospitality in relation to the teaching and ministry of Jesus in the Gospels and the gentile version of the appeal to hospitality in relation to the teaching and ministry of the apostles to gentiles.

Enter through the Narrow Gate: Jesus, Inclusion, and Restriction

As an appeal to Jesus, the appeal to hospitality pleads a case that both goes beyond and falls short of the Jesus of the Gospels. The appeal to hospitality is correct this far: Jesus did model a practice of hospitality that crisscrossed social boundaries, contravened cultural conventions, upended structural hierarchies, and offended religious sensibilities, earning himself the epithet "friend of tax collectors and sinners" (Luke 7:34; cf. 5:29–32; 7:31–50; 14:12–14; 15:1–2).[34]

Yet there is no evidence that Jesus's hospitality entailed revisions relevant to the present matter. The Gospels do not present Jesus giving any instruction or making any decision that would license the church to revise sexual norms

32. Grimsrud contrasts "restrictive" and "inclusive" views, aligns hospitality with "inclusion," and aligns "inclusion" with affirmation of same-sex union. See Grimsrud, "Toward a Theology of Welcome," 129–30.

33. See Gushee, *Changing Our Mind*, 170–72. Gushee, *Changing Our Mind*, 42, characterizes maintaining a traditional view of sex and marriage as an "exclusionist" option that is "far worse than" all other options.

34. See Kraybill, *Upside-Down Kingdom*; Grimsrud, "Toward a Theology of Welcome," 137–41.

or redefine marriage in the name of inclusive hospitality—or in the name of love or justice or any other gospel imperative. To the contrary, Jesus drew strict lines around lust, adultery, divorce, and sexual immorality: in matters of sex and marriage, Jesus intensified rather than weakened the law's force, tightened rather than loosened the law's application. Jesus's hospitality was more *inclusive* of "sinners," "tax collectors," and others deemed "unclean" than that of the Pharisees. At the same time, Jesus's teaching was more *restrictive* concerning sex and marriage than that of the Pharisees.

Again, the appeal to hospitality is correct this far: Jesus welcomed those who were excluded from the synagogue or outcast from society. He welcomed the many who were wearied and burdened; and he offered the weary rest and the burdened relief. Jesus's welcome was not an easy invitation to God's kingdom, however. Jesus's invitation was also an exhortation to those he welcomed, that they listen to him and learn from him: "Come to me, all you that are weary and carrying heavy burdens, and I will give you rest. Take my yoke upon you, and learn from me; for I am gentle and humble in heart, and you will find rest for your souls. For my yoke is easy, and my burden is light" (Matt. 11:28–30). Jesus's welcome is twofold: first, an offer of rest to the weary and relief to the burdened; second, a directive: "Take my yoke . . . and learn from me"—a directive to submit oneself to him as teacher and to bind one's life to his teaching. Jesus taught his disciples to entrust themselves to God's care in all things and strive for God's righteousness above all else (6:25–33). Jesus warned the disciples to avoid the wide gate and easy road that leads to destruction, which is traveled by many, and exhorted the disciples to enter through the narrow gate and walk the hard road that leads to life, which is found by few (7:13–14). Jesus intended this teaching not only for Israel but also for gentiles. The risen Jesus commissioned his disciples to go in his authority and "make disciples of all nations," baptizing them and "teaching them to obey everything" that Jesus had commanded them (28:18–20). Jesus's message thus paralleled Isaiah's vision: the nations come to God's mountain, to God's Messiah, to receive God's law and convert to God's ways.

In his practice of hospitality, accordingly, Jesus called people to a changed life. Jesus did include people who were marginalized or despised. And he did so not only for the sake of meeting their immediate needs (acceptance, forgiveness, healing, rescue, etc.) but also with a view toward their turning from sin and converting to righteousness. After calling the "sinful man" Peter (Luke 5:8) and the tax collector Levi, Jesus dines with sinners and tax collectors, proclaiming, "I have come to call . . . sinners to repentance" (5:32). Jesus "welcomes sinners and eats with them," announcing that heaven rejoices "over one sinner who repents" and returns to God (15:1–10). Jesus invites himself to dine with the despised tax collector Zacchaeus, who then repents from exploitation and acts to repair the wrong he has done (19:1–10).

Jesus's hospitality extends to those associated with or involved in sexual sin, even to the point of offending those who regard themselves as righteous. Jesus receives the intimate and affectionate attention of "a woman in the city, who was a sinner," and forgives her sins, declaring, "Your faith has saved you" (Luke 7:36–50). Jesus relates openly and perceptively with the Samaritan woman divorcée, to the effect that she becomes a bearer of the gospel that Jesus is the Messiah (John 4:7–26). Jesus intervenes to rescue a defenseless woman accused of adultery, refusing to condemn her yet exhorting her, "Do not sin again" (8:2–11; cf. 5:2–14). Yet Jesus's hospitality to sinners—forgiveness of prostitutes, compassion on divorcées, and mercy to adulterers—is not evidence that Jesus was "progressive" or "tolerant" in sexual matters.[35] In each case Jesus's words and deeds assume the need of repentance from sin and conversion to righteousness.

These twin emphases of Jesus's teaching and ministry—inclusion and restriction, invitation and exhortation—are evident also in Jesus's parables. Jesus's parables of God's kingdom are not simple stories of unqualified inclusion; they tell of invitation and inclusion and also of separation and exclusion. The fishers of God's kingdom cast a wide net and catch "fish of every kind," but when the net is full, Jesus will send his angels to sort the catch, keeping the "good" fish and throwing out the "bad" fish (Matt. 13:47–50; cf. 13:37–43). The messengers of God's kingdom invite "everyone" to the wedding banquet, but when the king comes to the banquet hall to greet the guests, he will instruct his attendants to throw out those who are "not wearing a wedding robe" (22:1–14). Jesus's parables celebrate the salvation of sinners who repent from sin and the lost ones who return to God (Luke 15). But Jesus's parables also highlight the judgment of those who do not repent or return and so remain lost: the "foolish" bridesmaids who fail to prepare for the bridegroom's coming are shut out of the wedding banquet, the "worthless" servant who has nothing to show his master is thrown into "outer darkness," and the "accursed" ones who neglect the poor and needy are sent away to "eternal punishment" (Matt. 25). According to Jesus's parables, God's kingdom will "separate the evil from the righteous" (13:49)—and "the righteous will shine like the sun in the kingdom of their Father" (13:43). God's kingdom, then, cannot be defined simply by inclusion: "For many are called, but few are chosen" (22:14).

Grimsrud writes that "Jesus modeled inclusiveness" and "Jesus models welcome." Yes, Jesus did include outsiders and welcome sinners. Yet how did

---

35. See Derrett, *Law in the New Testament*, 363.

Jesus model inclusivity and welcome? Gushee invokes a "Hebraic-prophetic-kingdom-of-God-love-justice-mercy-compassion Jesus." Yes, Jesus is the authoritative interpreter and interpretive center of Scripture. Yet does Gushee's Jesus fully represent the Jesus we meet in the Gospels?

Portraits of an "inclusive Jesus" fall short of the full Jesus of the whole Gospels. Jesus's hospitality comprises social inclusion *and* ethical restriction.[36] Jesus's welcome is an invitation to follow him in the path of striving for God's righteousness: all may enter the narrow gate and walk the hard way that leads to life, but "there are few who find it" (Matt. 7:13–14). Jesus's teaching of God's kingdom concludes with a warning of the perils of hearing but not obeying his teaching: going one's own way leads to destruction (7:24–27). God's kingdom in Jesus's teaching is defined by faith and obedience: "Not everyone who says to me, 'Lord, Lord,' will enter the kingdom of heaven, but only the one who does the will of my Father in heaven" (7:21–23; cf. 12:48–50). Jesus's invitation to rest in God's kingdom follows his warning of judgment to those who refuse to repent in response to his proclamation of God's kingdom (11:20–24, 28–30).

Appeals to a welcome-and-inclusion Jesus or love-and-compassion Jesus or justice-and-mercy Jesus, then, portray a simplified Jesus that reflects a selective reading of the Gospels. This portrait neglects the call-to-repentance Jesus and strive-for-righteousness Jesus and warning-of-judgment Jesus to whom also the Gospels testify. The "inclusive Jesus" of the hospitality appeal thus appears to be a Jesus neatly tailored to fit a desired conclusion. The Jesus of the Gospels, and the gospel of Jesus, cannot be reduced to "inclusion." As disciples of Jesus, we would do well to take our direction in discernment from the full Jesus of the whole Gospels and the full gospel of the Gospels' Jesus. The same Jesus who said "Come to me all . . ." (Matt. 11:28–30) also said "Enter through the narrow gate" (7:13–14).[37]

No Longer Live as the Gentiles: The Apostles, Inclusion, and Restriction

The appeal to hospitality, as an extension of the analogy to gentiles, presumes that practicing hospitality not only entails redrawing membership boundaries but also warrants, or even requires, revising sexual norms and redefining marriage. This begs the question, for that is precisely the matter that the Jerusalem Council was discerning.

36. Jesus's inclusive hospitality and restrictive ethic cuts across the categories—"inclusive" vs. "restrictive"—by which Grimsrud frames the matter.

37. See also Gagnon, *Bible and Homosexual Practice*, 185–228; Swartley, *Homosexuality*, 39–49.

The question discerned by the Jerusalem Council can be rephrased in terms of hospitality: What should be the terms of hospitality for welcoming gentile believers? Prompted by action of the Holy Spirit and guided by interpretation of Scripture, the apostles and elders discerned that the church should welcome gentile believers as equal members with Jewish believers. The church decided on terms of hospitality that were belonging-inclusive with respect to ethnic identity (Jews and gentiles welcome) but behaving-restrictive with respect to sexual conduct (no *porneia*). The Jerusalem Council's terms of hospitality regarding gentile believers were thus inclusive *and* restrictive. In this way, the hospitality discerned by the church—ethnic inclusion plus ethical restriction—extended the model of Jesus.

The apostles continued teaching these terms of hospitality regarding gentile believers. In his general letter to several churches in Asia Minor, Paul affirms both inclusion of gentile believers and restriction of gentile behaviors. Paul proclaims "the mystery of Christ," that "the Gentiles have become fellow heirs, members of the same body, and sharers in the promise in Christ Jesus through the gospel" (Eph. 3:1–6). At the same time, Paul teaches gentile believers that, because they have been "brought near by the blood of Christ" (2:13) and become "members of the household of God" (2:19), they should conduct themselves according to their new status: "Lead a life worthy of the calling to which you have been called" (4:1); "You must no longer live as the Gentiles live" (4:17); "You were taught to put away your former way of life" (4:22). In place of the old self with its old ways, Paul exhorts gentile believers, "Be renewed in the spirit of your minds, and . . . clothe yourselves with the new self, created according to the likeness of God [i.e., Jesus Christ] in true righteousness and holiness" (4:23–24). In calling gentile believers to lead lives made new through Christ, Paul emphasizes a radical reordering of sexual conduct as a central arena of holy living. The gentile believers, while living in "ignorance and hardness of heart," had given themselves over to "licentiousness" and "impurity" (4:18–19). Now that they belong in God's household, they must give up their former practices of "sexual immorality" (*porneia*) and "impurity," because "these are not fitting for the saints" (5:3 NET; see also 1 Thess. 4:1–7; Col. 3:1–11).

In his general letter to gentile believers in Asia Minor, Peter exhorts these "aliens and exiles" (1 Pet. 2:11) from the surrounding society to adopt the distinctive habits of a holy life that befit belonging to God's people. The gentile believers have been "ransomed from the futile ways inherited from [their] ancestors . . . with the precious blood of Christ" (1:18–19). Having redeemed gentile believers through Christ, God has called them "out of darkness into his marvelous light," separating them from the nations. Now, having received

God's mercy, they are "a holy nation, God's own people" (2:9–10). Because they now belong to God's people, Peter exhorts the gentile believers: "Do not be conformed to the desires that you formerly had in ignorance. Instead, as he who called you is holy, be holy yourselves in all your conduct" (1:13–15). They have been "sanctified by the Spirit to be obedient to Jesus Christ" (1:2), such that their purification from uncleanness comes by "obedience to the truth" (1:22). And this obedience to truth in Christ entails "conformity to a new standard" that effects "a new reorientation of one's life."[38] Peter, like Paul, names reorientation of sexual conduct as central to the holy living that befits God's people and separates gentile believers from unbelieving gentiles: "Live . . . no longer by human desires but by the will of God. You have already spent enough time in doing what the Gentiles like to do, living in licentiousness, passions, . . ." (4:1–4).[39] Echoing the apostolic decree of Acts 15, Peter urges the gentile believers to "abstain" from acting on "the desires of the flesh that wage war against the soul" (2:11).[40]

The apostles' teaching orients inclusion toward holiness, calling forth in the believer a new way of being human patterned after Christ and thus a new pattern of conduct throughout all life. "This conduct, by the standards of the nations, will be unusual. According to both Paul and Peter, it is characterized by a resolute *refusal to conform* to the ways of the nations."[41] The early church welcomed gentiles as members of Christ's body so that gentile believers and Jewish believers together might become a holy people fulfilling the calling of a holy God by imitating the way of Jesus, the holy One of God.[42]

The New Testament—Jesus and apostles, Gospels and epistles—consistently *both* invites gentiles (and other "aliens" and "outsiders") to belong by faith to God's people *and* exhorts gentile believers to a spiritual transformation of personal character and ethical reorientation of sexual conduct. This crucial point—that the reception of gentiles is also the repentance of gentiles—is evident in the Jerusalem church's response to Peter's report that the Holy Spirit had come upon the gentile believers at Cornelius's house: "God has given even to the Gentiles the repentance that leads to life" (Acts 11:18). The gospel of Jesus welcomes gentile believers; at the same time, inclusion in God's people by baptism into Christ transforms what it is to be "gentile." Gentile believers should no longer be conformed in character and conduct to

38. Edwards, *1 Peter*, 73.
39. See Edwards, *1 Peter*, 170–71.
40. See Edwards, *1 Peter*, 101. The same verb "abstain" (*apechō*) appears in Acts 15:20, 29 and 1 Pet. 2:11.
41. Kreider, *Journey toward Holiness*, 186 (emphasis original).
42. See Kreider, *Journey toward Holiness*, 176–205.

their native desires and inherited habits but rather are to become transformed by learning Christ (Eph. 4:20–21). Wesley Hill writes, "The New Testament never seems to envision Gentile inclusion without an accompanying radical transformation of characteristically Gentile passions and behaviors. The Gentiles remain Gentiles [i.e., uncircumcised] when they become Christians, but they don't remain Gentiles *in the same way* they were before they became Christians."[43] Gentile believers belonged as gentiles (i.e., without circumcision) to God's people. And precisely because they now belonged to God's people, they were no longer to behave as gentiles customarily did but rather were to adopt the holy habits of a peculiar people.

Questions for Discernment

Appealing to hospitality, therefore, falls short of providing warrant for overriding the consistent biblical witness concerning same-sex intercourse for the sake of sanctioning same-sex union. Emphasizing "inclusivity" is inadequate to characterize the vision of the prophets, the ministry of Jesus, and the teaching of the apostles: the nations coming to God's mountain are to convert to God's ways; the way of God's kingdom is the narrow way of faith and obedience; the baptism of the gentiles is the repentance of the gentiles. An appeal to inclusive hospitality to warrant sanctioning same-sex union privileges an ideology of inclusion over the invitation to holiness.[44]

An appeal to hospitality, nonetheless, generates questions for innovationists and challenges for traditionalists.

Hospitality How Far?

The hospitality appeal raises further questions. How far should inclusive hospitality extend into sexual practices? Innovationists who appeal to hospitality typically intend that sexual inclusion extends only as far as marriage but not beyond marriage (promiscuity or adultery).[45] That still begs a question: What should be the outer boundary of marriage inclusion?

Take nonmonogamy as a test case. If the church's no to same-sex union is contrary to hospitality, is the church's no to nonmonogamy also contrary to hospitality? If denying blessing to same-sex couples is unwelcoming of sexual

43. Hill, "Transformation of the Gentiles" (emphasis original). Hill applies this to himself: "I don't *stop* being gay (or at least *I* haven't, nor have many of my other same-sex-attracted Christian friends), but neither do I *remain* gay in the way my culture tells me to be gay. I'm fully included in the church, I trust, as a gay man; but I'm not thereby exempted from the call to a costly discipleship that will leave no corner of my gayness untransformed" (emphasis original).

44. See Nation, "Ideology of Inclusion."

45. See Grimsrud, "Toward a Theology of Welcome," 129–30; Gushee, *Changing Our Mind*, 101–4.

minorities, is it unwelcoming of sexual minorities also to deny blessing to open-marriage couples or polyamorous "throuples"?

Many innovationists would agree that the church should not affirm non-monogamy. Some innovationists, however, have advocated rescinding the restriction of sex to monogamy because this "heteronormative" pattern does not fit the experiences or reflect the self-understandings of sexual minorities. So, what would be the inclusionary rationale for excluding nonmonogamy from the church's sanction of sex? Having expanded the boundary of marriage to include same-sex union, why not, in the name of inclusion, further expand the boundary of sex to include nonmonogamy? Having removed union of "man and woman" from the definition of marriage to suit some sexual minorities, why not rescind restriction to "one and one" in sex to suit all sexual minorities? After all, Israel's patriarchs practiced polygamy, which Jesus never condemned. N. T. Wright presses these questions: "If Jesus' message is about inclusivity, why not include people whose instincts run to multiple simultaneous partners? If the New Testament normally relaxes tight Old Testament restrictions, in the interests of . . . openhanded inclusivity, how much more should Jesus' followers be prepared to recognize the propriety . . . of the multi-marriages which were apparently common in the Old Testament and are never explicitly prohibited in the New?"[46] Why, biblically and theologically, should the church be hospitable toward same-sex union but be *in*hospitable toward nonmonogamy?

The inclusion problem extends to near-kin union. Why include same-sex union but exclude near-kin union? After all, marriage within families, even between siblings, is an ancient practice evident in a prominent biblical couple: Abraham and Sarah. The inclusion problem is evident in Grimsrud's response to the incest question: "Concerning siblings having sex . . . [,] this seems like a universal taboo that, for Christians, surely also follows from a sense that the Bible clearly opposes it."[47] The same may be said of same-sex union; in fact, the same set of biblical laws opposes both sibling sex and same-sex intercourse (Lev. 18). And Israel's ancestors practiced sibling marriage, which Jesus never condemned. So why include same-sex union, which is consistently opposed in Scripture, but exclude sibling marriage, which could claim some support in Scripture? Why, biblically and theologically, bless a David-Jonathan union but not an Abraham-Sarah union?

Marriage innovationists have an inclusion problem. It remains the responsibility of innovationists to explain why the church should privilege the

---

46. N. T. Wright, *Scripture and the Authority of God*, 178.
47. Grimsrud and Nation, *Reasoning Together*, 192–95.

hospitality imperative over the consistent biblical witness on same-sex intercourse but then practice selective inclusion, welcoming same-sex couples but not polyamorous "throuples" or near-kin couples.

Hospitality and Holiness

God's people are called to practice hospitality toward the "alien" as our grateful response to God's gracious redemption and our obedient participation in God's salvation plan. Israel was to treat the "resident alien" with justice because they themselves had been "aliens in the land of Egypt," where God had provided for them and from which God had delivered them (Exod. 20:2; 22:21; 23:9). Believers in the church are to "welcome one another" as a reflection of how "Christ has welcomed [them]"; Christ's work of faithful service to confirm God's covenant promise to Israel continues through the church, whose work of hospitality fulfills God's plan to gather gentiles into God's people, all for God's glory (Rom. 15:7–12). Practicing hospitality—welcoming strangers, sinners, even enemies—is not optional for God's people (cf. Rom. 12:13, 20; 14:1; Heb. 13:2).[48]

Seeking holiness, also, is not optional for God's people. Yet can a hospitable people be a holy people? Hospitality (welcoming strangers) seems to press against holiness (separating from worldly ways). The apostles assured the early church that hospitality is not opposed to holiness. Paul taught that the attitudes suitable for practicing hospitality—compassion, kindness, gentleness, humility, patience, forbearance, forgiveness, and love—are the clothing proper to "God's chosen ones, holy and beloved" (Col. 3:12–14). Likewise, to those whom God called to be "a holy nation, God's own people," Peter gave the instruction that acts of love, hospitality, and service toward one another are the work appropriate to God's holy people (1 Pet. 2:9–10; 4:8–10). According to the apostles, hospitality and holiness are not opposites but complements: the church practices hospitality for the sake of calling people of all nations into God's holy nation; and the holiness of God's people is manifest in attitudes and actions that promote hospitality. In Jesus hospitality and holiness are united and perfected.

That hospitality and holiness are complementary implies two things: welcoming strangers into God's people without calling them to walk the way of holiness is not Jesus-like hospitality; and separating from worldly ways by wariness of welcoming strangers into God's people is not Jesus-like holiness. The church may not, in the name of Jesus, either privilege hospitality over holiness or pit holiness against hospitality. The church must, for the sake of Jesus, manifest holiness through the practice of hospitality and practice hospitality along the journey toward holiness. While we dare not make the

---

48. On the biblical theology and ethic of hospitality, see Pohl, *Making Room*.

way of God's kingdom wider than the way of Jesus, we dare not make the welcome to God's kingdom narrower than the welcome of Jesus.

The church's calling to Jesus-like hospitality and holiness poses a challenge to traditionalists. In the context of the current debate, traditionalists hear calls to "welcome" and "include" gay folks in the church as code words for altering or diluting the church's doctrine of sex and marriage. Traditionalists tend to treat such calls with skepticism and suspicion. Having armed themselves with skepticism and suspicion, however, traditionalists might neglect to clothe themselves with compassion and love. There is a danger here: if we lack clothing fitting for saints, we might see gay folks—as Samaritans, eunuchs, and gentiles were once seen—as threatening the holiness of God's people. Such an unholy, inhospitable attitude might deter gay believers that have left the church but desire to return; it might even induce the gay children of our congregations, despite their faith in God and love for Jesus, to join the "aliens" and "exiles" outside the church.[49] Jesus, we do well to remember, warned of severe judgment for those who put stumbling blocks before the "little ones" who believe in him and whom he welcomes (Matt. 18:1–7).

The biblical imperative of hospitality and the biblical precedents of inclusion (the baptizing of Samaritans, eunuchs, and gentiles) should shape a posture and practice in the church that intentionally invites and incorporates various "outsiders" (such as persons with physical or developmental disabilities or mental illnesses, immigrants and refugees, and sexual minorities) who have been previously excluded from or marginalized within the church. Hospitality and holiness need not be enemies and, among the followers of Jesus, should be friends.[50] Inviting all folks to (re)join the family of faith and follow Jesus, training all believers to turn from worldly ways and walk in God's way—such holy hospitality, or hospitable holiness, is the calling proper to God's people.

Better to Marry than to Burn: Appeal to Paul

A Pauline Marriage Proposal

The analogy to gentiles and the appeal to hospitality augur for welcoming gay folks in the church but fall short of warranting sanction of same-sex

49. According to Marin, *Us versus Us*, more than 80 percent of LGBT people in the United States are reared in Christian faith communities; roughly half of LGBT people reared in the church leave the church as young adults; yet some three-fourths of LGBT people are open to returning to the faith communities from which they have left, including those reared in theologically conservative traditions.

50. See Butterfield, *Gospel Comes with a House Key*; Yuan, *Holy Sexuality and the Gospel*; Otto, *Oriented to Faith*, 85–97 (on "compassionate traditionalism").

union. Rather than precedents or imperatives of inclusion, one might appeal to ethical casuistry and pastoral concession as warrant for overriding the consistent biblical pattern of male-female marriage and prohibition of same-sex intercourse in order to sanction same-sex union.

Some innovationists appeal to Paul's counsel on celibacy and marriage to make a "Pauline case" for same-sex union.[51] On account of sexual immoralities among the Corinthian believers, Paul commends conjugal fidelity within monogamous marriage to guard against sexual immorality. Paul practices celibacy and, convinced that "the present form of this world is passing away" (1 Cor 7:31), wishes all believers would forgo marriage for the sake of God's kingdom (7:7, 25–40). Accordingly, Paul praises self-control (*enkrateia*; Gal. 5:23), a fruit of life in the Spirit that enables one to bridle passions and abstain from sexual immorality (5:16–25). Yet Paul acknowledges that some believers lack the self-control necessary to celibacy. Concerned that believers lacking self-control would be tempted into sexual immorality, Paul advises unmarried and widowed believers: "I say that it is well for them to remain unmarried as I am. But if they are not practicing self-control, they should marry" (1 Cor. 7:8–9). Paul commends celibacy for the sake of serving God but concedes marriage for the sake of avoiding immorality: "It is better to marry than to be aflame with passion" (7:9). Or in the memorable phrasing of the King James Version: "It is better to marry than to burn."

The church today, one might argue, could apply Paul's counsel to the case of gay believers and affirm an analogous concession of same-sex union. Christians have often associated gay sexuality with sexual promiscuity. Yet congregations have excluded gay believers from the socially recognized and spiritually sanctioned form of sexual relationship in which fidelity could be observed and promiscuity avoided—marriage. "If they've been left to 'burn,' as Paul said, it's because they could not marry."[52] Seeing the plight of gay believers in light of Paul's counsel, one might make a Pauline marriage proposal: it would be better for gay believers to take on the yoke of committed monogamy within the faith community than to burn with desire and fall into promiscuity. Ethical casuistry and pastoral concession, one might argue, warrant sanction of same-sex union.

Weighing the Pauline Proposal

Paul emphasizes that his counsel is not the Lord's command but Paul's opinion (1 Cor. 7:25). It is thus fitting to consider this Pauline proposal in

---

51. See Schlabach, "What Is Marriage Now?"; K. Wilson, *Letter to My Congregation*, 157–61; Keen, *Scripture, Ethics, and the Possibility of Same-Sex Relationships*, 68–82.
52. Schlabach, "What Is Marriage Now?," 27.

relation to Paul's views on sex and marriage in 1 Corinthians 5–7. I will do so in two stages: first, I will establish the conditions and examine the cogency of a concession of same-sex union in relation to Paul's concession of marriage (1 Cor. 7) and Paul's teaching of chastity (1 Cor. 6), respectively, in this section; then, in the next section, I will test the limits of a concession to same-sex union in relation to Paul's response to the reported case of immorality (1 Cor. 5).

A Conditional Exception

First, I will consider this Pauline proposal for sanctioning same-sex union in the context of Paul's concession of marriage. If this is to be a truly Pauline proposal, then it must take account of and be analogous to Paul's concession.

Obviously, conceding same-sex union within the church's sanction of marriage would be an exception to Paul's concession. The marriage that Paul conceded is man-woman monogamy: "Because of cases of sexual immorality, each man should have his own wife and each woman her own husband" (1 Cor. 7:2). Paul proposed conjugal fidelity between husband and wife as an acceptable alternative and effective antidote to sexual immorality. A Pauline concession of same-sex union would thus be an exception for gay believers unsuited to man-woman monogamy in a mixed-orientation couple.

Moreover, same-sex union would be conceded as a conditional exception to Paul's concession. Paul preferred that believers practice self-control in celibacy. Paul conceded marriage for avoiding immorality out of pastoral concern for believers lacking, or failing to exercise, self-control. Paul thus stated the concession conditionally: "If they are not practicing self-control, they should marry" (1 Cor. 7:9). Paul proposed marriage as a conditional concession for believers unable or unlikely to avoid immorality unless married. A Pauline concession of same-sex union would thus be a conditional exception for gay believers unable or unlikely to avoid promiscuity apart from monogamy. Same-sex union would be sanctioned, then, as a conditional exception to Paul's concession.

Now it should not be assumed that no gay believer would be suited to man-woman monogamy or could be capable of lifelong celibacy. Some gay believers have deliberately entered marriage and faithfully remained married in mixed-orientation male-female couples; some gay believers, like some straight believers, thrive socially and spiritually in celibacy with the Spirit's help. Nor can it be assumed that all gay believers are either suited to man-woman monogamy or capable of lifelong celibacy. Few gay believers, likely, will incline toward mixed-orientation marriage; many gay believers, like many straight believers, may consider lifelong celibacy undoable.[53] The concession

---

53. See Keen, *Scripture, Ethics, and the Possibility of Same-Sex Relationships*, 70–74.

of same-sex union, by analogy with Paul's concession of marriage, would apply to gay believers for whom neither man-woman monogamy nor lifelong celibacy seems a viable option.

A Nonanalogous Concession

Second, I will weigh this Pauline proposal in the scale of Paul's teaching. Paul pointedly warned believers to not deceive themselves about the spiritual consequences of sexual immorality, for individual and community: "Do you not know that" those who habitually practice sexual immorality (*pornoi*) "will not inherit the kingdom of God?" (1 Cor. 6:9–10); "Do you not know that a little yeast leavens the whole batch of dough?" (5:6). Paul emphatically exhorted believers to discipline their personal bodies by keeping chaste—"Flee sexual immorality!" (6:18 NET)—and to discipline their communal body by judging believers that persist unrepentantly in sexual immorality: "Drive out the wicked person from among you" (5:13). Whereas Paul's concession of marriage is casuistic, Paul's prohibition of immorality and exhortation to chastity are apodictic.

Construing Paul's concession of marriage in line with Paul's teaching on chastity constrains casuistic extension and pastoral application of Paul's concession. Paul conceded and commended conjugal fidelity "because of cases of sexual immorality" (1 Cor. 7:2). Because Paul commended marriage as an alternative and antidote to sexual immorality, we cannot suppose that Paul intended to concede practicing sexual immorality within marriage. Casuistic extension and pastoral application of Paul's concession, therefore, should respect the moral logic of Paul's concession: Paul conceded a good (marriage) in place of a better (celibacy), not an evil (immorality) in place of a good (marriage)—and thus conceded a believer's choice between two modes of chastity (celibacy or marriage), not between chastity and unchastity.

The proposal to extend Paul's concession to same-sex union would have the church concede a gay believer's choice between celibacy and monogamous same-sex partnership. To respect Paul's moral logic, this choice must be between a "better" and a "good." In Paul's concession, the "good" is man-woman marriage. The Pauline proposal thus requires a nontrivial assumption: that monogamous same-sex partnership is a moral good comparable to man-woman marriage.

Now same-sex couples could, and many actual couples do, demonstrate virtues of fidelity, charity, and stability. Some innovationists have argued that monogamous same-sex partnership can, in these ways, exhibit the "good of marriage" as characterized by Augustine.[54] Yet Augustine held that the good

---

54. See Schlabach, "What Is Marriage Now?"

of fidelity depends on the intent of one's fidelity and the activity in which one is faithful. "When fidelity is used to commit sin," he wrote, "we wonder whether it should still be called fidelity." Loyal partners in crime may keep "fidelity in the society of sin," but they break "fidelity to human society" by their criminal activity. Likewise, loyal partners in adultery may keep fidelity in their society of sin but break fidelity in the society of marriage by their immoral activity. Thus, someone unfaithful to a spouse but faithful to a lover "is still evil," even if betraying that lover for yet another "is worse." Adultery cannot be converted from vice into virtue by being done with fidelity.[55] In Augustine's assessment, fidelity—or charity or stability—with a partner in the practice of sexual immorality is tainted virtue. A monogamous partnership involving immoral activity would be at best the flawed good of "fidelity in the society of sin" and so would not be morally comparable to marriage.[56]

Weighing this Pauline proposal, then, hinges on whether a monogamous same-sex partnership involves sexual immorality—and thus on whether, in Paul's judgment, same-sex intercourse is inherently immoral or possibly righteous. Among wrongdoers who exclude themselves from God's kingdom by their wrongdoing Paul lists *arsenokoitai*, men engaging in sexual intercourse with men (1 Cor. 6:9). Scholarly discussion of Paul's term *arsenokoitai* has generated diverse opinions. Some scholars argue that, in Paul's cultural context, Paul's term referred to men engaged in nonmutual or nonconsensual sex through unloving practices (e.g., pederasty) or to men exploiting others or being exploited sexually through unjust practices (e.g., prostitution)—and thus does not apply to sexual partnerships that are loving and just. Other scholars argue that, in Paul's biblical context, Paul's term derived from the holiness law prohibiting male-male sexual intercourse (Lev. 18:22; 20:13) and included all forms of male-male sexual intercourse—and thus does apply to monogamous same-sex partnerships. Not surprisingly, innovationists tend to the former view, while traditionalists tend to the latter view.

I have concluded, from my own examination of 1 Corinthians 6 and Leviticus 18, that there are sound reasons to read Paul's vice list as deriving from biblical law and to interpret Paul's term *arsenokoitai* as including all forms of male-male sexual intercourse. Paul judged the practice of same-sex intercourse as inherently incompatible with a habit of life fitting for baptized believers, who have been "washed" and "sanctified" and "justified" (1 Cor. 6:11). In Paul's judgment, same-sex intercourse cannot be converted from vice into virtue by being practiced faithfully, lovingly, and justly: it is, simply,

---

55. Augustine, *On the Good of Marriage* 4, in Hunter, *Marriage in the Early Church*, 105–6.
56. See also S. Holmes, "Listening to the Past," 184–85.

vice.[57] One might interject that Paul's judgment was prejudiced by ignorance: Paul, in his historical situation, could not have known of mutual and faithful, loving and just same-sex partnerships, for which innovationists advocate church sanction. Yet historical research and textual evidence indicate that it is possible and plausible that Paul did know of such same-sex partnerships.[58]

Paul's prohibition of same-sex intercourse, like his prohibition of sexual immorality but unlike his concession of marriage, is apodictic, not casuistic. This renders the Pauline proposal problematic. It would concede not a good in place of a better but a lesser vice (monogamous same-sex intercourse) in place of a greater vice (promiscuous same-sex intercourse). It would have the church concede the gay believer's choice not between modes of chastity but between a mode of chastity (celibacy) and a mode of *un*chastity (same-sex intercourse). A pastoral concession of same-sex union would thus not be analogous to Paul's concession of marriage.

Those inclined to accept the Pauline proposal, likely, will disagree with my conclusion about Paul's prohibition. Whether or not my conclusion is correct, this much is true: affirming a pastoral concession of same-sex union analogous to Paul's concession of marriage requires assuming the ethical possibility of righteous same-sex intercourse. That assumption begs the question. The Pauline proposal for sanctioning same-sex union, therefore, does not resolve the question of same-sex union but returns us to the debate over Paul's prohibition of same-sex intercourse.

Questions for Discernment

The Pauline proposal, premised on the assumption that same-sex union is compatible with chastity, provides only a weak warrant for overriding the consistent biblical pattern of male-female marriage. Nonetheless, this proposal generates questions and challenges for both innovationists and traditionalists.

Limits of Concession

Suppose, for the sake of discussion, we provisionally grant this innovationist proposal the benefit of the doubt. I have already stated the conditions of a pastoral concession of same-sex union. What would be the limits of concession?

Take the reported case of sexual immorality among the Corinthian believers as a test case. A man was having a sexual relationship with his stepmother. Suppose it were proposed to extend pastoral concession to this couple: it is

---

57. See appendixes F and G in the online supplement.
58. See appendixes D and E in the online supplement.

better to publicly commit to monogamous partnership than to burn with passion and engage in immorality. Paul, of course, would have none of it: the church should grieve this relationship and, pending repentance, remove the man from fellowship (1 Cor. 5:1–2). Most innovationists, I would expect, would not grant a concession in this case. It is not obvious, however, how to distinguish, biblically and theologically, a monogamous near-kin partnership from a monogamous same-sex partnership.[59] Ethically, one might say, this man was taking advantage of a vulnerable woman; and the church should not concede sexual exploitation. Yet for all we know, it may be that the desire was mutual and the sex was consensual. If so, why not concede their relationship?

While near-kin marriage is uncommon in the modern West, nonmonogamy—such as open marriage and polyamory—is becoming common, among opposite-sex and same-sex couples,[60] and increasingly acceptable, even among Christians.[61] The social fact of nonmonogamy is thus pastorally relevant. Consider hypothetical scenarios akin to actual cases. A woman, married many years to a man, realizes that she experiences strong same-sex attraction and yearns for female intimacy; she asks her husband to allow her a same-sex relationship outside their marriage (or agree to divorce) so that she might fulfill her unmet need. The husband of a married couple acknowledges sexual dissatisfaction with a single partner; the wife has long experienced bisexual attraction; they discuss bringing a third partner into their marriage for mutual satisfaction of their unmet needs. Again, suppose it were proposed to extend pastoral concession in these cases: it is better to open your marriage (or divorce and remarry) than to engage in adultery; it is better that your relationship become polyamorous than to engage in adultery.

Assuming that many innovationists would not favor sanctioning nonmonogamy, such cases present a challenge. If the church should concede monogamy in same-sex partnerships so that same-sex-attracted/-oriented believers might avoid promiscuity, why not concede nonmonogamy in opposite-sex marriages so that same-sex- or bisex-attracted/-oriented believers might avoid adultery? If the unmet intimacy needs of same-sex-attracted/-oriented single believers warrant pastoral concession, why not also the unmet intimacy needs of same-sex- or bisex-attracted/-oriented married believers? One might reply that nonmonogamy would provoke jealously between spouses, undercutting fidelity and stability in marriage. Yet some advocates of nonmonogamy argue

59. See also Gagnon, "Bible and Homosexual Practice," 48.

60. See Dominus, "Not Just Us"; James, "Many Successful Gay Marriages Share an Open Secret"; Oppenheimer, "Married, with Infidelities"; Thrasher, "Master Bedroom, Extra Closet."

61. See Gordon et al., *Relationships in America Survey*, 51.

that open and polyamorous arrangements can preserve fidelity and stability while promoting flexibility and honesty in marriage.

The social fact of singleness in Western societies also is pastorally relevant. The average age at first marriage and the population portion of never-married adults have risen significantly over the last few generations. In this milieu, many believers remain single much longer into adulthood than expected, some believers reach middle age without marrying, and a few believers never marry. Do the unmet intimacy needs of involuntarily single believers qualify for pastoral concession? Should the church concede nonmarital sexual relationships for single believers, straight and gay, who neither see prospect of marriage nor find lifelong celibacy doable? The Pauline proposal thus implicates the traditional restriction of sex to marriage as well as the traditional definition of marriage.

Sanctioning same-sex union as a pastoral extension of Paul's concession prompts questions: Why override the biblical witness for pastoral concession but then practice selective concession, acknowledging unmet intimacy needs of some believers in certain cases but not others? Whose intimacy needs merit pastoral consideration?

Possibility of Accommodation

Although the Pauline proposal does not warrant sanctioning same-sex union as a pastoral concession, it does prompt considering whether the church might practice pastoral accommodation of same-sex couples. Accommodation is different from concession: whereas concession allows making choices of "good" over "better," accommodation allows existing situations falling short of "good." Accommodation is different also from agreeing to disagree: whereas a church body might resolve disagreement by suspending judgment in a "disputable matter," accommodation presupposes judgment of situations according to an agreed moral standard.

Some traditionalist congregations, in fact, already practice pastoral accommodation of morally imperfect marital situations: accepting divorced-remarried couples and never-married parents as members; overlooking premarital cohabitation of engaged couples; and so on. Several rationales might be offered for extending accommodation to same-sex couples.

First, the creation story: Genesis sets forth God's ideal for sex and marriage: man and woman, monogamous, for life. Jesus summed up the creational ideal: the "two" of "male and female" joined by God into "one flesh" (Matt. 19:4–6; Mark 10:6–8). Actual marriages might deviate from the creational ideal in various ways: divorce-remarriage sunders the "one flesh" and falls short of lifelong fidelity; polygamy exceeds the "two" of monogamy; same-sex union misses the mark of "male and female." Each deviates from God's design in a fundamental respect and so is inherently imperfect; but, judged according to the creational ideal, no one deviation is more awry than the others.[62] The church could consider divorce-remarriage, polygamy, and same-sex union as morally comparable.[63] Second, salvation history: God accommodated the incestuous and polygamous marriages of Abraham and Jacob in order to create a covenant people; God even used the incestuous and adulterous unions of Judah and David to bring forth the Messiah in order to save God's people. If God accommodated imperfect situations for the sake of God's plan of salvation, then the church may accommodate imperfect situations for the sake of pointing people to Jesus Christ. Third, church mission: Divorce, cohabitation, and same-sex union belong to the cultural milieu and missional context of Western churches just as polygamy belongs to the cultural milieu and missional context of African churches. As some African churches have discerned ways to accommodate polygamous situations without sanctioning polygamy, Western churches might discern ways to accommodate same-sex couples without sanctioning same-sex union.

Some traditionalists thus argue: While the church should continue teaching God's creational ideal for sex and marriage, and although the church should not sanction sexual unions that are inherently morally imperfect, the church may accommodate imperfect unions in exceptional situations. Thus, while the church would continue teaching that marriage is man-woman monogamy, and although the church would not bless same-sex couples, same-sex couples could be included alongside divorced-remarried couples, cohabitating couples, and never-married parents within the worship and fellowship of the church.[64]

The practice of pastoral accommodation, of course, encounters challenges: how to discern, case by case, whether a situation warrants accommodation or discipline; whether to accommodate openly, or quietly; whether temporarily, or indefinitely; how to avoid becoming accustomed to sinning by accommodating sinful situations; how to preach repentance while practicing accommodation.[65]

---

62. Christian tradition has often judged same-sex intercourse and bestial intercourse as worse sins than adulterous, incestuous, or promiscuous sex, sometimes categorizing the former as "irrational" or "unnatural" (cf. Rom. 1:26–27) and the latter as "illicit" or "unlawful." Yet each is contrary to created order; the Holiness Code prohibits all alike (Lev. 18; 20); and Paul lists adultery, promiscuity, and same-sex intercourse as vices incompatible with God's kingdom (1 Cor. 6:9–10). There seems no obvious biblical reason to judge these sins by different standards.

63. See Goldingay, *Old Testament Theology*, 3:382–83.

64. See Thielicke, "Theologicoethical Aspect of Homosexuality"; Reimer, "Homosexuality"; S. Holmes, "Listening to the Past," 190–93. See also Keen, *Scripture, Ethics, and the Possibility of Same-Sex Relationships*, 104–5.

65. For classic counsel, see Gregory the Great, *Book of Pastoral Rule* 2.10; 3.33, 38.

Every traditionalist congregation faces a challenge here. Congregations willing to extend accommodation to same-sex couples must ask themselves how they will teach that marriage is man-woman monogamy while accommodating same-sex couples and how they will accommodate same-sex couples while honoring gay believers committed to celibacy in obedience to Jesus Christ for the sake of God's kingdom. Congregations reluctant to extend accommodation to same-sex couples must ask themselves why they should accommodate some situations that deviate from the creational ideal, such as divorced-remarried couples and never-married parents, but not accommodate other situations that also deviate from the creational ideal, such as same-sex couples. Congregations that eschew accommodation and expect gay believers to practice self-denial and self-control in lifelong celibacy must ask themselves how they will bear the burden of brothers and sisters who are same-sex attracted/oriented as they strive to obey faithfully and abide fruitfully in Jesus Christ and how they will exhort all believers—men and women, married and single, straight and gay—to the costly discipleship of sexual chastity. Expecting sexual discipline of gay believers while accommodating the sexual sins of straight and married believers is simply hypocrisy.

The marriage debate within the church has mostly gone back and forth between innovationist and traditionalist sides. Considering the questions that have emerged in this chapter, I suggest that more robust deliberation is needed both among adherents of tradition and among advocates of innovation. Among innovationists, most needed is theological deliberation, especially between affirmation and liberation viewpoints—between those that advocate including same-sex union within monogamy and those that advocate liberating queer sexuality from marriage and monogamy.[66] The need for a cogent theological perspective is a pressing challenge for innovationists: Which vision of innovation should the church embrace, and why? Among traditionalists, most needed is pastoral deliberation, especially between discipleship and accommodation viewpoints—between those that would expect costly discipleship of gay believers and those that would accommodate same-sex couples.[67] The need for a compassionate pastoral approach is a pressing challenge for traditionalists: How might the church adhere to traditional doctrine and, at the same time, practice holy hospitality in the way of Jesus?[68]

66. See Holben, *What Christians Think about Homosexuality*, 153–224.
67. See Holben, *What Christians Think about Homosexuality*, 95–152.
68. See Wesley Hill's afterword to this book.

Segue

In part 3 I have examined several arguments supporting marriage innovation. I have considered arguments that appeal to precedents of change in church history (chap. 7) and arguments that appeal to precedents of inclusion or concession in Scripture (chap. 8). I have found in each case that the precedent provides only a weak warrant—hermeneutical, theological, or ethical—for overriding the consistent biblical pattern of male-female marriage and prohibition of same-sex intercourse in order to sanction same-sex union.

It will be helpful at this point to recapitulate the main argument across parts 1, 2, and 3. I have considered the question of same-sex union within the catholic consensus that marriage is man-woman monogamy—and have asked the innovationist to justify reforming marriage. Sanctioning same-sex union would entail altering the form, function, and figure of marriage. Substantially reforming a Scripture-based doctrine affirmed universally by the church requires the strongest of reasons, for which advocates of innovation bear the burden of responsibility. But innovationist arguments fall short of providing sufficient reasons that would justify altering the church's catholic doctrine of marriage to sanction same-sex union. The catholic consensus that marriage is man-woman monogamy, therefore, still seems to me sound doctrine to which the church should hold fast.

Discernment does not end here with a simple vindication of the traditionalist view, however. We should consider the possibility that, despite all the foregoing biblical, theological, ethical, and historical considerations, the Holy Spirit might be leading the church today in a new direction. We still need to ask: How can we discern which way the Holy Spirit is guiding the church? I will address that question in part 4.

PART 4

SEEKING
A
DIRECTION

WHICH WAY TO WALK

9

Testing the Spirits

CONSIDERING PATHS TO INNOVATION

> Beloved, do not believe every spirit, but test the spirits to see whether
> they are from God.
>
> 1 John 4:1

In part 3 I considered several innovationist arguments that appeal to historical precedents or biblical texts in favor of sanctioning same-sex union. Each
argument provides only weak warrant for sanctioning same-sex union. In this
chapter I consider innovationist proposals for moving the church along a path
toward sanctioning same-sex union without meeting a burden of proof—that
is, without arguing that sanctioning same-sex union can be justified from
Scripture. Each proposal appeals to Scripture in order to point the church
along a path beyond Scripture.

Let Both Grow Together: "Wheat and Weeds"

One proposed path to innovation suggests that we apply Jesus's parable of
wheat and weeds to the church today.[1] This parable, some argue, directs us
to allow both traditional and innovational views of sex and marriage to dwell

1. See Siker, "Gentile Wheat and Homosexual Christians," 147–49.

together in the church. This proposal compares innovationists and traditional-ists to wheat and weeds and suggests that, rather than distinguishing wheat from weeds, we treat all in the church as wheat.

Proposal: Treat All in the Church as "Wheat"

Jesus compared God's kingdom to a householder who sowed "good seed" in his "field" (Matt. 13:24–30). An "enemy" came in the night and "sowed weeds among the wheat." So both wheat and weeds sprouted and grew in the field. The servants, seeing the weeds mixed with the wheat, went to their master. Whence these weeds? they asked. "An enemy," the householder an-swered. Should we go and gather the weeds, they asked. No, the householder answered, for you might uproot the wheat along with the weeds. "Let both of them grow together until the harvest." At that time, I will send harvesters into the field to bundle the weeds for burning but bring the wheat into the barn. Later, Jesus explained the parable to his disciples (13:36–43): The Son of Man sows the good seed of kingdom children in the field of the world, while the devil sows the weeds of evil children. The harvest is "the end of the age," and the harvesters are "angels" acting under Jesus's authority. At the end of the age the angels will remove from God's kingdom and dispatch for destruction "all causes of sin and all evildoers," but "the righteous will shine like the sun" in God's kingdom.

We might put the church today in parallel with the parable. Many tradi-tionalists see themselves as kingdom children sprouted from the good seed sown by Jesus—Jesus's teaching of marriage, call to chastity, and life of celibacy—and see support for same-sex union as sprouted from the evil seed of false doctrine and lax morals sown by the devil. Many innovationists see themselves as kingdom children sprouted from the good seed sown by Jesus—Jesus's teaching of love, mission of justice, and practice of inclusion—and see defense of traditional marriage as sprouted from the evil seed of hatred and bigotry sown by the devil. Such perceptions have yielded actions. Some traditionalist leaders, zealous to cleanse the church of error and immorality, have sought to defrock pastors and discipline congregations that affirm same-sex union or bless same-sex couples. Some innovationist leaders, zealous to transform the church into an inclusive community, have employed processes and implemented policies that have effectively excluded traditionalists from conversations and congregations.

Suppose instead that traditionalists and innovationists give each other the benefit of the doubt and treat each other as wheat rather than weed. Jeffrey Siker writes: "Essentially, the parable instructs us to treat one another as wheat.

. . . When in doubt, assume wheat and not weeds. Tolerance and patience are to be our guides. We must not rush to exclude and uproot one another."[2] Traditionalists and innovationists should heed the householder's decision and patiently tolerate one another in the church. This proposal implies that the church would consider both traditionalist and innovationist views as sprouted from good seed sown by Jesus and thus allow both male-female union and same-sex union to be blessed by the church. Traditionalists would allow without censure innovationist blessings of same-sex couples, while innovationists would allow without scorn traditionalist refusal to bless same-sex couples. Traditionalist congregations would accept without suspicion innovationist members, and vice versa; innovationist denominations would accept without prejudice traditionalist congregations, and vice versa. In this way, traditionalists and innovationists would leave it to God's judgment whether same-sex union is righteous or not.

Evaluating the Proposal

What to think of this proposal depends on how to interpret the parable. As Siker sees it, the problem in the parable is epistemic: "What is wheat and what is weed? Ultimately that is for God to determine, for we are apt to mistake one for the other."[3] Other commentators offer similar interpretations: "It is possible that Matthew's faith community (like our own faith communities) is at risk of trying to do the 'sorting out' prematurely—confident of its capacity to distinguish between 'weeds' and 'wheat.' . . . It is best to let the mixture grow together until the harvest rather than make premature judgments. That way we do not mistakenly exclude any of God's beloved."[4] Because we are susceptible of overconfidence in distinguishing weed from wheat and likely to mistake wheat for weed, we should refrain from weeding and even suspend making judgments between wheat and weeds and instead consider all as wheat. The church should thus adopt a posture of gracious inclusion and patient tolerance toward all.

This interpretation, I think, misses the mark. While Jesus might have had in mind a weed that resembles wheat until the heads of grain appear (darnel or "false wheat"), at no point in telling or explaining the parable does Jesus say or imply that the problem is epistemic. The parable states that the plants had formed heads of grain (Matt. 13:26), which would have visibly differentiated the false wheat from the true wheat. The servants reported seeing weeds among the wheat; and the householder's response indicates that he believed they have seen correctly. The householder neither chided the servants for

2. Siker, "Gentile Wheat and Homosexual Christians," 148.
3. Siker, "Gentile Wheat and Homosexual Christians," 148.
4. Case-Winters, *Matthew*, 178.

overconfidence in their ability to distinguish wheat from weeds nor instructed them to consider all growing in the field as wheat. Instead, the householder instructed the servants to consider the weeds as the enemy's work.

The problem is not epistemic but organic. Pulling weeds might uproot wheat, not because you mistake wheat for weed and grab wheat instead of weed, but because wheat and weeds take root in the same soil. The householder pinpointed the problem precisely: "For in gathering the weeds you would uproot the wheat along with them" (Matt. 13:29). Because they are growing together in common ground, the root systems of wheat and weed overlap and intertwine: pulling one might uproot the other. That wheat and weeds take root in the same soil is important. The parable does not divide the world into two realms, God's and the devil's; there is one field, the world, the whole of which is God's to rule and judge. The weeds are growing inside, not outside, God's kingdom; in the end, the weeds are collected *out* of God's kingdom. This implies three things: that both the Son of Man and the devil are active in God's kingdom; that both "children of the kingdom" and "children of the evil one" (13:38) are present in God's kingdom; and that God allows this to be so for now. At the same time, the parable assumes that Jesus's disciples, like the householder's servants, can and should distinguish wheat and weeds, and it assures them that Jesus, like the householder, will separate weeds from wheat when he executes God's judgment.[5]

The parable of wheat and weeds may be put alongside the parables of the sower (Matt. 13:3–9, 18–23) and the dragnet (13:47–50). Matthew precedes the parable of wheat and weeds with the parable of the sower. We may imagine that the householder has sowed good seed on the foot path and rocky ground and weedy ditch as well as on the good soil of the tilled field—and that the "enemy" has sowed evil seed likewise. Now wheat and weeds are growing together in the tilled feed, their roots entwined. Were the servants to pull weeds before the wheat is ready for harvest, they might uproot wheat before the grain heads are fully formed. To allow the wheat to produce a full yield, leave the weeding until the harvest. Matthew follows the explanation of the wheat and weeds with the parable of the dragnet. As the farmer allows wheat and weeds to grow until the harvest is ready, so the fishers catch good and bad fish until the net is full; as the angels will store the wheat and destroy the weeds, so the angels will keep the good and cast out the bad fish. The proclamation of God's kingdom will draw in many, good and evil, but the judgment of God's kingdom will separate good from evil, the righteous to salvation and the wicked to destruction. To allow the net to bring in a full catch, leave the sorting until the boat returns to shore.

5. See Gardner, *Matthew*, 213–16.

Farmers sowing seed and fishers casting nets symbolize God's kingdom at work in this world. Taken together, these parables depict worldwide proclamation of the gospel and indiscriminate invitation to the kingdom. These parables thus portray God's grace announced in the gospel and God's providence in fulfilling God's purpose. These parables also depict removal of evil from God's kingdom and consignment of evildoers to destruction. These parables thus portray also God's judgment assured in the gospel and God's patience in executing judgment.

So Jesus's parable of wheat and weeds is a story of generous invitation to God's kingdom and patient trust in God's providence. But it is not a story of inclusive tolerance: God does not tolerate evil and evildoers, which are destined for exclusion from God's kingdom. Jesus's disciples are to be gracious, sowing seed generously, casting nets widely, and inviting everyone. Jesus's disciples are to wait patiently and humbly on God, neither preempting the day of God's judgment nor usurping God's authority to judge. Yet Jesus's disciples are to be discerning, distinguishing truth from error and good from evil.

Wisdom of the Lord

I don't see the parable of wheat and weeds as pointing the church along a path of inclusive tolerance on marriage. Yet this parable does offer Jesus's wisdom to the church today. I will draw out this wisdom by connecting the parable to three teachings of Jesus in Matthew.

When sending out his disciples as apostles, with authority to proclaim the kingdom, Jesus warns them: "See, I am sending you out like sheep into the midst of wolves; so be wise as serpents and innocent as doves" (Matt. 10:16). Jesus's disciples, like Jesus, will face opposition and suffer persecution in a world that resists God's rule. Beware of wolves but do not fear them, Jesus says, for you are in God's care and God is trustworthy (10:17–31). Putting this together with the parable, we may hear Jesus saying to his disciples: You are in the world as sheep among wolves, as wheat among weeds. So be wise to evildoers: look for weeds amid the wheat, especially weeds resembling wheat; watch for wolves among the sheep, especially wolves wearing wool (cf. 7:15–20). Yet be innocent of wrongdoing: leave judgment to Jesus, put trust in God, and endure patiently (cf. Ps. 37). Stanley Hauerwas comments: "The parable of the wheat and tares is not Jesus's justification for the mixed character of the church. . . . The parable is given to encourage Christians to endure in a world that will not acknowledge the kingdom that has come in Christ."[6]

---

6. Hauerwas, *Matthew*, 133.

Jesus's parable of wheat and weeds directs disciples to exercise Godlike patience in dealing with evil(doers) in the world. Jesus's teaching on discipline and forgiveness instructs his disciples to exercise Godlike patience also when dealing with sinners in the church. If another believer sins, Jesus says, point out the sin but do so privately; if the believer won't listen, take along one or two others as witnesses; if the believer still won't listen, then bring the matter to the assembly of believers (*ekklēsia*); and if the believer still won't listen, only then "let such a one be to you as a Gentile and a tax collector" (Matt. 18:17)—that is, as one needing to hear again the gospel call to repent from sin and follow Jesus (cf. 9:9–13; 28:19–20). Jesus teaches the church a patient discipline that allows for repentance and aims at restoration: if the believer listens, "you have regained that one" (18:15). But what if that believer sins against me, Peter asks? How many times should I forgive? Does this patience have a limit? No, Jesus answers, your forgiveness should be unlimited (18:21–22). He then tells the parable of the unmerciful servant to emphasize the point: God's patience in forgiving you should be reflected in your patiently forgiving others (18:23–35; cf. 6:14–15). Jesus's disciples are to exercise Godlike patience, by faithful endurance in a weedy world and restorative discipline of wayward believers.

In the parable of wheat and weeds, the "enemy" sowed evil seed "while everybody was asleep" (Matt. 13:25). The "enemy" was working while the servants were sleeping. The parable thus underscores the disciple's duty of vigilance. In the days before his death, Jesus repeatedly exhorts his disciples to "be ready" and "stay awake"—for your "time of trial" by evildoers and "the hour" of judgment by Jesus will come when you don't expect it (24:36–44; 25:1–12; 26:36–46). Blessed is the "faithful and wise" servant in charge of the household, Jesus says, who is dutifully at work rather than taking leisure and falling asleep when the master comes at an unexpected hour (24:45–51). Jesus's disciples are to exercise vigilant patience in this "weedy" world, ready for the "enemy" while waiting for Jesus and praying to God: "Do not bring us to the time of trial, but rescue us from the evil one" (6:9–13).[7]

Let Each Be Convinced: "Disputable Matters"

Another proposed path to innovation suggests that we apply Paul's approach to "disputable matters" (Rom. 14:1 NIV) at Romans 14 to this dispute. Some have proposed that, rather than debating Romans 1 to decide the same-sex-

---

7. On the importance of patience in the early church, see Kreider, *Patient Ferment of the Early Church*.

union question, we would do well to follow Romans 14 as a guide for dealing with protracted and intractable disagreement.[8] Others have proposed that Romans 14 points congregations along a "third way" toward "full inclusion."[9] Each compares the marriage debate in the church today to the food dispute in the early church.

Proposal: Treat Same-Sex Union as a "Disputable Matter"

Disagreement over whether or not believers may eat meat and whether or not believers should observe special days had generated "quarreling over opinions" among the Roman house churches (Rom. 14:1).[10] Some (the "strong" in conscience) believed in eating everything, meat and vegetables alike, and not observing special days; others (the "weak" in conscience) believed in eating vegetables only and observing special days. The "strong" despised the "weak," and the "weak" judged the "strong."[11] Paul admonished both parties: "Those who eat must not despise those who abstain, and those who abstain must not pass judgment on those who eat; for God has welcomed them" (14:3). Mindful that each of us will stand or fall before God's judgment, Paul counseled, let us no longer despise or judge one another; instead, "Let all be fully convinced in their own minds" (14:5). Paul himself was convinced that no food is intrinsically unclean but is unclean only for the one who considers it unclean. Accordingly, one may be convinced that certain meat is clean and eat, while another may be convinced that such meat is unclean and abstain; yet each honors God by thanking God for what one eats.

We can easily draw a parallel with the present debate: Innovationists believe that the church should bless all couples, male-female and same-sex alike, in covenanted union; traditionalists believe that the church should bless only male-female couples in marriage. Some innovationists despise traditionalists as homophobic bigots; some traditionalists judge innovationists as Bible-repudiating apostates. And we can readily translate Paul's counsel into advice for the church today: each of us, whether innovationist or traditionalist, has been welcomed by God; so let us stop despising and judging each other and

8. See Finger, "What Can We Do When We Don't Agree?"

9. See K. Wilson, *Letter to My Congregation*, 79–132, 190.

10. Paul does not specify whether the meat at issue was from unclean animals forbidden by the law and thus offensive to faithful Jews or was from animals sacrificed in temples and thus offensive also to some gentile converts. Nor does Paul specify whether the days at issue were Sabbaths observed by Jews or were festivals observed by Greeks and Romans. Possibly both were involved in both disputes.

11. The weak/strong divide did not necessarily correlate with the Jew/gentile distinction: Paul does not define the groups by ethnicity; and Paul, a Jew, counts himself among the "strong" (Rom. 15:1). See Grieb, *Story of Romans*, 126–27.

allow each one to make up his or her own mind about the matter; mindful that all are accountable to God, let all be convinced in their own minds. Accordingly, one may be convinced that monogamous same-sex partnership is righteous and bless same-sex couples, while another may be convinced that all same-sex intercourse is sinful and abstain from blessing same-sex couples; yet each seeks to honor God. By mutual accommodation between traditionalists and innovationists, the church may bless and embrace both male-female couples and same-sex couples.

Evaluating the Proposal

The point of comparing the same-sex-union debate in the church today to the food dispute in the early church is to argue that we would do well to deal with our dispute in like manner: "Therefore, if in both cases, believers are disagreeing on fundamental issues, Paul's principles should apply to both situations."[12] Applying Paul's approach to both disputes assumes that the respective matters—food in the one case, sex in the other case—are substantively comparable. That assumption needs testing. As this proposal appeals to Paul, it is fitting to test that assumption against Paul's own view. Would Paul have considered these as comparable matters and thus advised dealing with them in similar ways?

Paul counseled the Romans that matters of food could be left to individual conviction because, he was convinced, food does not matter to God's kingdom: "For the kingdom of God is not food and drink but righteousness and peace and joy in the Holy Spirit" (Rom. 14:17). Would Paul say also that matters of sex may be left to individual conviction because sex does not matter to God's kingdom? I will consider this question in the context of Paul's counsel to the Corinthians, which addressed disputes about both sex and food.

The sex dispute in Corinth concerned whether believers are free from law in matters of sex, including whether believers may participate in sexual relationships or engage in sexual activities forbidden by biblical law. Some Corinthians held that the believer's freedom from law included sex just as it included food: food and sex are each means to satisfy the needs and desires of the body, and the body is destined for death, so neither what we eat nor how we have sex matters to the Christian life. Paul repudiated such thinking regarding sex: the body is not destined for destruction in the grave but for resurrection by God; the body has been redeemed by God through Christ and is indwelled by the Holy Spirit; the body is not for sexual immorality but belongs to God and is for God's glory (1 Cor. 6:12–20).

---

12. Finger, "What Can We Do When We Don't Agree?," 218.

The food dispute in Corinth concerned whether believers could eat food offered to idols, which included most meat sold in markets and served at banquets. The "strong" argued that because they know that there is only one God and that the "gods" do not really exist, they could eat such foods without worshiping false gods. The "weak" had become so habituated to idols that despite now confessing the one God, they could not eat such foods without damaging their conscience. Paul was convinced that neither eating nor abstaining makes one better or worse in relation to God. Paul thus allowed believers to buy meat in the market or eat meat at a banquet without question of conscience, for the earth's abundance belongs to God; but if one is informed it was offered to an idol, then abstain for the sake of others. At the same time, Paul summoned "strong" believers to show concern for "weak" believers, lest the "strong" "sin against Christ" by wounding another's conscience (1 Cor. 8:1–13; 10:23–33).

Regarding whether Christians may eat idol food at temple feasts, however, Paul makes no allowance for conscience (1 Cor. 10:14–22). Paul compared eating in temples and having sex with prostitutes. He drew parallel depictions: partnering with a prostitute in sex violates union with Christ in spirit; eating idol food at a temple feast is partnering with demons, which is incompatible with participating in Christ by eating holy food from the Lord's table (6:15–17; 10:16–21). He issued parallel injunctions: "Flee [*pheugete*] sexual immorality" and "Flee [*pheugete*] from idolatry" (6:18; 10:14 NET).[13] Paul insisted that how we dispose our bodies in sexual activity, as much as how we devote ourselves in worship, does matter to God's kingdom: "Fornicators, idolaters, adulterers . . . —none of these will inherit the kingdom of God" (6:9–10; cf. Gal. 5:16–21; Eph. 5:3–5).

In Paul's view, food and sex belong to different arenas: whereas food belongs to the arena of conscience and choice, sex belongs to the arena of discipline and chastity.[14] God's kingdom is indifferent to food choices, so believers are not bound by biblical law in food choice; there is allowance for conscience in whether to eat or abstain from meat, but believers must never eat in temples and should show concern for others. By contrast, God's kingdom is incompatible with sexual immorality, so believers are bound by biblical law in sexual conduct; there is no allowance for conscience in whether to engage in or abstain from what biblical law condemns as sexual immorality. Paul,

---

13. See Hays, *First Corinthians*, 166; Thiselton, *1 Corinthians*, 156.
14. See K. Bailey, *Paul through Mediterranean Eyes*, 153–292.

then, did not consider sex comparable to food.[15] I thus think it doubtful that Paul would advise us to deal with the same-sex-union question as a "disputable matter."

Counsel of the Apostle

Although I doubt that Paul would consider the same-sex-union question a "disputable matter," I think Paul would have counsel for us in our discernment. Consider again Paul's counsel to the Romans. Paul did not say simply, "Let everyone make up his or her own mind and do what you want." Paul balanced permission with exhortation: "Let us then pursue what makes for peace and for mutual upbuilding" (Rom. 14:19). One should use conscience to serve neighbor and community.

Paul advised the "strong" in particular that they should take concern for others in how they practice their convictions. Paul was especially concerned that the actions of the "strong" might grieve or distress the "weak" to the point of causing them to stumble theologically or bringing them to ruin spiritually. Paul admonished the "strong" that they had the obligation to bear with the "weak" and thus should act for their neighbor's good rather than to please themselves. Paul appealed to the work and example of Jesus, who died for all and did not act to please himself.[16] The "strong" would do well to keep their conviction to themselves before God, Paul advised, rather than "condemn themselves because of what they approve" (Rom. 14:13–15:3).

Translating Paul's counsel for the church today requires identifying the "strong" and the "weak." Theologically, the "strong" believers were "progressive" and the "weak" believers were "conservative."[17] If we identify "strong" and "weak" in the same-sex-union debate by theological conviction, innovationists would be the "strong" and traditionalists would be the "weak." Paul might thus advise innovationists: "The faith you have, keep to yourself before God. Blessed is the one who does not judge himself by what he approves" (Rom. 14:22 NET).

Paul's terms "strong" and "weak" also had political and social significance in the Roman context: the "strong" might refer to a numerical majority able to impose its will upon a powerless minority; or the "strong" might refer to educated and wealthy believers able to exercise influence over lower-class believers.[18] Insofar as we identify "strong" and "weak" in the same-sex-union

---

15. See also K. DeYoung, *What Does the Bible Really Teach about Homosexuality?*, 74.
16. See Elias, *Remember the Future*, 387–88.
17. See Finger, "What Can We Do When We Don't Agree?," 213–15.
18. See Finger, "What Can We Do When We Don't Agree?," 216; Toews, *Romans*, 342–43.

debate by political power and social position, translating Paul's counsel for the church today depends on the polities of denominations. Suppose we identify the "strong" by political power in church assemblies: innovationists might be the majority of a congregation but the minority of a denomination, or vice versa. Suppose we identify the "strong" by social position in church leadership: traditionalists might predominate in a congregation's leadership while innovationists predominate in a denomination's offices, institutions, and publications, or vice versa. Whether traditionalists or innovationists are "stronger" politically or socially, sexual-minority believers tend to be in vulnerable positions throughout the church. Most vulnerable within the church may be sexual-minority believers who maintain traditional beliefs on sex and marriage: these believers have been assailed from *both* sides of the debate, judged by some traditionalists as suspect of theological error (for identifying as "gay") and denounced by some innovationists as complicit in spiritual violence (for not affirming same-sex union).

Whichever way we identify "strong" and "weak," Paul counsels that the "strong" should not practice their convictions or use their power or positions in ways that distress or grieve the "weak." Traditionalists should beware the effects of their actions on innovationists, and vice versa. Whoever is "strong" politically or socially should take concern for and bear with whoever is vulnerable spiritually and socially. Heeding Paul's counsel, both traditionalists and innovationists would do well to exercise special concern for, and bear burdens of, gay believers.

All the Truth: A New Dispensation

In chapters 7, 8, and 9, I have considered arguments and proposals for marriage innovation that draw from "what is old" (Matt. 13:52)—Scripture, tradition, and church history. In my estimation, all these arguments and proposals fall short of providing sufficient reason to justify sanctioning same-sex union. A plausible justification for marriage innovation, I conclude, will need to draw from "what is new." The only plausible justification for sanctioning same-sex union, it seems to me, is to claim that God is giving the church today a new teaching through the Holy Spirit. I will consider this possibility.

Proposal: Recognize Same-Sex Union as a New Teaching

Dan Via acknowledges that sanctioning same-sex union can't be justified from Scripture. What justifies sanctioning same-sex union, he says, is a "new revelation." Sanctioning same-sex union is "a new position that supersedes"

Scripture's consistent pattern of male-female union and prohibition of same-sex intercourse. This claim, he argues, "is no more than an effort to appropriate what Scripture promises." Jesus told his disciples that the Spirit would come to remind them of what he had taught them and would lead them into all the truth, including many things that they could not bear now (cf. John 14:26; 15:26; 16:12–13). The Holy Spirit would thus lead Jesus's disciples "into implications of Jesus's redemptive mission and message that [had] not yet come to explicit expression." Although neither Jesus's teaching nor Jesus's promise refers explicitly to it, we may see sanctioning same-sex union "as a hitherto unrecognized and unacknowledged aspect of all the truth that comes in Jesus."[19]

Eugene Rogers sees the church's blessing of same-sex couples as a new dispensation of the Holy Spirit, analogous to the new era of God's grace begun with the baptism of gentile believers. "Like the claim that the Spirit of Christ is joining the gentiles to the tree in baptism," he writes, "the claim that the same Spirit is building up the body of Christ by joining together gay and lesbian couples is a pneumatological one—a claim, that is, about what the Spirit is doing new in the church." As God grafted gentiles into God's covenant people by the Holy Spirit, "so God grafts gay and lesbian couples . . . by a new movement of the Spirit onto the domestic, married covenants of straight women and men." Those who fail "to accept faithful, monogamous gay and lesbian marriages" put themselves "in danger of their salvation." "Marriage for gay and lesbian spouses depends upon the work of the Holy Spirit no less than baptism for the gentiles, and disbelief in either risks blasphemy against the Spirit." In this new dispensation, "we must mine Scripture and tradition under the Spirit, who will rule new rules for us."[20]

This proposal presents blessing same-sex couples as God doing "a new thing" in the church. The Holy Spirit is giving a new teaching for God's people, beginning a new era of God's blessing, surpassing the old era and its teaching. Same-sex union is a new dispensation; those who resist marriage innovation resist the Holy Spirit.

Evaluating the Proposal

The church must remain open to God doing a new thing. Salvation history, especially the incarnation and resurrection of Jesus, testifies to God's doing new things to accomplish God's purpose and fulfill God's promise (Isa. 43:16–21). At the same time, the church must discern whether a new thing

---

19. Via, "Bible, the Church, and Homosexuality," 38–39.
20. E. Rogers, "Sanctification, Homosexuality, and God's Triune Life," 226–27, 230, 238.

is God's doing or not. The apostles, aware that false prophets were leading believers astray, counseled the early church: "Do not despise the words of the prophets, but test everything" (1 Thess. 5:20–21); "Do not believe every spirit, but test the spirits to see whether they are from God" (1 John 4:1).[21] How, then, should the church test the spirit of this proposal to see whether it is from God? Jesus and his apostles have given the church criteria by which to discern whether a new teaching is truly of the Holy Spirit.

First, a teaching truly of the Holy Spirit will be true to the teaching of Jesus that we have received through the testimony of the apostles. Jesus's promise to his disciples that the Father would send the Holy Spirit "to teach [them] everything" and "guide [them] into all the truth" includes several qualifications: the Holy Spirit would come "in [Jesus's] name" and "remind [them] of all" that Jesus had said to them (John 14:26); "The Spirit of truth . . . will testify on my behalf" (15:26); "The Spirit of truth . . . will not speak on his own. . . . He will take what is mine and declare it to you" (16:13–14). The Spirit would come in Jesus's name and testify on Jesus's behalf, speaking Jesus's word by Jesus's authority. Jesus also told his disciples, "You also are to testify because you have been with me from the beginning" (15:27). Jesus authorized his apostles to testify to Jesus. A new teaching of the Holy Spirit, therefore, must accord with what Jesus has taught and his apostles have testified. Any teaching that contradicts Jesus's teaching or his apostles' testimony is not from God.

Second, a teaching truly of the Holy Spirit will present the same Jesus and proclaim the same gospel. Concerned that some believers were falling for "another Jesus" (2 Cor. 11:4) and "turning to a different gospel" (Gal. 1:6), Paul gave this test for discernment: "If anyone [even an angel from heaven] proclaims to you a gospel contrary to what you received, let that one be accursed!" (Gal. 1: 9; cf. 2 Cor. 11:3–4). Concerned that believers will be "carried away by all kinds of strange teachings," the writer of Hebrews gave this test for discernment: "Jesus Christ is the same yesterday and today and forever" (Heb. 13:8–9). A new teaching of the Holy Spirit, therefore, must accord with the Jesus the church has believed and the gospel the church has received by the apostolic preaching. Any teaching that alters Jesus or distorts the gospel is not from God.

Third, a teaching truly of the Holy Spirit will maintain a true confession of Jesus. The apostle John gave this test for discernment: "By this you know the Spirit of God: every spirit that confesses that Jesus Christ has come in the flesh is from God, and every spirit that does not confess Jesus is not from

---

21. See Verhey, *Remembering Jesus*, 18–19.

God" (1 John 4:2–3). To this he adds: "We have seen and do testify that the Father has sent his Son as the Savior of the world. God abides in those who confess that Jesus is the Son of God" (4:14–15). A new teaching of the Holy Spirit, therefore, must accord with the apostolic confession that Jesus is the Son of God, come in the flesh, to be the Savior of the world. Any teaching that denies or doubts the divinity, incarnation, or salvation of Jesus is not from God.

I will apply these tests to the innovationist proposal that sanctioning same-sex union is justified by a new teaching through the Holy Spirit. The first test of a new teaching is whether it is consistent with Jesus's teaching according to the apostles' testimony. Sanctioning same-sex union would alter marriage from sex-unitive to sex-neutral, such that "man and woman" would not be constitutive of marriage. According to the apostles, Jesus taught that God ordained marriage from the beginning of creation as "the two" of "male and female" joined into "one flesh" (see chap. 4). Sanctioning same-sex union, evidently, would not accord with Jesus's teaching.

An innovationist might avoid discord between new teaching and Jesus's teaching by proposing a second path of new dispensation: Jesus, through the Holy Spirit, is giving the church today a teaching different from what he gave his apostles. One way to distinguish what Jesus taught his apostles from what Jesus teaches us today, proposed by a seminary professor of mine, is this: the test for discernment is not what Jesus *did* teach but what Jesus *would* teach. Had Jesus been asked whether same-sex union is approved by God, surely he would have said no. Yet what Jesus said about marriage to his disciples *then* in response to *their* question (divorce) is not the issue. What matters for us is what Jesus says about marriage to us *now* in response to *our* question (same-sex union). The church today might thus discern that Jesus would teach that same-sex union is approved by God.

Another way to distinguish what Jesus taught his apostles from what Jesus teaches us today, proposed by a pastor friend of mine, is the hermeneutic of accommodation: what Jesus taught his apostles about marriage was accommodated to their perspective. Jesus's comment on Genesis, that God joined "male and female" into "one flesh," reflects the common belief of that historical-cultural context—but it neither represents God's eternal will for marriage nor states Jesus's plain teaching of marriage. The Holy Spirit is leading the church today beyond Jesus's accommodation of common belief— and into Jesus's plain teaching that God blesses all loving, faithful couples.

If this second path of new dispensation is of the Holy Spirit, then the church should be willing to follow it wherever it leads. We should thus allow the possibility that, regarding other marriage matters, Jesus now would say yes to what Jesus then said no to. Whereas Jesus then said that marriage is the two of male and female becoming one flesh, that divorcing one's spouse and marrying another is committing adultery, and that even lusting for someone not one's spouse is committing adultery, maybe Jesus now would say that marriage is any number of any gender joined in covenant, that divorcing agreeably and remarrying is pursuing happiness, and that indulging lust by using pornography is healthy sexuality. Maybe biblical standards of monogamy, fidelity, and chastity also were accommodations to historical-cultural contexts, which we may leave behind by the Holy Spirit's leading in our context. This possibility is not only hypothetical: some innovationists actually claim that the Holy Spirit is leading the church in such ways.[22]

Aside from implications for marriage, this second path of new dispensation implies disparity between "Jesus then" and "Jesus now." One might parse this disparity in alternative ways. One might distinguish between Jesus of apostolic testimony and Jesus of Holy Spirit testimony, discerning God's will for marriage by the latter rather than the former. Then, the apostles testified, Jesus taught that God created marriage as male-female union; but now, the Holy Spirit testifies, Jesus teaches that God blesses male-female and same-sex union. This distinction carries an implication: the apostles were mistaken about Jesus's true teaching of marriage. Yet Jesus empowered his apostles with the Holy Spirit to "be [his] witnesses" (Acts 1:8). This distinction thus generates questions: If the church today should discern God's will for marriage by Holy Spirit testimony, is apostolic testimony a reliable guide in other matters? Are the apostles unreliable witnesses to Jesus despite the power of the Holy Spirit?

Alternatively, one might distinguish between Jesus the belief-accommodator and Jesus the plain-teacher, discerning God's will for marriage by the latter rather than the former. Then, the Gospels record, Jesus accommodated common belief about marriage in teaching his disciples; but now, the church discerns, Jesus teaches us plain truth about marriage through the Holy Spirit. This distinction causes a conundrum: Why did Jesus let his apostles teach a common-but-mistaken view of marriage to the church? This distinction also makes an assumption: belief accommodation has passed, plain truth has come. Yet it could be that the Holy Spirit's leading the church beyond accommodation into plain truth is still to come. This assumption thus begs the question: If Jesus then, by referencing the male-female pattern of marriage, was accommodating a common-but-mistaken belief of that historical-cultural context, it could be that the church now, by sanctioning same-sex

---

22. See Bolz-Weber, *Shameless*.

union, is accommodating a common-but-misguided belief of this historical-cultural context. If the apostles (mis)interpreted Jesus's teaching of marriage through their cultural lens, then innovationists might be (mis)interpreting Jesus's teaching of marriage through their cultural lens.

However one parses disparity between "Jesus then" and "Jesus now," this second path of new dispensation suggests that, concerning marriage, either the church today is to discern God's will by the teaching of "another Jesus" than the Jesus of apostolic testimony—or Jesus, in some way, is not "the same yesterday and today and forever."

An innovationist might avoid disparity between "Jesus then" and "Jesus now" by proposing a third path of new dispensation: God, through the Holy Spirit, is giving the church a new teaching surpassing whatever Jesus taught or would teach. God's blessing of same-sex union indicates that just as God's dispensation through Jesus surpassed God's dispensation through Moses, the church today has received a new dispensation through the Holy Spirit that surpasses God's dispensation through Jesus. As "law indeed was given through Moses" and "grace and truth came through Jesus" (John 1:17), so inclusive love has come through the Holy Spirit, surpassing both Moses and Jesus. As then "something greater" than law and temple, prophets and sages, had come in Jesus (Matt. 12:1–8, 38–42; Heb. 3:1–6), so now "something greater" than Jesus has come by the Holy Spirit.

This third path of new dispensation has historical precedent: Montanism. We encountered this second-century movement in the figure of Tertullian (see chap. 5). The Montanists took a rigorist stance on marriage that exceeded and contradicted the teachings of Jesus and the apostles. Before the eschatological renewal, they taught, God has abolished the old order of marriage and procreation. Celibacy is evidence of the Spirit, marriage is permitted only for controlling lust, and second marriage is forbidden even for widows. Tertullian defended this rigorist stance by claiming a new dispensation from the Holy Spirit, who supposedly had given the "spiritualists" a previously unrevealed prophecy. As the "new law" through Jesus had revoked the "old law" conceding divorce yet permitted second marriage, so the "new prophecy" through the Holy Spirit has forbidden second marriage.

Now, ancient Montanism and modern innovationism diverge on sex and marriage: whereas Montanists retained marriage unaltered and adopted a more restrictive discipline of sex, innovationists advocate altering marriage and a less restrictive discipline of sex. Nonetheless, ancient Montanism and modern innovationism converge on discernment: as Tertullian justified forbidding remarriage by claiming a "new prophecy" from the Holy Spirit that surpassed Jesus and the apostles, so this innovationist proposal justifies sanctioning same-sex union by claiming a "new revelation" from the Holy Spirit that surpasses Jesus and the apostles. In that sense, marriage innovation may be seen as a neo-Montanist movement.

This third path of discernment prompts questions regarding not only Jesus and marriage but also Jesus and salvation. If the church has received a post-Jesus teaching from the Holy Spirit, has the church entered a post-Jesus era of salvation history? Are we still saved by Jesus, who came in the flesh, or has Savior Jesus been left behind? This third path of new dispensation, implicitly, casts doubt on the apostolic confession of Jesus.

Seeking the Spirit

The innovationist proposal that we recognize same-sex union as a new dispensation claims that sanctioning same-sex union is justified not by (even revisionist interpretations of) old teachings of Scripture and tradition but by a new teaching through the Holy Spirit. This proposal claims that the church today has received revelation from the Holy Spirit that surpasses and corrects the apostolic testimony to Jesus—which suggests that the church today has entered a new era of salvation history.[23] I have recalled three tests for discernment that Jesus and his apostles have given to the church, and I have considered three paths of new dispensation. Judging by these tests, that the spirit of this proposal is from God seems doubtful to me.

Yet the church today does need to seek direction of the Holy Spirit. I thus suggest that we look again to the discernment of the apostles and elders at the Jerusalem Council, which "seemed good to the Holy Spirit," for guidance in our discernment.

---

23. See also Greene-McCreight, "Logic of the Interpretation of Scripture," 251, 256–58; O'Donovan, *Church in Crisis*, 60–62.

10

It Seemed Good to the Holy Spirit

GUIDANCE FOR DISCERNMENT

For it has seemed good to the Holy Spirit and to us . . .

Acts 15:28

The apostles and elders convened in Jerusalem to discern together the theological question of whether gentile believers could be saved as gentiles (i.e., without circumcision) and, correspondingly, the ethical question of what would be required of gentile believers as members of God's people. The discernment of the apostles and elders took account of three things: the Spirit's activity to incorporate gentiles into God's people; the prophets' testimony to God's plan for a renewed Israel; and the law's standards of holiness and righteousness. Accordingly, the apostles and elders discerned a way that recognized gentile believers as equal members of God's people and, at the same time, reinforced biblical norms of ethical conduct for God's people. Acting "with the consent of the whole church," the apostles and elders sent emissaries from Jerusalem to Antioch with a decree concerning what "seemed good to the Holy Spirit and to [the council]" (Acts 15:22, 28).[1]

1. On the Jerusalem Council and apostolic decree, see appendix H in the online supplement.

The importance of this council and of the decree it issued is reflected in the fact that it is the only such decree officially issued by the early church recorded in the Acts of the Apostles.[2] Regarding both process of discernment and substance of decision, the Jerusalem Council has set an enduring precedent that can serve as a trustworthy guide for discernment in our present situation.[3]

The Jerusalem Council

Background to Discernment: Spirit and Salvation

The apostolic mission in Jerusalem and Judea had attracted believers in Jesus who were Jews and thus already belonged to God's people in the accustomed way, by receiving circumcision and observing Torah. By repenting from sin and confessing their faith, enacted and expressed through receiving baptism "in the name of Jesus Christ" (Acts 2:38), they now belonged to God's renewed Israel (Acts 2–3). The success of this mission engendered the expectation that all believers in Jesus would belong to God's renewed Israel in the same way, such that receiving circumcision and observing Torah would remain the standard of obedience for the whole people of God. That expectation, borne from experience, was buttressed by Scripture. God's covenant with Abraham had declared that circumcision would mark those belonging to God's people and receiving God's promise (Gen. 17:1–14). God's instruction to Moses had made circumcision prerequisite for partaking of the Passover meal, which celebrated God's salvation of God's people (Exod. 12:43–49).

The success of the apostolic mission beyond Jerusalem and Judea, which generated an influx of gentiles into the church from Samaria (Acts 8), Caesarea (Acts 10), Cilicia and Syria (Acts 11), and Asia Minor (Acts 13–14), disrupted this presumed order of initiation and discipline. The apostles' testimony that God had given to gentile believers "the repentance that leads to life" (11:18) through the Holy Spirit and baptism confounded the expectation that gentiles would belong to God's people by becoming Jews (i.e., receiving circumcision and observing Torah). Indeed, Peter testified, God's salvation of gentiles by conversion through the Holy Spirit revealed the unexpected in God's plan: rather than gentiles being saved as Jews, Jews would be saved in the same way as gentiles—by the grace of Jesus (15:11)![4]

---

2. L. Johnson, *Acts of the Apostles*, 268.

3. L. Johnson, *Scripture and Discernment*, 89–106, also looks to the Jerusalem Council as a paradigm for the church.

4. See L. Johnson, *Acts of the Apostles*, 263.

Process of Discernment: Spirit and Scripture

God's saving activity through the Holy Spirit pressed this question upon the church: What should be required of gentile believers who, not having received circumcision, have received baptism in the name of Jesus? This question, Luke reports, generated "no small dissension" and "much debate" (Acts 15:1–7).

At one end of the debate, Luke tells us, was the position advocated by Jewish believers of the Pharisee party in Jerusalem, which argued that gentile believers were acceptable to God only by *becoming Jews—and thus* that all those belonging to God's renewed Israel, including gentile believers, should be required to receive circumcision and observe the whole Torah (Acts 15:1, 5). At the other end of the debate, we might imagine, was the position advocated by gentile believers of a "liberty" party in Antioch, which argued that gentile believers were acceptable to God *as gentiles—and thus* that, in Christ, bondage under the yoke of law has been replaced by freedom in the law of love (cf. Gal. 5:1–6) such that gentile believers are in no way bound by Torah. The Jerusalem Council adopted *neither* of these opposed positions. Instead, the apostles and elders discerned a way of *both* gentiles belonging in Jesus *and* gentiles observing Torah: gentiles baptized into Jesus belong as gentiles (without circumcision) to God's renewed Israel—and are enjoined to observe those laws that God had given for gentiles.

The apostles and elders reached this Spirit-approved consensus by listening to experience and interpreting Scripture. Recalling God's giving gentiles the Holy Spirit, to which Peter was witness, Peter pressed the assembly to consider whether gentile believers are acceptable to God without circumcision and thus without observing the whole Torah (Acts 15:7–11). "The whole assembly kept silence, and listened" as Paul and Barnabas reported what God was doing among gentile believers (15:12; cf. 15:3–4). The spiritual experience of gentile believers, however, was not the sole basis or final arbiter of the council's decision.

The testimony of Peter and Paul to the saving work of the Holy Spirit among gentiles prompted the assembly to research the Scriptures and reread the prophets to discern God's will concerning gentiles. James, president of the council, premised his decision on Scripture's confirmation of Peter's testimony: Scripture agrees with God acting to save gentiles, James declared, for the prophets had long ago testified to God's will to draw gentiles into God's people (Acts 15:13–18). Gentile experience of the Spirit, to which Peter and Paul testified, was submitted to the testing of the church; and God's will to incorporate gentiles into God's people was discerned by interpreting Scripture in light of that testimony. Discernment at the Jerusalem Council was guided, therefore, by interpretation of Scripture prompted by experience of the Spirit, experience witnessed by the community and confirmed by Scripture.

The process of the Jerusalem Council was open to the activity of God's Spirit among gentiles, witnessed by the apostles, and bound to the testimony of God's will for gentiles, spoken by prophets. In this way, the Jerusalem Council took account of both experience and Scripture in discerning God's will for God's people. The Jerusalem Council illustrates how testimony to God's saving work through the Spirit can contribute to discernment by interpretation of Scripture: the prophets' testimony to God's will for gentile salvation is seen afresh in light of the Spirit's action to bring gentiles to Jesus.

Substance of Decision: Scripture and Tradition

I have observed how the Jerusalem Council interpreted the word of Scripture in light of the work of the Spirit. I now consider how the Jerusalem Council drew from the treasury of Scripture and tradition. While the process of their discernment took account of "what is new," the substance of their decision took account of "what is old."

The Jerusalem Council decided two things together: to baptize gentile believers without circumcision and to enjoin gentile believers to observe certain ethical mandates. The apostles and elders, with the church consenting and the Spirit approving, decreed that gentile believers should abstain from eating food offered to idols, blood, or meat of strangled animals, and from sexual immorality (Acts 15:20, 22, 28–29). These "essentials" or "necessities" were neither arbitrary nor novel but were derived from Scripture and tradition.

Luke's account of the Jerusalem Council does not cite a biblical source for the ethical mandates. Probably, they derived from the Holiness Code in Leviticus, which makes certain laws binding on non-Israelites residing among Israelites. Those laws prohibited idolatry, drinking blood or eating meat with blood, and various forms of illicit sex, including same-sex intercourse, as well as blasphemy and murder (Lev. 17:8–18:30; 24:10–22). Or, possibly, they were a version of Noachian laws derived from Genesis (Gen. 9:1–7), which delineated God's will for "the nations" of Noah's descendants and defined "righteous gentiles" (e.g., Cornelius, Acts 10:1–2). Rabbinic tradition codified seven laws, which forbade idolatry, eating meat torn from living animals, and various forms of illicit sex, including same-sex intercourse, as well as blasphemy, murder, and theft. Or, plausibly, the Jerusalem Council may have drawn from both biblical sources.[5]

---

5. On the source and rationale of the apostolic decree, see appendix H in the online supplement.

The decision to baptize gentile believers without circumcision did not imply that the church had set aside the old law or that the Holy Spirit had dispensed or inspired a new law. The apostles and elders discerned not *whether* biblical law is applicable to gentile believers but *which* biblical laws are appropriate for gentile observance. Luke Timothy Johnson comments: "The elimination of Mosaic *ethos* (custom) [i.e., circumcision] for the Gentiles does not mean the elimination of Torah, but rather the fulfillment of its prophetic intention, 'made known from long ago' (15:18), as well as the continuation of those aspects of Torah that have always applied to the proselyte and sojourner."[6] The apostles and elders applied to gentile believers in the church those laws that God had already given for non-Israelite residents in Israel and gentiles generally. Those biblical laws were summarized in the ethical mandates of the apostolic decree issued by the Jerusalem Council. Markus Bockmuehl comments: "It is the covenant's terms of membership, not its moral and spiritual intention, which the coming of Christ opens up: in the very fact of messianic fulfillment lie both the reformation of the covenant relationship and the continuity of its substance and purpose. . . . This suggests that the Scriptures retain their moral force even for Gentile conduct."[7] The apostles and elders, therefore, did not presume authority to either nullify old law or devise new law. The Jerusalem Council, with approval of the Holy Spirit, upheld the continuing validity and appropriate applicability of biblical laws for gentile believers.

By enjoining gentile believers to observe biblical laws, moreover, the Jerusalem Council adhered to tradition. Applying biblical laws to gentile believers, Bockmuehl comments, was traditional, not innovational: "The New Testament authors make very substantial use of a traditional *halakhah for Gentiles*, which can be traced from the Pentateuchal laws for resident aliens all the way to the rabbinic Noachide Commandments. Ever since the Levitical Holiness Code and the prophets, these views had concentrated on the prohibitions of idolatry, sexual immorality, and blood offences."[8] The Jerusalem Council's adherence to tradition, alongside the innovation of baptism without circumcision, is important for our discernment. Willard Swartley comments: "The Jerusalem Council reaffirmed certain tenets of Jewish faith that were not to be compromised in the admission of uncircumcised Gentiles into the community. Since one of these tenets is proscription of sexual immorality, it becomes difficult to 'bracket' this conclusion when utilizing this process for discernment on the homosexuality issue."[9] The church discerned with

---

6. L. Johnson, *Acts of the Apostles*, 268.
7. Bockmuehl, *Jewish Law in Gentile Churches*, 169.
8. Bockmuehl, *Jewish Law in Gentile Churches*, 232–33 (emphasis original).
9. Swartley, *Homosexuality*, 124.

the Spirit's agreement that biblical laws and traditional teaching concerning sexual holiness were neither relegated to an old era of God's providence nor restricted to Jewish believers among God's people.

Within Hellenistic Judaism, these biblical laws had been gathered into a common stock of synagogue teaching concerning ethical standards for gentiles.[10] James justified applying these biblical laws to gentile believers by appealing to this teaching tradition: "For in every city, for generations past, Moses has had those who proclaim him, for he has been read aloud every sabbath in the synagogues" (Acts 15:21). James emphasized the universality ("in every city"), antiquity ("for generations past"), and regularity ("every sabbath") of this teaching tradition, which confirmed the reasonability of the council's decision: the ethical mandates of the apostolic decree were "not trouble" for "those Gentiles who are turning to God" (15:19–20), James argued, because God's law for gentiles had been proclaimed by Scripture reading and ethics teaching in the synagogues. Presumably, "God-fearing" gentiles who associated with synagogues in Greek cities would already have heard and been observing these laws even before hearing the gospel and believing in Jesus.[11] For these reasons—because God had given these laws for gentiles, because Jews had recognized these laws as God's will for gentiles, and because gentiles had received these laws as God's will—the apostles and elders saw gentile observance of these laws not as an unreasonable burden but rather as appropriate practice for gentile members of God's people.

The gentile believers in Antioch saw it the same way, evidently. When Paul and Barnabas returned from the Jerusalem Council, they gathered the congregation and delivered the council's letter. "When its members read it, they rejoiced at the exhortation" (Acts 15:30–31). After reception of the council's decision in Antioch, Paul revisited congregations in Syria, Cilicia, and Asia Minor, transmitting this tradition: "They passed on [*paredidosan*] the decrees [*dogmata*] that had been decided on by the apostles and elders in Jerusalem for the Gentile believers to obey" (16:4 NET).

The Jerusalem Council's decision was not a negotiated compromise. The apostles and elders did not serve in the role of neutral mediators between opposing parties. James did not simply take the two end-point positions (all Torah versus no Torah) and settle on something in the middle (some Torah) to partially please both sides. The apostolic decree was not merely a modus vivendi, a useful agreement to facilitate cooperation between disagreeing factions in a difficult situation. The gathered church, prompted by personal

10. See J. Collins, *Between Athens and Jerusalem*, 155–85; Rosner, *Paul, Scripture and Ethics*, 38–58; Runesson, "Entering a Synagogue with Paul."

11. See L. Johnson, *Acts of the Apostles*, 267, 273.

testimony and guided by the Holy Spirit, researched Scripture and consulted tradition to discern God's will for God's people. The council's decision, which "seemed good to the Holy Spirit and to [them]" (Acts 15:28), bears divine authority that precedes and exceeds human authority.[12]

The Jerusalem Council and the Church Today

As did the question of gentile salvation, the question of same-sex union has generated "no small dissension" and "much debate." The Jerusalem Council, regarding both process of discernment and substance of decision, can guide us well in the church today. To follow the process and honor the substance of the Jerusalem Council, we must hold together testimony to the Spirit, interpretation of Scripture, and teaching of tradition.

Discernment: Spirit and Scripture

The discernment process of the Jerusalem Council was guided by both experience of the Spirit and interpretation of Scripture: the assembly reread the prophets' testimony to God's will for gentiles in light of the apostles' testimony to the Spirit's work among gentile believers. The church today, likewise, should listen to the testimonies of gay believers to the Spirit's work in their lives and then, in that light, research Scripture. I have witnessed the Spirit's working in and through gay believers for the good of the church and to the glory of God.

I will focus here on testimonies of gay believers who, by God's grace and the Spirit's help, have committed themselves and their lives to obedience, celibacy, and service in Christ.[13] Bridget Eileen, a gay celibate believer, explains why their testimonies are significant for the church's discernment of God's will: "God delights in saving the most unlikely of peoples. And who is considered less likely to follow the traditional teachings of Scripture than an LGBT+ person? . . . Where the Gospel is most unlikely, that's where the glory of God shines brightest. . . . Our testimony glorifies God precisely because it's so unlikely."[14] In what follows, I offer one way the church might research Scripture in light of the testimonies of these believers.[15]

---

12. See also Ash, *Marriage*, 90–99.

13. See the writings by Ron Belgau, David Bennett, Gregory Coles, Bridget Eileen, Martin Hallett, Wesley Hill, Greg Johnson, Ed Shaw, Eve Tushnet, Pieter Valk, and Christopher Yuan listed in the bibliography.

14. Eileen, *8 Essential Thoughts*, 54–55.

15. Focusing on testimonies of other believers could suggest other paths of researching Scripture. Testimonies of gay believers in mixed-orientation marriages might prompt us to reread biblical stories of intermarriages (e.g., Boaz and Ruth) and reconciliation in that

The testimonies of gay celibate believers lead me first to Jesus, who honored among his disciples those "who have made themselves eunuchs for the sake of the kingdom of heaven" (Matt. 19:12). In Jesus's vision of God's kingdom, those who forgo marriage and children for the sake of obeying God and following Jesus are promised spiritual family in this age and eternal life in the age to come (Matt. 19:29; Mark 10:29–30; Luke 18:29–30). Celibacy both anticipates the surpassing of marriage in the future age of God's people and demonstrates what is possible in the present age among God's people by God's power. Rereading the Gospels, we may see gay celibate believers as faithful disciples of Jesus, whose lives bear God's promise, display God's power, and prefigure God's future for all faithful disciples.

Jesus's praise of "eunuchs for the kingdom" leads me to the prophet Isaiah, who spoke God's promise to "eunuchs who . . . hold fast [the LORD's] covenant." Eunuchs faithful to God's covenant will receive an honored place in God's "house" and "an everlasting name" among God's people. God gave the same promise to "foreigners who join themselves to the LORD" and who "hold fast" God's covenant. God will bring them to God's "holy mountain," where they will worship in God's "house of prayer." In Isaiah's vision of God's kingdom, God's promise to eunuchs and proselytes is part of God's plan to gather "the outcasts of Israel" and "others to them besides" (Isa. 56:3–8). Rereading the Prophets, we may see God's promise being fulfilled in the faithful obedience and fruitful service of gay celibate believers, who are partaking of God's plan to gather "outcasts" and "others" into God's people.

Isaiah's word to eunuchs and proselytes, Jews and gentiles, leads me to the apostle Paul, who proclaimed that among baptized believers, "there is neither Jew nor Greek, there is neither slave nor free, there is neither male nor female" (Gal. 3:28 NET). Everyone "baptized into Christ" is "clothed . . . with Christ," so that, regardless of ethnicity or status or gender, "all . . . are one in Christ Jesus" (3:27–28 NET) and "Christ is all and in all" (Col. 3:11 NET). All baptized believers are adopted as God's children, becoming heirs of God's promise and receiving the Holy Spirit as God's pledge and power (see Rom. 8:1–17; 2 Cor. 1:21–22; Gal. 3:26–4:7; Eph. 1:13–14). In Paul's vision of God's kingdom, we regard no baptized believer "according to the flesh," because anyone "in Christ" is a "new creation" (2 Cor. 5:16–17; my translation). Rereading the apostles, we may see gay celibate believers as children of

---

light. Testimonies of gay believers in same-sex partnerships, as noted in previous chapters, have prompted some to reinterpret biblical stories of same-sex friendships (e.g., David and Jonathan), unconventional marriages (e.g., Joseph and Mary), and outsider inclusion (e.g., eunuchs) in that light.

God who are "clothed . . . with Christ" (Gal. 3:28) and "marked with the seal of the promised Holy Spirit" (Eph. 1:13) and thus manifest "new creation."

Paul's word of "new creation" leads me to the apostle John, to whom the Spirit gave the vision of "a new heaven and a new earth." John saw "the holy city, the new Jerusalem" descending from heaven to earth, "prepared as a bride adorned for her husband." In John's vision of God's kingdom, heaven and earth are reconciled and all creation is restored through the marriage of Christ and the church, by which God will dwell with God's people (Rev. 21:1–4). Rereading Revelation, we may see gay celibate believers, adorned with faith, hope, and love, as already preparing the church for her holy destiny as the "bride of Christ."

Rereading Scripture in light of God's giving the Holy Spirit to gentile believers refreshed the apostles' vision of salvation and the church. The Spirit's bringing gentiles to faith in Jesus signaled the next stage in God's plan—gathering gentiles into God's people. This realization refreshed their vision of God's salvation: "We believe that [Jews] will be saved through the grace of the Lord Jesus, just as [Gentiles] will" (Acts 15:11). Consequently, regarding salvation in Christ, "neither circumcision nor uncircumcision counts for anything; the only thing that counts is faith working through love"—all that matters in Christ is "new creation" (Gal. 5:6; 6:15). This realization refreshed their vision of the church as encompassing all nations in Christ—Jews and gentiles—and thus comprising "a house of prayer for all peoples" (Isa. 56:7).

Rereading Scripture in light of testimonies of gay celibate believers may also refresh our vision of salvation and the church. The Spirit's working among gay celibate believers indicates God's purpose in the present—creating a community of disciples to make God's way of righteousness visible and God's word of salvation credible to all peoples. The Spirit's working among gay celibate believers also signifies God's promise for the future—renewing all creation by life beyond birth and death in resurrection beyond marriage and procreation. This realization refreshes our vision of salvation: straight and married believers will be saved the same way as gay and single believers, by the grace of Jesus. Regarding salvation in Christ, neither marital status nor sexual identity counts for us or against us—all that matters is faith working through love as we become a new creation by God's power. This realization refreshes our vision of the church as the Spirit's gathering of believers in Jesus from all nations into God's people. God's people, who live even now in God's promise of resurrection by God's power that raised Jesus, are called by God's purpose to a new life in which all believers—male and female, married and single, straight and gay—belong together as brothers and sisters of one family and labor together as servants in God's household.

Decision: Scripture and Tradition

The Jerusalem Council decided to baptize gentile believers while enjoining them to observe certain biblical laws. Some might propose a seemingly Jerusalem-like decision for the church today: bless same-sex couples in marriage while enjoining gay believers to observe monogamy. This decision would reject both extremes of the debate—excluding gay believers from marriage and liberating sex from monogamy—and affirm a middle position embracing both tradition (monogamy) and innovation (same-sex union). Such a proposal would view the Jerusalem Council's process as a negotiation and their decision as a compromise: a middle way to partly please both sides. This view, however, falls short of Luke's account.

The Jerusalem Council, recognizing the Spirit's work in gentile believers, addressed the question of God's will for gentile believers. In discerning God's will for gentile believers, the apostles and elders drew from Scripture and tradition: biblical laws God had given to Israel for non-Israelites and traditional teaching of biblical laws for gentile observance. The church today, recognizing the Spirit's work in gay believers, must address the question of God's will for gay believers. Here we are discerning whether God declares same-sex union to be holy marriage. To honor the substance of the Jerusalem Council's decision in our discernment, we should draw from Scripture and tradition to discern this question.

Scripture, consistently, presents a single picture of marriage and approves a single pattern of sexual relations: male-female union. Jesus summarizes this witness: "the two" of "male and female" joined into "one flesh." The Holy Spirit has woven this pattern of holy union throughout Scripture, from Genesis to Revelation, in the form, function, and figure of marriage. Tradition, East and West, also has consistently taught a single standard of sex and marriage: marriage is man-woman monogamy; all sex outside man-woman monogamy is sin. This doctrine has been taught always by the church, beginning with the apostles' testimony to Jesus's teaching; it has been proclaimed throughout the worldwide church, among all peoples in every place and epoch, as God's will for sex and marriage; it has been articulated by apologetic writings and theological treatises, transmitted through baptismal catechesis and canonical discipline, celebrated in monastic vows and nuptial rites. On account of the consistency of this teaching in Scripture and the catholicity of this teaching in tradition, because the church has long proclaimed to believers and nonbelievers alike that this is God's will for sex and marriage, it is reasonable that the church today continue this biblical-traditional teaching.

One might doubt whether anyone who isn't straight would willingly or gladly accept this teaching. Biblical-traditional teaching on sex and marriage, some critics assert, is a heterosexist dogma that the straight majority has unfairly forced onto sexual minorities. The discipline of chastity, some Christians protest, is a burden that even straight believers have not been able to bear and from which gay believers should be liberated. Traditionalists would change their minds on sex and marriage, some innovationists suggest, were they "blessed" by "transformative encounters" with gay believers.[16] Were it true that only straight believers accept the traditional view, while all (or nearly all) gay believers reject the traditional view in favor of an innovational view, which might indicate heterosexist bias in the traditional view, it would put a serious reservation in my mind whether the traditional view adequately reflects God's will. But it is not true.

As Bridget Eileen observes, "Sexual and gender minorities who willingly affirm the historic teachings of the Bible seem utterly impossible to the world-at-large."[17] Yet, as Scripture testifies, what seems impossible to humans is possible for God (Gen. 18:14; Luke 1:37; 18:27). Surprising as it may seem, many gay believers in the church today, like the gentile believers in Antioch, have "rejoiced at the exhortation" (Acts 15:31) of church teaching. Many gay believers—men and women, celibate and married—have gladly received and willingly keep the biblical-traditional teaching of sex and marriage and have shared their testimonies with the church. This reception is evident especially in the Revoice gathering, which annually draws hundreds of gay believers, as well as straight believers, for worship and fellowship, teaching and witness, all while affirming the orthodox faith and traditional ethic of the church catholic.[18] This reception is evident also in online forums such as Spiritual Friendship, which features diverse voices of gay believers reflecting as disciples on faith, vocation, and sexuality.[19] It is evident further in parachurch ministries such as EQUIP, which supports gay believers in living faithfully and fruitfully as followers of Jesus and equips congregations to love and serve gay believers with compassion and integrity.[20] And it is evident in numerous books, articles, and blogs written by gay believers that affirm or defend the biblical-traditional ethic of sex and theology of marriage.[21] By the Holy Spirit, gay believers in the church today are receiving and keeping the biblical-traditional teaching as God's will for sex and marriage.

16. See Gushee, *Changing Our Mind*, 109–10.
17. Eileen, *8 Essential Thoughts*, 55.
18. Find Revoice online at https://revoice.us/.
19. Find Spiritual Friendship online at https://spiritualfriendship.org/.
20. Find EQUIP online at https://equipyourcommunity.org/.
21. See the writings by Ron Belgau, David Bennett, Gregory Coles, Nate Collins, Bridget Eileen, Rachel Gilson, Martin Hallett, Wesley Hill, Greg Johnson, Ed Shaw, Eve Tushnet, Pieter Valk, and Christopher Yuan listed in the bibliography.

Continuing biblical-traditional teaching, however, does not entail excluding gay believers from marrying in the church. The church may, and should, affirm the blessing of "mixed orientation" man-woman couples. Continuing biblical-traditional teaching, moreover, does not imply simply imposing burdens on gay believers. While it is reasonable for the church to ask gay believers to accept the burden of this teaching, it is *not* reasonable for the church either to expect gay believers to bear this burden alone or to ask only gay believers to accept this burden.

The Jerusalem Council did decide to "burden" gentile believers with biblical laws of sexual holiness (Acts 15:28–29). And the apostles did call gentile believers in the early church to the holy discipline of sexual chastity. Yet that burden was not imposed apart from the prior gift of God's grace, nor was it meant to be borne apart from the mutuality and solidarity of the faith community. And that discipline was mandated to all believers: even as the apostles recognized that God saves by grace, Jew and gentile equally, they discerned that biblical laws of sexual holiness apply to all God's people, gentile and Jew equally.

The church today, guided by the Jerusalem Council, should decide to "burden" gay believers with biblical laws of sexual holiness. Pastors should call gay believers to the holy discipline of sexual chastity. At the same time, the church should apply biblical laws of sexual holiness to all believers: sexual chastity should be a communal practice, not a special discipline for gay believers. Pastors, acknowledging that sexual chastity burdens believers who are gay or single differently than believers who are straight or married, should also exhort believers who are straight or married to bear burdens with believers who are gay or single: sexual chastity summons us to communal solidarity, not heroic feats of individual sacrifice. The church today should call all baptized believers—male and female, married and single, straight and gay—to chastity and solidarity.

In receiving guidance from the Jerusalem Council, the church today must remember the words of Jesus Christ. Jesus calls to himself all those who are "weary" and "carrying heavy burdens." Jesus says of himself, "I am gentle and humble in heart," and of his teaching, "my yoke is easy" and "my burden is light" (Matt. 11:28–30). Jesus also warns us against "experts in the law" who "tie up heavy burdens" for others to bear but are "unwilling to lift a finger" to help others bear their burdens (23:2–4). Paul, accordingly, exhorts the church to "fulfill the law of Christ" by teaching and disciplining with "a spirit of gentleness" and by bearing one another's burdens (Gal. 6:1–2). As Nate Collins observes, "One uncomfortable implication of this verse is that straight people who resist carrying the unique burden of their gay brothers and sisters are disobeying the law of Christ."[22] The church today dare not use biblical-traditional teaching to simply tie up heavy burdens to be grimly borne by gay believers. Traditionalists, especially, have a responsibility to build communities of charity, fidelity, and solidarity in which keeping the holy discipline of sexual chastity is viable for all believers.[23]

Discerning New and Old: Then and Now

In chapter 1, I set before us Jesus's saying about the "scribe trained for the kingdom" who discerns "what is new and what is old" (Matt. 13:52). At the Jerusalem Council, the apostles and elders, as wise scribes well trained for God's kingdom, discerned both new and old in God's will for God's people. They discerned what is new by listening to the testimony of the apostles to the salvation of gentiles who feared God and did right. Their stories testified to God's giving the Spirit and baptism to those who had not been circumcised. Rereading the prophets' visions of God's plan of salvation for the nations, in the fresh light of those testimonies, the apostles and elders discerned that the Holy Spirit was gathering gentile believers into God's people. At the same time, the apostles and elders discerned what is old by looking into the treasury of Torah and tradition: God's law given for gentiles through Israel, proclaimed among the nations in the synagogues. The Torah of God taught by Israel in the synagogues had long proclaimed among gentiles that God calls people of all nations to abstain from unclean practices and immoral behaviors. Drawing from the storehouse of Torah and tradition, the apostles and elders discerned God's will that gentile believers in the church should abstain from unclean practices and immoral behaviors that God had always forbidden for all nations.

In our discernment, we would be wise and do well to do likewise, discerning both what is new and what is old in God's will for the church today. We discern what is new by listening to the testimonies of gay believers who are living faithfully and serving fruitfully as followers of Jesus. Their stories testify to Jesus calling them to walk the difficult road of costly discipleship, and to the Holy Spirit blessing them with gifts for doing God's work through the church. Their stories testify to love of God and neighbor, a love too often unrecognized and unrequited within the church. Rereading the biblical story of God's salvation, in the fresh light of these testimonies, we discern the Holy Spirit gathering

22. N. Collins, *All but Invisible*, 37.
23. See Wesley Hill's afterword to this book. See also Eileen, *8 Essential Thoughts*, 3–30; Hill, *Washed and Waiting*, 51–79; Shaw, *Same-Sex Attraction and the Church*, 135–51; Callaway, *Breaking the Marriage Idol*, 213–41; Hitchcock, *Significance of Singleness*, 132–40.

gay believers into God's people. At the same time, we discern what is old by looking into the treasury of Scripture and tradition: the consistent testimony of Scripture, confirmed by the authoritative teaching of Christ and conserved through the consensus teaching of the church, that God ordained marriage as man-woman monogamy and blessed sex within marriage. It is from that treasury that I have drawn in offering counsel to the church.

Afterword

WESLEY HILL

Well, here you are. You've reached the end of one of the most careful, judicious, and cogent defenses of the so-called traditional Christian view of marriage and sexuality that we now have. And perhaps, having read this far, you, like Agrippa, are almost persuaded (see Acts 26:28 KJV). But one question probably lingers: *Is this Christian vision of marriage and sexuality actually livable, especially by those who know themselves to be lesbian, gay, or bisexual?*[1]

Theologian Stephen Holmes, remarking on the Appalachian churches who handle poisonous snakes as part of their worship, has pointed out that there *is* an exegetical case to be made for the practice: "Those who believe," Jesus says in the longer (and canonical) ending of Mark, "will pick up snakes in their hands" (16:18). Yet, says Holmes, snake handling "seems so self-evidently ridiculous, on account of the threat to health involved, that I see no reason to give time to exploring its supposed justifications; they simply must be wrong." Similarly, perhaps, despite having now read the formidable exegetical and theological case for traditional marriage presented in this book, you can only conclude that it must be flawed somewhere. It cannot actually be right: "The conclusion pressed is so self-evidently wrong, again on account

---

1. I intentionally leave out the question of how far this vision is embraceable for trans*, queer, intersex, and asexual people and other sexual minorities, believing the issues raised by those communities are sufficiently distinct as to require a fuller treatment. For a useful orientation to some of the issues and questions involved, see Cornwall, *Theology and Sexuality*, chap. 3.

of the threat to health involved, that arguments for it [must be] assumed to be inadequate."[2]

We arrive, then, at "the plausibility problem."[3] Exegetical and theological argument can only take us so far. For many readers, the final hurdle to embracing the conclusion this book presses isn't intellectual; it's personal, communal, relational, moral. How can the conclusion that marriage is designed by God to be the lifelong union of a man and woman who are open to the gift of children actually be good news for LGB people? How could it ever lead to their—*our*, for I include myself in their number—flourishing?

But I want to approach these questions from the other side, as it were. I have written at length elsewhere about the fact that I happen to be gay as well as convinced by the arguments this book makes.[4] And so I ask myself: What must *I* and my fellow "traditionalist" Christians do in order to make the vision of this book plausible for those who are not yet persuaded by it? Sociologists have long recognized that if people undergo a change of heart and mind, it is usually because some persons and communities have made that change seem possible by the way they live.[5] How might someone like me become such a person—someone who by their life and behavior helps make this book's conclusions embraceable by those who might otherwise deem them to be wrong, pernicious, or both? The answers to that question are many, but let me mention three important ones here.

⸻

The first thing I would say to myself and my fellow Christian "traditionalists" is, *Prioritize repentance and advocate for the wronged.*

Since writing my two books about being gay and celibate, I have met dozens of other LGBTQ Christians who have told me stories of the discrimination and rejection they've endured solely because of their decision to be honest about their sexual desires. For example, at the first annual Revoice conference in St. Louis in 2018, a conference for LGBTQ Christians who wish to adhere to a traditional Christian sexual ethic, a celibate gay Christian named Ray

2. S. Holmes, "On Not Handling Snakes," in Noble, Whittle, and Johnston, *Marriage, Family and Relationships*, 256.

3. See Shaw, *Same-Sex Attraction and the Church* (UK edition: *Plausibility Problem*).

4. See my books *Washed and Waiting* (exp. ed., 2016) and *Spiritual Friendship*.

5. See the comments of Newbigin, *Gospel in a Pluralist Society*, 227: "How is it possible that the gospel should be credible, that people should come to believe that the power which has the last word in human affairs is represented by a man hanging on a cross? I am suggesting that the only answer, the only hermeneutic of the gospel, is a congregation of men and women who believe it and live by it." Newbigin draws here on the work of Peter Berger on "plausibility structures" (*Sacred Canopy*, 45, 192).

Low told of applying for youth ministry positions, only to be denied on the basis of his sexual orientation. "I had one interview with a church that lasted no longer than 15 minutes before I was told that I was not a good fit, which is the most diplomatic way that a church likes to put it," he said. "And I had somebody tell me in another church that on paper, I was the perfect candidate, but my sexuality made it difficult for them to hire me."[6]

Chris Damian, a gay Catholic attorney, tells a similar tale: "I was [once] offered a prestigious position working for the Church. In the spirit of full disclosure, I shared with some stakeholders my sexuality and my public work on homosexuality and Catholicism. I made clear that all of my work aimed at promoting the teachings of the Catholic Church in their entirety. But after further consideration, they rescinded the offer, saying that the current tensions between the Church and the LGB community would make my work unnecessarily complicated, both for myself and for the Church. Another—straight—Catholic got the job."[7] More than one blogger at Spiritual Friendship (spiritualfriendship.org), the website I coedit for LGBTQ/same-sex-attracted Christians who adhere to the traditional Christian sexual ethic, has been fired from a Christian institution for disclosing their sexual orientation to superiors. Ron Belgau, my fellow blogger there, has highlighted the injustice of this in stark terms: "In each case, the Christian bosses agreed that the person they were terminating was not guilty of any sin, nor did he hold any belief about sexuality at odds with Christian orthodoxy. It was simply that they were unwilling to have an employee with same-sex attraction, even if he was completely committed to orthodox belief and obedient to orthodox teaching."[8] Were all of this not bad enough, I have also heard stories from numerous gay Christians about their fear and experiences of physical aggression and violence—not because of any actions or behaviors on their part (which wouldn't justify violence in any case) but purely because of their sexual orientation.

In short, injustice toward LGBTQ people is still very much alive and well in conservative religious communities, and that's not even to mention the wider problem of antigay animus in secular spaces.[9]

In light of these disturbing realities, the first thing Christians who wish to make a traditional view of marriage and sexuality plausible must cultivate

6. Ray Low, "General Session 2: Lament" (plenary address, Revoice 2018, Memorial Presbyterian Church, St. Louis, MO, July 27, 2018), https://www.youtube.com/watch?v=SHe2y2SVjIc.

7. Chris Damian, "Discrimination in the Catholic Church," *Chris Damian* (blog), August 17, 2017, https://chrisdamian.net/2017/08/17/discrimination-in-the-catholic-church/.

8. Belgau, "Brief Note on Phil Robertson and Double Standards."

9. The problem of LGBTQ youth homelessness, often the direct result of religiously motivated exclusion from families of origin, looms large here; see Human Rights Campaign Staff, "New Report on Youth Homeless."

is what Saint Paul calls "godly grief" (2 Cor. 7:9). Antigay injustice is still, troublingly, bound up with Christian culture-warring zeal.[10] And still Christians claim the moral high ground; "Ought you not rather to mourn?" (1 Cor. 5:2 RSV). Indeed, Christians ought to mourn publicly the ways they have not only actively harmed lesbian, gay, and bisexual people but also passively stood by while their basic human freedoms (such as the right to visit a hospitalized partner) were being trampled on. The first—and continual—posture Christians wishing to defend biblical teaching on marriage ought to adopt is a posture of repentance. Furthermore, Christians should commit themselves to the costly work of advocating for those who are vulnerable to the kind of discrimination described above.

There's an apocryphal Luther quote that goes like this: "If I profess with the loudest voice and clearest exposition every portion of the Word of God except precisely that little point which the world and the devil are at that moment attacking, I am not confessing Christ, however boldly I may be professing Him." Traditionalist Christians are fond of using this quote to insist that we must stand up for the truth of the historic Christian sexual ethic even as it is being attacked in contemporary Western cultures and that to fail to do so is to fail to be biblical and orthodox. In a mainline Protestant church like the one I belong to, I feel the force of this. These days it can seem easy to preach Christ in every way *but* the way that he challenges progressive sexual mores.

And yet "the world" that "Luther" mentions in the quotation above is not always the world of progressive secularism. Sometimes "the world" attacks the truth of Christ by tempting Christians to demean, disdain, ignore, overburden, or otherwise harm LGBTQ people. "The world" and "the devil" can manifest themselves in so-called progressivism, yes—*and* they can manifest themselves just as easily whenever a Christian heaps shame on LGBTQ people ("There's something more askew in your life than there is in that of heterosexuals," is what a pastor once told me), or offers a quick solution to their complex dilemmas ("Find a wife!" is advice I have been given by more than one Christian), or caricatures their sex lives ("Gay culture is inherently and always promiscuous"), or damages their faith ("If you want healing from same-sex attraction, it *is* available, and you have only to say yes," I have been promised by Christians numerous times, with the implication that my lack of faith is the reason I am still gay), or in any number of other ways attacks their dignity. If you are in a so-called conservative church and you are loudly proclaiming the truth about homosexuality at every point *but* at the point where that truth insists on the worth, dignity, and basic humanity of LGBTQ

---

10. For a searing account of one person's experience of this injustice, see Conley, *Boy Erased*.

people—if you are binding up heavy burdens on them and not lifting a finger to help (Matt. 23:4)—then you are not proclaiming Christian truth, no matter how much you claim otherwise.[11]

The *Catechism of the Catholic Church*, that great compendium of Christian teaching, stresses two things at once in its discussion of homosexuality: "Basing itself on Sacred Scripture, which presents homosexual acts as acts of grave depravity, tradition has always declared that 'homosexual acts are intrinsically disordered,'" and "men and women who have deep-seated homosexual tendencies . . . must be accepted with respect, compassion, and sensitivity. Every sign of unjust discrimination in their regard should be avoided."[12] Contemporary Christian defenders of traditional teaching on marriage and sexuality have often been faithful in proclaiming the Catechism's first point, the moral wrongness of same-sex sexual intimacy (though this is often done insensitively and with disproportionately harsh discipline). They have been rather less faithful in emphasizing the second. We must repent of this unfaithfulness and set ourselves to fight for justice on behalf of lesbian, gay, and bisexual people with every bit as much moral alacrity as that with which we have tried to fight against attempts to evade Scripture's challenging witness on sexuality. We must seek to "first take the log out of [our] own eye, and then [we] will see clearly to take the speck out of [our] neighbor's eye" (Matt. 7:5).

———•———

The second recommendation I have is this: *Recognize the call to an ascetic transformation of desire and reframe the church's debate over same-sex relations accordingly.*

Stephen Holmes has remarked memorably: "[The] story of warped desires being disciplined and re-ordered seems to me to be somewhere near the heart of a biblical theology of sexuality."[13] As Holmes goes on to make clear, this is just as much the case for so-called heterosexual persons as it is for lesbian, gay, and bisexual persons—if not more so. That there exists now, in a world disfigured by Adam's fall, a sexuality that is "normal" and "natural" as opposed to ones that are "disordered" and "broken" is a pious chimera. *All* sexualities as we experience them now are, in Holmes's words, "fallen and multiply broken; all our desires are warped and twisted out of their proper shape."[14] And this means that the call on straight Christians, in particular, is

11. The last two paragraphs of this section are adapted from Hill, "Where the World Attacks."
12. Roman Catholic Church, *Catechism of the Catholic Church*, §2357.
13. S. Holmes, "Homosexuality & Hermeneutics."
14. S. Holmes, "Homosexuality & Hermeneutics."

to renounce self-righteousness and stand in solidarity with so-called sexual minorities, as we, together, seek to submit our desires to "the crucible of divine desire."[15]

Several years ago, the conservative religious journal *First Things* caused an online ruckus when it published the provocatively titled essay "Against Heterosexuality" by a young Catholic layman named Michael Hannon. In the piece, Hannon called on Christians to forsake identifying themselves by their sexuality at all, and he insisted that this was an urgent matter for so-called straight people above all:

> The most pernicious aspect of the orientation-identity system is that it tends to exempt heterosexuals from moral evaluation. . . . As a general rule, identifying as a heterosexual person today amounts to declaring oneself a member of the "normal group," against which all deviant sexual desires and attractions and temptations are to be measured. Such hetero-identification thus ushers in a pathetically uncritical and—hopefully it goes without saying—unmerited self-assurance, not to mention an inaccurate measure for evaluating temptation. . . . It is true that homosexuality may be distinguished by an inappropriate despair, accepting sinful inclinations as identity-constituting and thereby implicitly rejecting the freedom bought for us by the blood of Christ. But heterosexuality, in its pretensions to act as the norm for assessing our sexual customs, is marked by something even worse: pride, which St. Thomas Aquinas classifies as the queen of all vices.[16]

There were some problems with Hannon's piece (he failed, for instance, to discuss in any depth how and why sexual minorities have often had their identifying terms forced upon them [e.g., "queer"] and why it has often felt necessary to sexual minorities to reclaim, reimagine, and retain them), but its basic thesis still strikes me as essential: there is no such thing as a "normal" sexuality on this side of Eden, and therefore all of us, without exception, are summoned to a long and arduous journey of sexual sanctification, with no room for arrogant disdain at all.

Were we to adopt such a perspective, it would become harder to characterize lesbian, gay, and bisexual people as the "broken" ones in need of sexual healing and straight people as living out a "natural" sexuality. Instead, we would together be pursuing parallel projects of self-denial, seeking to surrender more and more to the ever-beckoning lure of God's prior love for us. My friend and coauthor Stephen Holmes, already mentioned above, has written

15. See Coakley, *God, Sexuality, and the Self*, 52.
16. Hannon, "Against Heterosexuality," 27–34.

an essay in memory of the Baptist theologian Stanley Grenz, who once authored a book about homosexuality entitled *Welcoming but Not Affirming*. The title encapsulates Grenz's argument: the church is called to herald the unconditional welcome of Jesus Christ to any and all sexual sinners, regardless of sexual orientation; and, at the same time, it is not given to the church to baptize what God has called sinful (namely, same-sex sexual acts), and so not every felt inclination and identity of sexual sinners can simply be rubber-stamped by the church. The pastoral theology so encapsulated, Holmes maintains, is good as far as it goes: LGB people are extravagantly welcomed; LGB people's behaviors and identities are subject to the profound transformations of discipleship.[17] The problem, says Holmes, is when we begin to think that the "welcoming but not affirming" posture is for LGB people only; in fact, it is for everyone, LGB and straight alike: "While we say 'some are welcome and need no change; others need change before they can be welcomed' we have failed very badly."[18]

The more we can recover a vision of sexual holiness that exposes all of us, without exception, as in need of forgiveness, liberation, and sanctification and that beckons all of us, without exception, into a lifelong process of having our desires confronted, challenged, and transformed by the love of God in Christ, the closer we will be to approaching the life mission and message of Jesus Christ. By contrast, any theology or pastoral strategy that leaves LGB people with the message that they are somehow worse off than other sexual sinners is actively undermining its own plausibility.

Finally, I would recommend that we *foreground the question of vocation*.

The Catholic writer Andrew Sullivan, himself a gay man, has written movingly about the experience of growing up in the church with a longing to love other men and the unmet hope for some pastoral guidance as to how to go about doing so:

> In my adolescence and young adulthood, the teaching of the Church was merely a silence, an increasingly hollow denial even of the existence of homosexuals, let alone a credible ethical guide as to how they should live their lives. It is still true that in over thirty years of weekly churchgoing, I have never heard a homily that

17. Cf. Hays, *Moral Vision of the New Testament*, 401: Hays's gay friend Gary is quoted as saying, "Are homosexuals to be excluded from the community of faith? Certainly not. But anyone who joins such a community should know that it is a place of transformation, of discipline, of learning, and not merely a place to be comforted and indulged."

18. S. Holmes, "Should We 'Welcome' and 'Affirm'?," 133.

attempted to explain how a gay man should live, or how his sexuality should be expressed. I have heard nothing but a vast and endless and embarrassed silence, an awkward, unexpressed desire for the simple nonexistence of such people, for their absence from the moral and physical universe, for a word or a phrase, like "objective disorder," that could simply abolish the problem they represented and the diverse humanity they symbolized.[19]

My experience in the church tracks closely with Sullivan's. But even more, I am interested in the way he puts his finger on a lack of *positive* (as opposed to merely prohibitive) Christian reflection on the matter of homosexuality. How should a gay man or woman *live*, how should a same-sex-attracted person like me *express* his sexuality, rather than merely repress or try to deny its existence? For surely, like every other Christian, I am to live a life that includes both self-denial *and* an embrace of a positive calling, both no and yes. Surely, as the theologian Oliver O'Donovan has put it, I ought to try to see how my experiences as a gay man can "be clothed in an appropriate pattern of life for the service of God and discipleship of Christ."[20]

Another Catholic writer, the celibate lesbian Catholic author Eve Tushnet, has punchily insisted, "Right now gay [people] hear a robust 'Yes!' from the mainstream media and gay culture. From the Church, they hear only a 'No.' And you can't have a vocation of not-gay-marrying and not-having-sex. You can't have a vocation of No."[21] I recall when I first read that sentence and how much of an impact it made on me. I realized I *had*, in fact, heard only a no from my fellow Christians: no gay sex, no gay lust, no gay marriage, no sexual fantasizing, no masturbation, no pornography. But I hadn't heard much at all about what I might be called *toward*. I hadn't heard anyone cast a vision of what a life of devotion, fidelity, service, and self-giving—in short, a life of love—might look like for someone in my shoes. And so my sense of my vocation was essentially negative: God is asking me to refrain from something, to flee from something, full stop.

If we are to persuade anyone, going forward, of the truthfulness of the claims found in the book you now hold in your hands, it will be because we Christians have found a way to call lesbian, gay, and bisexual people into their unique callings, their specific vocations—their particular ways of participating in and furthering the love and beauty and justice of God's world. We have spent far too much time spelling out what LGB people ought to reject; we

19. Sullivan, *Love Undetectable*, 42.
20. O'Donovan, *Church in Crisis*, 117. The two preceding paragraphs are adapted from my essay "Christ, Scripture, and Spiritual Friendship."
21. Tushnet, "Botany Club."

have barely begun to explore what LGB people are invited into, are already gifted to offer and poised to pursue.

Writer Elizabeth Scalia, a "traditionalist" on marriage and sexuality herself, has written movingly: "I have a theory that our gay brothers and sisters are, in fact, planned, loved-into-being 'necessary others,' and that they are meant to show us something of God from a perspective that we cannot otherwise broach."[22] When Christians relearn how to speak like that, then perhaps we can begin to expect that our message might prove enticing—beckoning, beguiling—to the lesbian, gay, and bisexual members of our human family, who, knowingly or not, are searching for the love that is only found in Jesus Christ.

22. Scalia, "Homosexuality: A Call to Otherness?"

Bibliography

Editor's note: Entries that include a parenthetical reference to *ANF* or *NPNF*[1] or *NPNF*[2] are works found, respectively, in the indicated volume of *The Ante-Nicene Fathers* or of Series 1 or 2 of *The Nicene and Post-Nicene Fathers*, each of which has its own bibliography entry.

Achtemeier, Mark. *The Bible's Yes to Same-Sex Marriage: An Evangelical's Change of Heart.* Louisville: Westminster John Knox, 2014.

Aelred of Rievaulx. *Spiritual Friendship.* Collegeville, MN: Cistercian Publications, 2010.

Allen, Mike. "Wait a Minute, a Mixed What?" *Spiritual Friendship*, January 26, 2015. https://spiritualfriendship.org/2015/01/26/wait-a-minute-a-mixed-what/.

Alter, Robert. *The Art of Biblical Narrative.* Rev. ed. New York: Basic Books, 2011.

American Psychological Association. "Sexual Orientation & Homosexuality." Accessed August 13, 2020. https://www.apa.org/topics/lgbt/orientation.

Anderson, Bernhard W. *From Creation to New Creation: Old Testament Perspectives.* Minneapolis: Fortress, 1994.

Anderson, Matthew Lee. *Earthen Vessels: Why Our Bodies Matter to Our Faith.* Minneapolis: Bethany House, 2011.

Anscombe, Elizabeth. *Contraception and Chastity.* London: The Incorporated Catholic Truth Society, 2017. Kindle.

The Ante-Nicene Fathers. Edited by Alexander Roberts and James Donaldson. 1885–87. 10 vols. Available in the Christian Classics Ethereal Library. https://ccel.org/.

Apostolic Constitutions. In *ANF* 7.

Aquinas, Thomas. *On Law, Morality, and Politics.* Edited by William P. Baumgarth and Richard J. Regan, SJ. Indianapolis: Hackett, 1988.

———. *Summa Contra Gentiles.* Translated by Joseph Rickaby, SJ, as *Of God and His Creatures: An Annotated Translation.* London: Burns & Oates, 1905. https://ccel.org/ccel/aquinas/gentiles/.

Aristotle. *The Basic Works of Aristotle.* Edited by Richard McKeon. New York: Random House, 1941.

Ash, Christopher. *Marriage: Sex in the Service of God.* Vancouver: Regent College Publishing, 2003.

Athanasius. *On the Incarnation.* Translated by John Behr. Yonkers, NY: St. Vladimir's Seminary Press, 2011.

Augustine. *Concerning the City of God against the Pagans.* Translated by Henry Bettenson. London: Penguin Classics, 1984.

———. *Confessions.* Translated by Henry Chadwick. Oxford: Oxford University Press, 1992.

———. *The Enchiridion on Faith, Hope, and Love.* Translated by J. F. Shaw. Washington, DC: Regnery Gateway, 1961.

———. *Essential Sermons.* Edited by Boniface Ramsey. Translated by Edmund Hill, OP. Hyde Park, NY: Free City Press, 2007.

———. *On Christian Teaching.* Translated by R. P. H. Green. Oxford: Oxford University Press, 1997.

———. *On the Good of Marriage.* Translated by David G. Hunter. In Hunter, *Marriage in the Early Church*, 102–21.

———. *Sermons to the People.* Translated and edited by William Griffin. New York: Doubleday, 2002.

Azumah, John J. "Through African Eyes: Resisting America's Cultural Imperialism." *First Things*, October 2015, 41–46.

Bailey, J. Michael, Paul L. Vasey, Lisa M. Diamond, S. Marc Breedlove, Eric Vilain, and Marc Epprecht. "Sexual Orientation, Controversy, and Science." *Psychological Science in the Public Interest* 17 (2016): 45–101.

Bailey, Kenneth E. *Paul through Mediterranean Eyes: Cultural Studies in 1 Corinthians.* Downers Grove, IL: IVP Academic, 2011.

Balch, David L., ed. *Homosexuality, Science, and the "Plain Sense" of Scripture.* Grand Rapids: Eerdmans, 2000.

Banner, Michael, Markus Bockmuehl, Timothy Bradshaw, Oliver O'Donovan, Ann Holt, William Persson, and David Wright. "St. Andrew's Day Statement." In Bradshaw, *Way Forward?*, 5–11.

Batchelor, Edward, Jr., ed. *Homosexuality and Ethics.* New York: Pilgrim, 1980.

Bauckham, Richard. *The Bible and Ecology: Rediscovering the Community of Creation.* Waco: Baylor University Press, 2010.

———. "James and the Gentiles (Acts 15.13–21)." In *History, Literature, and Society in the Book of Acts*, edited by Ben Witherington III, 154–84. Cambridge: Cambridge University Press, 1996.

———. "James and the Jerusalem Church." In *The Book of Acts in Its Palestinian Setting*, edited by Richard Bauckham, 415–80. Grand Rapids: Eerdmans, 1995.

Beckett, Joshua. "Desire in Singleness: Ascetics and Eternity (Or, Why Christians Don't Need to Get Married)." In Callaway, *Breaking the Marriage Idol*, 193–211.

Belgau, Ron. "A Brief Note on Phil Robertson and Double Standards." *Spiritual Friendship*, December 19, 2013. https://spiritualfriendship.org/2013/12/19/a-brief-note-on-phil-robertson-and-double-standards/.

Belgau, Ron, and Beverly Belgau. "Always Consider the Person: Homosexuality in the Family." *Spiritual Friendship*, September 26, 2015. http://spiritualfriendship.org/2015/09/26/always-consider-the-person-homosexuality-in-the-family/.

Bennett, David. *A War of Loves: The Unexpected Story of a Gay Activist Discovering Jesus.* Grand Rapids: Zondervan, 2018.

Berger, Peter. *The Sacred Canopy: Elements of a Sociological Theory of Religion.* New York: Doubleday, 1967.

Bettenson, Henry, and Chris Maunder, eds. *Documents of the Christian Church.* 4th ed. Oxford: Oxford University Press, 2011.

Bird, Phyllis. "The Bible in Christian Ethical Deliberation concerning Homosexuality: Old Testament Contributions." In Balch,

Homosexuality, Science, and the "Plain Sense" of Scripture, 142–76.

Blackwell, Richard J. *Galileo, Bellarmine, and the Bible*. Notre Dame, IN: University of Notre Dame Press, 1991.

Blanchard, Kathryn D. "The Gift of Contraception: Calvin, Barth, and a Lost Protestant Conversation." *Journal of the Society of Christian Ethics* 27, no. 1 (2007): 225–49.

Blosser, Don. "Why Does the Bible Divide Us? A Conversation with Scripture on Same-Gender Attraction." In Kraus, *To Continue the Dialogue*, 121–47.

Blount, Brian K. "Reading and Understanding the New Testament." In Seow, *Homosexuality and Christian Community*, 28–38.

Bockmuehl, Markus. *Jewish Law in Gentile Churches: Halakhah and the Beginning of Christian Public Ethics*. Grand Rapids: Baker Academic, 2000.

Bolz-Weber, Nadia. *Shameless: A Sexual Reformation*. New York: Convergent Books, 2019.

Bontrager, Marion G., Michele Hershberger, and John E. Sharp. *The Bible as Story: An Introduction to Biblical Literature*. Newton, KS: Workplay Publishing, 2016.

Boswell, John. *Christianity, Social Tolerance, and Homosexuality: Gay People in Western Europe from the Beginning of the Christian Era to the Fourteenth Century*. Chicago: University of Chicago Press, 1980.

———. *Same-Sex Unions in Premodern Europe*. New York: Villard Books, 1994.

Bouteneff, Peter C. *Beginnings: Ancient Christian Readings of the Biblical Creation Narratives*. Grand Rapids: Baker Academic, 2008.

Bradshaw, Timothy, ed. *The Way Forward? Christian Voices on Homosexuality and the Church*. 2nd ed. Grand Rapids: Eerdmans, 2003.

Brawley, Robert L., ed. *Biblical Ethics and Homosexuality: Listening to Scripture*. Louisville: Westminster John Knox, 1996.

Bristow, John Templeton. *What Saint Paul Really Said about Women: An Apostle's Liberating Views on Equality in Marriage, Leadership, and Love*. San Francisco: HarperSanFancisco, 1988.

Brooten, Bernadette J. *Love between Women: Early Christian Responses to Female Homoeroticism*. Chicago: University of Chicago Press, 1996.

Brown, Peter. *The Body and Society: Men, Women, and Sexual Renunciation in Early Christianity*. New York: Columbia University Press, 1988.

Brownson, James V. *Bible, Gender, Sexuality: Reframing the Church's Debate on Same-Sex Relationships*. Grand Rapids: Eerdmans, 2013.

Brundage, James A. *Law, Sex, and Christian Society in Medieval Europe*. Chicago: University of Chicago Press, 1987.

Burtchaell, James Tunstead. *The Giving and Taking of Life: Essays Ethical*. Notre Dame, IN: University of Notre Dame Press, 1989.

Butterfield, Rosario Champagne. *The Gospel Comes with a House Key: Practicing Radically Ordinary Hospitality in Our Post-Christian World*. Wheaton: Crossway, 2018.

———. *Openness Unhindered: Further Thoughts of an Unlikely Convert on Sexual Identity and Union with Christ*. Pittsburgh: Crown and Covenant, 2015. Kindle.

———. *The Secret Thoughts of an Unlikely Convert: An English Professor's Journey into Christian Faith*. Exp. ed. Pittsburgh: Crown and Covenant, 2014.

Cahill, Lisa Sowle. "Homosexuality: A Case Study in Moral Argument." In Siker, *Homosexuality in the Church*, 61–74.

Callaway, Kutter. *Breaking the Marriage Idol: Reconstructing our Cultural and Spiritual Norms*. Downers Grove, IL: InterVarsity, 2018.

Campbell, Joan Cecelia. *Phoebe: Patron and Emissary*. Collegeville, MN: Liturgical Press, 2009.

Cannon, Mae Elise, Lisa Sharon Harper, Troy Jackson, and Soong-Chan Ra. *Forgive Us: Confessions of a Compromised Faith*. Grand Rapids: Zondervan, 2014.

The Canons of the Holy Fathers Assembled at Gangra, Which Were Set Forth after the Council of Nice. In NPNF² 14.

The Canons of the Synod Held in the City of Laodicea, in Phrygia Pacatiana, in Which Many Blessed Fathers from Divers Provinces of Asia Were Gathered. In NPNF² 14.

Case-Winters, Anna. *Matthew*. Belief: A Theological Commentary on the Bible. Louisville: Westminster John Knox, 2015.

Chevasse, Claude. *The Bride of Christ: An Enquiry into the Nuptial Element in Early Christianity*. London: Religious Book Club, 1940.

Chrysostom, John. *A Comparison between a King and a Monk; Against the Opponents of the Monastic Life: Two Treatises*. Translated by David G. Hunter. Lewiston, NY: Mellen, 1988.

———. *Homily V on 1 Thessalonians*. In NPNF¹ 13.

———. *Homily XVII on Matthew 3*. In NPNF¹ 10.

———. *Homily XXX on Romans*. In NPNF¹ 11.

———. *Instructions to Catechumens*. In NPNF¹ 9.

———. *On Marriage and Family Life*. Translated by Catherine P. Roth and David Anderson. Crestwood, NY: St. Vladimir's Seminary Press, 1986.

———. *On Virginity; Against Remarriage*. Translated by Sally Rieger Shore. Lewiston, NY: Mellen, 1983.

———. *On Wealth and Poverty*. Translated by Catherine P. Roth. Crestwood, NY: St. Vladimir's Seminary Press, 1981.

———. *Six Books on the Priesthood*. Translated by Graham Neville. Crestwood, NY: St. Vladimir's Seminary Press, 1977.

Coakley, Sarah. *God, Sexuality, and the Self: An Essay 'On the Trinity.'* Cambridge: Cambridge University Press, 2013.

Coles, Gregory. *Single, Gay, Christian: A Personal Journey of Faith and Sexual Identity*. Downers Grove, IL: InterVarsity, 2017.

Collins, John J. *Between Athens and Jerusalem: Jewish Identity in the Hellenistic Diaspora*. 2nd ed. Grand Rapids: Eerdmans, 2000.

Collins, Nate. *All but Invisible: Exploring Identity Questions at the Intersection of Faith, Gender, and Sexuality*. Grand Rapids: Zondervan, 2017.

Collins, Nate, and Sara Collins. "A Simple Reason to Get Married: 'We Were in Love.'" *Spiritual Friendship*, February 3, 2015. https://spiritualfriendship.org/2015/02/03/a-simple-reason-to-get-married-we-were-in-love/.

Collwell, John. "Christ, Creation, and Human Sexuality." In Bradshaw, *Way Forward?*, 86–98.

Conley, Garrard. *Boy Erased: A Memoir of Identity, Faith, and Family*. New York: Riverhead, 2017.

Conrad, Sue L. "The Gift and Celibacy." In Hershberger, *Sexuality*, 211–29.

Cornwall, Susannah. *Theology and Sexuality*. London: SCM, 2013.

Countryman, L. William. *Dirt, Greed, and Sex: Sexual Ethics in the New Testament and Their Implications for Today*. Rev. ed. Minneapolis: Fortress, 2007.

Crowe, Michael J. *Modern Theories of the Universe from Herschel to Hubble*. New York: Dover Publications, 1994.

Cummings, Brian, ed. *The Book of Common Prayer: The Texts of 1549, 1559, and 1662*. Oxford: Oxford University Press, 2011.

Cyril of Jerusalem. *Catechetical Lectures: Lecture III on Baptism*. In NPNF² 7.

———. *Lectures on the Christian Sacraments: The Procatechesis and the Five Mystagogical Catecheses Ascribed to St. Cyril of Jerusalem*. Translated by Maxwell E. Johnson. Yonkers, NY: St. Vladimir's Seminary Press, 2017. Kindle.

Damian, Chris. "Discrimination in the Catholic Church." Chris Damian, August 17, 2017. https://chrisdamian.net/2017/08/17 /discrimination-in-the-catholic-church/.

Danylak, Barry. *Redeeming Singleness: How the Storyline of Scripture Affirms the Single Life*. Wheaton: Crossway, 2010.

Davidson, Richard M. *Flame of Yahweh: Sexuality in the Old Testament*. Peabody, MA: Hendrickson, 2007.

Davies, W. D., and Dale C. Allison. *Matthew 19–28*. Vol. 3 of *A Critical and Exegetical Commentary on The Gospel according to Saint Matthew*. International Critical Commentary. London: T&T Clark, 2004.

Davis, James Calvin. *Forbearance: A Theological Ethic for a Disagreeable Church*. Grand Rapids: Eerdmans, 2017.

Dawn, Marva J. *Sexual Character: Beyond Technique to Intimacy*. Grand Rapids: Eerdmans, 1993.

Dearman, J. Andrew. "Marriage in the Old Testament." In Brawley, *Biblical Ethics and Homosexuality*, 53–67.

DeFranza, Megan K. "Journeying from the Bible to Christian Ethics in Search of Common Ground." In Sprinkle, *Two Views on Homosexuality, the Bible, and the Church*, 69–101.

———. "Rejoinder." In Sprinkle, *Two Views on Homosexuality, the Bible, and the Church*, 119–23.

Dehlin, John P., Renee V. Galliher, William S. Bradshaw, Daniel C. Hyde, and Katherine A. Crowell. "Sexual Orientation Change Efforts among Current or Former LDS Church Members." *Journal of Counseling Psychology* 62, no. 2 (April 2015): 95–105.

Derrett, J. Duncan M. *Law in the New Testament*. London: Darton, Longman & Todd, 1970.

DeYoung, Kevin. *What Does the Bible Really Teach about Homosexuality?* Wheaton: Crossway, 2015.

DeYoung, Rebecca Konyndyk. *Glittering Vices: A New Look at the Seven Deadly Sins and Their Remedies*. Grand Rapids: Brazos, 2009.

Diamond, Lisa M. *Sexual Fluidity: Understanding Women's Love and Desire*. Cambridge, MA: Harvard University Press, 2008.

Dillenberger, John. *Protestant Thought and Natural Science*. Notre Dame, IN: University of Notre Dame Press, 1960.

Dominus, Susan. "Not Just Us: Is an Open Marriage a Happier Marriage?" *New York Times Magazine*, May 14, 2017, 34–59.

Douthat, Ross. *Bad Religion: How We Became a Nation of Heretics*. New York: Free Press, 2012.

Dresner, Samuel H. "Homosexuality and the Order of Creation." *Judaism* 40 (1991): 309–21.

Driggers, Ira Brent. "New Testament Appropriations of Genesis 1–2." In Greenwood, *Since the Beginning*, 45–75.

Driver, Tom F. "Homosexuality: The Contemporary and Christian Contexts." In Batchelor, *Homosexuality and Ethics*, 14–21.

Dunn, James D. G. *The Theology of Paul the Apostle*. Grand Rapids: Eerdmans, 1998.

Durso, Laura E., and Gary J. Gates. *Serving Our Youth: Findings from a National Survey of Youth Providers Working with Lesbian, Gay, Bisexual, and Transgender Youth Who Are Homeless or at Risk of Becoming Homeless*. Los Angeles: Williams Institute, 2012.

Edwards, Dennis R. *1 Peter*. The Story of God Bible Commentary. Grand Rapids: Zondervan, 2017.

Eileen, Bridget. *8 Essential Thoughts: The Ultimate Guide to My Lesbian Thought Life*. Self-published, 2019.

Eisen, Ute E. *Women Officeholders in Early Christianity: Epigraphical and Literary Studies*. Collegeville, MN: Liturgical Press, 2000.

Elias, Jacob W. *Remember the Future: The Pastoral Theology of Paul the Apostle*. Scottdale, PA: Herald, 2006.

Ephrem the Syrian. *The Harp of the Spirit: Poems of Saint Ephrem the Syrian*. 3rd ed. Translated by Sebastian Brock. Cambridge: Aquila Books, 2013.

———. *Hymns on Paradise*. Translated by Sebastian Brock. Crestwood, NY: St. Vladimir's Seminary Press, 1990.

Epp, Eldon Jay. *Junia: The First Woman Apostle*. Minneapolis: Fortress, 2005.

Eskridge, William N., Jr., and Darren R. Spedale. *Gay Marriage: For Better or for Worse?* New York: Oxford University Press, 2006.

Evangelicals and Catholics Together. "The Two Shall Become One Flesh: Reclaiming Marriage." *First Things*, March 2015, 23–31.

Evdokimov, Paul. *The Sacrament of Love: The Nuptial Mystery in Light of the Orthodox Tradition*. Crestwood, NY: St. Vladimir's Seminary Press, 1985.

Fairchild, Mark R. *Christian Origins in Ephesus and Asia Minor*. Istanbul: Akeoloji, 2015.

Fantoli, Annibale. *The Case of Galileo: A Closed Question?* Notre Dame, IN: University of Notre Dame Press, 2012.

Farley, Margaret A. *Just Love: A Framework for Christian Sexual Ethics*. New York: Continuum, 2006.

Farrow, Douglas. "Beyond Nature, Shy of Grace." *International Journal of Systematic Theology* 5 (November 2003): 261–86.

Finger, Reta Halteman. "What Can We Do When We Don't Agree? Christian Tolerance in Romans 14:1–15:6." In Kraus, *To Continue the Dialogue*, 209–22.

Finn, Thomas M. "Sex and Marriage in the *Sentences* of Peter Lombard." *Theological Studies* 72 (2011): 41–69.

Fitzmyer, Joseph A., SJ. *Romans: A New Translation with Introduction and Commentary*. Anchor Bible 33. New York: Doubleday, 1993.

Ford, David C. *Women and Men in the Early Church: The Full Views of St. John Chrysostom*. South Canaan, PA: St. Tikhon's Seminary Press, 1995.

Fortson, S. Donald, III, and Rollin G. Grams. *Unchanging Witness: The Consistent Christian Teaching on Homosexuality in Scripture and Tradition*. Nashville: B&H, 2016.

Fox, Robin Lane. *Pagans and Christians*. New York: Knopf, 1987.

Fredrickson, David E. "Natural and Unnatural Use in Romans 1:24–27: Paul and the Philosophic Critique of Eros." In Balch, *Homosexuality, Science, and the "Plain Sense" of Scripture*, 197–222.

Fretheim, Terence E. *God and World in the Old Testament: A Relational Theology of Creation*. Nashville: Abingdon, 2005.

Furnish, Victor Paul. "The Bible and Homosexuality: Reading the Texts in Context." In Siker, *Homosexuality in the Church*, 18–35.

Gagnon, Robert A. J. "The Bible and Homosexual Practice: Key Issues." In *Homosexuality and the Bible: Two Views*, by Dan O. Via and Robert A. J. Gagnon, 40–92. Minneapolis: Fortress, 2003.

———. *The Bible and Homosexual Practice: Texts and Hermeneutics*. Nashville: Abingdon, 2001.

Galileo Galilei. *Discoveries and Opinions of Galileo*. Translated by Stillman Drake. New York: Doubleday, 1957.

Gardner, Richard B. *Matthew*. Believers Church Bible Commentary. Scottdale, PA: Herald, 1991.

Gathercole, Simon J. "Sin in God's Economy: Agencies in Romans 1 and 7." In *Divine and Human Agency in Paul and His Cultural Environment*, edited by John M. G. Barclay and Simon J. Gathercole, 158–72. London: T&T Clark, 2006.

Geddert, Timothy J. *Mark*. Believers Church Bible Commentary. Scottdale, PA: Herald, 2001.

Gilliam, Connally. *Revelations of a Single Woman: Loving the Life I Didn't Expect*. Wheaton: Tyndale, 2006.

Gilson, Rachel. *Born Again This Way: Coming Out, Coming to Faith, and What Comes Next*. Epsom, UK: Good Book Company, 2020.

———. "I Never Became Straight." *Christianity Today*, October 2017, 50–54.

Girgis, Sherif, Ryan T. Anderson, and Robert P. George. *What Is Marriage? Man and Woman: A Defense*. New York: Encounter Books, 2012.

Goddard, Andrew. *God, Gentiles, and Gay Christians: Acts 15 and Change in the Church*. Cambridge: Grove Books, 2001.

Goldingay, John. *Genesis for Everyone, Part One: Chapters 1–16*. Old Testament for Everyone. Louisville: Westminster John Knox, 2010.

———. *Old Testament Theology*. 3 vols. Downers Grove, IL: InterVarsity, 2003–9.

González, Justo L. *The Early Church to the Dawn of the Reformation*. Vol. 1 of *The Story of Christianity*. Revised and updated. New York: HarperOne, 2010.

Good, Meghan Larissa. *The Bible Unwrapped: Making Sense of Scripture Today*. Harrisonburg, VA: Herald, 2018.

Gordon, David, Austin Porter, Mark Regnerus, Jayne Ryngaert, and Larissa Sarangaya. *Relationships in America Survey*. Austin: The Austin Institute for the Study of Family and Culture, 2014.

Gorman, Michael J. *Abortion and the Early Church: Christian, Jewish, and Pagan Attitudes in the Greco-Roman World*. Downers Grove, IL: InterVarsity, 1982.

Gould, Stephen Jay. *The Mismeasure of Man*. Revised and expanded. New York: Norton, 1996.

Grant, Jonathan. *Divine Sex: A Compelling Vision for Christian Relationships in a Hypersexualized Age*. Grand Rapids: Brazos, 2015.

Greenberg, David F. *The Construction of Homosexuality*. Chicago: University of Chicago Press, 1988.

Greene-McCreight, Kathryn. "The Logic of the Interpretation of Scripture and the Church's Debate over Sexual Ethics." In Balch, *Homosexuality, Science, and the "Plain Sense" of Scripture*, 242–60.

Greenwood, Kyle R, ed. *Since the Beginning: Interpreting Genesis 1 and 2 through the Ages*. Grand Rapids: Baker Academic, 2018.

Gregory of Nazianzus. *On God and Christ: The Five Theological Orations and Two Letters to Cledonius*. Translated by Frederick Williams and Lionel Wickham. Crestwood, NY: St. Vladimir's Seminary Press, 2002.

———. *On God and Man: The Theological Poetry of St. Gregory of Nazianzus*. Translated by Peter Gilbert. Crestwood, NY: St. Vladimir's Seminary Press, 2001.

Gregory the Great. *The Book of Pastoral Rule*. Translated by George E. Demacopolous. Crestwood, NY: St. Vladimir's Seminary Press, 2007.

Grenz, Stanley J. *Sexual Ethics: An Evangelical Perspective*. Louisville: Westminster John Knox, 1990.

———. *Welcoming but Not Affirming: An Evangelical Response to Homosexuality*. Louisville: Westminster John Knox, 1998.

Grieb, A. Katherine. *The Story of Romans: A Narrative Defense of God's Righteousness*. Louisville: Westminster John Knox, 2002.

Griffith, R. Marie. *Moral Combat: How Sex Divided American Christians and Fractured American Politics*. New York: Basic Books, 2017.

Grimsrud, Ted. "Toward a Theology of Welcome: Developing a Perspective on the 'Homosexuality' Issue." In Grimsrud and Nation, *Reasoning Together*, 129–66.

Grimsrud, Ted, and Mark Thiessen Nation. *Reasoning Together: A Conversation on Homosexuality*. Scottdale, PA: Herald, 2008.

Gryson, Roger. *The Ministry of Women in the Early Church*. Collegeville, MN: Liturgical Press, 1976.

Guroian, Vigen. *The Orthodox Reality: Culture, Theology, and Ethics in the Modern World*. Grand Rapids: Baker Academic, 2018.

Gushee, David P. *Changing Our Mind*. 3rd ed. Canton, MI: Read the Spirit Books, 2017.

Hallett, Martin. *Still Learning to Love: A Personal Journey to Wholeness in Christ*. Wirral, UK: HOW Publications, 2004.

Hannon, Michael W. "Against Heterosexuality." *First Things*, March 2014, 27–34, https://www.firstthings.com/article/2014/03/against-heterosexuality.

Harper, Kyle. *From Shame to Sin: The Christian Transformation of Sexual Morality in Late Antiquity*. Cambridge, MA: Harvard University Press, 2013.

———. "*Porneia*: The Making of a Christian Sexual Norm." *Journal of Biblical Literature* 131 (2011): 363–83.

Hartney, Aideen M. *John Chrysostom and the Transformation of the City*. London: Duckworth, 2004.

Hauerwas, Stanley. "Love's Not All You Need." *Cross Currents* (Summer–Fall 1972): 225–37.

———. *Matthew*. Brazos Theological Commentary on the Bible. Grand Rapids: Brazos, 2006.

Hauerwas, Stanley, and William H. Willimon. *Resident Aliens: Life in the Christian Colony*. Nashville: Abingdon, 1989.

Hays, Richard. *First Corinthians*. Interpretation: A Bible Commentary for Teaching and Preaching. Louisville: John Knox, 1997.

———. *The Moral Vision of the New Testament: A Contemporary Introduction to New Testament Ethics*. San Francisco: HarperSanFrancisco, 1996.

———. "Relations Natural and Unnatural: A Response to John Boswell's Exegesis of Romans 1." *Journal of Religious Ethics* 14 (1986): 184–215.

Helminiak, Daniel A. *What the Bible Really Says about Homosexuality*. Millennium ed. Tajique, NM: Alamo Square, 2000.

Hershberger, Anne Krabill, ed. *Sexuality: God's Gift*. 2nd ed. Scottdale, PA: Herald, 2010.

Hiestand, Gerald, and Todd Wilson, eds. *Beauty, Order, and Mystery: A Christian Vision of Human Sexuality*. Downers Grove, IL: IVP Academic, 2017.

Hill, Wesley. "Christ, Scripture, and Spiritual Friendship." In Sprinkle, *Two Views on Homosexuality, the Bible, and the Church*, 124–47.

———. "How Should Gay Christians Love?" In Hiestand and Wilson, *Beauty, Order, and Mystery*, 31–43.

———. "Rejoinder." In Sprinkle, *Two Views on Homosexuality, the Bible, and the Church*, 163–65.

———. "Response to Megan K. DeFranza." In Sprinkle, *Two Views on Homosexuality, the Bible, and the Church*, 108–12.

———. "Response to William Loader." In Sprinkle, *Two Views on Homosexuality, the Bible, and the Church*, 55–60.

———. *Spiritual Friendship: Finding Love in the Church as a Celibate Gay Christian*. Grand Rapids: Brazos, 2015.

———. "The Transformation of the Gentiles." *Spiritual Friendship*, September 5, 2016. https://spiritualfriendship.org/2016/09/05/the-transformation-of-the-gentiles/.

———. *Washed and Waiting: Reflections on Christian Faithfulness and Homosexuality*. Grand Rapids: Zondervan, 2010. Rev. and exp. ed., 2016. (Page references are to the 2010 ed. except where noted.)

———. "Where the World Attacks." *Spiritual Friendship*, July 25, 2018. https://spiritualfriendship.org/2018/07/25/where-the-world-attacks/.

Hirsch, Debra. *Redeeming Sex: Naked Conversations about Sexuality and Spirituality*. Downers Grove, IL: InterVarsity, 2015.

Hitchcock, Christina S. *The Significance of Singleness: A Theological Vision for the Future of the Church*. Grand Rapids: Baker Academic, 2018.

Hoff, Colleen C., Sean C. Beougher, Deepalika Chakravarty, Lynae A. Darbes, and Torsten B. Neilands. "Relationship Characteristics and Motivations behind Agreements among Gay Male Couples: Differences by Agreement Type and Couple Serostatus." *AIDS Care* 22 (July 2010): 827–35.

Holben, L. R. *What Christians Think about Homosexuality: Six Representative Views*. North Richland Hills, TX: BIBAL Press, 1999.

Hollinger, Dennis P. "The Church as Apologetic: A Sociology of Knowledge Perspective." In *Christian Apologetics in the Post-Modern World*, edited by Timothy R. Phillips and Dennis L. Okholm, 182–93. Downers Grove, IL: InterVarsity, 1995.

———. *The Meaning of Sex: Christian Ethics and the Moral Life*. Grand Rapids: Baker Academic, 2009.

Holmes, Michael W. *The Apostolic Fathers: Greek Texts and English Translations*. Rev. ed. Grand Rapids: Baker, 1999.

Holmes, Stephen R. "Homosexuality & Hermeneutics: Creating Counter-Cultural Communities." Evangelical Alliance, January 15, 2013. https://www.eauk.org/church/stories/homosexuality-and-hermeneutics.cfm.

———. "Listening to the Past and Reflecting on the Present." In Sprinkle, *Two Views on Homosexuality, the Bible, and the Church*, 166–93.

———. "On Not Handling Snakes: Late-Modern Cultural Assumptions about Sexuality." In *Marriage, Family and Relationships: Biblical, Doctrinal and Contemporary Perspectives*, edited by Thomas A. Noble, Sarah K. Whittle, and Philip S. Johnston, 256–75. London: Apollos, 2017.

———. "Response to Megan K. DeFranza." In Sprinkle, *Two Views on Homosexuality, the Bible, and the Church*, 113–18.

———. "Response to William Loader." In Sprinkle, *Two Views on Homosexuality, the Bible, and the Church*, 61–65.

———. "Should We 'Welcome' and 'Affirm'? Reflecting on Evangelical Responses to Human Sexuality." In *Revisioning, Renewing, Rediscovering the Triune Center: Essays in Honor of Stanley J. Grenz*, edited by Derek J. Tidball, Brian S. Harris, and Jason S. Sexton, 121–34. Eugene, OR: Cascade Books, 2014.

Hopko, Thomas. *Christian Faith and Same-Sex Attraction: Eastern Orthodox Reflections*. 2nd ed. Chesterton, IN: Ancient Faith Publishing, 2015.

House, H. Wayne, ed. *Divorce and Remarriage: Four Christian Views*. Downers Grove, IL: InterVarsity, 1990.

Hubbard, Thomas K., ed. *Homosexuality in Greece and Rome: A Sourcebook of Basic Documents*. Berkeley: University of California Press, 2003.

———. "Peer Homosexuality." In *A Companion to Greek and Roman Sexualities*, edited by Thomas K. Hubbard, 128–49. Oxford: Wiley Blackwell, 2014.

Human Rights Campaign Staff. "New Report on Youth Homeless Affirms that LGBTQ Youth Disproportionately Experience Homelessness." Human Rights Campaign, November 15, 2017. https://www.hrc.org/blog/new-report-on-youth-homeless-affirms-that-lgbtq-youth-dis proportionately-ex.

Hunter, David G., trans. and ed. *Marriage in the Early Church*. Sources of Early Christian Thought. Minneapolis: Fortress, 1991.

Instone-Brewer, David. *Divorce and Remarriage in the Bible: The Social and Literary Context*. Grand Rapids: Eerdmans, 2002.

Irenaeus of Lyons. *On the Apostolic Preaching*. Translated by John Behr. Crestwood, NY: St. Vladimir's Seminary Press, 1997.

James, Scott. "Many Successful Gay Marriages Share an Open Secret." *New York Times*, January 29, 2010. https://www.nytimes.com/2010/01/29/us/29sfmetro.html.

Jeal, Roy R., ed. *Human Sexuality and the Nuptial Mystery*. Eugene, OR: Cascade Books, 2010.

———. "Ideology, Argumentation, and Social Direction in Romans 1." In Jeal, *Human Sexuality and the Nuptial Mystery*, 27–44.

———. "Visions of Marriage in Ephesians 5." In Jeal, *Human Sexuality and the Nuptial Mystery*, 116–30.

Johnson, Greg. "I Used to Hide My Shame. Now I Take Shelter under the Gospel." *Christianity Today*, May 20, 2019. https://www.christianitytoday.com/ct/2019/may-web-only/greg-johnson-hide-shame-shelter-gospel-gay-teenager.html.

Johnson, Luke Timothy. *The Acts of the Apostles*. Sacra Pagina. Collegeville, MN: Liturgical Press, 1992.

———. "Disputed Questions: Debate and Discernment, Scripture and the Spirit." In E. Rogers, *Theology and Sexuality*, 367–72.

———. *The Gospel of Luke*. Sacra Pagina. Collegeville, MN: Liturgical Press, 1991.

———. *Scripture and Discernment: Decision Making in the Church*. Nashville: Abingdon, 1996.

———. "Scripture and Experience." *Commonweal*, June 15, 2007, 14–17.

Jones, Beth Felker. "Embodied from Creation through Redemption: Placing Gender and Sexuality in Theological Context." In Hiestand and Wilson, *Beauty, Order, and Mystery*, 21–30.

———. *Faithful: A Theology of Sex*. Grand Rapids: Zondervan, 2015.

Jones, Jeffrey M. "Americans Hold Record Liberal Views on Most Moral Issues." Gallup, May 11, 2017. https://news.gallup.com/poll/210542/americans-hold-record-liberal-views-moral-issues.aspx.

Jones, Rachel K., and Joerg Dreweke. *Countering Conventional Wisdom: New Evidence on Religion and Contraceptive Use*. New York: Guttmacher Institute, 2011.

Jones, Stanton L., and Mark A. Yarhouse. *Ex-Gays? A Longitudinal Study of Religiously Mediated Change in Sexual Orientation*. Downers Grove, IL: IVP Academic, 2014.

———. *Homosexuality: The Use of Science in the Church's Moral Debate.* Downers Grove, IL: IVP Academic, 2000.

Kanagy, Conrad. "2014 Survey of Credentialed Leaders in Mennonite Church USA." Mennonite Church USA, March 5, 2015. http://mennoniteusa.org/resource /2014-survey-of-credentialed-leaders-in -mennonite-church-usa/.

Kass, Leon R. "Man and Woman: An Old Story." *First Things*, November 17, 1991, 14–26.

Katz, Jonathan N. *The Invention of Heterosexuality.* Chicago: University of Chicago Press, 1995.

Keen, Karen R. *Scripture, Ethics, and the Possibility of Same-Sex Relationships.* Grand Rapids: Eerdmans, 2018.

Keener, Craig S. *Acts: An Exegetical Commentary.* Vol. 3, *15:1–23:35.* Grand Rapids: Baker Academic, 2014.

———. *And Marries Another: Divorce and Remarriage in the Teaching of the New Testament.* Peabody, MA: Hendrickson, 1991.

———. *Paul, Women & Wives: Marriage and Women's Ministry in the Letters of Paul.* 1992. Reprint with a new preface, Grand Rapids: Baker Academic, 2013.

Keller, Marie Noël. *Priscilla and Aquila: Paul's Coworkers in Christ Jesus.* Collegeville, MN: Liturgical Press, 2010.

Kelly, J. N. D. *Golden Mouth: The Story of John Chrysostom—Ascetic, Preacher, Bishop.* Ithaca, NY: Cornell University Press, 1995.

Kevles, Daniel J. *In the Name of Eugenics: Genetics and the Uses of Human Heredity.* Cambridge, MA: Harvard University Press, 1995.

King, Philip J. *Amos, Hosea, Micah: An Archaeological Commentary.* Philadelphia: Westminster, 1988.

Kinnaman, David, and Gabe Lyons. *unChristian: What a New Generation Really Thinks about Christianity . . . and Why It Matters.* Grand Rapids: Baker Books, 2007.

Kirk, J. R. Daniel. "Embracing the Gentiles." *Storied Theology* (blog), January 30, 2016. Patheos. http://www.patheos .com/blogs/storiedtheology/2016/01/3 0/embracing-the-gentiles/.

Kraus, C. Norman. "The 'H' Words: Hermeneutics and Homosexual." In Kraus, *To Continue the Dialogue*, 25–44.

———. "Making Theological and Ethical Decisions: Contextualizing the Bible," In Kraus, *To Continue the Dialogue*, 256–79.

———, ed. *To Continue the Dialogue: Biblical Interpretation and Homosexuality.* Telford, PA: Pandora Press U.S., 2001.

Kraybill, Donald B. *The Upside-Down Kingdom.* Rev. ed. Scottdale, PA: Herald, 1990.

Kreider, Alan. *Journey toward Holiness: A Way of Living for God's Nation.* Scottdale, PA: Herald, 1987.

———. *The Patient Ferment of the Early Church: The Improbable Rise of Christianity in the Roman Empire.* Grand Rapids: Baker Academic, 2016.

Lamb, David T. *Prostitutes and Polygamists: A Look at Love, Old-Testament Style.* Grand Rapids: Zondervan, 2015.

Lawrence, Raymond J. "Bench Marks for a New Sexual Ethics." *Saint Luke's Journal of Theology* 28, no. 2 (March 1985): 93–106.

Lee, Justin. *Torn: Rescuing the Gospel from the Gays-vs.-Christians Debate.* New York: Jericho Books, 2012.

Lenow, Evan. "Protestants and Contraception." *First Things*, January 2018, 15–17.

Levering, Matthew. "Thomas Aquinas on Sexual Ethics." In Hiestand and Wilson, *Beauty, Order, and Mystery*, 165–80.

Lewis, C. S. *Mere Christianity.* London: HarperCollins, 1977.

Livingston, Gretchen. *Four in Ten Couples Are Saying "I Do," Again: Growing Numbers of Adults Have Remarried.* Washington, DC: Pew Research Center, 2014.

Loader, William. "Homosexuality and the Bible." In Sprinkle, *Two Views on Homosexuality, the Bible, and the Church,* 17–48.

———. *Making Sense of Sex: Attitudes towards Sexuality in Early Jewish and Christian Literature.* Grand Rapids: Eerdmans, 2013.

———. "Response to Megan K. DeFranza." In Sprinkle, *Two Views on Homosexuality, the Bible, and the Church,* 102–7.

———. *Sexuality in the New Testament: Understanding the Key Texts.* Louisville: Westminster John Knox, 2010.

Lombard, Peter. *The Sentences, Book 2: On Creation.* Translated by Giulio Silano. Toronto: Pontifical Institute of Medieval Studies, 2008.

———. *The Sentences, Book 4: On the Doctrine of Signs.* Translated by Giulio Silano. Toronto: Pontifical Institute of Medieval Studies, 2010.

Madigan, Kevin, and Carolyn Osiek, eds. *Ordained Women in the Early Church: A Documentary History.* Baltimore: Johns Hopkins University Press, 2005.

Malherbe, Abraham J. *Paul and the Popular Philosophers.* Minneapolis: Fortress, 1989.

Mangina, Joseph L. *Revelation.* Brazos Theological Commentary on the Bible. Grand Rapids: Brazos, 2010.

Mann, Thomas W. "Stars, Sprouts, and Streams: The Creative Redeemer of Second Isaiah." In *God Who Creates: Essays in Honor of W. Sibley Towner,* edited by William P. Brown and S. Dean McBride Jr., 135–51. Grand Rapids: Eerdmans, 2000.

Marin, Andrew. *Love Is an Orientation: Elevating the Conversation with the Gay Community.* Downers Grove, IL: InterVarsity, 2009.

———. *Us versus Us: The Untold Story of Religion and the LGBT Community.* Colorado Springs: NavPress, 2016.

Martin, Dale B. *Sex and the Single Savior: Gender and Sexuality in Biblical Interpretation.* Louisville: Westminster John Knox, 2006.

Mason, Matthew. "The Wounded It Heals: Gender Dysphoria and the Resurrection of the Body." In Hiestand and Wilson, *Beauty, Order, and Mystery,* 132–47.

Mast, Carrie A., and Gerald J. Mast. *Human Sexuality in Biblical Perspective: A Study Guide.* Telford, PA: Cascadia, 2016.

Matlock, Michael D. "Interpretation of Genesis 1–2 in Second Temple Jewish Literature." In Greenwood, *Since the Beginning,* 23–43.

Mauser, Ulrich W. "Creation and Human Sexuality in the New Testament." In Brawley, *Biblical Ethics and Homosexuality,* 3–15.

———. "Creation, Sexuality, and Homosexuality in the New Testament." In Seow, *Homosexuality and Christian Community,* 39–49.

Mayer, Lawrence S., and Paul R. McHugh. "Sexuality and Gender: Findings from the Biological, Psychological, and Social Sciences." *New Atlantis* 50 (Fall 2016): 1–143.

Mayer, Wendy, and Pauline Allen. *The Early Church Fathers: John Chrysostom.* London: Routledge, 2000.

McCarthy, David Matzko. "The Relationship of Bodies: A Nuptial Hermeneutics of Same-Sex Unions." In E. Rogers, *Theology and Sexuality,* 200–216.

McGuckin, John Anthony. *The Path of Christianity: The First Thousand Years.* Downers Grove, IL: IVP Academic, 2017.

McKnight, Scot. *The Letter to Philemon.* New International Commentary on the

New Testament. Grand Rapids: Eerdmans, 2017.

———. *Sermon on the Mount.* The Story of God Bible Commentary. Grand Rapids: Zondervan, 2013.

McMullin, Ernan, ed. *The Church and Galileo.* Notre Dame, IN: University of Notre Dame Press, 2005.

———. "Galileo's Theological Venture." In McMullin, *Church and Galileo,* 88–116.

Meeks, Wayne A. *The First Urban Christians: The Social World of the Apostle Paul.* 2nd ed. New Haven: Yale University Press, 2003.

———. *The Origins of Christian Morality: The First Two Centuries.* New Haven: Yale University Press, 1993.

Meilaender, Gilbert. *Bioethics: A Primer for Christians.* 3rd ed. Grand Rapids: Eerdmans, 2013.

Mennonite Church USA. *Confession of Faith in a Mennonite Perspective.* Elkhart, IN: Mennonite Church USA, 1995. http://mennoniteusa.org/confession-of-faith/.

Methodius. *Symposium.* In ANF 6.

Meyendorff, John. *Marriage: An Orthodox Perspective.* 3rd rev. ed. Yonkers, NY: St. Vladimir's Seminary Press, 1975.

Milavec, Aaron. *The Didache: Faith, Hope, and Life of the Earliest Christian Communities, 50–70 C.E.* New York: Newman, 2003.

Miles, Carrie A. *The Redemption of Love: Rescuing Marriage and Sexuality from the Economics of a Fallen World.* Grand Rapids: Brazos, 2006.

Milgrom, Jacob. *Leviticus: A Book of Ritual and Ethics.* Continental Commentaries. Minneapolis: Fortress, 2004.

Miller, David M. "Reading Law as Prophecy: Torah Ethics in Acts." In Wendel and Miller, *Torah Ethics and Early Christian Identity,* 75–91.

Miller, Patrick D. "Creation and Covenant." In *Biblical Theology: Problems and Perspectives,* edited by Steven J. Kraftchick, Charles D. Myers Jr., and Ben C. Ollenburger, 155–68. Nashville: Abingdon, 1995.

Milliner, Matthew J. "One Soul in Two Bodies: Icons of Sergius and Bacchus Then and Now." In Hiestand and Wilson, *Beauty, Order, and Mystery,* 181–95.

Moberly, Walter. "The Use of Scripture in Contemporary Debate over Homosexuality." *Theology* 103 (2000): 251–58.

Nation, Mark Thiessen. "The Ideology of Inclusion." In Grimsrud and Nation, *Reasoning Together,* 167–82.

Nelson, James B. "Sources for Body Theology: Homosexuality as a Test Case." In Siker, *Homosexuality in the Church,* 76–90.

Newbigin, Lesslie. *The Gospel in a Pluralist Society.* Grand Rapids: Eerdmans, 1989.

The Nicene and Post-Nicene Fathers. Series 1. Edited by Philip Schaff. 1886–89. 14 vols. Available in the Christian Classics Ethereal Library. https://ccel.org/.

The Nicene and Post-Nicene Fathers. Series 2. Edited by Philip Schaff and Henry Wace. 1890–1900. 14 vols. Available in the Christian Classics Ethereal Library. https://ccel.org/.

Nissinen, Martti. *Homoeroticism in the Biblical World: A Historical Perspective.* Minneapolis: Fortress, 1998.

Noll, Mark A. *The Civil War as a Theological Crisis.* Chapel Hill: University of North Carolina Press, 2006.

Noonan, John T., Jr. *Contraception: A History of Its Treatment by the Catholic Theologians and Canonists.* Enlarged ed. Cambridge, MA: Harvard University Press, 1986.

O'Brien, Brandon. "A Jesus for Real Men: What the New Masculinity Movement Gets Right and Wrong." *Christianity Today,* April 2008, 48–52.

O'Donovan, Oliver. *Church in Crisis: The Gay Controversy and the Anglican Communion.* Eugene, OR: Cascade Books, 2008.

———. "Homosexuality in the Church: Can There Be a Fruitful Theological Debate?" In Bradshaw, *Way Forward?*, 20–36.

———. *Resurrection and Moral Order: An Outline for Evangelical Ethics.* 2nd ed. Leicester, UK: Apollos, 1994.

———. *Transsexualism: Issues and Arguments.* Cambridge: Grove Books, 2007.

Ollenburger, Ben C. "Isaiah's Creation Theology." *Ex Auditu* 3 (1987): 54–71.

O'Loughlin, Thomas. *The Didache: A Window on the Earliest Christians.* Grand Rapids: Baker Academic, 2010.

Oppenheimer, Mark. "Married, with Infidelities." *New York Times Magazine*, July 3, 2011, 22–37.

O'Reilly, Matt. "What Makes Sex Beautiful? Marriage, Aesthetics, and the Image of God in Genesis 1–2 and Revelation 21–22." In Hiestand and Wilson, *Beauty, Order, and Mystery*, 197–212.

Otto, Tim. *Oriented to Faith: Transforming the Conflict over Gay Relationships.* Eugene, OR: Cascade Books, 2014.

Paris, Jenell Williams. *The End of Sexual Identity: Why Sex Is Too Important to Define Who We Are.* Downers Grove, IL: InterVarsity, 2011.

Patricios, Nicholas N. *The Sacred Architecture of Byzantium: Art, Liturgy and Symbolism in Early Christian Churches.* New York: I. B. Tauris, 2014.

Paul, Ian. *Same-Sex Unions: The Key Biblical Texts.* Cambridge: Grove Books, 2014.

Paul VI. *Humane Vitae: Encyclical Letter of the Supreme Pontiff Paul VI.* Vatican: Libreria Editrice Vaticana, 2017. Kindle.

Payette-Bucci, Diane. "Voluntary Childlessness." *Direction: A Mennonite Brethren Forum* 17 (Fall 1988): 26–41.

Pearcey, Nancy R. *Love Thy Body: Answering Hard Questions about Life and Sexuality.* Grand Rapids: Baker Books, 2018.

Pelikan, Jaroslav. *The Emergence of the Catholic Tradition (100–600).* Vol. 1 of *The Christian Tradition: A History of the Development of Doctrine.* Chicago: University of Chicago Press, 1971.

Perry, Jackie Hill. *Gay Girl, Good God: The Story of What I Was and Who God Has Always Been.* Nashville: B&H, 2018.

Perry, Tim. "Forbid Them Not: The Place of Children in a Theology of Marriage." In Jeal, *Human Sexuality and the Nuptial Mystery*, 148–64.

Pittenger, W. Norman. "The Morality of Homosexual Acts." In Batchelor, *Homosexuality and Ethics*, 139–45.

Plato. *The Collected Dialogues.* Edited by Edith Hamilton and Huntington Cairn. Princeton: Princeton University Press, 1961.

Pohl, Christine D. *Making Room: Recovering Hospitality as a Christian Tradition.* Grand Rapids: Eerdmans, 1999.

Radner, Ephraim. *Hope among the Fragments: The Broken Church and Its Engagement with Scripture.* Grand Rapids: Brazos, 2004.

———. "The Nuptial Mystery: The Historical Flesh of Procreation." In Jeal, *Human Sexuality and the Nuptial Mystery*, 85–115.

Reimer, A. James. "Homosexuality: A Call for Compassion and Moral Rigor." In Kraus, *To Continue the Dialogue*, 174–86.

Reno, R. R. *Genesis.* Brazos Theological Commentary on the Bible. Grand Rapids: Brazos, 2010.

Reynolds, Philip Lyndon. *Marriage in the Western Church: The Christianization of Marriage during the Patristic and Early Medieval Periods.* Leiden: Brill, 2001.

Rine, Abigail. "What Is Marriage to Evangelical Millennials?" *First Things*, May 14,

2015. https://www.firstthings.com/web
-exclusives/2015/05/what-is-marriage-to
-evangelical-millennials.

Roberts, Christopher C. *Creation and Covenant: The Significance of Sexual Difference in the Moral Theology of Marriage.*
London: T&T Clark, 2007.

Robinson, James M., ed. *The Nag Hammadi
Library.* Leiden: Brill, 1978.

Rogers, Eugene F., Jr. "Sanctification, Homosexuality, and God's Triune Life." In E.
Rogers, *Theology and Sexuality,* 214–46.

———, ed. *Theology and Sexuality: Classic
and Contemporary Readings.* Oxford:
Blackwell, 2002.

Rogers, Jack. *Jesus, the Bible, and Homo-
sexuality: Explode the Myths, Heal the
Church.* Louisville: Westminster John
Knox, 2006.

Roman Catholic Church. *Catechism of the
Catholic Church.* 2nd ed. Vatican: Libreria Editrice Vaticana, 2012.

Rosner, Brian S. *Paul, Scripture and Ethics:
A Study of 1 Corinthians 5–7.* Grand
Rapids: Baker, 1994.

Ruden, Sarah. *Paul among the People: The
Apostle Reinterpreted and Reimagined
in His Own Time.* New York: Image
Books, 2010.

Rueger, Matthew. *Sexual Morality in a
Christless World.* St. Louis: Concordia,
2016.

Runesson, Anders. "Entering a Synagogue
with Paul: First-Century Torah Observance." In Wendel and Miller, *Torah Ethics and Early Christian Identity,* 11–26.

Ryan, Caitlyn, David Huebner, Rafael M.
Diaz, and Jorge Sanchez. "Family Rejec-
tion as a Predictor of Negative Health
Outcomes in White and Latino Lesbian,
Gay, and Bisexual Young Adults." *Pediat-
rics* 123, no. 1 (January 2009): 346–52.

Ryan, Caitlyn, Stephen T. Russell, David
Huebner, Rafael Diaz, and Jorge Sanchez.
"Family Acceptance in Adolescence and

the Health of LGBT Young Adults."
*Journal of Child and Adolescent Psychi-
atric Nursing* 23, no. 4 (November 15,
2010): 205–13.

Scalia, Elizabeth. "Homosexuality: A Call to
Otherness?" *First Things,* June 14, 2011.
https://www.firstthings.com/web-exclu
sives/2011/06/homosexuality-a-call-to
-otherness.

Schafer, Steven. *Marriage, Sex, and Procreation: Contemporary Revisions to Augustine's Theology of Marriage.* Princeton
Theological Monograph Series 240. Eugene, OR: Pickwick Publications, 2019.

Schlabach, Gerald W. "What Is Marriage
Now? A Pauline Case for Same-Sex Marriage." *Christian Century,* October 29,
2014, 22–25, 27.

Schmemann, Alexander. *For the Life of the
World: Sacraments and Orthodoxy.*
St. Vladimir's Seminary Press Classics
Series 1. Yonkers, NY: St. Vladimir's
Seminary Press, 2018.

Schmidt, Thomas E. *Straight and Narrow?
Compassion and Clarity in the Homo-
sexuality Debate.* Downers Grove, IL:
InterVarsity, 1995.

Schroeder, David. "Homosexuality: Biblical,
Theological, and Polity Issues." In Kraus,
To Continue the Dialogue, 62–75.

Scroggs, Robin. *The New Testament and
Homosexuality: Contextual Background
for Contemporary Debate.* Philadelphia:
Fortress, 1983.

Selmys, Melinda. *Sexual Authenticity: An
Intimate Reflection on Homosexuality
and Catholicism.* Huntington, IN: Our
Sunday Visitor, 2009.

Seow, Choon-Leong, ed. *Homosexuality and
Christian Community.* Louisville: Westminster John Knox, 1996.

———. "Textual Orientation." In Brawley,
Biblical Ethics and Homosexuality, 17–34.

Sevilla, Aidyn. "I Walk Between." *Christianity Today,* April 2014. http://www

.christianitytoday.com/pastors/2014
/april-online-only/i-walk-between.html.

Sevilla, Joy. "We All Walk Between." *Christianity Today*, April 2014. http://www
.christianitytoday.com/pastors/2014/april
-online-only/we-all-walk-between.html.

Shaw, Ed. *Same-Sex Attraction and the Church: The Surprising Plausibility of the Celibate Life*. Downers Grove, IL: InterVarsity, 2015. Published in the UK as *The Plausibility Problem: The Church and Same-Sex Attraction*. London: Inter-Varsity, 2015. Page references are to *Same-Sex Attraction and the Church*.

Shellnutt, Kate. "My Pregnancy, Not My Baby: Surrogacy Meets Christian Bioethics." *Christianity Today*, March 2018, 28–35.

Siker, Jeffery S. "Gentile Wheat and Homosexual Christians: New Testament Directions for the Heterosexual Church." In Brawley, *Biblical Ethics and Homosexuality*, 137–51.

———. "Homosexual Christians, the Bible, and Gentile Inclusion: Confessions of a Repenting Heterosexist." In Siker, *Homosexuality in the Church*, 178–94.

———, ed. *Homosexuality in the Church: Both Sides of the Debate*. Louisville: Westminster John Knox, 1994.

Smith, James K. A. *You Are What You Love: The Spiritual Power of Habit*. Grand Rapids: Brazos, 2016.

Smith, Mark D. "Ancient Bisexuality and the Interpretation of Romans 1:26–27." *Journal of the American Academy of Religion* 64, no. 2 (1996): 223–56.

Sobel, Dava. *Galileo's Daughter: A Historical Memoir of Science, Faith, and Love*. New York: Penguin Books, 2000.

Song, Robert. *Covenant and Calling: Towards a Theology of Same-Sex Relationships*. London: SCM, 2014.

Sprinkle, Preston. *People to Be Loved: Why Homosexuality Is Not Just an Issue*. Grand Rapids: Zondervan, 2015.

———, ed. *Two Views on Homosexuality, the Bible, and the Church*. Grand Rapids: Zondervan, 2016.

Staniforth, Maxwell, and Andrew Louth, trans. *Early Christian Writings: The Apostolic Fathers*. London: Penguin Books, 1987.

Stark, Rodney. *The Rise of Christianity: How the Obscure, Marginal Jesus Movement Became the Dominant Force in the Western World in a Few Centuries*. San Francisco: HarperSanFrancisco, 1996.

Stewart, Alistair C. *On the Apostolic Tradition*. Popular Patristics Series 22. Yonkers, NY: St. Vladimir's Seminary Press, 2015.

Strong, David K. "The Jerusalem Council: Some Implications for Contextualization, Acts 15:1–35." In *Mission in Acts: Ancient Narratives in Contemporary Context*, edited by Robert L. Gallagher and Paul Hertig, 196–208. Maryknoll, NY: Orbis Books, 2004.

Stuart, Elizabeth. "Dancing in the Spirit." In Bradshaw, *Way Forward?*, 71–85.

———. *Just Good Friends: Towards a Lesbian and Gay Theology of Relationships*. London: Mowbray, 1995.

Sullivan, Andrew. *Love Undetectable: Notes on Friendship, Sex, and Survival*. New York: Vintage, 1998.

Swartley, Willard M. *Homosexuality: Biblical Interpretation and Moral Discernment*. Scottdale, PA: Herald, 2003.

———. *Slavery, Sabbath, War, and Women: Case Issues in Biblical Interpretation*. Scottdale, PA: Herald, 1983.

Tannehill, Robert C. *The Acts of the Apostles*. Vol. 2 of *The Narrative Unity of Luke-Acts: A Literary Interpretation*. Minneapolis: Fortress, 1990.

Tatian. *Fragments*. In *ANF* 2.

Taylor, Aaron. "Can One Be Gay and Christian?" *First Things*, April 22, 2013. https://
www.firstthings.com/web-exclusives/2013
/04/can-one-be-gay-and-christian.

Tertullian. *An Exhortation to Chastity.* Translated by David G. Hunter. In Hunter, *Marriage in the Early Church*, 39–40.

———. *On Monogamy.* In *ANF* 4.

———. *On the Veiling of Virgins.* In *ANF* 4.

———. *To His Wife.* Translated by David G. Hunter. In Hunter, *Marriage in the Early Church*, 33–39.

Thatcher, Adrian. *Liberating Sex: A Christian Sexual Theology.* London: SPCK, 1993.

Thielicke, Helmut. "The Theologicoethical Aspect of Homosexuality." In Batchelor, *Homosexuality and Ethics*, 96–104.

Thiselton, Anthony C. "Can Hermeneutics Ease the Deadlock? Some Biblical Exegesis and Hermeneutical Models." In Bradshaw, *Way Forward?*, 145–96.

———. *1 Corinthians: A Shorter Exegetical and Pastoral Commentary.* Grand Rapids: Eerdmans, 2006.

———. *The First Epistle to the Corinthians: A Commentary on the Greek Text.* New International Greek Testament Commentary. Grand Rapids: Eerdmans, 2000.

Thorne, Gary. "Friendship: The End of Marriage." In Jeal, *Human Sexuality and the Nuptial Mystery*, 45–64.

Thrasher, Steven W. "Master Bedroom, Extra Closet: The Truth about Gay Marriage." *Gawker*, June 19, 2013. https://gawker .com/master-bedroom-extra-closet -the-truth-about-gay-marri-514348538.

Timbol, Emily. "The Fruitful Callings of the Childless by Choice." *Christianity Today*, September 16, 2013. https://www .christianitytoday.com/women/2013/sept ember/fruitful-callings-of-childless-by -choice.html.

Toews, John A. *Romans.* Believers Church Bible Commentary. Scottdale, PA: Herald, 2004.

Trakatellis, Demetrios. *Authority and Passion: Christological Aspects of the Gospel according to Mark.* Translated by George K. Duvall and Harry Vulopas. Brookline, MA: Holy Cross Orthodox Press, 1987.

Trenham, Josiah B. *Marriage and Virginity according to St. John Chrysostom.* Platina, CA: St. Herman of Alaska Brotherhood, 2013.

Trible, Phyllis. *Texts of Terror: Literary-Feminist Readings of Biblical Narratives.* Overtures to Biblical Theology. Philadelphia: Fortress, 1984.

Turner, Philip. "Sex and the Single Life." *First Things*, May 1993, 15–21.

Tushnet, Eve. "Beyond Sexual Identity: Not Whether but How." *Eve Tushnet* (blog), March 5, 2015. Patheos. http://www .patheos.com/blogs/evetushnet/2015/03 /beyond-sexual-identity-not-whether -but-how.html.

———. "The Botany Club: Gay Kids in Catholic Schools." *American Conservative*, May 30, 2012. https://www.theameri canconservative.com/the-botany-club -gay-kids-in-catholic-schools/.

———. *Gay and Catholic: Accepting My Sexuality, Finding Community, Living My Faith.* Notre Dame, IN: Ave Maria, 2014.

———. "Vows of Friendship." *America: The Jesuit Review of Faith and Culture* 216 (February 6, 2017): 24–31.

Valk, Pieter. "I'm Gay." *EQUIP*, September 20, 2018. http://equipyourcommunity.org /blog/im-gay.

Varcoe, Gillian. "Marriage." In *The Oxford Guide to the Book of Common Prayer: A Worldwide Survey*, edited by Charles Hefling and Cynthia Shattuck, 509–17. Oxford: Oxford University Press, 2006.

Vasey, Michael. *Strangers and Friends: A New Exploration of Homosexuality and the Bible.* London: Hodder & Stoughton, 1995.

———. "Travelling Together?" In Bradshaw, *Way Forward?*, 60–70.

Verhey, Allen. *Remembering Jesus: Christian Community, Scripture, and the Moral Life*. Grand Rapids: Eerdmans, 2002.

Verhey, Allen, and Joseph S. Harvard. *Ephesians*. Belief: A Theological Commentary on the Bible. Louisville: Westminster John Knox, 2011.

Via, Dan O. "The Bible, the Church, and Homosexuality." In *Homosexuality and the Bible: Two Views*, by Dan O. Via and Robert A. J. Gagnon, 1–39. Minneapolis: Fortress, 2003.

Vibert, Simon. "Divine Order and Sexual Conduct." In Bradshaw, *Way Forward?*, 113–27.

Vines, Matthew. *God and the Gay Christian: The Biblical Case in Support of Same-Sex Relationships*. New York: Convergent Books, 2014.

Waetjen, Herman C. "Same-Sex Sexual Relations in Antiquity and Sexuality and Sexual Identity in Contemporary American Society." In Brawley, *Biblical Ethics and Homosexuality*, 103–16.

Walton, John H. *The Lost World of Genesis One: Ancient Cosmology and the Origins Debate*. Downers Grove, IL: IVP Academic, 2009.

Wannenwetsch, Bernd. "Old Docetism—New Moralism? Questioning a New Direction in the Homosexuality Debate." *Modern Theology* 16, no. 3 (July 2000): 353–64.

Ware, Timothy. *The Orthodox Church*. New ed. London: Penguin Books, 1993.

Webb, William J. *Slaves, Women and Homosexuals: Exploring the Hermeneutics of Cultural Analysis*. Downers Grove, IL: InterVarsity, 2001.

Weed, Josh, and Lolly Weed. "Devoutly Mormon. Happily Married. Undeniably Gay." Evangelicals for Social Action, November 29, 2014. http://www.evangelicalsforsocialaction.org/sexual-justice/devoutly-mormon-happily-married-undeniably-gay/.

———. "Turning a Unicorn into a Bat." *The Weed*, January 25, 2018. http://joshweed.com/2018/01/turning-unicorn-bat-post-announce-end-marriage/.

Weiner, Rabbi Moshe. *The Divine Code: The Guide to Observing God's Will for Mankind, Revealed from Mount Sinai in the Torah of Moses*. 2nd ed. Pittsburgh: Ask Noah International, 2011.

Wendel, Susan J., and David M. Miller. *Torah Ethics and Early Christian Identity*. Grand Rapids: Eerdmans, 2016.

Westfall, Cynthia Long. *Paul and Gender: Reclaiming the Apostle's Vision for Men and Women in Christ*. Grand Rapids: Baker Academic, 2016.

Wheeler, Sondra. "Creation, Community, Discipleship: Remembering Why We Care about Sex." *Ex Auditu* 17 (2001): 60–72.

Whitaker, Richard E. "Creation and Human Sexuality." In Seow, *Homosexuality and Christian Community*, 3–13.

White, Mel. *Stranger at the Gate: To Be Gay and Christian in America*. New York: Plume, 1995.

Williams, Craig A. *Roman Homosexuality*. 2nd ed. Oxford: Oxford University Press, 2010.

Williams, Rowan D. "The Body's Grace." In E. Rogers, *Theology and Sexuality*, 309–21.

Willitts, Joel. "Bent Sexuality and the Pastor." In Hiestand and Wilson, *Beauty, Order, and Mystery*, 119–33.

Wilson, Ken. *A Letter to My Congregation: An Evangelical Pastor's Path to Embracing People Who Are Gay, Lesbian, Bisexual, and Transgender into the Company of Jesus*. 2nd ed. Canton, MI: Read the Spirit Books, 2014.

Wilson, Todd. *Mere Sexuality: Rediscovering the Christian Vision of Sexuality*. Grand Rapids: Zondervan, 2017.

Wink, Walter. "Homosexuality and the Bible." *Christian Century*, November 7, 1979, 1082–86.

Winner, Lauren F. *Real Sex: The Naked Truth about Chastity*. Grand Rapids: Brazos, 2005.

Witte, John, Jr. *From Sacrament to Contract: Marriage, Religion, and Law in the Western Tradition*. 2nd ed. Louisville: Westminster John Knox, 2012.

Wold, Donald J. *Out of Order: Homosexuality in the Bible and the Ancient Near East*. 2nd ed. San Antonio: Cedar Leaf, 2009.

Woodhead, Linda. "Sex in a Wider Context." In *Sex These Days: Essays on Theology, Sexuality and Society*, edited by Jon Davies and Gerard Loughlin, 98–120. Sheffield, UK: Sheffield Academic, 1997.

Wright, Brian J. *Communal Reading in the Time of Jesus: A Window into Early Christian Reading Practices*. Minneapolis: Fortress, 2017.

Wright, David F. "Homosexuality: The Relevance of the Bible." *Evangelical Quarterly* 61, no. 4 (1989): 291–300.

———. "Homosexuals or Prostitutes? The Meaning of *ARSENOKOITAI* (1 Cor. 6:9, 1 Tim. 1:10)." *Vigiliae Christianae* 38 (1984): 125–53.

Wright, N. T. "From Genesis to Revelation: An Anglican Perspective." In *Not Just Good, but Beautiful: The Complementary Relationship between Man and Woman*, edited by Steven Lopes and Helen Alvaré, 85–96. Walden, NY: Plough Publishing, 2015.

———. *Scripture and the Authority of God: How to Read the Bible Today*. New York: HarperOne, 2011.

———. *Surprised by Hope: Rethinking Heaven, the Resurrection, and the Mission of the Church*. New York: HarperOne, 2008.

Yarhouse, Mark. *Homosexuality and the Christian: A Guide for Parents, Pastors, and Friends*. Minneapolis: Bethany House, 2010.

Yoder, Perry B. *Leviticus*. Believers Church Bible Commentary. Harrisonburg, VA: Herald, 2017.

Yoder Neufeld, Thomas R. *Ephesians*. Believers Church Bible Commentary. Scottdale, PA: Herald, 2002.

———. *Killing Enmity: Violence in the New Testament*. Grand Rapids: Baker Academic, 2011.

Yuan, Christopher. *Holy Sexuality and the Gospel: Sex, Desire, and Relationships Shaped by God's Grand Story*. Colorado Springs: Multnomah, 2018.

Yuan, Christopher, and Angela Yuan. *Out of a Far Country: A Gay Son's Journey to God; A Broken Mother's Search for Hope*. Colorado Springs: WaterBrook, 2011.

Zehnder, Markus. "Observations on the Relationship between David and Jonathan and the Debate on Homosexuality." *Westminster Theological Journal* 69 (2007): 127–74.

Index of Scripture and Ancient Christian Literature

Index of Subjects